INTEGRATED PRODUCTION AND INVENTORY MANAGEMENT

REVITALIZING THE MANUFACTURING ENTERPRISE

D1312285

The Business One Irwin/APICS Library of Integrated Resource Management

Customers and Products

Marketing for the Manufacturer   *J. Paul Peter*

Field Service Management: An Integrated Approach to Increasing Customer Satisfaction
Arthur V. Hill

Effective Product Design and Development: How to Cut Lead Time and Increase Customer Satisfaction   *Stephen R. Rosenthal*

Logistics

Integrated Production and Inventory Management: Revitalizing the Manufacturing Enterprise
Thomas E. Vollmann, William L. Berry, and D. Clay Whybark

Purchasing: Continued Improvement through Integration   *Joseph Carter*

Integrated Distribution Management: Competing on Customer Service, Time and Cost
Christopher Gopal and Harold Cypress

Manufacturing Processes

Integrative Facilities Management   *John M. Burnham*

Integrated Process Design and Development   *Dan L. Shunk*

Integrative Manufacturing: Transforming the Organization through People, Process and Technology   *L. Scott Flaig*

Support Functions

Managing Information: How Information Systems Impact Organizational Strategy   *Gordon B. Davis and Thomas R. Hoffman*

Managing Human Resources: Integrating People and Business Strategy   *Lloyd S. Baird*

Managing for Quality: Integrating Quality and Business Strategy   *V. Daniel Hunt*

World-Class Accounting and Finance   *Carol J. McNair*

INTEGRATED PRODUCTION AND INVENTORY MANAGEMENT

REVITALIZING THE MANUFACTURING ENTERPRISE

Thomas E. Vollmann
William L. Berry
D. Clay Whybark

Business One Irwin
Homewood, Illinois 60430

Executive editor: Jeffrey A. Krames
Project editor: Jess Ann Ramirez
Production manager: Mary Jo Parke
Designer: Laurie Entringer
Compositor: Publication Services
Typeface: 11/13 Times Roman
Printer: Book Press, Inc.

Library of Congress Cataloging-in-Publication Data

Vollmann, Thomas E.
    Integrated production and inventory management : revitalizing the
manufacturing enterprise / Thomas E. Vollmann, William L. Berry,
D. Clay Whybark.
      p.   cm.
    ISBN 1-55623-604-2
    1. Production management. 2. Inventory control. I. Berry,
William L. II. Whybark, D. Clay. III. Title.
TS155.V65   1993
658.5—dc20   92–11159

Printed in the United States of America
1 2 3 4 5 6 7 8 9 0 BP 9 8 7 6 5 4 3 2

FOREWORD

Integrated Production and Inventory Management is one book in a series that addresses the most critical issue facing manufacturing companies today: integration—the identification and solution of problems that cross organizational and company boundaries—and, perhaps more importantly, the continuous search for ways to solve these problems faster and more effectively! The genesis for the series is the commitment to integration made by the American Production and Inventory Control Society (APICS). I attended several brainstorming sessions a few years ago in which the primary topic of discussion was, "What jobs will exist in manufacturing companies in the future—not at the very top of the enterprise and not at the bottom, but in between?" The prognostications included:

- The absolute number of jobs will decrease, as will the layers of management. Manufacturing organizations will adopt flatter organizational forms with less emphasis on hierarchy and less distinction between white collars and blue collars.

- Functional "silos" will become obsolete. The classical functions of marketing, manufacturing, engineering, finance, and personnel will be less important in defining work. More people will take on "project" work focused on continuous improvement of one kind or another.

- Fundamental restructuring, meaning much more than financial restructuring, will become a way of life in manufacturing enterprises. The primary focal points will be a new market-driven emphasis on creating value with customers, as well as greatly increased flexibility, a new business-driven attack on global markets which includes new deployment of information technology, and fundamentally new jobs.

- Work will become much more integrated in its orientation. The payoffs will increasingly be made though connections across organizational and company boundaries. Included are customer and vendor partnerships, with an overall focus on improving the value-added chain.
- New measurements that focus on the new strategic directions will be required. Metrics will be developed, similar to the cost of quality metric, that incorporate the most important dimensions of the environment. Similar metrics and semantics will be developed to support the new uses of information technology.
- New "people management" approaches will be developed. Teamwork will be critical to organizational success. Human resource management will become less of a "staff" function and more closely integrated with the basic work.

Many of these prognostications are already a reality. APICS has made the commitments to *leading* the way in all of these change areas. The decision was both courageous and intelligent. There is not future for a professional society not committed to leading-edge education for its members. Based on the Society's past experience with the Certification in Production and Inventory Management (CPIM) program, the natural thrust of APICS was to develop a new certification program focusing on integration. The result, Certification in Integrated Resource Management (CIRM) is a program composed of 13 building block areas which have been combined into four examination modules, as follows:

Customers and products
    Marketing and sales
    Field service
    Product design and development
Manufacturing processes
    Industrial facilities management
    Process design and development
    Manufacturing (production)
Logistics
    Production and inventory management
    Procurement
    Distribution

Support functions
   Total quality management
   Human resources
   Finance and accounting
   Information systems

As can be seen from this topical list, one objective in the CIRM program is to develop educational breadth. Managers increasingly *must* know the underlying basics in each area of the business: who are the people who work there, what are day-to-day *and* strategic problems, what is state-of-the-art practice, what are the expected improvement areas, and what is happening with technology? This basic breadth of knowledge is an absolute prerequisite to understanding the potential linkages and joint improvements.

But it is the linkages, relationships, and integration that are even more important. Each examination devotes approximately 40 percent of the questions to the connections *among* the 13 building block areas. In fact, after a candidate has successfully completed the four examination modules, he or she must take a fifth examination (Integrated Enterprise Management), which focuses solely on the interrelationships among all functional areas of an enterprise.

The CIRM program has been the most exciting activity on which I have worked in a professional organization. Increasingly, manufacturing companies face the alternative of either proactive restructuring to deal with today's competitive realities, or just sliding away—giving up market share and industry leadership. Education must play a key role in making the necessary changes. People working in manufacturing companies need to learn many new things and "unlearn" many old ones.

There were very limited educational materials available to support CIRM. There were textbooks in which basic concepts were covered and bits and pieces which dealt with integration, but there simply was no coordinated set of materials available for this program. That has been the job of the CIRM series authors, and it has been my distinct pleasure as series editor to help develop the ideas and facilitate our joint learning. All of us have learned a great deal, and I am delighted with every book in the series. But the spirit of continuous improvement is built into the CIRM program and into the book series.

Thomas E. Vollmann
Series Editor

PREFACE

This volume is designed to provide a managerial understanding of the production and inventory management (PIM) activities in a manufacturing company. It is a part of integrated resource management because of its centrality to the planning and control of all activities that produce and deliver products for customers.

Understanding the activities performed in production and inventory management and their relationships to other functions in the firm is key to integrating them into the management systems of the company as a whole. Because integrated management resources are key in achieving world-class performance, this book provides a step in that direction. Moving to higher levels of overall performance in manufacturing requires an integrated view. Effectively using resources to produce high-value products also requires this view. Hence the role of this book in the development of professionals dedicated to integrated resource management.

A key step in the process of improving *your* ability to manage integrated resources is to become certified. The American Production and Inventory Control Society sponsors the examinations that lead to Certification in Integrated Resource Management (CIRM). This book is designed to help prepare you for that exam. It covers material that is primarily found in the Logistics and Manufacturing Processes part of the exam. It also provides linkages to all areas of CIRM, some more than others because some are more closely linked to production and inventory management. It does not., however, cover everything in *any* one examination and it also presents material covered in several other exams—because this is the nature of "integrated resource management." Moreover, the book is primarily written not for passing an examination, but to provide you with a broad understanding of this resource area. In the last analysis, it is your skill as a manager that counts!

The Manager and the Professional

It is important to distinguish this book from others that have the objective of education for professionals working directly in the field of production and inventory management. This book does not cover enough of the technical material, provide the depth of theory, nor give enough of the details necessary for the professional production and inventory management person. Instead, it is intended for managers who have the responsibility to integrate production and inventory management into the firm as a whole. It is for "driving the car," not "repairing the engine."

The approach of the book is, therefore, one of laying out concepts and management issues as opposed to developing the detailed techniques and theory. The material presented is sufficient to understand the major concepts without unnecessary detail. A second aspect of the presentation is the description of the interconnections with other areas of the firm. Again this is done to help you understand the management issues involved in order to help with integration of the areas.

ACKNOWLEDGMENTS

We first want to acknowledge the support of our editor, Jeff Krames, who has enthusiastically supported the integrated resource management series for BusinessOne and deserves much credit for his vision. The rest of the staff at BusinessOne have also been very supportive.

We have had the great pleasure of being involved with manufacturing executives and general managers over many years. These contacts have come through executive programs in many countries and our associations with research roundtables and centers. These people have been invaluable in keeping us connected with the real issues facing managers and the central role of production and inventory management. Without the occasional sanity check from them, our perspectives would be much more narrow.

The Deans that have given us the time to work on this book have been extremely tolerant. We would like to thank Paul Rizzo of North Carolina for indulging us, Juan Rada of IMD (the international management school in Switzerland) for his support, and Tim Hall of Boston University for believing that whatever we wanted to do was OK.

Of course, none of this would have been possible without the tolerance of three very great people, Tani Vollmann, Jane Berry, and Neva Whybark. Thanks for putting up with us!

Finally, we would like to dedicate this book to Elwood Buffa: He started it *all!*

Thomas E. Vollmann
William L. Berry
D. Clay Whybark

CONTENTS IN BRIEF

CONTENTS

INTEGRATED RESOURCE LINKAGES

SECTION 1

INTRODUCTION

There is only one chapter in this introductory section, but it is an important one. This is the chapter that places production and inventory management in its context for integrated resource management. In this chapter, we describe the philosophy and approach of the book along with its strengths and limitations. We discuss, in general terms, the functions performed in doing integrated production and inventory management (PIM). We touch upon the people involved, their decisions, and the implications of their actions. Framework and basic concepts for integrated production and inventory management are presented, including our model of PIM activities that is followed throughout the book. Also presented is an overview of key linkages of PIM with other resource activities. We recommend that you start with this section in order to understand the structure of the text. Thereafter, it is possible to proceed in whatever order appeals to you as a reader.

CHAPTER 1

INTRODUCTION

Integrated Production and Inventory Management! The key word in the title is "management." Improved management practice is the objective of production and inventory management (PIM), and management also depicts the perspective of this book. Our goal is to provide you with a conceptual understanding of the scheduling of production processes, the inventories that result from this scheduling, and how PIM connects with other critical problems in manufacturing. The word "integrated" is key to this understanding. PIM does not take place in isolation; it must be integrated with other areas of the business. Successful management of production and inventories requires integration of all the steps in the value-adding process—from product design and purchasing, to raw materials, through manufacturing and distribution, to use by customers.

Many of the resource inputs coordinated through PIM are provided by other parts of the organization. Furthermore, all of the production outputs are passed on to other parts of the company or to third parties (most importantly, customers). These connections are critical to understanding the task of PIM and its role in meeting overall corporate objectives. This mandates that the book provide an integrative understanding of these input and output resources. The flows of resources cross functional boundaries (sales, accounting, marketing, finance, engineering, and so on) and corporate entities (customers, suppliers, subcontractors, and so on). Different objectives, performance measurements, standards, cultures, languages, and expectations come into play in coordinating these diverse resources.

Effective integration and management across functional and corporate boundaries grows in complexity with each passing day. The imperatives of global competition, world-class product standards, increased customer input in product design, shorter product life cycles, and greater flexibility all place demands on PIM and the resource management areas with which it connects. World-class performance requires managers that understand and are effective in integrated resource management. In the spirit of furthering knowledge about integrated resource management, this book is devoted to providing the perspective for production and inventory management.

APPROACH OF THE BOOK

The perspective of the book is production and inventory management. The key focus is on the flow of materials: acquiring them, transforming them, storing them, moving them, and, ultimately, selling them. Each of these activities requires resources (capacities) often under the control of other groups in the company—and in other companies—giving rise to the integrative imperatives of PIM. The process of scheduling and controlling production and inventory implies planning, measuring, adjusting, and multiple tradeoffs.

The Bathtub Theory of Production

In many firms, the relationship between production and inventory is not well understood. The two are considered independently and are managed separately. Such firms often issue fiats such as "reduce inventories by 20 percent," failing to recognize the fundamental relationship between production, sales, and inventories. Inventories result from mismatches between production and sales. They are the residual that measures unsold production, but they are not a management lever in their own right.

The amount of production is a function of the resources applied—material, equipment capacities, people, information, and working capital—and how well they are applied. The amount of sales achieved is a function of underlying customer demand, the appeal of the products, sales, and promotional efforts—and even a bit of luck. In periods when production exceeds sales, inventories will build. The only way to reduce them, *even if production is stopped,* is to sell them, scrap them, or give them away. Without proper efforts to integrate production and sales, the company can end up with unwanted inventories and insufficient product to sell, the worst of all situations. A major objective in PIM is to ensure that this unhappy situation does not occur.

The relationship between inputs and outputs is summarized in the "bathtub" model of PIM illustrated in Figure 1.1. The total capacity available for production is determined by the resources made available. The amount of production (the input) can be no greater than allowed by the resource constraints, but it *can* be less. The output is determined by the underlying demand, sales efforts, intercompany transfers, scrap, and so on. The mismatch between input and output is modeled in Figure 1.1 by the amount of "water" in the tub. The job of PIM professionals is to monitor input and output, adjust the capacity actually used, coordinate production flows to get the right goods at the right times, minimize the inventories, and integrate with the other functions (there are a few wags who also believe that PIM professionals need to *walk* on the water!).

Scope of the Book

The major part of this book describes the activities of integrated production and inventory management (PIM) managers. What are the decisions they make and how are they carried out? What systems are available to help make these decisions? How do activities of PIM managers integrate with activities in other functions in the company? How do the different

FIGURE 1.1
The Bathtub Model of Production and Inventory Management

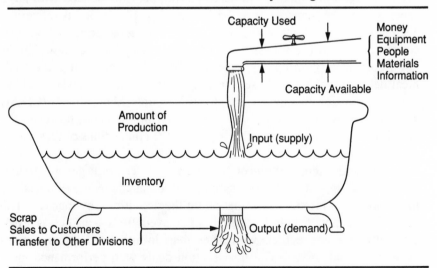

PIM activities relate to one another? How do PIM systems respond to the dynamics of the day-to-day world. How do changes in the business environment get reflected in PIM practices?

Throughout the book, the perspective is managerial and conceptual. Each chapter begins with the important production and inventory management concepts for the topic covered. Next, these concepts are illustrated using examples drawn from actual company operations. Then, material on other issues is presented. These other issues might include the managerial concerns involved in putting production and inventory concepts into practice, new developments in the area, or extensions of the basic concepts. Finally, key principles are presented and important linkages with other integrated resource management activities are highlighted.

The managerial focus of the book means that technical treatment of production and inventory management concepts will be limited to that necessary to understand the underlying problems and basic approaches. The objective is to describe the management of integrated resources, not to develop functional specialists. Some of the terminology of the specialist will be defined and some fundamental technical material will be presented, but not to the degree required of a PIM professional.

There are other important limitations to the book as well. The book will not treat production and inventory management for large-scale projects (such as the construction of a cruise ship or large office building). Neither will it address in depth the problems associated with large process industry firms such as basic chemical plants or oil refineries. Technical details of the equipment used in manufacturing will not be covered, nor will the details of product or process engineering. This is not a commentary on their importance, but a recognition that the technical details involved in those topics are better treated elsewhere. Other books in the Certification in Integrated Resource Management (CIRM) series do indeed treat some of these subjects. In this book, however, the goal is to focus on the integrative aspects—the connections of these areas with PIM.

The next major section of this chapter describes a general framework for the jobs of PIM professionals, discusses the nature of decisions they make, and provides information on the activities they manage. The following section details the benefits achieved from world-class PIM. Thereafter, the connections with other areas in integrated resource management are addressed. The final section deals with performance measurement in PIM and related challenges facing the profession today.

A FRAMEWORK FOR PIM

There are several ways to describe the job of integrated production and inventory management. One approach would be to frame the discussion around organization charts, job titles, and the hierarchical relationships of the people who perform the work. Another would be to frame the dialogue around the techniques and theoretical concepts in PIM. But we believe that a better approach here is to focus on the work—the processes and activities that need to be performed in PIM. As the activities are described, the associated job descriptions and technical issues will be included—but only as necessary to understand the processes and activities. Furthermore, our approach to describing the activities is to start with those closest to the market; thereafter the more detailed PIM processes inside the manufacturing facility will be described and linked to the marketplace.

Integrated Production and Inventory Management Processes

Figure 1.2 presents the framework for integrated production and inventory management that will be used in this book. Each block in the framework represents a management process or activity that must be performed in every manufacturing organization. The quality with which

FIGURE 1.2
Framework for Integrated Production and Inventory Management

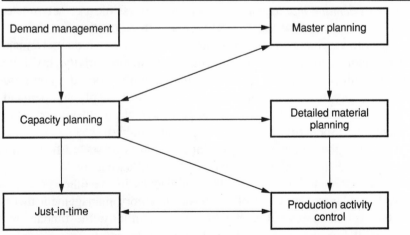

these processes and activities are accomplished has a major impact on the efficiency of manufacturing, and determines, to a large extent, manufacturing product costs. How well these functions are integrated with the other functions of the organization determines how effective the firm will be. That is, integration of PIM defines how well the firm serves its customers and gains a competitive advantage in the marketplace.

Each of these processes is treated as a section of the book. In some cases, more than one chapter is devoted to a section. In some sections this is necessary to cover all the concepts involved; in others the more technical material is broken out and covered separately. Each of the processes is related to other processes in the framework and other functions in the firm. These relationships will be described in the appropriate sections.

The activities of planning, scheduling, and controlling occur in all of the processes, though with varying degrees of emphasis. The blocks are not intended to indicate exclusivity, but rather to describe the process in general terms. In the same vein, there are many more feedback loops of information than those shown in Figure 1.2. In order to keep the framework readable and not unnecessarily cluttered, only the major connections are shown.

There is also an overall feedback loop for the entire system that is not shown. As conditions in the factory, marketplace, competitive arena and/or legislative context change, the company may need to replan, reschedule, and develop new control mechanisms to stay abreast of the new situation. These outside events can affect one or all of the processes in the framework.

The description of integrated production and inventory management starts with *demand management*. This is the process most closely related to the marketplace. It serves as the link between production and the market for both the input of resources and the output of product. Demand management is very much an information-centered activity, involving gathering information from customers, maintaining information on product availability, and monitoring the match between supply and demand. In the terms of Figure 1.1, this is the process that provides information to match the production rate with the output required.

Because the demand management material is presented first, some basic technical material and theory is presented as part of that section. Much of that material underlies the approaches in the other processes as well. For example, some of the basic inventory management theory will be applied in several of the functions. Similarly, the fundamental concepts of forecasting apply throughout the framework.

The *master planning* section describes the concepts employed in developing the production plan and master production schedule. These two plans are the key links between the top management of the company and production. The master planning process links the plans of each of the other major functional groups (sales, marketing, finance, and so forth) to those of production. The activities in this process have been termed "top management's handle on the business." The section covers the topics of production planning and master production scheduling in two separate chapters.

Capacity planning is the most comprehensively linked process in the framework. The capacity available sets constraints on what can be produced. In Figure 1.1, capacity planning determines the size of the input pipe and, in the same analogy, the water supply that will feed it in the future. Production is limited not only by the availability of material, people, and capital in the short run, but also by physical space and other long run limitations. The linkages of capacity planning to the other processes indicate the importance of communicating these limitations in order to adjust other plans or expectancies in the organization.

Whereas the master planning process sets overall output plans for manufacturing, the *detailed material planning* process translates them into the exact raw materials, parts, components, and subassemblies needed to meet the plans. Schedules for these detailed requirements are prepared for both purchasing and internal production. This process is very closely linked with the physical production process and scheduling production is constrained by the capacity available. One of the chapters in this section describes the process of deriving the detailed plans.

A typical manufacturing company processes a large number of parts and components that feed into an assembly process. The volume of activity and the dynamic nature of the production process create a factory floor in a constant state of change. This dynamism is not always on track; things will go wrong and do! The close relationship between the physical production process and detailed material planning means that there must be constant revision of plans in light of the changes that take place on the factory floor. The dynamic nature of the detailed plans is discussed in this section.

A second aspect of the high levels of activity is the sheer volume of schedules that are produced by the detailed material planning process. When combined with the dynamism of the floor, there is a resultant need for managing the flows of information, data base, and systems that keep it all together. This is such an integral part of the detailed planning process that there is a separate chapter devoted to the issue.

One of the most significant forces of change in manufacturing in the last two decades has been the *just-in-time* (JIT) movement and all of its variations. No treatise on integrated production and inventory management would be complete without a section on it. An early understanding of just-in-time was as an inventory control system in which the objective was to produce a part just-in-time to be used at a subsequent work center or by a customer, thus eliminating the need for inventory. Over time, the concept of just-in-time has been transformed into a philosophy of manufacturing in which all waste (non value-added activities) is to be eliminated, not just inventory. These understandings are sometimes distinguished as "little JIT" and "big JIT."

In the just-in-time process considered here, the perspective is that of big JIT. In one chapter of the section, some of the philosophical underpinnings of JIT are described. These involve organizational concerns, the required state of mind, and fundamental building blocks. The other aspects of JIT that are discussed here include some of the techniques used to achieve the philosophical objectives. These include significant changes in the layout of the factory, the quality of the parts produced, and the resources (including time) required to produce them. The impact of these physical changes on production and inventory management practices is profound. As the linkages imply, they influence both the effective capacity of the firm and the control of the production activities.

A chapter is devoted to the changes that are taking place in the way people are utilized in the newly configured factory and to the requirements that the new systems put on the people that use them. These changes will perhaps have an even more fundamental effect on the management of production than the physical changes that are taking place.

The final process in the framework is *production activity control (PAC)*. This is the activity in which production performance is monitored against plans and schedules, with changes made to correct problems. The control activities in this process are not only for the manufacturing facility of the company; they extend to the supplier base as well. The perspective taken here is that the control of outside capacity is as important as that of inside capacity.

Each of these sections contains a series of decisions made by the people that perform integrated production and inventory control. Let us now turn to the nature of these decisions and the people who make them.

Production and Inventory Management Decisions

The planning, scheduling, and control decisions required to keep products flowing to the customers all involve capacities and materials. The integrated production and inventory management processes, shown in Figure 1.2, indicate where these decisions are made and the other processes that most directly provide information or constraints on those decisions.

Planning decisions rely on estimates of marketplace needs and other sources of demand for materials or capacities. In Figure 1.1 these are the determinants of output at the bottom of the bathtub. The quality of PIM decisions is strongly influenced by the completeness and quality of these estimates. The requirements for detail and accuracy are more stringent the closer one gets to the time the customer needs the product.

An often overlooked aspect of the inputs to the planning decisions is the need for complete information on all of the sources of demand. The need to supply display or demonstration products to marketing or products for destructive testing to quality assurance places demands on manufacturing every bit as real as those from end users. Improper planning for these demands can lead to mismatches in demand and supply. Similarly, changes in quality levels affect the yield or amount of scrap, changing the supply available for other demands. Proper planning for yields can be particularly important for businesses in situations such as state-of-the-art integrated circuits manufacturing.

Output planning leads to input planning, but here it is necessary to plan capacities as well as materials. To the extent that the outputs are relatively constant, the inputs can also be constant, with uniform utilization of capacities and minimal inventory levels. When this is not the case, companies are faced either with building inventories to level capacity or with creating flexibility in manufacturing (and PIM) to respond to actual demands with reduced inventories. World-class manufacturing practice is shifting toward this latter approach, that is, toward flexibility and responsiveness.

Long-range capacity planning decisions are based on aggregate estimates of demand, leading to investments in plant and equipment—which create the capacities. These decisions necessarily involve expanding physical capacity, vertical integration, subcontracting, labor availability, automation, and so forth. They also have a strategic element in terms of how to achieve increased flexibility. These decisions are critical to the long-term success of the firm because they are generally costly, enduring in nature, and hard to reverse. Economic feasibility is critical since decisions may hinge on changing the demands as well as building capacity.

When overall input and output planning are completed, detailed material planning decisions are made to match the exact product features with demand requirements. For the more distant future, these decisions are in aggregated units such as dollars, units of average product, gallons, tons, and so on. The units indicate the levels of business, not the precise products to be delivered. In the immediate future, the decisions must be in terms of exact product configurations, customer orders, delivery requirements, and expected scrap losses.

Detailed material and equipment scheduling decisions are constrained by the overall input planning decisions of the past. These schedules specify who gets what product, in what configuration, and when. Detailed schedules are also constrained by past material scheduling decisions concerning the availability of raw material and components.

Flexibility in short- and medium-term equipment scheduling is achieved with overtime, extra shifts, and subcontracting. As in the longer-term capacity decisions, economic feasibility is important. In cases in which the cost of increasing short-term capacity is too high, the decision may be to change the material plans and revise customer expectations.

Plans and schedules, however, cannot anticipate all the conditions of the future. Responding to changes in a timely manner, without overcompensating, requires continuous and careful monitoring and detailed decision making. This includes changing the priorities for producing particular components and products, adjusting capacities to overcome problems, and changing near-term schedules—all to match the detailed product flows with market needs.

Production and Inventory Management People

The wide variety of PIM decision making is accomplished by different people in different companies. All of the processes in the framework of Figure 1.2 are carried out somewhere in the firm, but the titles, organizational homes, styles, and even approaches can vary greatly. Some of these differences depend on the nature of the firm, some on historical patterns, and some on personalities. The key point, however, is that all of the processes must be performed.

Demand management is one of the more recently recognized activities in production and inventory management. The forecasting aspects have long been associated with the sales and marketing departments, with other departments being involved as necessary. Matching the outbound products with customer demands has historically been the province of distribution, logistics, transportation order entry, and customer service. Combining these activities is relatively rare in practice, although the need for integrating them is clear. Some companies are moving in the direction of better integration of demand management, focusing on the overall process or stream of activities to support the need, rather than on the particular organizational units. Materials management forms of organization are one attempt to house these activities in a more integrated fashion.

In most firms the demand management process is likely to be performed in several departments and under several different titles. Integration of the activities is accomplished with committees, by overarching additional functions, or on an ad hoc basis. This is a process for which clear integrative roles and responsibilities will become increasingly important as firms strive to become more customer driven. It is also a process that can often be improved significantly—in terms of both cost and performance!

Master planning is generally a responsibility of top management, at least for the production planning aspects. Master production scheduling is often found in the manufacturing organization, typically carried out by someone with a title such as "master production scheduler." Sometimes both production planning and master production scheduling will be delegated to a production planning and control group, which serves as a staff group inside manufacturing. However, if master planning is to truly be "top management's handle on the business," there can be no real delegation of decision-making responsibility. Badly made decisions in this function have devastating effects on the company, and because master planning must be closely integrated with many other departments and functional groups, it is rare to see full responsibility for this function exclusively in manufacturing.

Capacity planning is another process with long-range impact. Overall capacity is a function of detailed individual resources that are planned and managed in different functional departments. Often individual decisions are made on an ad hoc basis, but capacity decisions are increasingly being coordinated through the master planning process. Capacity decisions must be consistent with the material plans in order to ensure successful execution without costly excess capacities.

Capacity planning has been termed the missing link in production and inventory management because of the ad hoc nature of much of the decision making. As in the demand management process, many different people get involved with capacity decisions; integration of the decisions is an increasingly significant management concern, particularly in today's turbulent competitive environment.

The detailed material planning function is the first in the framework that is almost always housed in manufacturing, often with persons with job titles such as material or inventory planner. The development of the technical details of manufacturing, which are necessary to meet the production plan, would certainly seem to belong to manufacturing. In some cases, however, the heavy information and computer requirements of this function have led to its being housed in the data processing department. We certainly do not advocate this location, but we also believe that almost any organization can be made to work; conversely, few organizational changes are a guarantee of improvement.

Just-in-time activities cross many departments. In the last analysis, JIT is a philosophy, requiring fundamental changes in the company's culture, organization, and control systems. Decisions affecting human resource management are increasingly integrated into day-to-day manufacturing, but rely on enlightened personnel departments for support and guidance. The product movement aspects of JIT are again carried out by manufacturing, with significantly reduced interaction with formal PIM groups. JIT also leads manufacturing to undertake new forms of interaction with engineering, many other internal departments, and outside companies.

The production activity control process is primarily concerned with detailed scheduling of individual operations of particular parts as they go through manufacturing conversion stages. The activities are largely performed by manufacturing personnel, although some of the reporting and comparisons of performance are done by accounting people. Much of the responsibility for this process lies with the workers on the manufacturing floor itself, particularly for processing transaction information on production status, problems, or changes. Similarly, the responsibility for taking action and initiating changes may rest with the floor, again utilizing information nearest to the source.

PAYOFFS FROM PIM

The improvement of manufacturing management has been characterized as "doing better things," and "doing things better." Aligning the production capabilities with the strategic needs of the company is the substance of "doing better things" in manufacturing. Included are strategic issues such as what markets to serve, how to serve them, which competencies to develop, what products to focus on, and building the manufacturing capabilities to routinely support the strategy.

"Doing things better" is concerned with the efficiency with which things get done. This is traditionally a direct concern of manufacturing and the engineering functions. It is also an issue for the routine activities of all functional areas of the PIM processes detailed in Figure 1.2. Integrated production and inventory management is devoted to doing things better on a routine basis. *Changes* in the design of PIM, on the other hand, are often focused on doing better things.

Integrating PIM with Company Strategy

The process of integrating production and inventory management with overall company strategy is so important to effective PIM that we devote the entire closing chapter to it. The development of strategy begins in the marketplace. As seen in Figure 1.3, the business situation is based on an assessment of the market characteristics, competitive situation, and company strengths and weaknesses. The specific approach to the business situation defines the company's strategy. Market selection, product specifications, and competitive posture are driven by market characteristics and other factors, and they form the basis for development of company strategy. This in turn leads to determination of the manufacturing task. The manufacturing task is a summary of what is required of manufacturing to support the company strategy in terms of product, process, and the key competitive competencies. Does the strategy demand low cost, high quality, rapid response to new customer requirements, reliability in delivery, or something else?

The PIM infrastructure provides support for executing the manufacturing task. This infrastructure consists of all the processes listed in Figure 1.2 that support the overall manufacturing function. The key message here is that PIM must be different for different companies. They all face different market requirements, and have unique company strategies

---

FIGURE 1.3

Deriving the Required Production and Inventory Management Infrastructure

---

Market characteristics
Competitive situation   ⇒   Business situation
Company strengths/weaknesses
            ⇓   ⇓
Market selection
Product specifications   ⇔   Company strategy
Competitive posture
            ⇓   ⇓
Product design
Process requirements   ⇔   Manufacturing task
Competencies required
            ⇓   ⇓
Utilization of capacity   Production and
Variety of products   ⇔   inventory management
Responsiveness to change   infrastructure

---

that best leverage their unique capabilities. Producing large volumes of a few products at low cost, for example, mandates a different PIM infrastructure than is the case for a company producing a large number of different products in low volumes. The system must be consistent with the company's strategic needs.

The rewards for correctly aligning the production and inventory management processes with the strategic objectives can be substantial. Consider the following examples:

- An industrial packaging company implemented a make-to-stock master production scheduling system designed to support the greatly increased requirements during the peak selling season of a major soft drink customer. This superior customer service could not be easily duplicated by their competitors and the payoffs to the company included premium prices and excellent margins.

- An industrial battery company reduced manufacturing lead times with a JIT program and improved its ability to provide shorter delivery lead times to its customers by installing an improved master production scheduling system. As a result, the company was able to achieve major sales growth in a down market by taking market share from its competitors.

- By carefully assigning production to the appropriate plants around the world, a company in the copier and printer business was able to achieve important cost advantages over the competition and gain substantial market share.
- A medical products company has so closely integrated its customers into the production and inventory management functions that the customers are now part of the decision process. This is a significant barrier to any potential competitor.

Operational Payoffs from Production and Inventory Management

The payoffs from well-performed production and inventory management activities are not limited to strategic benefits. Significant and pervasive changes have led to savings in many operational areas of the company and have provided distinct profit advantages for many firms. The payoffs include not only cost savings, but also increased sales through better customer service, lower prices, and/or improved product design. In fact, we often tell managers that if you have not made a significant improvement in your PIM systems in the last five years, you should review them very carefully. State-of-the-art PIM practice is improving at a rapid pace. Several examples illustrate the inventory reductions that are being achieved:

- A heavy equipment manufacturer reduced total inventory levels by 50 percent during a period when production volume grew by 40 percent.
- A large telecommunications equipment manufacturer reduced the number of days of inventory on hand by 25 percent. This was after a major program had already made it one of the best in its industry.
- The benefits are not just for large companies. A 300-person firm that supplies the copier and printer industry realized overall inventory reductions of 15 to 20 percent and some instances of 80 to 90 percent reductions, in less than one year.

Operating costs are improved by getting people to work on the right things and having the capacity available to do so. This is an important function of integrated production and inventory management. Further efficiencies can be derived from having the support of the other areas of the firm. Generally, when operating savings are discussed the first thought is labor savings, but they can also involve equipment, material, indirect labor, and costs of "confusion." Some recent examples follow:

- A small telecommunications equipment manufacturer reduced labor costs by 46 percent during a period in which labor turnover *dropped* from 46 percent a year to 8 percent.
- A corrugated container company increased production volumes by 57 percent (achieving the highest levels ever) without adding new equipment.
- A hospital equipment manufacturer received a large unexpected order from the Middle East. The new PIM system allowed them to simulate the impact of accepting the order, plan the additional requirements, and deliver on schedule—without "panic" operations.
- An automobile manufacturer achieved a 58 percent reduction in assembly hours per car over several years of effort.

Time-based competition has recently received considerable management interest. The intent is to reduce manufacturing lead times, promise delivery in less time than the competition, and respond to unexpected demands in short time periods. The ability to execute a time-based competition strategy requires effective execution of the PIM processes. If the material is not there when needed, if the capacity is not available, or if there is no clear understanding of the customer's need, the best of efforts are bound to fail. When the elements all come together, however, the payoffs can be substantial. Some companies have recently reported these results:

- A communication equipment manufacturer reduced total manufacturing lead times (from raw material to finished product) by more than 50 percent in a two-year time period.
- By integrating the customer contact and logistics activities into the production and inventory management functions, a consumer products manufacturer reduced total cycle time (from customer contact to delivery to the customer) by more than 50 percent. An automobile manufacturer achieved nearly a 70 percent reduction with the same integration.
- A global audio equipment manufacturer has been able to realize on time delivery performance in excess of 98 percent overall, with 100 percent performance for some segments of their business.

INTEGRATION WITH OTHER RESOURCE AREAS

Production and inventory management decisions affect many other resource management problems. Several linkages have already been pointed out. In this section we look at relationships from the point of view of the other resource areas, rather than starting from the PIM vantage point. In the remaining chapters of the book, some of these relationships will be described in considerably more detail.

Human Resources

The human resource management (HRM) function helps in the recruiting and selecting of labor resources for PIM processes. HRM also aids in career planning, training, performance appraisal, and ongoing job redesign. All of these activities are important, and none of them belongs exclusively to HRM. Developing and maintaining a skilled core of PIM people is a shared responsibility, as the dynamism of PIM requires substantial and continual skill-building and training. The responsibility for initiating that training rests with the PIM managers, but the training can be facilitated by the human resource department.

The human resource dimension of PIM is growing in importance. At one time, PIM activities represented the largest deployment of overhead personnel in most manufacturing companies. This is still true in some cases, but the technology has changed. More and more PIM processes are being performed as a part of the basic manufacturing infrastructure. PIM that formerly was done in offices, removed from the action, is now done in real time on the shop floor by factory workers. This means that redeployment, retooling, and outplacement has been and is still occurring in the field of PIM.

In a similar vein, the changes in company strategy—toward time-based competition, globalization, faster responses, and greater flexibility—require major changes in PIM. The human resource dimension of these changes is critical. It is not enough to have good ideas; one needs to sell the ideas—and to implement them.

A related linkage between the human resource management department and PIM comes with the growing importance of JIT. The JIT philosophy calls for considerable training of direct labor employees in topics such as problem solving, group relationships, and continual improvement processes—as well as in cross-functional training to support evolution in JIT applications. These efforts are part of PIM as well as the general manufacturing effort. JIT makes a *major* impact on job design, which is felt in PIM, in human resource management, and in general management.

Information Systems

Even for relatively small companies, PIM requires computer-based systems, with an enormous amount of information processed in order to plan and control the flow of materials. Continual changes in status, conditions, and demands require information that is up to date, with important changes highlighted for actions by the PIM group. The information must be accurate, timely, and in the appropriate format. The expertise for providing this information has historically been in the management information systems area. The responsibility for system design specifications, however, rests with the PIM managers.

In recent times, the dependence of PIM on information systems professionals has declined as ever-higher levels of computer literacy are achieved by PIM professionals. More importantly, computer systems are becoming increasingly user friendly. Commercial software is readily available for PIM use, and these packages can be used with a much lower dependence on outside help.

Changes in company needs, technology, and PIM capabilities mean that periodic enhancements to the PIM system are desirable. The critical question is *how* these enhancements are to be achieved. Historically, in the interface between PIM and information systems, PIM professionals were asked to specify their change requirements very precisely; thereafter, the information systems professional disappeared to write the computer code. This has changed dramatically in state-of-the-art applications. Many of the enhancements can be made by the users themselves, because they merely represent new ways of presenting data that are not fundamentally altered in the basic computer system. For those changes that *do* represent new software technology, there are two basic choices: write your own or choose a package that is being constantly improved, ride the upgrades, and *never* allow anyone to change the basic code. As soon as basic code is changed you are on your own because upgrades usually require more custom patches.

Although we strongly advocate packaged software, "plain vanilla" applications, and riding software upgrades, there still comes a time when the basic system needs to be replaced. Constant attention to the packaged software marketplace is an important activity for the information systems professional. If your PIM information systems have not been upgraded in the last five years, it is very likely that you are missing out on a major improvement opportunity.

Total Quality Management

PIM has a growing relationship with total quality management (TQM). We have audited several PIM systems that we were told were not working properly. Orders were being completed late, customer promise dates were missed, and a great deal of overtime and other "panic mode" operations were evident. But on closer examination we found that in the vast majority of cases, the faults were not in the PIM systems; they occurred because of quality problems. Indeed, we concluded in one case that the "M" in MRP does not stand for "miracle."

To the extent that quality problems can be minimized, scheduling and other PIM activities are much more straightforward. TQM is founded on the basic premise of prevention rather than detection, so implementation of TQM makes PIM an easier task. But the interaction is not one way. Best-practice PIM also supports better quality. An example will illustrate the point:

> A large defense contractor was paid with progress payments—which encouraged bad practices as far as work-in-process and throughput times. The average time to insert components on printed circuit boards was six months, while the average amount of work was less than one hour. The boards were typically processed only partially because of component shortages, then held as work-in-process until more components were available. Matching the right components with the right boards was "a work of art." Since boards were assembled in ad hoc ways, there was no way to truly assign causes to defects. When this problem was cleaned up, the work-in-process levels were reduced by more than 90 percent, and no circuit boards were released to manufacturing unless they had *all* components. Thereafter, boards were assembled as indicated in their engineering routings. The company expected to see the work-in-process decreased, but they were extraordinarily surprised by the improvements in quality. Major sources of variability had been removed.

Another interaction between TQM and PIM stems from integrated data bases. Production activity control is designed to track the progress of each component part and assembly as it is made. But TQM requires much of the same data, so the best practice is to combine these data streams, both for economy and to achieve better consistency, higher accuracy, and better early warning signals for when quality problems will necessitate PIM replanning.

In Figure 1.1, the role of scrap as a demand on capacity is clear. Accounting for this loss requires transaction processing that should be tied both to TQM activities and to PIM. As more scrap is produced, less capacity is available for production sold to customers. Even more important is the *particular* scrap produced; it only takes one part to keep a large product from completion and shipment.

Another impact of TQM on PIM is the need to plan for a product that is to be tested in quarantine, destroyed, or otherwise used by the quality department. Quarantine is often merely a lead time offset, and some firms are making creative use of PIM to decrease the overall inventory investment. Several drug companies push their products out to the distributors before the quarantine period is complete, with hold procedures in place so no one can purchase the drugs before they are authorized.

A more fundamental aspect of the quality/PIM role comes from the notions of continual improvement in quality, building quality in at the source, and striving for zero defects. All of these programs are fundamental to JIT, and are part of the practices of world-class firms today.

Accounting and Finance

The relationship between accounting and PIM is primarily concerned with joint information collection and the use of common data for solving problems in both resource areas. The vast majority of accounting information for operations (labor costs, inventory levels, materials used, and capacities utilized) comes from the data base accumulated to accomplish the PIM processes, which includes the detailed tracking information used for scheduling the operations to make component parts. The same data provide detailed information on the amount of machine and labor time each operation requires. These data are accumulated into actual cost data, and provide the comparison with the standard cost data (also based on PIM information) that provide variance analysis (materials, labor, and so on). Similarly, PIM data coming from purchasing provide the basis for material price variance analysis. The data are generated in manufacturing, and are used for PIM purposes and for cost accounting. The responsibility for accuracy in data collection often falls to PIM managers.

Accounting provides data for PIM management and for analyses of various kinds. For example, accounting often supplies cost estimates to PIM managers for project proposals, justifications, or assessments. It also provides estimates of costs and revenues for capital expenditures such as new equipment. Newer approaches in accounting, such as activity-based accounting, are also intimately linked to PIM. The main issue facing firms attempting to use these approaches is how to properly apply the costs of transactions such as material movements.

Another important interrelationship between accounting and PIM is the development and use of performance measures. These measures must provide the right incentives to achieve the objectives of PIM in particular, manufacturing in general, and the enterprise in total. This implies changing performance measurements as changes occur in strategic objectives, or in tactical plans. Similarly, the incentives must be right for the other parts of the organization that relate to PIM. The new breed of accountants is getting out of their offices and spending time on the shop floor—helping managers to find new ways to improve competitive performance.

As far as finance is concerned, it is important to remember that PIM decisions drive a very high proportion of the cash flows in the company. Money to pay for labor and material and to support inventory represents a negative outflow of cash, which will ideally be offset by inflows from sales of product. To the extent that PIM is done better, the time gap between outflows and inflows is reduced.

An important activity in finance is estimating the cash requirements. This requires information about cash outflows and inflows. The best source of these data is PIM, which makes it possible to estimate these cash flows very accurately. The cash flow projections are necessary for finance to provide loan schedules, lines of credit, and other sources of funds to pay for resources used in manufacturing.

Another link between PIM and finance is in the justification for projects to improve PIM performance. New computer software, relayout projects, and expenditures on facilities to support PIM activities may all have to satisfy a financial justification for capital allocation throughout the company.

Marketing and Sales

Many firms have implemented a drive toward "market focus," "customer delight," "maximizing customer prosperity," "customer problem solving," or "customer partnerships." There are minor differences among these, but all have an orientation toward closer relations with key customers, which invariably requires linking of information between customers and suppliers. The primary linkage is in PIM systems, because detailed linking of customer needs with these systems provides major improvements in customer satisfaction.

Examples include customers who have direct input into supplier scheduling systems, computer-to-computer planning and scheduling without intervention, separation of buying and selling from order placement and delivery, customers who purchase "capacity" at vendors—thereafter filling the capacity at a later date with specific items and joint customer/vendor engineering—where the bills of material and manufacturing routings are *jointly* determined.

Marketing/manufacturing integration is also being driven by the move toward "strategic business units," or SBUs. The SBU concept focuses on the overall flow of goods and ideas, from product design to customer, again breaking out of the functional silo syndrome. Typically, manufacturing units are specifically devoted to the service of a defined business segment or group of customers. PIM decisions are made to serve this market group, and PIM systems are tailored accordingly. "Hidden factory" transaction costs are reduced, response times are cut, and "bundles of goods and services" are produced as a unit.

> An example is seen in a very large Japanese electronics manufacturer. It found that for certain markets, the same customers would be serviced by several independent sales units, so it reorganized into SBUs. In the case of nuclear power plants, one integrated team was formed to provide basic hardware, electrical equipment, software, and systems integration. This required a newly trained sales force, marketing that dealt with *total* customer needs in this industrial sector, and manufacturing/design/research/development that was focused on the overall nuclear industry. It also mandated new PIM systems to provide coordinated deliveries of all items, project management of the installation, and coordinated support of new product developments (in all areas).

Another manifestation of marketing/manufacturing integration is seen in Europe, post 1992—particularly in consumer products. There has been a large growth in hypermarkets in Europe, and alliances are being formed to compete in the Common Market. The result is more power for the retailer, and less for the manufacturers. Competing as a manufacturer is more difficult; the pressures are on to reduce prices, help retailers turn their inventories faster, reduce paperwork costs, and provide other services. All of these have a big impact on PIM systems. PIM activities are being more closely integrated with marketing, chiefly through the demand management activity.

The relationship of sales to production and inventory management is again primarily through the demand management function, but here the emphasis is on day-to-day coordination. The exact product mix that goes out the door is largely dictated by the sales activity. The task for PIM is to anticipate this mix—and to respond to deviations from the predictions with as much responsiveness to customers as possible. As the actual sales take place, they consume the production planned by PIM systems.

Sales activities can have a great impact on production and inventory management, as sales promotions, quotas, and bonuses strongly influence the timing of demand. There are many stories of companies inducing seasonality in demand by scheduling sales promotions or discounts. In some cases this has been severe (the firm's own worst enemy is found by looking in the mirror).

Product Design and Development

The primary interaction between product design and development and PIM comes from the decreasing product life cycle and ever-greater product variety demanded by the marketplace. More and more new products are being scheduled into manufacturing, and changes to those products are accelerating. This means that PIM *must* be designed to move products through manufacturing more rapidly in order to avoid obsolescence—and in order to avoid the extraordinarily high (often hidden) costs of making changes to components and products as they are being produced.

> An example is a CAD/CAM terminal producing company that reduced its manufacturing throughput time from 20 weeks to four days—by implementing JIT. Its obsolescence costs were reduced to practically zero; because all customer orders were made to order, there were no finished goods; and work-in-process inventories were minuscule. Moreover, engineering changes were very straightforward; they were always for products that had not yet started manufacture, and could be implemented by the direct labor workers.

A second cut at the interaction between design and PIM comes when the design activity itself is scheduled—with PIM systems. Some firms, particularly those fabricating large custom products, use the same PIM systems for scheduling engineering design, drafting, and release as those used in manufacturing. This provides smoother, faster transitions from design to manufacturing.

Another growing link between the outside world and engineering is in the increasing practice of engineering communications with customers' and suppliers' engineers. This communication needs to be somewhat unconstrained, but at some point the result will be specifications of product designs, delivery dates, and schedules. To the extent that communication becomes a partnership or strategic alliance, the joint activities in both firms are enhanced by compatible PIM approaches and systems.

Field Service

The most immediate connection of PIM to field service is in the management of field service inventories. In many companies, large inventories of spare parts are held to satisfy customer demands for service parts. For some products, down time of equipment is so critical that inventories are kept at major airports and managed with real time computer systems. The basic design of all field service inventory systems is similar to that used in manufacturing enterprises that produce goods for stock.

An interesting issue, which we encounter fairly frequently, is whether to segregate field service parts from production parts—both physically and in terms of the planning systems used for them. Although there is not a generic answer to this question, we tend to believe that well-run firms should be able to use one system and one warehouse (though this is obviously not the case for companies in which field service is so large as to be a business by itself). The standard argument against this posture is that manufacturing will "steal" field service parts. This is neither necessary nor undesirable—under the right set of conditions. The key is to have one stockroom, with field service parts "allocated" or mortgaged to the field service group. If manufacturing needs a part, they must ask permission from field service. The opposite condition also holds; sometimes parts are necessarily "stolen" from manufacturing to satisfy emergency field service requirements. The point is that sharing and borrowing is facilitated with one inventory and one system, and duplication of warehousing costs is avoided.

In some cases, field service has its own "factory" to repair returns from the field and to manufacture items that the main plant no longer makes. In these instances, a formal PIM system is required—with most of the same problems encountered in manufacturing for new product PIM systems. One difference is the necessary planning for product lives, and the population of equipment that uses the spare parts. Another difference is often found in the bills of material that have to be maintained at different levels of change; a part returned for repair sometimes needs to be refurbished to a different engineering revision level. A final difference comes from the fact that many times field service must not only schedule parts, but must also schedule the people who will go into the field and perform the necessary work.

When field service does not have its own factory, it is necessary to incorporate the requirements of field service into PIM systems. Field service is a source of demand for capacity, and it is also a "customer." One issue that always arises in manufacturing is what priority to give field service orders. The issue is complicated by the extent to which orders are for real customer needs versus simply going into field service inventories—or even into customer spare-part inventories. The greater the "visibility" of the PIM systems in the demand requirements, the greater the possibility for overall company optimization and tradeoffs of conflicting needs.

A final issue in field service/PIM integration is how to design the customer order entry and order servicing activities. Can order entry for field service parts and services be done by the same group as order entry for products? Again, there is not a cookie cutter answer. A great deal depends upon the volume of orders in each stream and the complexity of the order entry. For some field service applications, order entry becomes partially a diagnostic service for the customers (Have you tried X? Is light Y on or off? What happens when switch Z is activated?). The point here is not to prescribe. What is worth doing is closely examining the procedures (a detailed process analysis) for order entry and customer servicing in both field service and regular business. What are the differences, and why are they necessary? Are there synergies that could be exploited? What would be required to combine the two systems? What are the basic systems used in each—and how do they connect to PIM? How can we make them more identical?

Distribution

There is probably no other resource area as directly linked to PIM as distribution. One view is that the outputs of manufacturing are the inputs to distribution. What gets scheduled and produced by PIM is sent to the customers by distribution. A rather different viewpoint is that what the customers need is provided by distribution and made by manufacturing. This is more than a question of tails and dogs. Moreover, the issues are complicated when the ideas are extended backward to supplying companies. Distribution necessarily encompasses inflows as well as outflows, and the question is how to best coordinate both of them with PIM. In many companies, an overall "stream" view is adopted of distribution and PIM: systems are designed so that goods can flow much like a stream—unimpeded—from suppliers through manufacturing to customers.

In many cases, there are indeed "impediments" in the flows—called inventories. Distribution inventories are usually held in distribution warehouses (sometimes at the factories), in distribution centers near the customers, or sometimes at the customer location (perhaps on consignment). In any case, managing distribution inventories is often accomplished with many of the same tools used in PIM inside the factory.

What is more interesting, however, is to not manage distribution inventories independently, but in fact to connect them with PIM approaches. This is often accomplished with a system called distribution requirements planning (DRP), which provides data to the demand management process. The logic is the same as that used for planning and scheduling inside the factory with material requirements planning, (MRP). The master production scheduler provides the critical linkage between the two systems.

A related dimension of "stream" thinking is to plan and monitor all the steps necessary to fill customer orders. That is, the emphasis here is on "order management," including the communications and monitoring of the internal orders as well—which plan and control the movement of products through the entire chain of supply. A large portion of order management is in fact PIM. The difference between order management and DRP may be small in terms of actual systems used, but there is a difference in concept. Order management starts with a customer focus; customer satisfaction is the primary driver for system design and evaluation. Competitive advantage presumably goes to the firm that provides the best deliveries, is most responsive to customer demands, and continually seeks new ways to satisfy customers.

The impact of changes on the design of the order management system, and particularly on PIM, is significant. PIM systems will continually be assessed in terms of how improvements might further the objectives of order management. This will call for periodic updating of software and occasional major changes in manufacturing approaches, such as cellular manufacturing or JIT.

A final impact of distribution on PIM comes from a "product mix" issue. The PIM processes plan and control production of the products that distribution has to get to the customers. Because the customers may be highly geographically dispersed, the product mix problem takes on another dimension. The relationship between PIM and distribution now rests on whether the mix is right for the set of customer deliveries that is needed. Have the right products been produced for the customer mix (and planned delivery schedule)? Not having the right products available to meet customer orders means increased distribution costs and/or poorer customer service.

The product mix issue is complicated even further by trying to integrate PIM activities with distribution to minimize transportation costs. Often there is substantial economy in making shipments in full carload quantities, and producing in a fashion that will accomplish this result can lead to significant transportation savings. Full carload lots become particularly important when shipments are of relatively bulky items shipped in pooled cars, which is the case in the furniture industry, for example. This also holds true for firms that collectively pool their shipments to a major customer in JIT deliveries, as is fairly common for automotive suppliers. In both of these cases, PIM decisions are strongly influenced by the transportation costs.

Procurement

The relationship between procurement and PIM is very close; often the activities are even grouped together organizationally, under a materials management form of organization. There are many interdependencies. For example, the planning activities of PIM are dependent upon vendor lead time information, quality of vendor products, and reliability of vendor delivery promises. This information has to be monitored by the purchasing group and updated for PIM as necessary. The detailed actions of procurement are dictated by many of the same tradeoffs and models used for PIM. Decisions need to be made concerning the quantities to be purchased and when these orders will be placed. The quantity decisions are typically based on lot-sizing models (which include purchase discounts), where the tradeoff is between the cost to place a purchase order and the costs associated with carrying inventory. The timing decisions are most often based on material requirements planning (MRP) systems, which time phase the requirements for component parts with the master production schedule.

An interesting change in integration of PIM and procurement has occurred with introduction of well-functioning MRP systems. Previously, many companies used documents such as a "traveling requisition," which in essence was an authorization for purchasing to buy—issued by the PIM process. This was necessary because it was only those working with the details of the day-to-day schedule who could be sure of procurement needs. This is no longer necessary with reliable systems: the system informs *everyone* as to the best estimates of needs, and there is no longer any need for procurement to receive authorizations from PIM. This has generated major cost savings in many companies, as procurement can now make decisions based on long-term plans—for all the parts purchased from a particular vendor, not just the immediate need for a single part, with full knowledge of the particular vendor's purchase discount policies.

The procurement process has also changed in other ways with the introduction of excellent PIM systems. Many firms now separate the activities of "buying" from "order placement." The former is a creative activity requiring negotiation, vendor partnership development, establishment of communication linkages between different functional areas in the two firms (e.g., engineering to engineering), and the overall contractual arrangements. The latter is a clerical activity, best served with minimal "hidden factory" costs, rapid response, and flexibility. Some firms have people on the shop floor transmit requirements each day, by FAX or telephone, to the vendors.

A more profound connection is to hook up the purchasing firm with its suppliers by electronic data interchange (EDI). In this way, the entire contents of an MRP system that affect a particular vendor can be readily accessed. This satisfies both the immediate needs and the long-term requirements.

The implementation of a just-in-time (JIT) approach to PIM has a profound impact on procurement. Best practice has been for companies to first implement JIT in their own operations before trying to institute JIT with vendors. This is because it is critical to understand not only the techniques, but also the change in mindsets and company culture associated with JIT. Once these are in place, it is possible and desirable to teach vendors how to implement JIT, and to connect the companies in more fundamental ways. A major thrust in all of this is the PIM philosophy of JIT; this calls for profound changes in vendor education and evaluation—as well as for major changes in the procurement activities.

In the section on production activity control in this book, a related aspect of procurement/PIM integration will be discussed in some detail. The idea there is to have relations with vendors be the same as those with a shop inside the factory. That is, the vendor is regarded as the "external shop," with the same approaches to priority setting and scheduling. The management of the outside shop would be similar, if not exactly the same, as the management of an inside shop. This approach pervades current thinking on procurement and vendor relations.

Manufacturing

On a day-to-day basis, PIM serves a key role in integrating the activities of the entire manufacturing enterprise, as detailed plans and schedules in manufacturing are themselves "integrated" by PIM. There must be internal consistency between the overall plans for manufacturing and the detailed shop floor scheduling activities, so PIM also connects the factory with the rest of the manufacturing organization. Customer orders are matched to manufacturing plans. Cash flows result from purchases of material, inventory buildups and reductions, and sales of finished goods. Engineering designs are "put into production"—scheduled by PIM. The requirements of PIM also help to frame strategic decision making—leading to the company "game plan." This game plan sets the stage for development of the production plan that links strategy with the master production schedule and detailed PIM execution.

There are many fundamental connections between manufacturing and PIM. In essence, the entire Certification in Integrated Resource Management (CIRM) program is devoted to "manufacturing." And the emphasis is on the entire manufacturing enterprise—not just on the manufacturing function. There are enormous changes occurring in manufacturing companies. One set of those changes is to achieve "world-class manufacturing." But increasingly, world-class manufacturing is becoming the "ante to play in the game." Every company has to have excellent quality, fast throughput times, simplified systems, continuous improvement, and excellent systems. But winning the competitive game now requires restructuring—an ongoing series of fundamental changes, or "strategic leaps"—*in addition to* the small steps of continuous improvement.

Achieving world-class manufacturing status itself requires major changes in PIM activities. Typically, just-in-time production methods are implemented in one form or another, and one of the major results is a decrease in resources required for PIM activities. Detailed scheduling is no longer an issue, and most PIM tasks are done on the shop floor—as part of the basic manufacturing infrastructure. Similarly, total quality management (TQM) also has a major impact on the PIM process. When quality is uncertain, a great deal of effort is expended in PIM to clean up the resultant messes.

Going beyond the usual definitions of world-class manufacturing leads to a focus on rapid innovation, flexibility, cross-functional integration, new product introduction, and process designs that support organizational learning. In all of these cases, PIM is affected. As the underlying data base for product creation, and the means for planning and scheduling product creation, PIM activities must be changed—sometimes fundamentally—in order to support the new manufacturing enterprise mandates.

Process Design and Development

Process design and engineering is concerned with developing and implementing the processes required to make goods and services available to customers. The integration with PIM comes primarily through the establishment of process routings for the manufacture of parts and assemblies. That is, process design and development specifies the way each component part and assembly is to be fabricated. The resultant routings are used for detailed shop floor scheduling, as well as for estimating the required lead times to make the parts and finished products. All of these data are part of the PIM data base and are used for planning and scheduling. Technical changes in the routings, equipment, and/or times required for manufacturing must all be coordinated with the development of the material plans.

Process design and development plays a key role in the physical aspects of JIT, changing the layouts of the plant, integrating pieces of equipment, and reconfiguring the factory for quicker throughput. These activities are often combined with some of the human resource activities to make substantial changes in the way the product is made. These changes, of course, must be integrated with the PIM plans.

A related interaction of process design and development with PIM occurs when cellular manufacturing is implemented. Manufacturing engineers spend a great deal of time identifying the particular parts to process in a cell—the "family" of parts. Typically, these choices are based on processing similarity and common routings. Some of these data are found in the PIM data base. After the family is identified and the cell is installed, the scheduling for cellular parts needs to change. What was before scheduled in detailed routing steps for parts—or even assemblies—is now scheduled at the piece part or assembly level, without detailed scheduling of the individual conversion steps. This often causes problems with accounting systems that are based on collecting data from routing steps.

Scheduling of major process design and development improvements is typically done with project scheduling approaches. Many of these are PIM models, and some companies use the same systems for scheduling projects (of any kind) as they use for routine PIM scheduling.

A final process design and development activity that influences PIM comes from the increasing attention being given to environmental problems. Firms are increasingly determined to keep close control over hazardous materials, and to account for their quantities and disposal exactly. There is a physical set of requirements to make this a reality, including design and maintenance of equipment. There is also the necessary recordkeeping associated with these activities, which can largely be accommodated with "standard" PIM software applications, rather than using specially designed systems and approaches. The advantages are common models and understanding of issues inside the company, and "transparency" of results.

Facilities Management

Facilities management is concerned with planning, installing, and maintaining the plant facilities and equipment required to produce the products and services offered by the company. There are several relationships with PIM. Perhaps the most fundamental connection is with capacity planning. In the long run, capacities need to be estimated based on projections of market demands and particular manufacturing methods. The rough-cut capacity planning methods are presented in the section on capacity planning. The importance of the resultant projections is critical to industrial facilities management, because it provides estimates of required equipment as well as expected hours of operation—so that maintenance requirements can also be better anticipated.

Another linkage with PIM is in scheduling maintenance on the equipment. Although not a product demand, this is a demand on capacity. Maintenance might be included in Figure 1.1, but the demands are quite different than the product demands. The schedules of these demands affect the use of the equipment for regular production and, therefore, must be integrated with PIM planning activities.

Capacity planning models can also be used to generate "scenarios" of different demand patterns, different equipment choices, and different intensities of running the equipment (e.g., three shifts). All of these have an impact on facilities planning and maintenance.

Maintenance part inventories also require planning. Many PIM concepts are being adapted for this purpose, including lot-sizing models, price discounts, and some of the issues discussed under procurement. Additionally, some firms are using the time-phasing applications of MRP to better anticipate the requirements for maintenance parts. The basic approach is to anticipate a requirement by placing a time-phased requirement in the future (based on mean time to failure data) whenever a new part is installed. These estimates can be planned and updated based on actual hours of operation.

Total productive maintenance (TPM) uses PIM concepts even more. Preventive maintenance is planned, scheduled, and carried out *before* equipment problems arise. These activities need to be coordinated with other demands on equipment, and with personnel who perform the maintenance. In fact, TPM requires complex scheduling of equipment, materials, and people—many of which have competing demands. Coordination requires the same skills and approaches used in PIM.

PIM also has a link with integrated facilities management in the process of setup time reduction associated with JIT. Smaller batches (a goal of lot size = one) require many process changeovers. Included are the equipment itself, tooling, location of tools, and planning systems for scheduling changeovers. PIM systems can be applied to help with some of these issues. Some firms establish "bills of material" for tooling and changeovers, and use their PIM systems to identify when the particular tooling requirements are needed—and where they are to be sent. As flexibility is increased in JIT systems, scheduling of changeovers becomes more critical. In many cases, the scheduling is delegated to the shop floor personnel. The objective is to have the facilities available to workers at all times so that changeovers can be made without delay.

PIM AND PERFORMANCE MEASUREMENT

One gets what one measures! Further, it is not what one *expects,* it is what one *inspects!* Figure 1.4 depicts a necessary alignment between strategy, actions, and measures. If the strategic directions for the company change, it is necessary to change the measures—both to achieve implementation of the new strategic directions and to operate under the new strategy. Thus, if "Quality is Job One" (to quote Ford Motor Company), then measures will have to be changed to achieve *and* maintain quality. Management cannot issue platitudes about quality and then beat people over the head to push products out the door. If after some time a firm feels that its quality is just fine, it may choose a new strategic direction (but not at the expense of quality) such as time-based competition. Again, measures will have to be changed.

A similar congruence needs to exist between actions and measures. If just-in-time manufacturing is now a major action program in the company, it is necessary to install measures to support JIT implementation.

FIGURE 1.4
The Strategy, Actions, Measures Alignment

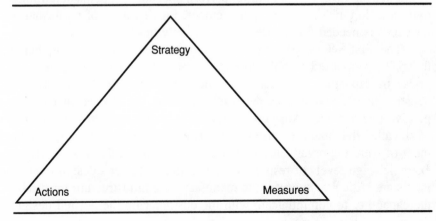

Moreover, it is critical to eliminate practices and measures that impede progress toward JIT. Examples are found in accounting-based measures that drive toward better capacity utilization—at the expense of work-in-process inventory levels.

Finally, measurement changes should be seen not only as keeping up with changes in strategy and actions, but also as a powerful lever to mobilize an organization. Some firms, for instance, have recognized that labor costs are a relatively small percentage of overall costs; they are largely fixed in nature, and the firm has extra capacity. In this situation, many companies have concluded that material velocity is the game. Measures that focus on inventory reduction, linkages across the value-added chain, changeover speed, and flexibility will drive the firm toward concrete changes.

All of these changes have a major impact on PIM. As the source of planning and coordination, PIM needs to be synchronized with the desired modifications in operations. Moreover, PIM in many companies is the largest source of "hidden factory" activities, and so it is not unusual to find more overhead people deployed in PIM than anywhere else in the company. One goal is to reduce this cost—to find alternative PIM methods that allow PIM personnel to be redeployed to solve other problems.

Setting Performance Standards

Setting performance standards can be divided into a hierarchy with four levels. The first level is for the organization as a whole. The second is concerned with the performance of the manufacturing function. The third standard deals with manufacturing performance against plans determined by production and inventory management. Finally, a set of performance measures is needed for the detailed PIM activities.

The first set of performance standards deals with "doing better things"—as opposed to only "doing things better." These measures appraise overall strategic success for the entire enterprise. The primary question here is: what does the firm need to do to succeed in its competitive marketplace? Answers to this question, in turn, set out what is often called the "manufacturing task." The manufacturing task is a statement of what the organization should be doing particularly well. If, for example, high levels of responsiveness to the customer's design requirements are critical to success, the manufacturing infrastructure must have the capability to communicate with the customer on the desired design.

Explicit measures then need to be formulated to assess the firm's performance in this area. The key point here is that it is better to measure the right thing—even if imperfectly – than to define the measurements on some other more readily measurable basis.

Alternatively, if the manufacturing task is defined as low cost, then cost/price objectives relative to the competition need to be set and evaluated periodically. If reliability of delivery is the task, the measures need to focus on performance—from the *customer's* point of view. How well is our company performing relative to our competitors? The critical issue in this case is to not only measure one's performance internally, but also to see how the customers see us—on a relative basis, where the game is constantly changing.

The next level of performance measurement involves the manufacturing function, which partially depends upon the capability of PIM. But performance of the overall manufacturing function depends on other activities as well. The line organization has to deliver the goods—with satisfactory cost and quality performance. Engineering must design the right products and roll them out in proper time frames. Procurement needs to find ways to integrate vendor capabilities with those possessed by the company. Manufacturing processes need to be designed concurrently with product design, and continually improved. Distribution must also be assessed with a continual improvement philosophy.

Within the manufacturing function, there is also a pivotal issue associated with tradeoffs. Today's competition requires that the classic tradeoff questions be rephrased as *and* rather than *or.* Best practice requires low cost and flexibility, low inventories and high customer service levels, a wide product line offering and focused facilities, low overhead costs and strong support services, and so forth. Measures must be formulated that support these combined objectives. Are the periods of inventory supply decreasing without any sacrifice in customer service? Is unit cost decreasing despite the increasing product line? Are the measures of customer service improving, along with cost reduction? These combined metrics underscore the need for continuous improvement in manufacturing performance—on several dimensions simultaneously.

The third level of performance standards relates to manufacturing performance in terms of PIM plans. These measures define efficiency and effectiveness in meeting the most basic activity in manufacturing: execution of the schedule and customer satisfaction. The key performance standard here is whether or not manufacturing hit the schedule. Was it able to build the products planned and deliver them to the customers on time? How closely did it come to the inventory targets? How about the cost targets? Did vendor performance measure up to expectations?

PIM sets the pace for a great deal of what takes place thereafter in manufacturing. Resources are planned and provided to execute the PIM plans and cash flow projections can be based on PIM expectations of when component parts and supplies will be purchased and when finished goods can be invoiced to customers. Machine and labor capacities are planned as well. The key question in all of this is, how well did actual operations match the plans as determined by PIM?

The final set of standards pertains to operation of the PIM group itself and its performance in helping the manufacturing function. A primary standard for the group is set in terms of the cost (and the improvement in cost) to do its job. Is it reducing the overhead costs by continuously getting more efficient at the PIM activities? Is it taking less and less cost per unit of product or manufacturing work center to develop the production plans, material schedules, and other activities? Is it easier to react to the control system signals for changes?

A related set of issues has to do with the quality of PIM activities. That is, in addition to doing the work for less cost, firms also need to continuously improve their PIM activities. JIT, cellular manufacturing approaches, and all the other latest concepts should be studied to see if they fit the company. If so, they need to be implemented—and promptly. The PIM activity must be evaluated in terms of its relation to state-of-the-art practices.

Auditing PIM

The procedure for auditing PIM needs to be consistent with the four-stage hierarchy delineated above. The first issue is to be sure that all performance standards and measures reflect the strategic objectives—or at the very least are not inconsistent with these overarching objectives. The objectives for the manufacturing function also need to be examined at many lower levels in the organization to search for inconsistencies. The audit of actual manufacturing practices in executing PIM plans requires a focus on problems in execution and their underlying causes. Recurring problems are to be particularly studied for similarities, root causes, and basic changes required. Within the PIM activity itself, the audit focuses quite a bit on benchmarking—against best practices. Where are there chances for improvement? How quickly is progress being made? What is impeding improvement? What needs to be done to quicken the pace?

Outside auditing of manufacturing operations involves first gaining an understanding of what the fundamental business objectives are and how they have been formulated for the manufacturing function. Is there a well-articulated manufacturing strategy statement that has been widely disseminated? How do the PIM systems support it? Who is the person who explains these systems? Is it only someone from the computer department? A next step is to review actual system outputs, whether on paper or on video terminals. Do the data make sense? Is there face validity (e.g., no negative inventory balances)? Next, it is necessary to go to the factory floor to see if the system is *really* in use. Foremen need to be asked for their shop reporting systems. Do these come out of their pockets, or is there a blank stare? Finally, data base integrity needs to be verified. Are all boxes of parts on the shop floor clearly identified, with proper paper work?

Finally, the audit has to focus on what might be, on continuous improvement, and on the "strategic leaps" that might be possible with very different approaches to manufacturing—and to the other functional areas in terms of better solving customer problems.

Keeping the Faith

In addition to periodic auditing, performance measures need to be in place that measure accomplishment on a routine basis. The measurements must be relatively frequent; once a week is not too occasional to collect some of the information. Group performance should be made public soon after the measures are taken, or even at the same time.

Best practice provides rewards for good performance and frequent celebration of accomplishments. The rewards need not be exotic; in fact, simple rewards publicly given have had great impact on motivating continued improvements in performance. These can be in the form of public displays (dinners, photos in the company newspaper, trips to other divisions, and so on).

It is important to make sure that supporting organizations share the feelings of accomplishment. If the management information systems department was instrumental in changing software that made it possible for the PIM group to make major improvements, recognition of both groups is vital.

The Impact on the PIM Functions

One clear objective for the PIM function is an ongoing process of "raising the bar." Today's best systems and solutions are tomorrow's average performance. PIM practices must evolve quickly in order to keep up with global competition and best practices. In the strategic area, this means more carefully assessing the required manufacturing task and deriving the resultant PIM infrastructure required. It also means determining the role of new technical aids, such as hardware and software, designed to manage material flows in the factory. In the last analysis, the *real* need is for increased PIM professionalism.

Several professional societies are working hard to provide the new levels of professionalism required. The American Production and Inventory Control Society (APICS), in particular, was an early provider of certification examinations for professionals involved in PIM. That program is called Certification in Production and Inventory Management (CPIM). Now APICS, recognizing the ever-increasing need for integration, has developed an examination program for Certification in Integrated Resource Management (CIRM).

In the rest of this book, production and inventory management—from an integrative point of view—will be described in detail. The intent is to provide sufficient background for the certification exams. But the examination process is only a short-term objective. In the last analysis, our goal must be to provide insights for leading edge manufacturing practice.

SECTION 2

DEMAND MANAGEMENT

This section contains a chapter that focuses directly on the demand management activity, and two more containing technical material for those of you who would like more background on PIM basics before launching into the rest of the book. The concept of demand management is rela-

Production and Inventory Management

tively new. There are some that would argue that demand management is an oxymoron. Demand cannot be managed. We do not hold to that concept. Not only can demand be planned, but it can also be shifted when it is of value to the customer, or if major economies can be achieved. The key point is that demand cannot simply be allowed to happen (as though Christmas was a surprise each year) and then have the company react. It must be anticipated and planned for explicitly. This is a key role of integrated production and inventory management.

In addition to the initial chapter on demand management, there are two chapters in this section that cover background material that underlies not only demand management, but many of the other chapters as well. Forecasting serves as an input to virtually every management decision in the book. Chapter 3 is devoted to some of the management issues underlying short-term forecasting for operational decisions. If you have a background in forecasting, you can easily skip this chapter.

The chapter on inventory theory is very basic, but does present some classical background that is useful in understanding the systems that are currently in place in many companies. The roles of inventory are described, and some of the trade-offs taken into account in the development of inventory policy are presented. Chapter 4 also points out the difference between independent demand and dependent demand, which is helpful in understanding some of the notions that pervade modern material requirements planning systems.

CHAPTER 2

DEMAND MANAGEMENT

We begin with demand management because that is where all production and inventory management begins and ends—with the customer. It is here that the needs of the customer are determined and satisfied.

Demand management is an important activity because it relates the factory to the customer, and synchronizes manufacturing accordingly. It is an area in which a great deal of change is happening. The customer-driven firm realizes how important it is to forge links with its customers. These links are part of the demand management function. Regardless of the type of firm, the customer-driven company will strive to provide value-enhanced products. Thus, in all company environments there may be much more to learn about customer needs than just the quantity and timing of the product requirements. Such things as packaging, quality, nonstandard sizes, and positioning on the carrier might all be important to some customer. These needs establish the overall bundle of goods and services provided.

Through demand management, all potential demands on manufacturing capacity are collected and coordinated. This activity manages the day-to-day interactions between customers and the company. A well-developed demand management module within production and inventory management (PIM) brings significant benefits. Proper planning of all externally and internally generated demands means that capacity can be better planned and controlled. Timely and honest customer order promises are possible, and physical distribution activities can be improved significantly. This chapter illustrates how these benefits can be achieved.

The approach to demand management depends on two important factors: the degree of product customization and the level of service to be provided to the customer. When products are sold on a *make-to-stock* basis, forecasting how many of each product will be demanded over some time period is the essential task. In other environments, demand management can involve much more than just quantity determination. In *make-to-order* companies, for example, it might be necessary to work out the exact specifications of the product, even while it is being manufactured. In *assemble-to-order* firms, customers communicate the product options they would like and a delivery date must be provided to them.

In this chapter, we show examples of the demand management function in make-to-stock, assemble-to-order, and make-to-order firms. The chapter is organized around three topics:

- Demand management in production and inventory management: What role does demand management play in PIM?
- Company examples: How is effective demand management put into practice?
- Managing demand: How do we live with demand management on a day-to-day basis?

DEMAND MANAGEMENT IN PIM

Demand management encompasses forecasting, order entry, order delivery date promising, customer order service, physical distribution, and other customer-contact-related activities. Demand management also concerns other sources of demand for manufacturing capacity, including service-part demands, intracompany requirements, and pipeline inventory stocking. All quantities and timing for demands must be planned and controlled.

For many firms, planning and control of demand quantities and timings are a day-to-day interactive dialogue with customers. For other firms, particularly in the process industries, the critical coordination is in scheduling large inter- and intracompany requirements. For still others, physical distribution is critical, as the factory must support a warehouse replenishment program which can differ significantly from the pattern of final customer demand.

Demand management is a gateway module in PIM that provides the link to the marketplace. Activities performed here provide coordination between manufacturing and the marketplace, sister plants, and warehouses. Through demand management, we maintain a channel of communication between PIM and the customers. Specific demands initiate actions, which ultimately result in product delivery and consumption of materials and capacities.

Figure 2.1 depicts external aspects of the demand management module as the double-ended arrow connected to the marketplace outside the PIM boundary. One implication of this connection is the need to forecast demand as a prerequisite to the other PIM activities. An important aspect is providing forecasts at the appropriate level of detail. It may also imply constraining forecasts to meet certain overall requirements of the company. Both considerations are taken into account in the demand management process.

The importance of identifying all sources of demand is obvious, but sometimes overlooked. If material and capacity resources are to be planned effectively, we must identify *all* sources of demand: spare parts, distribution, inventory changes, new items, promotions, and so on. Only when we have accounted for all demand sources can we develop realistic PIM plans.

Demand Management and Production Planning

The exact linkage of demand management and production planning depends to some extent on how the firm handles production planning. If the production plan is a quarterly statement of output in dollars or some other financial measure, then the key requirement for demand planning is synchronization with this target. If delivery timings for significant customer orders affect the production plan, this information must be communi-

FIGURE 2.1
Key Linkages of Demand Management

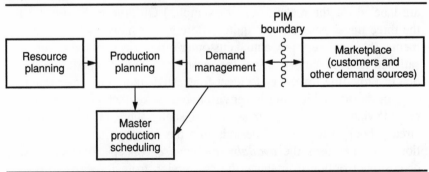

cated to production planning. Similarly, a major change in distribution inventory policy might influence the production plan.

In addition to the role of synchronization and communication between market activities and the production plan, a key activity in the demand management module is ensuring the completeness of demand information. All sources of demand for manufacturing resources must be identified and incorporated in the production and resource planning processes. Sometimes this is more difficult than it appears, especially for companies with a significant number of interplant transfers. We have often heard plant managers complain that their worst customer is a sister plant or division.

To get a complete picture of the requirements for manufacturing capacity and material, we collect such sources of demand as spare-parts demand, intercompany transfers, promotion requirements, pipeline buildups, quality assurance needs, exhibition or pilot project requirements, and even charitable donations. The principle is clear, although specifics differ from firm to firm: We must take all sources of demand into account. All must be included in the production plan to provide synchronization with other PIM activities.

Demand Management and Master Production Scheduling

Interactions of demand management and master production scheduling (MPS) are frequent and detailed. Details vary significantly between make-to-stock, assemble-to-order, and make-to-order environments. In all instances, however, the underlying concept is that forecasts are consumed over time by actual customer orders, as Figure 2.2 shows. In each case, forecast future orders lie to the right and above the line, while actual customer orders are to the left and below the line. (These areas are labeled for the make-to-order example.) Observe in Figure 2.2 that the three lines' positions are quite different. For make-to-stock environments, there are very few actual customer orders, as demand is generally satisfied from inventory. Thus, the master production scheduling task is one of providing inventory to meet forecasted future customer orders.

In the assemble-to-order environment, a key scheduling task is to provide viable customer promise dates. Usually, there are customer orders already booked for several periods into the future. The master production scheduler uses the *available-to-promise* concept for each module or customer option to manage the conversion from forecasts to booked orders.

FIGURE 2.2
MPS Time Fences—Forecasts Consumed by Orders

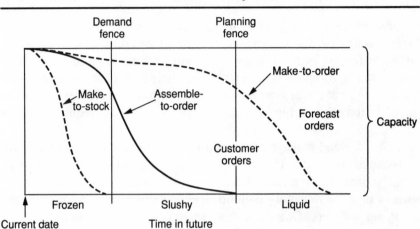

Still different demand management/MPS problems confront the firm with a make-to-order environment, even though there is a relatively large backlog of customer orders. Some orders can be in progress, even though they are not completely specified and engineered. This means that the master production scheduler is concerned with controlling these custom orders as they progress through all steps in the process. This involves engineering activities, which affect resource requirements as well as manufacturing. In addition, all this has to be coordinated with customers as the orders become completely specified.

In each company environment, the demand management module's objective is to bridge the firm and the customer. This is facilitated by the time fences (the demand and planning fences) in Figure 2.2. The two fences result in three areas sometimes termed "frozen," "slushy," and "liquid." The authority for making changes, as well as the way the MPS is stated, differs among these areas. Fences provide guidelines to help the master production scheduler as forecasts become actual orders.

Types of uncertainty also differ from company to company. One aspect of the relationship between master production scheduling and demand management is facilitating the buffering against this uncertainty. In the make-to-stock case, uncertainty is largely in the demand variations around the forecast at each of the inventory locations. Here, levels of safety stock (and/or safety lead time) must be set in order to provide the service levels required.

In the assemble-to-order case, the uncertainty involves not only the quantity and timing of customer orders but product mix as well. Safety stocks of options can be used, and hedging with components and/or materials is a valuable technique. For make-to-order environments, the uncertainty is often not the timing or quantity of the customer order, but rather how much of the company's resources will be required as the engineering is finally completed and exact requirements are determined.

The demand management task of specifying all sources of demand on manufacturing affects master production scheduling in several ways. Some sources are handled directly in the master production schedule, such as pipeline inventory buildup, special exhibition requirements, and interplant transfers. Others, such as spare parts, may not be.

The spare part issue can be complex in many firms. Demand for spare parts is typically forecast on an item-by-item basis, and added to the gross requirement data in the corresponding detailed material planning records. There may not be an explicit treatment of each spare part by a master production schedule. The actual spare-part demand, of course, varies around the forecast. Safety stocks can buffer variability. This simplified approach works reasonably well in firms in which it would take too long to manage each spare part by an MPS record.

Outbound Product Flow

Distribution activities are planned on the basis of the information developed in the demand management function. Customer delivery promise dates, inventory resupply shipments, interplant shipments, and so on, are all used to develop short-term transportation schedules.

Information used for master production schedules can be integrated with distribution planning as well. We can use the information to plan and control warehouse resupply. Moreover, transportation capacity, warehouse capacity, and the other resources in which the day-to-day distribution function operates can also be better planned and controlled with this information.

Integration of distribution with master production scheduling can have high payoffs for some firms. In essence, resupply shipping decisions are demand inputs, which the MPS must satisfy. Conversely, the MPS provides a set of product availabilities that we can use in the distribution planning system.

It is in demand management that we explicitly define service levels and resultant safety stocks. The requisite degree of flexibility for responding to mix or engineering design changes is set here as well, through the determination of buffer stocks and timings. The master scheduler is then responsible for maintaining the required level of buffer stocks and timings.

Through conversion of day-to-day customer orders into product shipments we realize the company's service levels. Careful management of actual demands can provide the stability needed for efficient production, stability which provides the basis for realistic customer promises and service. Booking actual orders also serves to monitor activity against forecasts. As changes occur in the marketplace, demand management can and should routinely pick them up, indicating when managerial attention is required.

Data Capture

Data capture and monitoring activities of demand management fall into two broad categories: the overall market and the detailed product mix. The activity most appropriate for production planning is overall market trends and patterns. Data should correspond to the units used in production planning. The intent is to determine on an ongoing basis the general levels of actual business for input to the production-planning process.

The second activity concerns managing the product mix for master production scheduling and customer order promising. Because final demand is in catalog numbers or stockkeeping units, day-to-day conversion of specific demands to MPS actions requires managing the mix of individual products.

For both the overall market and the detailed product mix, it is important to capture *demand* data where possible. Many companies use sales instead of demand for purposes of making "demand" projections. Unless all demands have been satisfied, sales can understate actual demand. In other instances, we know of firms that use shipments as the basis for projecting demands. In one such case, the company concluded that its demand was increasing because its shipments were increasing. Not until they had committed to increased raw-material purchases did they realize that the increased shipments were replacement orders for two successive overseas shipments lost at sea.

Dealing with Day-to-Day Customer Orders

A primary function of demand management is converting specific day-to-day customer orders into detailed PIM actions. Through the demand management function, actual demands consume the planned materials and capacities. Actual customer demands must be converted into production actions regardless of whether the firm manufactures make-to-stock, make-to-order, or assemble-to-order products. Details may vary depending on the nature of the company's manufacturing and marketing conditions.

In make-to-order environments, the primary activity is controlling customer orders to meet customer delivery dates. This must be related to the master production schedule to determine the impact of any engineering changes on the final customer requirement. While firms often perform this function the same way for assemble-to-order products, communication with the final assembly schedule may also be needed to set promise dates. In both of these environments, there is communication from the customer (a request) and to the customer (a delivery date) through the demand management activity. These aspects of demand management have such names as order entry, order booking, and customer order service.

In a make-to-stock environment, demand management does not ordinarily provide customer promise dates. Because material is in stock, the customer is most often served from inventory. If there is insufficient inventory for a specific request, the customer must be told when material will be available or, if there is allocation, told what portion of the request can be satisfied. Conversion of customer orders to MPC actions in the make-to-stock environment triggers resupply of the inventory from which sales are made. This conversion is largely through forecasting, as the resupply decision is in anticipation of customer orders.

In all these environments, extraordinary demands must often be accommodated. Examples include advance orders in the make-to-stock environment, unexpected interplant needs, large spare-part orders, provision of demonstration units, and increased channel inventories. These all represent "real" demands on the material system.

COMPANY EXAMPLES

In this section, we illustrate actual demand management practice as well as records that demonstrate key concepts discussed in this chapter. These illustrations use material gathered from Abbott Laboratories, the Tennant Company, and the Elliott Company.

Forecasting at Abbott Laboratories, Inc.

Abbott Laboratories, Inc., in North Chicago, Illinois, is a multinational health-care firm. Its product line includes pharmaceutical products for professional and personal use, medical electronics, cosmetics, and related chemical and pharmaceutical products. Products in this example are produced on a make-to-stock basis; the company has a reputation for maintaining a high level of customer service. Figure 2.3 shows the forecasting process for these products.

Abbott Laboratories' forecasting procedure uses several techniques. In this example, the first step in the process is to develop monthly forecasts by product. The initial input is a computer-developed forecast that uses data on customer demand and provides a basis for marketing review and approval. Figure 2.3 shows that marketing did not modify the forecast for April and May but changed it for June. Management judgment is used in reviewing the forecast for these monthly totals. Next, the forecast is broken down by distribution center using a computer program and the demand history data base.

The process of dividing up the forecast by distribution center begins with determining the historical percentage of each product sold by each distribution center. Step III in Figure 2.3 shows this. The computer then applies these percentage breakdowns to the approved total forecast to develop the monthly forecast by distribution center.

At Step IV in Figure 2.3, we break down the forecast further by week in the month. Again, the computer does this by taking into account split weeks, vacations, and so on. The result is a weekly forecast for each product at each distribution warehouse.

Abbott then utilizes these forecasts as detailed requirements data for time-phased records for each warehouse. The result of thereafter applying material requirements planning (MRP) logic is the planned shipments for replenishing inventory from the factory. Data on actual demand are

FIGURE 2.3
Developing Detailed SKU Forecasts at Abbott Laboratories

Illustration of Weekly Forecast
Development for a Product
(by distribution center)

	Month		
	April	*May*	*June*
Week*	1–4	5–8	9–12
Step I: Computer-developed forecast by product (preliminary forecast)	520	648	712
Step II: Marketing revision and/or approval (final forecast)	520	648	620
	(OK)	(OK)	(Revised by Mkt.)

Step III: Computer proration of monthly forecast by distribution center (DC)

DC	*Forecast*†	*Percent of total FC*
#218	155	‡31%
#233	310	62%
#244	35	7%
Total	500	100%

April	*May*	*June*
§160	200	192
320	400	394
40	48	44
520	648	620

Step IV: Development of weekly forecast

DC #218
     #233
     #244

Week:								
1	2	3	4	5	6	7	8	9
‖40	40	40	40	50	50	50	50	48
80	80	80	80	100	100	100	100	96
10	10	10	10	12	12	12	12	11

*Four weeks per month used to simplify example.
†Each DC forecast is done independently using an exponential smoothing technique based on past DC sales history.

   Sample of calculations (within computer):
         ‡155 ÷ 550 = 31%
         §31% × 520 = 160 (rounded)
         ‖160 ÷ 20 days/mo. × 5 days/wk. = 40/wk.

Source: D.C. Whybark, "Abott Laboratories, Inc.," in *Studies in Material Requirement Planning,* ed. E.W. Davis (Falls Church, Va.: American Production and Inventory Control Society, 1977), p. 17.

captured at the warehouses. Periodic replanning and safety stock are used to absorb fluctuations between sales and forecasts.

An interesting reaction occurred when warehouse supervisors first received these weekly projections of product sales at each warehouse. In many instances, they could use their knowledge of the local purchasing patterns to adjust the planned distribution of the weekly forecast for each month to better plan inventory resupply. Although the information was quite detailed, they could review weekly patterns and adjust them to the monthly totals provided by the computer breakdown of the marketing approved forecast.

Order Promising and Flexibility Management at Tennant Company

The Tennant Company manufactures industrial floor maintenance equipment and associated cleaning products, ranging from small walk-behind cleaners to larger operator-driven units. Machines are used for both indoor and outdoor applications. They are divided into families for planning and scheduling purposes. Within each family are a large number of customer-specified options and accessories for each machine.

Customer order promising is done explicitly from the machine availability plan prepared by the material planning and control system. Specifically, the order entry function does it using a report of machine status. Figure 2.4 provides an example. The first part of the document shows the status of machines in the E2 family. This report includes machines that have already been assembled, machines in various stages of preparation for customer delivery, and machines scheduled for future production. It shows that all but one of the machines scheduled for production in the next seven weeks are promised to customers. The earliest possible customer delivery date promise is for a machine in week 7 (manufacturing day 211, June 5). This report helps implement available-to-promise logic. It is used to allocate customer orders to the time periods in which machines will be available.

The next two parts indicate two of the options available for the E2 family: the gas and LP motor options. This provides a second level of order entry testing. The only machine that will be available in the week of June 5 is an LP machine. We see this because there is no commitment to the LP motor available in the week of June 5. This logic of testing product availability illustrates the process of order entry that matches customer requests to the availability of scheduled machines and options at Tennant.

FIGURE 2.4
Tennant's Report of Machine Status: The Customer Order Promising Document

D A I L Y   M A C H I N E   R E S E R V A T I O N   R E P O R T — MFG DATE 182

		1	2	3	4	5	6	7	8	9	10	11	12	13	14	15	LATER
	FINAL	182	186	191	196	201	206	211	216	221	226	231	236	241	246	251	
	LOGS	APE6	MYO1	MYO8	MY15	MY22	MY29	JNO5	JN12	JN19	JN26	JLO3	JL10	JL17	JL24	JL31	CMTMNT

16100 PARTS BASIC E2
PARTS-BASIC   E2LINE #16100

CRTO UNCH TEST RWRK ASSY PULO		1	2	3	4	5	6	7	8	9	10	11	12	13	14	15	LATER
3 4 1 1 1	SCHEDULED	1	1	1	2	2	2	1	2	1	1	1	1	1	1	1	1
	STOCK CMT																
1 1	1 OF 1 CUST CMT	–	–	–	–	–	–	–	–	–	–	–	–	–	–	–	–

17005 FINAL ASSY E2
PARTS-UNIQUE-GAS   E2LINE #16102

CRTO UNCH TEST RWRK ASSY PULO		1	2	3	4	5	6	7	8	9	10	11	12	13	14	15	LATER
1 2 1	SCHEDULED	1			2	2	1	1	1	1	1	1	1	1	1		1
	STOCK CMT																
1	1 OF 1 CUST CMT	–	–	–	–	–	–	–	–	–	–	–	–	–	–	–	–

17006 FINAL ASSY E2 LP
PARTS-UNIQUE-LP   E2LINE #16103

CRTO UNCH TEST RWRK ASSY PULO		1	2	3	4	5	6	7	8	9	10	11	12	13	14	15	LATER
2 2	SCHEDULED	1	1			1	1	1	1	1	1	1	1	1	1	1	1
	STOCK CMT																
2 1	CUST CMT			1													1

Source: W. L. Berry, T. E. Vollmann, and D. C. Whybark, *Master Production Scheduling: Principles and Practice* (Falls Church, Va.: American Production and Inventory Control Society, 1979), p. 163.

Figure 2.5 illustrates the production version of the same document in somewhat greater detail. This MPS control report has basic parts, unique gas parts, and unique LP parts, as did the order entry document. It is important to notice that exactly the same information is available to manufacturing as was available to order entry. Additional information in this report is of interest in illustrating flexibility management. First, we see specifically identified time fences for the basic parts at manufacturing day 276 and 436 (note the vertical lines of slashes), and different fences identified on the records for the gas and LP parts. These time fences are defined to indicate time frames in which management wants flexibility. For the basic parts, the fence set at manufacturing day 276 is a *volume hedge* fence. Its purpose is to provide flexibility to accommodate an increase in overall demand for the E2 family. The fence for the gas and LP engines provides flexibility for adapting to mix changes, which occur between these two options.

The hedge concept is applied as illustrated in Figure 2.5. For example, in the basic parts, the hedge unit indicated in period 276 has just crossed the time fence, and the master scheduler will move it out unless a management decision is made to increase the volume for the E2 family to include the hedge quantity. Fences for the options indicate the flexibility range for product mix changes. The number of gas and LP options within the time fences exceeds the basic parts scheduled, thus providing flexibility to adjust to day-to-day swings in demand for product options without having too large an inventory.

Tennant manages the hedge units explicitly, which means that the amount of flexibility is highly visible and reviewed continually. A great deal of computer information on time fences, hedge percentages, and current status is available to the master production scheduler to assist in managing the hedges. An important concept is to provide flexibility in volume and product mix only where necessary. This is noted by the fact that no hedge units are provided prior to manufacturing day 211. There is no need for flexibility before that time, because all available machines and options are covered by customer orders.

With all this system's formality and the support it provides planners, there is still a major element of management discipline that makes this system work. When asked what would happen if a salesperson tried to promise delivery of an E2 prior to week 211, Doug Hoelscher (director of manufacturing at the time these reports were gathered) replied, "We'd fire the person."

FIGURE 2.5
Tennant Flexibility Management Document

```
                    M A S T E R   S C H E D U L E   C O N T R O L   R E P O R T
                                              MFG DATE 1.82

E2 FAMILY
                        D.RATIO   SHORT RANGE HEDGE   TIME FENCES   BACKLOG   LONG RANGE HEDGE   LAST REVIEW
16100   PARTS-BASIC    EZLINE 100%  10%  15%  20%    00 20 52 00      2        %    %    %          417

SEQ 0560  -APR/-----MAY-----/-----JUN-----/-----JUL-----/-----AUG-----/-----SEP-----/----OCT
     ADJ. 161 166 191 196 201 206 211 216 221 226 231 236 241 246 251 256 261 266 271 276 281 286 291 296 301 306
PLANNED    1   1   1   2   2   1   1   2   1   1   1   1   1   1   1   1   2   1   1  1/   1   1   1   1   1   1

HEDGE
W/S                                                                                          1/
COMMITTED  1   1   2   2   2   1   1                                      2/                  2/  1   1   1   2   1

          ----/-----NOV-----/-----DEC-----/-----JAN-----/-----FEB-----/-----MAR-----/----APR
           311 316 321 326 331 336 341 346 351 356 361 366 371 376 381 386 391 396 401 406 411 416 421 426 431 436
PLANNED     1   1   1   1   1   1   1   1   1   2   1   1   1   1   1   2   1   1   1   1   1   1   1   2   1  1/

HEDGE                           1   1       1       1       1       1       1           1
W/S         1   1   1   2   1   2   1   2   1   2   1   3   1   1   1   2   1   2   1   2   1   2   1   2   1  1/
COMMITTED                                           /                                                        1/

          ----/-----MAY-----/-----JUN-----/-----JUL-----/-----AUG-----/-----SEP-----/----OCT
           441 446 451 456 461 466 471 476 481 486 491 496 501 506 511 516 521 526 531 536 541 546 551 556 561 566
PLANNED     1   1   1   1   1   2   1   1   1   1   1   1   1   1   1   1   2   1   1   2   1   1   1   1   2   1

HEDGE       1   1       1       1       1       1       1       1       1       1       1       1       1
W/S         1   1   1   1   2   1   1   1   2   1   1   1   1   1   1   2   1   1   1   2   1   1   1   2   1   1

          ----/-----NOV-----/-----DEC-----/-----JAN-----/-----FEB-----/-----MAR-----/----
           571 576 581 586 591 596 601 606 611 616 621 626 631 636 641 646 651 656 661 666 671 676 681 686 691 696
PLANNED     2   1   2   1   1   2   1   2   1   2   1   2   1   2   1   2   1   2   1   2   1   2   1   2   1   2

HEDGE       2   1   1   2   1   1   1   1   1   1   1   1   1   1   1   1   1   1   1   1   1   1   1   1   1   1
W/S         2   1   2   1   2   1   2   1   2   1   2   1   2   1   2   1   2   1   2   1   2   1   2   1   2   1
```

FIGURE 2.5
Tennant Flexibility Management Document (continued)

```
16102  PARTS--UNIQUE-GAS   B2LINE   D,RATIO   SHORT RANGE HEDGE   TIME FENCES   BACKLOG   LONG RANGE HEDGE   LAST REVIEW
                                      65%      45%  50%  55%       00 03 16 00      2        %    %    %          417

SEQ 0570
        -APR-/-------MAY------/-------JUN------/-------JUL------/-------AUG------/-------SEP------/------OCT
ADJ.    161 166 191 196 201 206 211 216 221 226 231 236 241 246 251 256 261 266 271 276 281 286 291 296 301 306
PLANNED  1   1  / 1  / 2   2   1   1   1   1   1   1   1   1   1   1   1   1  1/ 2   1   1   1   1   1   1   1

HEDGE           /   1   1                       1   1           1   1           1   1           1   1
W/S      1   1  / 2   2   1   1   1   1   1   1   1   1   1  1/ 2   1   1   1   1   1   1   1
COMMITTED 1  1  / 2   2   /

        -NOV-/-------DEC------/-------JAN------/-------FEB------/------MAR------/------APR
PLANNED 311 316 321 326 331 336 341 346 351 356 361 366 371 376 381 386 391 396 401 406 411 416 421 426 431 436
         1   1   1   1   1   1   1   1   1   1   1   1   1   1   1   1   1   1   1   1   1   1   1   1   1   1

HEDGE            1   1               1   1           1   1           1           1           1
W/S      1   1   1   1               1   2           1   2           1           1           1               1
COMMITTED

        -/-------MAY------/-------JUN------/-------JUL------/-------AUG------/------SEP------/------OCT
PLANNED 441 446 451 456 461 466 471 476 481 486 491 496 501 506 511 516 521 526 531 536 541 546 551 556 561 566
         1   1   1   1   1   1   1   1   1   1   1   1   1   1   1   1   1   1   1   1   1   1   1   1   1   1

HEDGE    1                                                               1
W/S      1   1   1   1   1   1   1   1   1   1   1   1   1   1   1   1   1   1   1   1   1   1   1   1   1   1

        -/-------NOV------/-------DEC------/-------JAN------/-------FEB------/------MAR
PLANNED 571 576 581 586 591 596 601 606 611 616 621 626 631 636 641 646 651 656 661 666 671 676 681 686 691 696
         1   1   1   1   1   1   1   1   1   1   1   1   1   1   1   1   1   1   1   1   1   1   1   1   1   1

HEDGE    1
W/S      1   1   1   1   1   1   1   1   1   1   1   1   1   1   1   1   1   1   1   1   1   1   1   1   1   1
```

FIGURE 2.5
Tennant Flexibility Management Document (continued)

PARTS-UNIQUE- LP	EELINE	D.RATIO 35%	SHORT RANGE HEDGE 45% 50% 55%	TIME FENCES 00 03 16 00	BACKLOG 2	LONG RANGE HEDGE % % %	LAST REVIEW 417

16103

SEQ 0580

```
-APR/----MAY----/----JUN----/----JUL----/----AUG----/----SEP----/----OCT
ADJ. 161 166 191 196 201 206 211 216 221 226 231 236 241 246 251 256 261 266 271 276 281 286 291 296 301 306
                                                                                              /
PLANNED   1/                                                          1    1    /    /
                                                                               /    /
HEDGE            /        1    1    1    1    1
W/S       1/                                         1    1    1         1         1
COMMITTED 1/
```

```
---/----NOV----/----DEC----/----JAN----/----FEB----/----MAR----/----APR
311 316 321 326 331 336 341 346 351 356 361 366 371 376 381 386 391 396 401 406 411 416 421 426 431 436
PLANNED   1    1    1         1    1    1    1    1    1    1    1    1    1    1    1    1    1    1    1    1
                                1
HEDGE                           1
W/S       1         1    1    1         1    1    1    1    1    1    1    1    1    1    1    1    1
COMMITTED
```

```
---/----MAY----/----JUN----/----JUL----/----AUG----/----SEP----/----OCT
441 446 451 456 461 466 471 476 481 486 491 496 501 506 511 516 521 526 531 536 541 546 551 556 561 566
PLANNED   1    1    1    1    1    1    1    1    1    1    1    1    1    1    1    1    1    1    1    1    1    1    1    1    1    1
HEDGE
W/S       1              1         1    1    1    1    1    1    1    1    1    1    1    1    1    1    1    1
```

```
---/----NOV----/----DEC----/----JAN----/----FEB----/----MAR----/
571 576 581 586 591 596 601 606 611 616 621 626 631 636 641 646 651 656 661 666 671 676 681 686 691 696
PLANNED   1    1    1    1    1    1    1    1    1    1    1    1    1    1    1    1    1    1    1    1    1    1    1    1    1    1
HEDGE
W/S       1    1    1    1    1    1    1    1    1    1    1    1    1    1    1    1    1    1    1    1    1    1    1    1    1    1
```

Source: W. L. Berry, T. E. Vollmann, and D. C. Whybark, *Master Production Scheduling: Principles and Practice* (Falls Church, Va.: American Production and Inventory Control Society, 1979), p. 166–167.

The discipline at Tennant runs through to manufacturing as well. Under the new responsibilities created by formal systems, the manufacturing mandate is to produce the scheduled products. If no customer order is available for an item approaching final assembly, management will release a stock commitment for that item. If no customer order is received by the time the item goes to final assembly, it is produced in an easily retrofitted model and goes into inventory. The top-management committee of Tennant owns this inventory. Top management feels that the commitment to meeting the plans, be they in manufacturing or marketing, is important enough that they will own any unsold finished goods. They recognize that, if marketing is to meet the sales plan, any currently unsold machines will be sold in the future.

Make-to-Order Products at Elliott Company, Division of Carrier Corporation

The Jeanette, Pennsylvania plant of the Elliott Company manufactures large air and gas compressors and steam turbine devices. Products are highly engineered using state-of-the-art manufacturing techniques and materials. Engineered apparatus products are designed and built to customer specifications to accomplish a specific function. Products typically weigh 50 tons and take a year or more to produce. Over half this lead time consists of order processing, design engineering, and purchasing.

Scheduling each customer order is based upon the assignment of an imaginary (planning) bill of material to each major piece of equipment. This bill is established by using elements of previously built products that are similar to the product on the customer order. This imaginary bill of material is then processed by standard MRP logic. Lead times to produce the components on the imaginary bill of material include estimated times to perform the engineering design and do the necessary drafting, as well as manufacturing lead times. The result is proper ordering of when each component should be designed, priorities for all customer orders relative to due dates, and a capacity requirement profile for each work center. Capacity profiles are produced for engineering and drafting work centers on a routine basis. Figure 2.6 shows one of the imaginary bills of material.

Figure 2.7 is part of an exception report showing behind-schedule project activities. For example, the first item on the list is nine weeks behind schedule, has project engineer A in charge, and is presently in engineering department H3P. The report is printed in order of those jobs

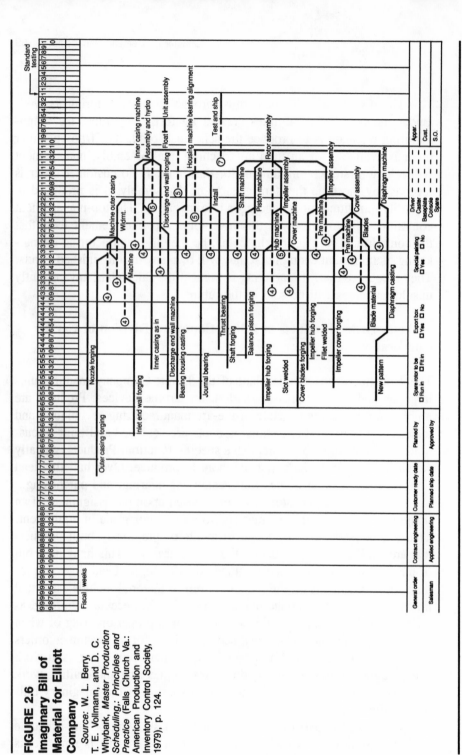

**FIGURE 2.6
Imaginary Bill of
Material for Elliott
Company**

Source: W. L. Berry,
T. E. Vollmann, and D. C.
Whybark, *Master Production
Scheduling: Principles and
Practice* (Falls Church Va.:
American Production and
Inventory Control Society,
1979), p. 124.

FIGURE 2.7
Late Project Status Report for Elliot Company

Report no. ELCH08391				Engineered apparatus project engineering records scheduled for action		
Shop order	Description	Quantity	Rel. no.	Project engineer	EAC Project engineering schedule	Status (weeks)
A528156000	Piping Agreement	1.0	H3P	A	356	−9
A528157000	Piping Agreement	1.0	H3P	A	376	−7
A628502000	Purchase Response	1.0	P3		326	−6
A628503000	Purchase Response		P3		326	−6
A628505000	Coupling	1.0	S5	V	326	−6
A528196000	Major Components	1.0	S5	A	466	−5
A628505000	Release of S2	1.0	S3	V	336	−5
A528164000	Coupling	1.0	S2T		356	−3
	Coupling	1.0	S2T		356	−3
A528187000	Oil Schematic	1.0	M1P	A	356	−3
	Piping Agreement	1.0	H3P	A	416	−3
V025094000	Pipe Agreement	1.0	M3P	O	376	−3
A528175000	Piping Agreement	1.0	H3P	A	366	−2
A528027000	Purchase Request	1.0	S2		376	−1
A528043000	Purchase Response	1.0	P2P		376	−1
	Major Components	1.0	S5	N	376	−1
A528131000	Lube Information	1.0	SAP		376	−1
	Firm Incomplete	1.0	S1A		376	−1
A528142000	Purchase Response	1.0	P3		376	−1

Source: W. L. Berry, T. E. Vollmann, and D. C. Whybark, *Master Production Scheduling: Principles and Practice* (Falls Church, Va.: American Production and Inventory Control Society, 1979), p. 125.

with the worst delays. Elliott uses production activity control and other PIM system modules to plan and control each customer order during the several months that each is in progress. In two years of using these systems, performance against customer promise dates improved 50 percent; inventory levels fell 23 percent; and meanwhile, sales volume rose 32 percent. The advantages stemmed from better planning and control of *all* aspects of the business, from order entry, through engineering, to the shop floor. Both hard and soft activities are planned and controlled with the PIM systems for project management.

MANAGING DEMAND

In this section we look at managerial issues related to the performance of day-to-day demand management tasks.

Organizing for Demand Management

Most companies already perform many if not all of the activities we have associated with demand management. In many instances, organizational responsibility for these activities is widely scattered throughout the firm. The finance or credit department performs credit checks and order screening associated with customer orders. Sales or customer service departments handle order entry or booking. Outbound product activities are associated with the distribution, traffic, or logistics departments of firms.

Some companies establish a materials management function to coordinate demand management activities. Organizational responsibility for demand management tends to be a function of the organization's history and nature. It is much less important, however, to have a unified organizational home for all activities than to appropriately define and coordinate them with one integrated data base.

In marketing-oriented firms (where success requires close contact with demand trends and good customer relations), demand management might well be performed by the marketing or sales organization. In firms in which product development requires close interaction between engineering and customers, a technical services department might manage demand. The materials management organization has grown up in firms that feel it is important to manage the flow of materials from purchasing raw materials through the production process to the customer. In such firms, which manufacture both industrial and consumer products, the demand management function can be part of materials management. In all instances, we must clearly assign responsibilities to make sure that nothing is left to chance.

If flexibility is a key objective, then management must carefully design and enforce rules for interacting with the system and customers so that the system can provide this flexibility. By this we mean that customer order processing must be established and enforced through the master production scheduling system. It involves carefully establishing rules for serving particular special customers. For example, if an extraordinarily large order is received at a field warehouse, procedures need to be established for determining whether that order will be allowed to consume a large portion of the local inventory or be passed back to the factory. We must define and enforce limits within which changes can be made. If any of these procedures is violated by a manager who says, "I don't care how you do it, but customer X must get his order by time Y," demand management is seriously undercut.

A useful technique for defining and managing these areas of responsibility is to tie them to time fences. Abbott Laboratories, Ltd. of Canada has developed a highly formalized set of time fences. Figure 2.8 shows the firm's four levels of change responsibility. As a change request affects the MPS nearer to the current date, responsibility for authorizing the change moves up in the organization. This procedure does not preclude a change, but it does force a higher level of review for schedule changes to be made in the near term.

The underlying concept for approval procedures is to take the informal bargaining out of the system. By establishing and enforcing such procedures for order entry, customer delivery date promising, changes to the material system, and responses to mix changes in the product line, everyone plays by the same rules. In the Abbott example, flexibility is part of the change procedure, but the difficulty of making a change increases as the cost of making that change increases. Clearly, this is more a matter of management discipline than technique. The ability to respond, "What don't you want?" to the "I have to have it right away" for a particular customer request helps to establish this discipline.

Managing Service Levels

One way to help the organization live with a formal system for placing demands on the manufacturing organization is to explicitly set levels of service and to publicize them throughout the organization. Substantial theoretical work has been performed concerning setting service levels for finished-goods inventory. This work indicates that inventory investment increases exponentially as service-level objectives are increased. More important is the need for discipline in the management of service levels. Simply stated, this means understanding that less than a 100 percent service-level target implies that occasionally there *will* be a stock-out. Truly understanding and living with that can be difficult. Often a stock-out or late delivery focuses so much attention on a given transaction that people respond to prevent its recurrence. This is frequently the origin of the impossible order given to many inventory clerks: "Keep the inventory low but don't stock out."

Determining appropriate service levels requires carefully considered trade-offs. With increasingly high costs of carrying inventory, levels of

FIGURE 2.8
Approval Fences for Master Scheduling Change at Abbott Laboratories, Ltd.

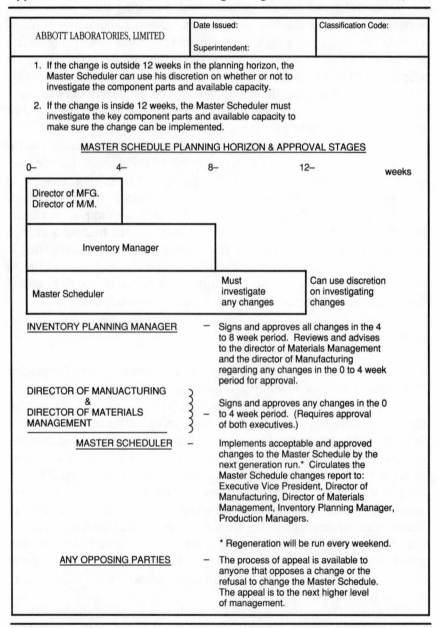

ABBOTT LABORATORIES, LIMITED	Date Issued:	Classification Code:
	Superintendent:	

1. If the change is outside 12 weeks in the planning horizon, the Master Scheduler can use his discretion on whether or not to investigate the component parts and available capacity.

2. If the change is inside 12 weeks, the Master Scheduler must investigate the key component parts and available capacity to make sure the change can be implemented.

MASTER SCHEDULE PLANNING HORIZON & APPROVAL STAGES

0—   4—   8—   12—   weeks

Director of MFG.
Director of M/M.

Inventory Manager

Master Scheduler | Must investigate any changes | Can use discretion on investigating changes

INVENTORY PLANNING MANAGER — Signs and approves all changes in the 4 to 8 week period. Reviews and advises to the director of Materials Management and the director of Manufacturing regarding any changes in the 0 to 4 week period for approval.

DIRECTOR OF MANUACTURING
&
DIRECTOR OF MATERIALS MANAGEMENT — Signs and approves any changes in the 0 to 4 week period. (Requires approval of both executives.)

MASTER SCHEDULER — Implements acceptable and approved changes to the Master Schedule by the next generation run.* Circulates the Master Schedule changes report to: Executive Vice President, Director of Manufacturing, Director of Materials Management, Inventory Planning Manager, Production Managers.

* Regeneration will be run every weekend.

ANY OPPOSING PARTIES — The process of appeal is available to anyone that opposes a change or the refusal to change the Master Schedule. The appeal is to the next higher level of management.

Source: W. L. Berry, T. E. Vollmann, and D. C. Whybark, *Master Production Scheduling: Principles and Practice* (Falls Church, Va.: American Production and Inventory Control Society, 1979), p. 83.

service provided to customers from a finished-goods inventory must be reevaluated very honestly. This means assessing the value of maintaining service levels versus the savings from reduced inventory. Statistical methods developed to solve the technical aspects of this trade-off do not solve the difficult managerial problem. Most firms recognize that 100 percent service (i.e., meeting every customer demand from inventory or at the time the customer requests it) is simply beyond the realm of financial possibility. For make-to-stock firms, 100 percent service implies huge inventories. For make-to-order firms, immediate delivery implies substantial idle capacity.

Lest we interpret these remarks as a plea for poor customer service, let us state emphatically that such is not the case. We firmly believe that major improvements are possible, but emotional responses are not the answer. PIM systems are designed to trade information for inventories and other kinds of slack—including poor delivery performances. By using systems well, we can be close-order coupled with customers; that is, demand management can often lead to substantial improvements in customer service *without* massive inventories or idle capacity.

Increasing use of just-in-time provides significant help as well. A CAD/ CAM terminal manufacturer reduced lead time from over 15 weeks to four days. At the same time, the company went from make-to-stock to make-to-order. All products are now built to exact customer order, and forecasts of exact orders are no longer necessary.

Using the System

An effective demand management module will gather marketing information, generate forecast information, screen and monitor performance information, and provide detailed action instructions for production and inventory management. Once implemented, we can use the system for routine tasks. A specific example is forecasting. The system can break out item sales within a product family, and management's attention can be focused on demand for the family itself. Focusing on the broader category both brings attention to bear where it is most needed and prevents squandering human resources on trying to reduce forecast error, which is unlikely. Only through support of the system can we redirect human resources.

The management control function also runs through formal PIM activities. Gathering intelligence on actual conditions in the marketplace provides the basis for deciding whether to change the organization's game plan (production plan, sales plan, budget, and so on) and for determining the appropriate level of flexibility. Again, the approach is to use the system to gather this information and then apply management talent where it is needed.

Perhaps the most important change that improved management in this area can effect is the ability to be honest with customers. In our experience, customers prefer honest answers (even if they are unpleasant) to inaccurate information. An effective production and inventory management system with discipline in order promising and service-level maintenance provides the basis for honest communication with customers. They can be told when to expect delivery or when inventory will be replenished—and they can count on it. Providing the basis for honest communication with customers can pay handsome dividends in terms of *customer loyalty.*

CONCLUDING PRINCIPLES

This chapter has focused on the integrative nature of demand management. It is necessary to capture all sources of demand, to maintain a proper demand management data base, and to carefully integrate demand management both with production planning and with the detailed MPS decision making. We see the following key principles as important to accomplishing these objectives:

- PIM systems must take into account *all* sources of demand, properly identified as to time, quantity, location, and source.
- Order promising must be coordinated with available capacity and materials.
- Customer service standards must be developed and maintained.
- Attaining more accurate forecasts may be an impossible dream. Management attention should focus on appropriate responses to actual conditions and forecast errors.
- To provide helpful stability in the factory, demand management and MPS activities need to be closely coordinated.
- Reliable customer promises should be the rule of the day, rather than wishful thinking.
- Clear definitions of authority and responsibility for demand management activities must be made to obtain the attendant benefits.

INTEGRATED RESOURCE LINKAGES

The most important linkage of demand management is with sales and marketing. Figure 2.1 shows this relationship explicitly, with the marketplace (and other demand sources) as a major input to demand management—as well as receiving information *from* demand management. The significance of the two-headed arrow in Figure 2.1 indicates that demand management responds to customer requests, but that the demand is *managed*.

This concept is also illustrated in Figure 2.2 where the three time zones, "frozen," "slushy," and "liquid," are shown. The underlying idea is that manufacturing should be responsive to marketplace needs, but it cannot do so without *any* constraints. In order to have some degree of stability in manufacturing—which allows for efficient operations—the company needs to place some restrictions on responsiveness and define the ways in which tradeoffs are to be evaluated.

Demand management is also closely related to logistics, in that the outward-bound product flow results in transportation schedule requirements. This flow also represents the input to distribution centers—and directly affects the customer service that can be provided by those distribution centers.

Demand management has several linkages with manufacturing strategy. The decision of whether to produce to order, to stock, or to assemble to order is a basic strategic issue—the manufacturing response to the marketplace. Thereafter, the management of customer orders, inventories, and/or a final assembly schedule is dictated by the strategic choice and by the way that demand data are integrated into PIM.

A linkage with management information systems follows from the strategic linkage. The ways in which data elements are described are important. For example, in a make-to-order approach, the customer order is essentially the bill of materials. It has to be uniquely defined, be managed through manufacturing, and serve as the basis for shipment, invoicing, and after-sales service. The information requirements are quite different for assemble-to-order or make-to-stock approaches.

The final significant linkage of demand management with the other resource areas is in field service. Field service is a source of demand to the company—both in terms of revenue and in terms of capacity requirements for materials, equipment, and personnel. An increasing trend in many companies is to combine the manufacturing facilities for both new products and repair items. Thus, several computer manufacturers will produce circuit boards for both new products and older products in the same facilities. We have also seen instances in which repairs are done in the same facilities.

If field service work is done in the same facility as regular production, it is clear that this source of demand needs to be planned and integrated with all other demands. But even if this is not the case, field service requirements represent an important source of demand for resources in many manufacturing companies. This demand needs to be captured, planned, and coordinated in PIM systems.

REFERENCES

Berry, W. L.; T. E. Vollmann; and D. C. Whybark. *Master Production Scheduling: Principles and Practice.* Falls Church, VA: American Production and Inventory Control Society, 1979.

Christopher, Martin. "Creating Effective Policies for Customer Service." *International Journal of Physical Distribution and Materials Management* 13, no. 2 (a special edition of the journal devoted to customer service, 1983), pp. xx–yy.

Kern, Gary M., and Hector H. Guerrero. "A Conceptual Model for Demand Management in the Assemble-to-Order Environment." *Journal of Operations Management* 9, no. 1 (January 1990), pp. 65–84.

Kuehne, W. A., and P. Leach. "A Sales Forecasting Pyramid for Dow Corning's Planning Endeavors." *Production and Inventory Management Review,* August 1984, pp. 6–11.

Ling, Richard C. "Sales and Operations Planning." *American Production and Inventory Control Society 1990 Annual Conference Proceedings,* pp. 161–64.

Martin, Andre. *DRP: Distribution Resource Planning.* 2nd ed. Essex Junction, VT: Oliver Wight Ltd., 1990.

Millen, R. "JIT Logistics, Putting JIT on Wheels," *Target,* 7, no.2, (Summer 1991), pp. 18–24.

Pyke, D. F., and M. A. Cohen. "Push and Pull in Manufacturing and Distribution Systems." *Journal of Operations Management* 9, no. 1, (January 1990), pp. 65–84.

Vaughn, O.; T. Perez; and B. Stemwedel. "Short Cycle Replenishment at 3M." *American Production and Inventory Control Society 1990 Annual Conference Proceedings,* pp. 515–18.

CHAPTER 3

SHORT-TERM
FORECASTING SYSTEMS

Among the sources of demand that place requirements on manufacturing are sales forecasts prepared by the marketing and sales functions. Because of lengthy lead times encountered in manufacturing and purchasing, sales forecasts are an important source of demand information in making production and inventory decisions. The process of developing sales forecasts for these decisions is the subject of this chapter.

Preparation of sales forecasts is an integrative effort involving a number of company areas. Known customer requirements, sales force expectations, potential market demand, recent trends in customer order entry (or sales quoting) activity, and planned sales promotions are incorporated into subjective forecasts by the sales and marketing staff. Likewise, the impact of macroeconomic factors is frequently introduced by the corporate economist, whereas new product developments and introductions are indicated by the research and development staff. Furthermore, information regarding financial targets and budgetary objectives often influences development of sales forecasts. Finally, where companies face critical shortages in purchased material, such as electronic components, sales forecast information is often converted to component requirements and checked against supplier capabilities.

The development of sales forecast information is, therefore, an essential activity in coordinating efforts of the various functional areas in a business, especially marketing and manufacturing. For production and inventory management (PIM), the sales forecasts provide information necessary to estimate material and capacity requirements, and are therefore an important input to production and inventory control decisions, especially in the case of make-to-stock products.

Our objective in this chapter is *not* to provide a detailed exposition of forecasting models. Rather, the goal is to provide an overview and "appreciation" of what is involved in forecasting practice, the implications for PIM, and the linkages with other resource management issues.

Although a variety of sales forecasts are prepared in a business, including long- and short-range as well as aggregate and individual product forecasts, in this chapter we concentrate on the less subjective problem of short-term forecasting for individual products. The goals of effective forecasting systems are low-cost routine forecasts and a set of monitors to indicate when forecasting problems are incurred. These forecasts of end items, spare parts, and other independent demand should be a key input to the high-level PIM planning process. A key objective is to provide one, and only one, source for forecast data; this source is to be unbiased and usable by all areas in the firm.

Forecasts used for production and resource planning can be of many types, including subjective estimates, econometric models, and Delphi techniques. A detailed exposition of all these is a book in itself. Although many techniques could be applied to forecasting demand for individual end items, we focus here on short-term forecasts based on observations of past actual demand. The chapter is organized around four topics:

- The forecasting problem: How is the forecasting problem defined for production and inventory management purposes?
- Forecasting in industry: How have forecasting techniques been put into practice?
- Comparisons of methods: Which forecasting techniques work best under which conditions? What are the lessons for managers?
- Using the forecasting system: How do we select initial forecasting parameter values and monitor forecast results?

THE FORECASTING PROBLEM

In this chapter, we deal primarily with the problem of making short-term demand forecasts the type most useful for routine decision making in PIM. However, other decision problems both in manufacturing and in other functional areas of the firm require different time horizons for forecasting. We will briefly discuss these other situations before delving more deeply into developing short-term forecasting approaches. We will also treat a vital forecasting question: How to evaluate a forecasting technique's performance.

Forecasting Perspectives

Managers need forecasts for a variety of decisions. Among these are long-run decisions involving such things as constructing a new plant, determining the type and size of aircraft for an airline fleet, extending a hotel's guest facilities, or changing the curriculum requirements in a university. Generally, these longer-run decisions require forecasts of aggregate levels of demand, utilizing such measures as annual sales volume, expected passenger volume, number of guest nights, or total number of students enrolled. In a sense this is fortunate, because aggregate levels of an activity can usually be forecast more accurately than individual activities. As an example, a university administration probably has a pretty good estimate of how many students will enroll next term, even though the enrollment forecast for an elective course may be off by a considerable amount.

For aggregate forecasts, we may be able to use causal relationships and the statistical tools of regression and correlation. For example, household fixture sales are closely related to housing starts. The number of vacationers at resorts is related to the economy's net disposable income level. In such instances, the relationship may be statistically modeled, thereby providing the basis for a forecasting procedure. Managerial insight and judgment are also used extensively in developing aggregate forecasts of future activities for long-run decisions. Both statistical and qualitative forecasting methods can also be applied for medium-run decisions, such as the annual budgeting process. It is tempting to classify forecasting techniques as long-run or short-run, but this misses the point of developing and using techniques appropriate to the decision and situation.

Throughout this chapter we will consider fairly mechanical approaches for making forecasts, specifically, models for "casting forward" historical information to make the "forecast." Implicit in this process is a belief that past conditions that produced the historical data will not change. Although the procedures we discuss are mechanical, we should not draw from this the impression that managers always rely exclusively on past information to estimate future activity. In the first place, in certain instances, we simply have no past data. This occurs, for example, when a new product is introduced, a future sales promotion is planned, a new competitor appears, or new legislation affects our business. These circumstances all illustrate the need for managerial review and modification of the forecast at times when special knowledge should be taken into account. Do not lose sight of this as we move into this chapter's details.

Forecast Evaluation

Ultimately, of course, the quality of any forecast is reflected in the quality of the decisions based on that forecast. This leads to suggesting that the ideal comparison of forecasting procedures would be based on the costs of producing the forecast and the value of the forecast for the decision. From these data, the appropriate trade-off between the cost of developing and the cost of making decisions with forecasts of varying quality could be made. Unfortunately, neither cost is easily measured. In addition, such a scheme suggests that a different forecasting procedure might be required for each decision, an undesirably complex possibility. As a result of these complications, we rely on some direct measures of forecast quality.

One important criterion for any forecast procedure is a low cost per forecast. For many manufacturing planning and control problems, we need to make forecasts for many thousands of items on a weekly or monthly basis; the result is the need for a simple, effective, low-cost procedure. There are only rare occasions when the decision is to add more factory capacity. But routine short-term decisions are made frequently for many items, and cannot require expensive, time-consuming forecasting procedures. Moreover, because the resultant decisions are made frequently, any error in one forecast can be compensated for in the decision next time. However, a large expenditure for an aggregate long-term forecast may well be justified for making a factory capacity decision.

At one time, the vast data storage requirements and computer time needed for producing forecasts for several thousands or tens of thousands of items were major concerns. But as computer time and storage costs decrease, this aspect of forecast procedure evaluation becomes less important. Nevertheless, we will concentrate on procedures that have the attribute of simplicity, are easy to use, and have low computer time and storage requirements. For any forecasting procedure we develop, an important characteristic is honesty, or lack of *bias*; that is, the procedure should produce forecasts that are neither consistently high nor consistently low. Forecasts should not be overly optimistic or pessimistic, but rather, should tell it like it is. Because we are dealing with projecting past data, lack of bias means smoothing out past data's randomness so that overforecasts are offset by underforecasts. To measure bias, we will use the *mean error*. The *forecast error* in each period is actual demand minus forecast demand for that period. Figure 3.1 shows an example calculation of bias.

As Figure 3.1 shows, when forecast errors tend to cancel each other out, the measure of bias tends to be low. Positive errors in some periods are offset by negative errors in others, which tends to produce an average error or bias near zero. In Figure 3.1 there is a bias, and the demand was overforecast by an average of 25 units per period for the four periods. Having unbiased forecasts is important in production and inventory management because the estimates, on average, are about right. But that is not enough.

We still need to be concerned with the errors' magnitude. Note, for the example in Figure 3.1, that we obtain the identical measure of bias when actual demand for the four periods is 100, 100, 5,500, and 100, respectively. (This is shown as part of the calculations in Figure 3.2.) However, the individual errors are much larger, and this difference would have to be reflected in buffer inventories if we were to maintain a consistent level of customer service.

Let us now turn to a widely used measure of forecast error magnitude, *the mean absolute deviation* (MAD). Figure 3.2 shows sample calculations.

FIGURE 3.1
Example Bias Calculation

		Period (i)			
		1	2	3	4
(1)	Actual demand	1,500	1,400	1,700	1,200
(2)	Forecast demand	1,600	1,600	1,400	1,300
	Error (1) − (2)	−100	−200	300	−100

$$\text{Bias} = \sum_{i=1}^{4} \text{error}_i/4 = (-100 - 200 + 300 - 100)/4$$
$$= -100/4 = -25 \tag{16.1}$$

FIGURE 3.2
Sample MAD Calculations

	Period (i)			
	1	2	3	4
(1) Actual demand	1,500	1,400	1,700	1,200
(2) Forecast demand	1,600	1,600	1,400	1,300
Error (1) − (2)	−100	−200	300	−100

$$MAD = \sum_{i=1} |error_i|/4$$
$$= (|-100| + |-200| + |300| + |-100|)/4 = 175 \quad (16.2)$$

	Period (i)			
	1	2	3	4
(1) Actual demand	100	100	5,500	100
(2) Forecast demand	1,600	1,600	1,400	1,300
Error (1) − (2)	−1,500	−1,500	4,100	−1,200

$$Bias = \sum_{i=1}^{4} error_i/4 = (-1500 - 1500 + 4100 - 1200)/4$$
$$= -100/4 = -25 \quad (16.1)$$

$$MAD = \sum_{i=1}^{4} |error_i|/4$$
$$= (|-1,500| + |-1,500| + |4,100| + |-1,200|)/4$$
$$= 8,300/4 = 2,075 \quad (16.2)$$

The mean absolute deviation expresses the size of the average error irrespective of whether it is positive or negative. Here it is the combination of bias and MAD that allows us to evaluate forecasting results. Bias is perhaps the more critical issue, as we can compensate for forecast errors through safety stocks, expediting, faster delivery means, and other kinds of responses. MAD indicates the expected compensation's size (e.g., required safety stock). However, if a forecast is consistently lower than demand, the entire material flow pipeline will run dry, and it will be necessary to start over again with raw materials. Other problems arise for a consistently high forecast. The good news is that routine monitoring techniques can identify bias when it is present. The bad news is that judgmental forecasts, such as those made by marketing groups, are often biased because forecasting incorporates other goals (e.g., stimulating the sales force). The key is to clearly separate the *process* of forecasting from the *use* of forecasting. The process's goals are no bias and minimum MAD. What is *done* with the forecast is another issue.

FORECASTING IN INDUSTRY

In this section we briefly describe the approach used by one firm, the Ethan Allen Furniture Company. The firm utilizes an exponential-smoothing-based forecasting system to forecast its products' demand. "Exponential smoothing" is a term that sounds much more sophisticated than it really is. Exponential smoothing is essentially a form of moving average-based forecasting, in which a proportion of the error in each forecast is added to the previous forecast. At Ethan Allen, forecasting models are part of an overall managerial system that provides for monitoring demand, developing forecasts, reviewing and modifying forecasts, aggregating information, producing sales history data, and developing a variety of other management reports. Figure 3.3 provides one example of the type of report that can be produced by the forecasting system. This particular report can be produced on request for any product that management might wish to scrutinize. (The forecasting model used to produce the forecasts in Figure 3.3 was a seasonally adjusted model.) The report shows monthly seasonal factors along with forecasts, actual demand, errors, and percent errors. Note also that manual adjustments can be made, and that MAD and the tracking signal can be reported.

Figure 3.4 is one of the monitoring reports produced by the system whenever a manual review is indicated. The first product in Figure 3.4, a governor's chair, has triggered a review because the error exceeds 50 percent of the forecast. (The limit of tolerance is shown at the top of the report.) The inclusion of this particular governor's chair on the sales screening report suggests possible manual correction. The report includes data on the last three forecasts, actual demand, MAD, and other review data. Adjustments are made manually, if needed, and will appear in subsequent runs of the report if actual demand continues to fall outside the limits for review. The next two items in Figure 3.4 are included in the report because one individual customer order was larger than the stated percentage of the total forecast. The report shows any information on past changes to the forecast as well, which keeps the entire process

FIGURE 3.3
Ethan Allen, Inc., Sales and Forecasts

MIRROR   FOR ITEM 11-9008-   225

AVG SALES 44.5

	JAN	FEB	MAR	APR	MAY	JUN	JUL	AUG	SEP	OCT	NOV	DEC
SEASONAL FACTORS	.74	1.12	1.39	.63	.72	.65	.79	1.17	1.73	1.01	.79	1.06

ADJUSTMENTS TO AMOUNT FOR   ADJUSTMENTS TO AMOUNT FOR   MAD   TRACK SGNL

NUMBER OF UNITS FORECAST AND SOLD

0...20...40...60...80...100..120..140..160..180..200..220..240

SALES	TOTAL FCST	ERROR	PCT ERROR	DATE
27				FEB
70				MAR
16				APR
20				MAY
28				JUN
29				JUL
66				AUG
53				SEPT
28				OCT
38	26	+12	+46%	NOV
53	37	+16	+43%	DEC
38	25	+13	+52%	JAN
52	38	+14	+36%	FEB
71	48	+23	+47%	MAR
	22			APR
	24			MAY
	29			JUN
	27			JUL
	40			AUG
	59			SEPT
	34			OCT

- TOTAL FORECAST
x SALES

FIGURE 3.4
Ethan Allen, Inc., Sales Screening Exception Report

FOR MAY

UPPER LIMIT PERCENT = 50%   LOWER LIMIT PERCENT = 50%   NUMBER OF MADS = 2.5

PERCENT/MAD LIMITS EXCEEDED — CHR GOV — FACTORY 018

ADJUSTED FORECAST	ACTUAL SALES	ERROR	PERCENT ERROR	MAD ERROR	SALES RANGE FROM – TO	AV SLS	SEAS	FORECAST	ADJUSTMENT	REASON	MAD	MAD/AV
268	84	-184	-68%	2.2	134 402	372.4	0.72	268			81.7	21%
232	282	+50	+21%		TWO MONTHS AGO			232				
534	379	-155	-29%		THREE MONTHS AGO			534				
434	236	-198	-45%		FOUR MONTHS AGO			434				

LARGE INDIVIDUAL ORDER — 30-6050-A

CUST ACCT NO 17-4870-0   218 R   CHR GOV CRVR   ORDER DATE 5/21   QUANTITY 12

CONSOLIDATION NO. 30-6050-A   218   FACTORY 018
AVERAGE SALES 97.9   ORDER % OF AV SLS 12%
MAD 97.9   MAD/AV 21%

PERCENTAGE LIMITS EXCEEDED — 30-6050-A

ADJUSTED FORECAST	ACTUAL SALES	ERROR	PERCENT ERROR	MAD ERROR	SALES RANGE FROM – TO	AV SLS	SEAS	FORECAST	ADJUSTMENT	REASON	MAD	MAD/AV
70	34	-36	-51%	0.8	35 105	97.9	0.72	70			40.8	41%
68	44	-24	-35%		TWO MONTHS AGO			68				
143	171	+28	+19%		THREE MONTHS AGO			143				
123	60	-63	-51%		FOUR MONTHS AGO			123				

CONSOLIDATION NO. 30-6050-A   218   FACTORY 018
AVERAGE SALES 97.9   ORDER % OF AV SLS 12%
MAD 40.8   MAD/AV 41%   MAD LIM 104%   CUMUL ERROR +225   TRACK SGNL +5.5

LARGE INDIVIDUAL ORDER — 30-6052-

CUST ACCT NO 35-3595-0   218 R   CHR CPTN   ORDER DATE 5/01   QUANTITY 12
CUST ACCT NO 13-5448-0   ORDER DATE 5/24   QUANTITY 24

CONSOLIDATION NO. 30-6052-   218   FACTORY 018
AVERAGE SALES 61.3   ORDER % OF AV SLS 19%
AVERAGE SALES 61.3   ORDER % OF AV SLS 39%

ADJUSTED FORECAST	ACTUAL SALES	ERROR	PERCENT ERROR	MAD ERROR	SALES RANGE FROM – TO	AV SLS	SEAS	FORECAST	ADJUSTMENT	REASON	MAD	MAD/AV
44	42	-2	-4%	0.0	0 0	61.3	0.72	44			26.4	46%
46	12	-34	-73%		TWO MONTHS AGO			46				
95	123	+28	+29%		THREE MONTHS AGO			95				
82	40	-42	-51%		FOUR MONTHS AGO			82				

CONSOLIDATION NO. 30-6052-   218   FACTORY 018
MAD 26.4   MAD/AV 46%   MAD LIM 116%   CUMUL ERROR +22   TRACK SGNL +0.7

PERCENTAGE LIMITS EXCEEDED — 30-6055-   218R   DRY SINK

ADJUSTED FORECAST	ACTUAL SALES	ERROR	PERCENT ERROR	MAD ERROR	SALES RANGE FROM – TO	AV SLS	SEAS	FORECAST	ADJUSTMENT	REASON	MAD	MAD/AV
30	9	-21	-70%	1.3	15 45	42.3	0.72	30			16.0	37%
28	23	-5	-17%		TWO MONTHS AGO			28				
56	77	+19	+32%		THREE MONTHS AGO			56				
52	20	-32	-61%		FOUR MONTHS AGO			52				

CONSOLIDATION NO. 30-6055-   218   FACTORY 022
MAD 16.0   MAD/AV 37%   MAD LIM 95%   CUMUL ERROR +109   TRACK SGNL +6.8

explicit to the reviewer. This sales screening process ensures that the ultimate responsibility for forecasting rests with management.

COMPARISONS OF METHODS

Some excellent work on comparing forecasting methods has been done by Spyros Makridakis and his colleagues. Their research and some later work evaluating focus forecasting will be overviewed here. The results contain a key message for practice: Simple models usually outperform more complex procedures, especially for short-term forecasting.

The Forecasting Competition

A variety of forecasting techniques have been developed, and more are being created all the time. They range from very simple to mathematically complex, from aggregate-business-oriented to stock-keeping-unit-oriented, and from very costly to relatively inexpensive. Among the techniques at the business planning level are those involving expert opinion and consensus, causal or regression approaches that link activities in one sector with those in another sector, and economic or business analysis approaches. For the more operations-oriented forecasts, techniques range from attempts to characterize past data by using mathematical approaches, to simple projections of past performance using moving averages or exponential smoothing.

Spyros Makridakis organized a forecasting competition in which seven experts evaluated 21 forecasting models. The competition was based on 1,001 different actual time series. Some of these were yearly, some quarterly, and some monthly. Some of the series were microdata (e.g., for business firms, divisions, or subdivisions); others were for macrodata (e.g., GNP or its major components). Some series were comprised of seasonal data; others were not. Expert proponents of a variety of forecasting models analyzed the data, determined appropriate model parameters, and made forecasts of the series. The forecasting horizon's length varied from 1 to 18 periods into the future. Forecasting accuracy was determined with five different measures.

There was no one model that consistently outperformed all the others for all series, all measures, or all forecasting horizons. Some models were better than others on macrodata, whereas others were better for microdata. Similarly, some models were better for monthly data than for quarterly or yearly data, and still others were good for longer forecasting horizons. Therefore, one conclusion that comes out of this work is that a forecast user can improve forecast accuracy by choosing a model that fits the criterion and the environment in which he or she is interested (e.g., microdata versus macrodata, short versus long horizon, and measure of accuracy).

Because we are concerned here with short-term horizons, the general conclusion that simple methods do better than the more sophisticated models, especially over short horizons for microdata, is important. Such techniques as simple exponential smoothing tend to outperform sophisticated methods, such as econometric models.

Figure 3.5 summarizes the rankings for some of the procedures (for one-period forecasting horizons). For most of the criteria shown, exponential smoothing models do quite well. Figure 3.5 is for all the 1,001 data series; the best techniques do even better for just the microdata. One of the research's surprises is the combination technique's performance. It supports the idea of continuously selecting the forecasting technique that produces the lowest error over the last several permits of demand, an approach known as "focus forecasting." The results of the Makridakis forecasting competition also suggest that it might be better to average the forecasts from the several models used for each period.

The Focus Forecasting Comparison

To further test the idea that averaging might be better than choosing a single technique, Flores and Whybark performed an experiment involving focus forecasting and an average of all the models' forecasts. Because the focus forecasting approach requires that several forecasting models be in place anyway, averaging forecasts from all the models was a simple extension of the technique. Averaging might lead to better results—and is also consistent with the desire for simplicity and understandability.

A focus forecasting system using seven different models was the basis for the experiment. The focus forecasting results were compared to the results of averaging all seven forecasts, and an exponential smoothing model without trend or seasonal adjustments was used for comparison. Both simulated and actual demand data were used to test the approaches.

MAD and MAPE were used as criteria to evaluate the three procedures' forecasting performance, and the results were the same for both criteria. For the simulated demand data, there were significant differences

---

FIGURE 3.5

Performance Rank for Forecasting Techniques among 21 Methods for a One-Period Planning Horizon

Criterion*

Method (all adjusted for seasonality)	MAPE (mean average percent error)	MSE (mean squared error)	Average ranking relative to all other techniques	Median APE (median value of percentage error)
Naive (Forecast = Current actual)	7	17	8	8
Moving average	15	20	10	11
Simple exponential smoothing	3	13	7	7
Exponential smoothing with trend	4	7	2	4
Exponential smoothing with trend and seasonal factors	4	7	2	2
Combination (an average of the forecasts from six methods)	1	10	1	1

*The best performance on the criterion is 1, the worst is 21.

Source: Makridakis et al., "The Accuracy of Extrapolation (Time Series) Methods: Results of a Forecasting Competition," *Journal of Forecasting* 1, no. 2 (1982).

---

among the three procedures—going from averaging (best) to exponential smoothing (worst). The rankings were changed and the level of significance was reduced when actual data were used; exponential smoothing performed best, but focus forecasting and averaging were not statistically different.

The pragmatic implications of these experiments are clear. Forecasting actual demand is difficult. Unfortunately, the results do not provide a consistently superior choice of forecasting technique, but they do support the use of simple forecasting models.

The important conclusion for practitioners is that more sophisticated and expensive models are not necessarily better. It means that those who advocate using complex forecasting models need to justify their choice. They need to clearly demonstrate that they can provide better forecasts than the simpler procedures, and that the error measures are more consistent with the needs of the decision makers. This "show me" attitude becomes even more important when we consider the preparation cost for using many of the sophisticated models. In addition to computer and other costs, we should also add the cost to the organization of using a procedure that is difficult for nonexperts to understand.

USING THE FORECASTING SYSTEM

Using the forecasting system requires a heavy dose of common sense. In this section, we will look at some methods for incorporating external information into the forecasting system. We will also look at the problems of establishing forecasting model parameters and of monitoring the forecasting model results. In forecasting, it is not enough to select the forecasting model that appears to provide minimum bias and MAD. We must continue to evaluate forecast quality to make sure that the model chosen is still appropriate, to determine whether market conditions have changed, and to learn quickly when something has gone awry. We first turn our attention to the topics of external information, getting started, and monitoring. Thereafter, we briefly raise some strategic issues relating to forecasting.

Incorporating External Information

Many kinds of information can and should be used to make good forecasts. For example, in a college town on the day of a football game, traffic around the stadium is a mess. An intelligent forecaster adjusts travel plans on game days to avoid the stadium traffic, if possible. He or she modifies the plans according to the game's impact on traffic. Forecasting models based on past observations during the week, however, would probably forecast little traffic around the stadium. We certainly would not use that forecast without adjusting it for game day. That simple principle is applicable to business forecasting as well, but it is surprising how often people fail to make these adjustments.

Examples of activities that will influence demand and perhaps invalidate the routine forecasting model are special promotions, product changes, competitors' actions, and economic changes. We have two primary ways to incorporate information about such future activities into the forecast. The first is to change the forecast directly; the second is to change the forecasting model. We might use the first method if we knew, for example, that there was to be a promotion of a product in the future, or that we were going to open more retail outlets, or that we were going to introduce a competing product. In these instances, we could adjust the forecast directly to account for the activities, just as we do for the game day. By recognizing explicitly that future conditions will not reflect past conditions, we can modify the forecast directly to reflect our assessment of the future.

The second method for dealing with future activities would be to change the model itself. This might work best when we are unsure of what these activities' effect will be. If, for example, we know that one of our competitors is going to introduce a new product, we suspect the market will change, but we may not be sure of the change's direction or magnitude. If the product is expensive, we may gain sales; if it is novel, we may lose sales. All we know is that there may be a change. In this instance, we could change the model to be more responsive to actual conditions in the marketplace, and thus incorporate changes into our forecasts more quickly. If we know something of what may happen, we could change both the forecast and the smoothing constant. Both methods help to incorporate information about the future into the forecasts before using the forecasts to make decisions.

Getting Started

When historical demand data are available, there is nothing like a plot of those data for getting started. If there is a pattern to the demand, we can easily plot it. The plots also help us to set the initial values for doing the forecasting in a way that is consistent with the historical data. If, for example, plots reveal seasonal factors, we can estimate the base value by taking the average for at least one seasonal cycle.

We can find seasonal indexes by averaging the indexes calculated for each period in the cycle. Similarly, a plot of the values for trend data would enable us to draw in a trend line (or we could average the period-to-period changes to estimate trend).

In every instance (constant data, trend data, or seasonal data), plots will help us determine whether it is desirable to use the more recent data in setting starting values.

It is also useful to make simulated forecasts, using the past few periods of historical data as test data. For instance, by using 75 percent of the historical data to estimate initial values, and then simulating forecasts for the remaining 25 percent of the data, the initial actual forecasts would already have been based on actual data.

The choice of forecasting model is a matter of balancing responsiveness with stability. This is not an easy balance. In practice, some simulation with past data can be useful, but we feel that this approach is of limited value, because the objective is to forecast well in the future. The issue always comes down to the stability-responsiveness trade-off, based on how stable the future environment is judged to be.

Demand Filter Monitoring

Forecasting models incorporate actual demand data into the forecasts as soon as the information is available. Therefore, actual demand data must be correct. One way to help ensure this is through demand filtering (i.e., checking actual demand against a range of reasonable values). An effective approach is to screen actual demand values against some limit, and to have some thinking person (not a computer) determine whether exceptions are correct. A common screening limit is four MADs in either direction of the forecast demand for the period, which provides a probability of less than .001 that the demand value is a random occurrence for normally distributed forecast errors. If an actual demand falls outside this limit, a manual review is applied.

Once the filter catches a value outside the limits, the review might consist of checking for a clerical error in recording demand, or some explainable cause for the big change. Perhaps conditions really have changed and demand will be changed significantly. If conditions are changing, the situation may call for techniques for modifying the forecasts.

The limits to use for filtering individual actual demand observations depend on a manual review's cost compared to an error's cost. The probabilities of exceeding the limits can be determined from statistical tables. This provides insight into setting limits on the observations.

Demand filtering can be very important in actual practice. We have seen many examples in which average demand for some product, such as a particular chair at Ethan Allen, might be, say, 20 units per month. All of a sudden an order comes along for 300 chairs at someone's new restaurant. Demand filtering will pick up this situation, first asking if a data entry error has occurred. The thinking analyst should not allow this order to influence the average or forecast. At Ethan Allen it would be treated as a "contract sale," which is only forecast in overall dollars, because it is too difficult to forecast the exact timings and actual items of contract sales.

Tracking Signal Monitoring

The approach of exponential smoothing can also be used to compute a useful statistic called the tracking signal, which helps in monitoring the forecast's quality. In essence, the signal is simply bias divided by MAD.

Note that MAD provides an estimate of the expected error (i.e., the average error) and the bias shows consistent over- or underforecasting. The tracking signal varies between -1 and $+1$. Either of these extreme values indicates that all the forecasts are of the same sign. If the forecast is unbiased, the tracking signal will be near zero, irrespective of the MAD's value. The tracking signal allows us to compute a measure of bias that is independent of the forecast error or MAD, one that will have the same numerical meaning for every item forecast. As the tracking signal deviates from zero in any significant way, manual review of the particular item is called for.

$$\text{Tracking signal} = \frac{\text{Bias}}{\text{MAD}}$$

where $-1 \leq \text{Tracking signal} \leq +1$.

The tracking signal is an indicator of forecast bias that is consistent for all observations. Its use is essentially the same as that described for demand filtering; that is, by isolating those items for which the tracking signal is deviating significantly from the nominal value of zero, we can take corrective actions. For example, if an item were forecast with the basic (no trend) model, and an underlying trend existed in the data, the tracking signal would move away from zero.

The issue of what tracking signal value to use for initiating a review is essentially the same as that for demand filtering. The closer the limit is to zero, the sooner poor forecasts are discovered. On the other hand, with small limits the number of times that a review will be necessary rises, and the chance for reaching an erroneous conclusion from the review rises with it.

Strategic Issues

There are a number of strategic and managerial questions about forecasting that we passed over rather rapidly, or did not discuss at all. Certainly we have not had space to discuss all possible forecasting models, and it would not be fair to leave this discussion without indicating that there are several approaches to short-term forecasting that we have not mentioned here.

It is often necessary to make longer-term decisions for which the item-level, short-term forecasts are simply not adequate. Among these decisions are capital expansion projects, proposals to develop a new product line, and merger or acquisition opportunities. For these long-term decisions, forecasts based on causal or econometric models (or simply based on managerial insight and judgment) can often produce improved results. Causal models are those that relate the firm's business to indicators that are more easily forecast or are available as general information. Substantial managerial judgment is required in reviewing forecasts that form the basis for making long-term decisions. The general principle indicated is that the nature of the forecast must be matched with the nature of the decision. The level of aggregation, the amount of management review, the cost, and the quality of the forecast needed really depend on the nature of the decision being made. Many short-term operating decisions do not warrant the use of expensive forecasting techniques, which has been one reason for focusing on short-term projection techniques. For strategic decisions, the investment in more expensive procedures (more management involvement) is needed. Figure 3.6 presents a general schema.

In the ongoing management of forecasts, strategic questions can also come about from a review triggered by forecast monitoring. For example, the forecasting model might be appropriate, but there are insufficient adjustments to account for known actions in the marketplace. Forecasting procedures must be managed to make sure that special knowledge is included in the forecasts.

A review might indicate that the model is no longer appropriate. There may be trend or seasonal effects that should now be included or

---

FIGURE 3.6
Applicability of Various Forecast Attributes to Decision Attributes

---

Decision attributes

Level	Frequency	Money	Time
Mission	Rare	Much	Long run
Strategic	Occasional	Some	Medium run
Tactical	Often	Little	Short run

Forecast attribute	Increasing aggregation	Item level	Product family	Total sales or output
	Cost/forecast	Low	Medium	High
	Degree of management involvement	Low	Medium	High
	Nature of forecast model	Projection technique	Econometric causal	Management judgment

*The darker the area the greater the applicability

---

dropped, or perhaps a compound model that has both trend and seasonal enhancements should be developed. In such cases, the model needs to be adjusted accordingly.

Yet another instance, in which the model may not be appropriate is when demand depends on other decisions in the firm. For example, demand for tires in an auto factory depends on the number of cars being produced. That is quite a different forecasting problem from trying to determine how many cars the public wants to buy. Before applying a model that assumes independent demand, a check for any dependent demand relationships should be made.

It is apparent that forecasting is a pervasive, central activity in managing operations. To be effective, the forecasting system must be linked closely to a number of other systems. Certainly, those decisions requiring forecast information must be linked directly to the forecasting system's output. Because all forecasting models require demand data, there must be close linkage between the order entry system and the forecasting system. Many firms will use sales data or shipment data instead of demand for adjusting their forecasts. At times when demand information is not available, this may be warranted; but there is a difference between sales, shipments, and demand.

Because it is demand we are interested in forecasting, the link with the order entry system should be capable of picking up demand information. If we do not have the stock available to make the sale or shipment, this will affect our customer service—but not the fact that there was a demand.

CONCLUDING PRINCIPLES

The development of sales forecasts is clearly an integrative effort, involving inputs from many areas in a company. However, the relationship between the sales/marketing and manufacturing functions is especially critical in managing the sales forecasting activity. Issues such as the development of unbiased forecasts which are independent of sales performance motivation factors, the assignment of responsibility for improving forecast accuracy, and the development of sales forecasts expressed in units instead of monetary value all affect the coordination of sales/marketing and manufacturing efforts in the preparation of sales forecasts, and can influence the quality of this information.

Forecasts provide an important input to PIM decisions. Although many kinds of forecasts are possible, this chapter has focused on short-term forecasts based on past data, using statistical models. We have tried to emphasize that forecasting is too important to leave to a forecasting model. Firms that use forecasting models wisely employ them to support, not to supplant, managerial judgment. The importance of taking external information into account is one example. Another is the necessary judgment required in a review resulting from forecast monitoring. For example, a tracking signal can indicate the need for a review. It takes a thinking person to decide precisely how to do the review, how (or whether) to change the model, and how to modify the forecasting model data.

We stress the following basic concepts or principles:

- Evaluative criteria must be chosen for the short-term forecasting system. The choices implied in this chapter are minimum bias, minimum MAD, low cost and simplicity.
- The most critical problem is for management to control bias. It is often easier to live with larger errors (larger MAD) if that is what it takes to reduce bias.
- Use of forecasts must be separated from the act of forecasting.
- Methods for monitoring forecasts over time must be installed.
- Forecasting needs to be embedded in a management structure.
- Forecasting is not a computer program, and the result should not be monitored by the computer department.
- Simple forecasting methods seem to work better than sophisticated procedures for short-term forecasts of microdata.

INTEGRATED RESOURCE LINKAGES

There are two resource areas to which short-term forecasting is most closely linked. The first is sales and marketing, which must be intimately involved with sales forecasting. In fact, sales and marketing should "own" this activity and be held accountable for its success. For many firms this is a *very* difficult requirement. Salespeople often produce either optimistic or pessimistic forecasts. Either situation can produce significant bias in a forecasting system. But if routine short-term forecasting methods are adopted, extrapolation of the past is the approach, and bias conditions are readily identified by the tracking signal.

Routine short-term forecasting must be understood as a *platform* for anticipating the future—but not as a straitjacket that does not allow for other input. Forecasting based on extrapolation is equivalent to driving a car by looking out the back window—one gets a great view of what has been run over! If the company is undertaking a major advertising campaign, a market special, opening new markets, or seeing a major change in competitive conditions, its knowledge should be used to temper the result of routine short-term forecasting systems.

The second close linkage of short-term forecasting is with logistics. Forecasting is the plan, logistics is the most immediate response. Many times forecasting errors can be compensated for by clever logistics. Examples include cross shipping between distribution centers, air freight for partial deliveries, and even knowledge of actual customer requirements being integrated into logistics system data bases.

Accounting and finance have a less direct linkage with forecasting, in that demand forecasts provide data on expected sales. These data can be used for revenue projections, cash flows, budgets, funds requirements, and pro forma financial statements.

Forecasting has a linkage with human resource management (HRM) in that sales projections imply needs for personnel. The resultant planning for personal requirements can be significant. This is particularly true when there are major changes in demand—either in total or in product mix, which requires personnel with different skill sets. In several firms we know quite well, the use of temporary workers is a key part of the HRM strategy. Good forecasts of labor requirements are essential for efficient use of this outside resource capability.

Purchasing is also linked with forecasting in that particular product requirements create demands for purchased components and services. Managing vendor capacities requires good knowledge of requirements, rapid updating of this information, and direct linkages with vendor PIM systems. This is often accomplished with electronic data interchange (EDI).

Facilities management and process engineering have a linkage with forecasting, because one needs forecasts that extend far enough into the future to plan facilities and make process choices. Typically, there are several ways to make products—the choice depends upon expected volumes over time.

Forecasting has a linkage with management information systems in that sales data need to be captured, maintained, and integrated into the PIM data base. The entire set of PIM computer systems all have to be linked, not only to forecasting.

Another linkage of forecasting systems is with field service. The demand for service parts needs to be anticipated, and in some cases this requires more complex models than those explained in this chapter. Models can be built that account for product life cycles, the population of equipment requiring service parts, and mean time between failure data.

REFERENCES

Artes, R. "Strategic Forecasting," *APICS–The Performance Advantage,* 2, no. 1, (January 1991), pp. 33–39.

Box, G. E. P., and G. M. Jenkins. *Time Series Analysis: Forecasting and Control.* New York: Holden-Day, 1970.

Brown, R. G. *Smoothing, Forecasting and Prediction of Discrete Time Series.* Englewood Cliffs, N.J.: Prentice Hall, 1962.

Chambers, J. C.; S. K. Mullick; and D. D. Smith. "How to Choose the Right Forecasting Technique." *Harvard Business Review,* July–August 1971, pp. 45–74.

Flores, B. E., and D. C. Whybark. "A Comparison of Focus Forecasting with Averaging and Exponential Smoothing Strategies." *Production and Inventory Management,* 3rd quarter 1986, pp. 96–103.

Gardner, Everette S., Jr., and E. McKenzie. "Seasonal Exponential Smoothing with Damped Trends." *Management Science* (Note) 35, no. 3 (March 1989), pp. 372–75.

Gupta, S., and P. C. Wilton. "Combination of Forecasts: An Extension." *Management Science* 33, no. 3 (March 1987), pp. 356–72.

Lawrence, M. J.; R. H. Edmundson; and M. J. O'Connor. "The Accuracy of Combining Judgmental and Statistical Forecasts." *Management Science* 32, no. 12 (December 1986).

Makridakis, S.; A. Andersen; R. Carbone; R. Fildes; M. Hibon; R. Lewandowski; J. Newton; E. Parzen; and R. Winkler. "The Accuracy of Extrapolation (Time Series) Methods: Results of a Forecasting Competition." *Journal of Forecasting* I (1982), pp. 111–53.

Smith, B. T. *Focus Forecasting Computer Techniques for Inventory Control.* Boston: CBI Publishing, 1978.

Trigg, D. W., and A. G. Leach. "Exponential Smoothing with an Adaptive Response Rate." *Operations Research Quarterly,* March 1967, pp. 53–59.

Wheelwright, S. C., and S. Makridakis. *Forecasting Methods for Management,* 5th ed. New York: Wiley, 1989.

Winters, P. R. "Forecasting Sales by Exponentially Weighted Moving Averages." *Management Science,* April 1960, pp. 324–42.

CHAPTER 4

INDEPENDENT DEMAND INVENTORY MANAGEMENT

Inventory is clearly created by PIM decisions when production occurs prior to demand. However, a company's inventory investment is also heavily influenced by decisions made in other areas of the company, particularly those of marketing and sales. For example, improvements in the accuracy of sales forecasts can reduce inventory requirements, whereas higher targets for customer service will increase inventory investment. Likewise, a strategic decision to provide "after-sales support" throughout the product life cycle can increase the investment in spare-parts inventory.

Strategic decisions in finance and accounting can also have a large influence on inventory management. For example, shifts in the cost of funds in the money markets, as well as improvements in cost estimation and control systems, can have an obvious impact on PIM. Increasingly, the effect on inventory of strategic manufacturing decisions is being recognized. As an example, a shift from line to batch production because of lower product volumes and increased product variety might introduce a major increase in work-in-process inventory investment . Likewise, a program to reduce equipment changeover times can dramatically reduce inventory investment.

The fact that a firm's inventory investment is determined by strategic and operational decisions in many different functions within a company means that it is important to be aware of some of the fundamentals of inventory management. Indeed, all of the chapters in this book are concerned with some aspect of inventory management.

This chapter is primarily concerned with independent demand and nonmanufacturing inventories, but the underlying concepts are applied to manufactured items. Independent. demand inventory items include finished goods in factory or field warehouses, spare-parts inventories, office and factory supplies, and maintenance materials. The inventory management methods described in this chapter are used to determine appropriate order quantities and timing for such items, and to manage multi-item systems. If we perform these functions well, we can provide appropriate levels of inventory or management costs. This chapter is organized around five topics:

- Basic concepts: What is independent demand and what are the functions of independent demand inventory?
- Management issues: How can routine inventory decisions be implemented and how is performance measured?
- Inventory-related costs: How are costs of the inventory system measured and and used?
- Order timing decisions: How can we determine timing of orders and set the level of safety stock?
- Multi-item management: What techniques are available for focusing management attention on the improtant items?

BASIC CONCEPTS

The investment in inventory typically represents one of the largest single uses of capital in a business, often over 25 percent of total assets. In this section, we discuss different types of inventory, distinguishing between independent and dependent demand inventories. We also describe functions of different types of inventories (transit, cycle, safety, and anticipation stock).

Independent Versus Dependent Demand Items

This chapter concerns managing independent demend inventories. The demand for items contained in independent demand inventories (such as those stocked in the field warehouses in Figure4.1) is primarily influenced by factors outside of company decisions. These external factors induce random variation in demand for such items. As a result, demand forecasts for these items are typically projections of historical demand patterns. Those forecasts estimate the average usage rate and pattern of random variation.

FIGURE 4.1
Dependent and Independent Demand Inventories

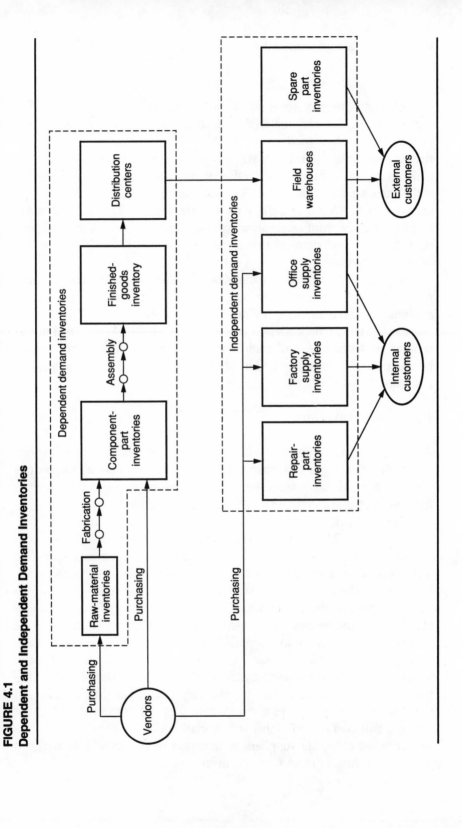

Demand for the items in the manufacturing inventories in Figure 4.1 (e.g., the raw material and component items) is directly dependent on internal factors well within the firm's control, such as the master production schedule (MPS); that is, demand for raw materials and component items is a derived demand, which we can calculate exactly once we have the MPS. For example, if the MPS calls for 4 red cars, we need 16 red wheels, plus 4 spare wheels. Therefore, demand coming directly from internal or external customers is called *independent demand,* and demand that is derived from PIM policies is called *dependent demand.*

Figure 4.1 gives other examples of independent demand inventories. Items subject to random use, such as spare parts for production equipment, office supplies, or production supplies used to support the process, all have independent demands. The techniques described in this chapter are suitable for all such items. Demand for these items cannot be calculated from a production schedule or other direct management program.

Functions of Inventory

An investment in inventory enables us to decouple successive operations or anticipate changes in demand. Inventory also enables us to produce goods at some distance from the actual consumer. This section describes four types of inventories that perform these functions.

Transit stock depends on the time to transport goods from one location to another. These inventories (along with those in distribution centers, field warehouses, and customers' locations) are also called *pipeline inventories.* Management can influence the magnitude of the transit stock by changing the distribution system's design. For example, in-transit inventory between the raw material vendor and factory can be cut by (1) changing the transportation method (e.g., switching from rail to air freight) or (2) switching to a supplier closer to the factory to reduce transit time. These choices, however, involve cost and service trade-offs, which need to be considered carefully. For example, shipping raw material by air freight instead of by rail may cut transit time in half and therefore reduce average pipeline inventory by 50 percent, but it might increase unit cost due to higher transportation costs. Therefore, the consequences of changing suppliers or transport modes should be weighed against investing in more (or less) inventory.

Cycle stock exists whenever orders are made in larger quantities than needed to satisfy immediate requirements. For example, a warehouse may sell two units of a given end item weekly. However, because of scale economies with larger shipping quantities, it might choose to order a batch of eight units once each month. By investing in cycle stock it can satisfy many periods of demand, rather than immediate need, and keep shipping costs down.

Safety stock provides protection against irregularities or uncertainties in an item's demand or supply, that is, when demand exceeds what is forecast or when resupply time is longer than anticipated. Safety stock ensures that customer demand can be satisfied immediately, and that customers will not have to wait while their orders are backlogged. For example, a portion of the inventory held at distribution centers may be safety stock. Suppose that average demand for a given product in a distribution center is 100 units a week with a restocking lead time of one week, and weekly demand might be as large as 150 units, with replenishment lead time as long as two weeks. To ensure meeting the maximum demand requirements in this situation, a safety stock of 100 units might be created.

An important management question concerns the amount of safety stock actually required; that is, how much protection is desirable? This question represents an inventory-investment trade-off between protection against demand and supply uncertainties and costs of investing in safety stock.

Anticipation stock is needed for products with seasonal patterns of demand and uniform supply. Manufacturers of children's toys, air conditioners, and calendars all face peak demand conditions when the production facility is frequently unable to meet peak seasonal demand. Therefore, anticipation stocks are built up in advance and depleted during the peak demand periods. Again, trade-offs must be considered. An investment in additional factory capacity could reduce the need for anticipation stocks.

MANAGEMENT ISSUES

Several issues surround the management of independent demand inventories. In this section we look at three: making routine inventory decisions, determining inventory system performance, and timing implementation.

Routine Inventory Decisions

Basically, only two decisions need to be made in managing independent demand inventories: *how much to order (size)* and *when to order (timing)*. These two decisions can be made routinely using any one of the four inventory control *decision rules* in Figure 4.2. The decision rules involve placing orders for either a fixed or a variable order quantity, with either a fixed or a variable time between successive orders. For example, under the commonly used order point (Q, R) rule, an order for a fixed quantity (Q) is placed whenever the stock level reaches a reorder point (R). Likewise, under the S, T rule, an order is placed once every T periods for an amount equaling the difference between current on-hand balance and a desired inventory level (S) upon receipt of the replenishment order.

Effective use of any of these decision rules involves properly determining decision rule parameter values (e.g., Q, R, S, and T).

Determining Inventory System Performance

A key management issue is determining the inventory control system's performance. We have already mentioned how large the investment in inventory can be. That investment's size makes it a visible performance measure. Because of this, some managers simply specify inventory reduction targets as the performance measure. Unfortunately, this is usually too simplistic; it does not reflect trade-offs between the inventory investment and other benefits or activities in the company.

FIGURE 4.2
Inventory Decision Rules

	Order quantity	
Order frequency	Fixed (Q)*	Variable (S)†
Variable (R)‡	Q,R	S,R
Fixed (T)§	Q,T	S,T

*Q = Order a fixed quantity (Q).
†S = Order up to a fixed expected opening inventory quantity (S).
‡R = Place an order when the inventory balance drops to (R).
§T = Place an order every (T) periods.

A common measure of inventory performance, *inventory turnover,* relates inventory levels to the product's sales volume. Inventory turnover is computed as annual sales volume divided by average inventory investment. Thus, a product with annual sales volume of $200,000 and average inventory investment of $50,000 has inventory turnover of 4. That is, the inventory was replaced (turned) four times during the year.

Turnover is often used to compare an individual firm's performance with others in the same industry or to monitor the effects of a change in inventory decision rules. High inventory turnover suggests a high rate of return on inventory investment. Nevertheless, although it does relate inventory level to sales activity, it does not reflect benefits of having the inventory.

To incorporate a major benefit of inventory, some firms use customer service to assess their inventory system performance. One common measure of customer service is the *fill rate* (the percentage of units immediately available when requested by customers). Thus, a 98 percent fill rate means that only 2 per cent of the units requested were not on the shelf when a customer asked for them. A 98 percent fill rate sounds good, but a 2 percent rate of unsatisfied customers does not. Furthermore, it may represent poorer service than that offered by competitors! Some firms now use a dissatisfaction measure to focus attention on continuous improvement of customer service.

Other measures of inventory-related customer service can be used, but all attempt to formalize trade-offs in costs and benefits. Among the alternatives, we find percentage of the different items ordered that were available, number of times any shortage occurred in a time period, length of time before the item was made available, and percentage of customers who suffered a lack of availability. The correct measure or measures depend upon the reason for having the inventory, the item's importance, the nature of the business, and the firm's competitive strategy.

Timing the Implementation

After analysis of the appropriate decision rules and performance measures, the critical management task is making the changes to improve inventory performance. Appropriate timing of these changes is important. Informal procedures may be quite effective for managing inventories in a small-scale warehouse, but as the number of products and sales volumes increases, more formal inventory control methods are needed to ensure continued growth. Further improvements might be warranted as the business grows and as inventory management technology improves.

Some inventory concepts require new mind-sets, such as the distinction between dependent and independent demand. Other concepts require new organizational objectives and role changes throughout the company. Both these issues must be explicitly considered in timing implementation. One final caveat in implementation, especially for highly automated computer systems, is that the basic systems must be in place first. If inventory accuracy is poor, computerizing only means that mistakes can be made at the speed of light! If the warehouse currently runs on informal knowledge of what is where and how much is available, or if some inventory is held back by salespersons for "their" customers, a formal system will not help. Basic disciplines and understandings must be in place before formal decision rules are developed.

INVENTORY-RELATED COSTS

Investment in inventory is not the only cost associated with managing inventories, even though it may be the most visible. This section treats three other cost elements: cost of preparing an order for more inventory, cost of keeping that inventory on hand until a customer requests it, and cost implied when there is a shortage of inventory. We will also discuss incremental costs in the context of inventory management.

Order Preparation Costs

Order preparation costs are incurred each time an inventory replenishment order is placed. Included are the variable clerical costs associated with issuing the paperwork, plus any one-time costs involved in transporting goods between plants and warehouses. Work measurement techniques, such as time study, can be used to measure the labor content of order preparation. Determining other order preparation costs is sometimes more subtle. For instance, the inventory balance might need to be verified before ordering. Sometimes there may be a fixed cost for filling out a form and a variable cost for each item ordered. Companies frequently bear large costs of maintaining files, con trolling quality, and verifying accurate receipts, as well as other hidden costs.

Inventory Carrying Costs

Inventory commits management to certain costs that are related to inventory quantity, items' value, and length of time the inventory is carried. By committing capital to inventory, a firm forgoes use of these funds for other purposes (e.g., to acquire new equipment, to develop new products, or to invest in short-term securities). Therefore, a cost of capital, which is expressed as an annual interest rate, is incurred on the inventory investment.

The cost of capital may be based on the cost of obtaining bank loans to finance the inventory investment (e.g., 10 to 20 percent), the interest rate on short-term securities the firm could earn if funds were not invested in inventory (e.g., 5 to 15 percent), or the rate of return on capital investment projects that cannot be undertaken because funds must be committed to inventory. For example, the cost of capital for inventory investment might be 25 percent when a new machine would yield a 25 percent return on investment. In any case, capital cost for inventory might be determined by alternative uses for funds. Cost of capital typically varies from 5 to 35 percent, but may be substantially higher in some cases.

The cost of capital is only one part of inventory holding cost. Others are the variable costs of taxes and insurance on inventories, costs of inventory obsolescence or product shelf life limitations, and operating costs involved in storing inventory—for example, rental of public warehousing space, or costs of owning and operating warehouse facilities (such as heat, light, and labor). Furthermore, overhead costs are also associated with operating PIM systems.

As an example, if capital cost is 10 percent and combined costs of renting warehouse space, product obsolescence, taxes, and insurance come to an additional 10 percent of the average value of the inventory investment, total cost of carrying inventory is 20 percent of the cost of an inventory item. In this example, an inventory item costing $1 per unit would have an inventory carrying cost of 20 cents per unit per year.

Shortage and Customer Service Costs

A final set of inventory-related costs are those incurred when demand exceeds the available inventory for an item. This cost is more difficult to measure than the order preparation or inventory carrying costs.

In some cases, shortage costs may equal the product's contribution margin when the customer can purchase the item from competing firms. In other cases, it may only involve the paperwork required to keep track of a back order until a product becomes available. However, this cost may be very substantial in cases where significant customer goodwill is lost. The major emphasis placed on meeting delivery requirements in many firms suggests that although shortage and customer service costs are difficult to measure, they are critical in measuring inventory performance.

Customer service measures are frequently used as surrogate measures for inventory shortage cost—for example, the fill rate achieved in meeting product demand (e.g., the percentage of demand supplied directly from inventory upon demand). If the annual demand for an item is 1,000 units and 950 units are supplied directly from inventory, a 95 percent fill rate is achieved.

The level of customer service can be measured in several ways, including the fill rate, average length of time required to satisfy back orders, and percentage of replenishment order cycles in which one or more units are back ordered. Level of customer service can also be translated into level of inventory investment required to achieve a given level of customer service. As an example, a safety stock of 1,000 units may be required to achieve an 85 per cent customer service level, whereas 2,000 units of safety stock may be required to achieve a 98 percent customer service level. Translating customer service level objectives into the inventory investment required is often useful in determining customer service level-inventory trade-offs.

Incremental Inventory Costs

Two criteria are useful in determining which costs are relevant to a particular inventory management decision: (1) Does the cost represent an actual out-of-pocket expenditure or a forgone profit? (2) Does the cost actually vary with the decision being made? Determining the item cost used in calculating inventory carrying cost is a good illustration of applying these criteria. The item's cost should represent the actual out-of-pocket cost of purchasing or producing the item and placing it in inventory (i.e., an item's variable material, labor, and overhead costs). An element of the overhead cost, such as a cost allocation for general administrative expenses, is not an actual out-of-pocket expenditure.

Another example involves measuring clerical costs incurred in preparing replenishment orders. If clerical staff size remains constant throughout the year, regardless of the number of replenishment orders placed, this cost is not relevant to the decision being made (i.e., the replenishment order quantity). These examples are not meant to be exhaustive, but rather to be illustrative of the careful analysis required in determining costs to be considered in evaluating inventory management performance.

Example Cost Trade-Offs

Order quantity decisions primarily affect the amount of inventory held in cycle stocks at the various stocking points in Figure 4.1. Large order quantities mean that orders are placed infrequently and lead to low annual costs of preparing replenishment orders, but they also increase cycle stock inventories and annual costs of carrying inventory. Determining replenishment order quantities focuses on the question of what quantity provides the most economic trade-off between order preparation and inventory carrying costs. An example item stocked in a field warehouse is used to illustrate this trade-off.

The Model 100 movie camera is sold to several hundred retail stores from a field warehouse. To avoid excessive inventories, stores place orders frequently and in small quantities. The demand for the movie camera at a typical field warehouse was obtained from past sales records. It averages 5 units per weekday (or 1,250 units per year). The movie camera can be obtained within a one-day lead time from the distribution center (DC) serving the field warehouse. This requires preparing an order and faxing it to the DC. The variable cost of preparing a replenishment order is estimated to be $6.25. The firm's cost of carrying inventory is estimated at 25 percent of the item cost per year, including variable costs of capital, insurance, taxes, and obsolescence. The camera's unit cost is $100, so inventory carrying cost is $25 per unit per year.

Currently, the field warehouse orders the Model 100 movie camera on a daily basis in lots of five units. The solid line in Figure 4.3 plots the inventory level versus time for this decision rule. This plot assumes that demand is constant at 5 units per day, and the resulting average inventory level is 2.5 units. Orders are placed daily, meaning that 250 orders are placed per year, costing a total of $1,562.50 per year ($6.25 × 250). The average inventory of 2.5 units represents an annual inventory carrying cost of $62.50 a year (2.5 × $25), yielding an overall combined cost of $1,625 per year for placing orders and carrying inventory.

FIGURE 4.3
Inventory Level versus Time for Model 100 Movie Camera

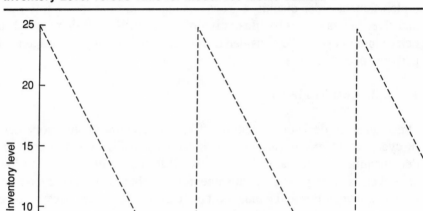

The dashed line in Figure 4.3 shows the inventory level plot for an alternative order quantity of 25 units, or placing orders weekly. In this case, average inventory is 12.5 units and 50 orders are placed annually. The larger order quantity in this case provides important savings in ordering cost ($312.50 versus the previous $1,562.50) with an increase in annual inventory cost ($312.50 versus the previous $62.50). Overall, a shift to a larger order quantity produces a favorable trade-off between ordering and inventory carrying costs, which cuts total cost to $625 per year.

A number of order quantities should be evaluated to determine the best trade-off between ordering and inventory carrying costs. The following economic order quantity model enables us to determine the lowest-cost order quantity directly:

$$EOQ = \sqrt{\frac{2AC_p}{C_h}}$$

where A = annual requirements

C_p = ordering cost

C_h = cost to hold one unit one year

In our movie camera example, the result is

$$\sqrt{\frac{2(1250)(6.25)}{25}} = 25 \text{ units}$$

ORDER TIMING DECISIONS

In this section, we describe timing of replenishment orders under the order point rule (Q, R) from Figure 4.2. This means calculating the re-order point (R). The inventory level is assumed to be under continuous monitoring (review), and when the stock level reaches the reorder point, a replenishment order for a fixed quantity (Q) is issued. Setting the re-order point is influenced by four factors: demand rate, lead time required to replenish inventory, amount of uncertainty in the demand rate and in the replenishment lead time, and management policy regarding the acceptable level of customer service.

When there is no uncertainty in an item's demand rate or lead time, safety stock is not required, and determination of the reorder point is straightforward. For example, if the Model 100 movie camera's demand rate is assumed to be exactly five units per day, and replenishment lead time is exactly one day, a reorder point of five units provides sufficient inventory to cover demand until the replenishment order is received.

Sources of Demand and Supply Uncertainty

The assumptions of fixed demand rate and constant replenishment lead time are rarely justified in actual operations. Random fluctuations in demand for individual products occur because of variations in the timing of consumers' purchases of the product. Likewise, the replenishment lead time often varies because of machine breakdowns, employee absenteeism, material shortages, or transportation delays in the factory and distribution operations.

The Model 100 movie camera illustrates the amount of uncertainty usually experienced in demand for end product items. Analysis of this item's warehouse sales and inventory records indicates that replenishment lead time is quite stable, requiring a one-day transit time from the distribution center to the field warehouse. However, daily demand (D) varies considerably for the camera. Although it averages five units, demands of from one to nine units have been experienced, as Figure 4.4 shows.

If the reorder point is set at five units to cover average demand during the one-day replenishment lead time, inventory shortages of one to four units can result when daily demand exceeds the average of five units; that is, when demand equals six, seven, eight, or nine units. Therefore, if we are to protect against inventory shortages when there is uncertainty in demand, the reorder point must be greater than average demand during the replenishment lead time. The difference between the average demand

FIGURE 4.4
Model 100 Movie Camera Daily Demand

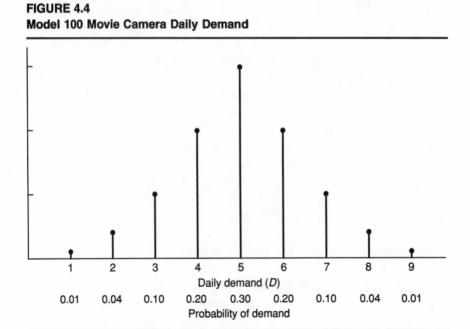

Daily demand (D)	1	2	3	4	5	6	7	8	9
Probability of demand	0.01	0.04	0.10	0.20	0.30	0.20	0.10	0.04	0.01

during lead time and the reorder point is called *safety stock* (*S*). Increasing the reorder point to nine units would provide a safety stock of four units, for example. It would also prevent any stock-outs from occurring if the Model 100 movie camera's his torical pattern of demand does not change.

The Introduction of Safety Stock

Figure 4.5 illustrates introducing safety stock into the reorder point setting. The reorder point (*R*) in this diagram has two components: safety stock level (*S*), and level of inventory (*R − S*) required to satisfy average demand (*d*) during the average replenishment lead time (*L*). The reorder point is the sum of these two: $R = d + S$. To simplify this explanation, lead time in Figure 4.5 is assumed to be constant while demand rate varies.

When a replenishment order is issued (at point *a*), demand variations during the replenishment lead time mean that the inventory level can drop

FIGURE 4.5
Safety Stock as a Buffer against Demand Variability

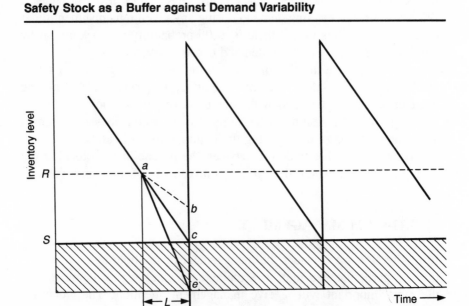

to *a* point between *b* and *e*. In the movie camera's case, inventory level may drop by one to nine units (points *b* and *e*, respectively) before a replenishment order is received. When demand equals the average rate of five units or less, the inventory level reaches a point between *b* and *c*, and the safety stock is not needed. However, when the demand rate exceeds the five-unit average and inventory level drops to a point between *c* and *e*, a stock-out will occur unless safety stock is available. (We can construct a similar diagram when both demand rate and lead time vary.)

Before deciding the safety stock level, we must establish a criterion for determining how much protection against inventory shortages is warranted. One of two different criteria is often used: the probability of stocking out in any given replenishment order cycle, or the desired level of customer service in satisfying product demand immediately out of inventory (the fill rate). We illustrate the first criterion using the demand distribution for the Model 100 movie camera in Figure 4.4.

Figure 4.4 provides demand distribution data for this analysis for the Model 100 movie camera. There is a .05 probability of demand exceeding seven units (i.e., a demand of either eight or nine units occurring). A safety stock level of two units (meaning a reorder point of seven units) would provide a risk of stocking out in 5 percent (1 out of 20) of the replenishment order cycles. This safety stock level provides a .95 probability of meeting demand during any given replenishment order cycle. Note that this means there is a .05 probability of stocking out by *either* one or two units when demand exceeds seven units.

We can reduce the risk of stocking out by investing more in safety stock; that is, with safety stock of three units, the probability of stocking out can be cut to .01, and with four units of safety stock the risk of stocking out is 0, assuming the demand distribution does not change. Thus, one method of determining the required level of safety stock is to specify an acceptable trade-off between the probability of stocking out during a replenishment order cycle and investment of funds in inventory.

MULTI-ITEM MANAGEMENT

In this section we consider the management of multiple items in inventory. In particular, we look at a method for categorizing items so that the most important will receive management attention. The technique is called *ABC analysis*. It is discussed first with a single criterion for classification, and then with multiple criteria.

Single-Criterion ABC Analysis

A single-criterion ABC analysis consists of separating the inventory items into three groupings according to their annual cost volume usage (unit cost x annual usage). These groups are: A items having a high dollar usage, B items having an intermediate dollar usage, and C items having a low dollar usage.

Figure 4.6 shows the results of a typical ABC analysis. For this inventory, 20 percent of the items are A items, which account for 65 percent of the annual dollar usage. The B category comprises 30 percent of the items and 25 percent of the dollar usage, and the remaining 50 percent of the items are C items accounting for only 10 percent of the annual dollar usage. Although percentages may vary from firm to firm, it is common to find a small percentage of the items accounting for a large percentage of the annual cost volume usage.

FIGURE 4.6
ABC Analysis

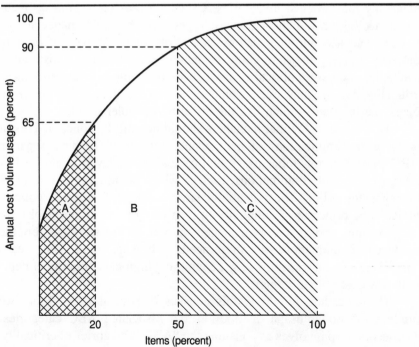

ABC analysis provides a tool for identifying which items will make the largest impact on the firm's overall inventory cost performance when improved inventory control procedures are implemented. A perpetual inventory system, improvements in forecasting procedures, or a careful analysis of the order quantity and timing decisions for A items will provide a larger improvement in inventory cost performance than will similar efforts on the C items. Therefore, ABC analysis is often a useful first step in improving inventory performance.

ABC analysis helps to focus management attention on what is really important. Managers concentrate on the "significant few" (the A items) and spend less time on the "trivial many" (the C items). Unfortunately, classifying items into A, B, and C categories based on just one criterion may overlook other important criteria.

Multiple-Criteria ABC Analysis

Several noncost criteria are important in inventory management. Among them are lead time, obsolescence, availability, substitutability, and criticality. Flores and Whybark looked into the use of noncost criteria in managing maintenance inventories. Criticality seemed to sum up managers' feelings about most noncost aspects of the maintenance items. It takes into account such factors as severity of the impact of running out, how quickly the item could be purchased, whether a substitute is available, and even political consequences of being out. Some of these criticality notions may even weigh more heavily than dollar usage in managing the item—much like the proverbial cobbler's nail.

That is not to say that managers should not still be concerned about dollar usage implications of maintenance inventory. To have separate ABC categories for dollar usage and criticality, however, could lead to a large number of combinations, each of which could require a different management policy. The potentially large number of different policies violates the principle of simplicity (a recurring theme in this book). To keep the number of inventory management policies to a workable few, the number of combinations of criteria needs to be kept small. This means combining criteria somehow (e.g., combining high-cost noncritical items with low-cost critical items).

The procedure for doing this consists of several steps. First, we produce the dollar usage distribution and associated ABC categories. The second step involves establishing the "ABC" categories of criticality.

To keep the confusion level down, we use I, II, and III to designate the criticality categories. The criteria to establish these categories are more implicit and intuitive. Category I, for example, might include items that would bring the plant to a stop and for which there is no easy substitute, alternative supply, or quick fix. A shortage in the III items, on the other hand, would cause little if any impact. The II items are the ones left over. Figure 4.7 shows the distributions of dollar usage and criticality for a sample of maintenance inventory items at a consumer durable manufacturing plant.

There is substantially less dollar usage in category I than in category A. This should not be surprising, given that the criteria for I include such things as impact of outage and ease of replacement. Figure 4.7 presents a matrix of the dollar usage and criticality classifications. There is an entry for every combination, which means that both low dollar usage and high dollar usage items can have high criticality (or low criticality). It also means that the problem of combining still remains.

There are nine possible combinations in Figure 4.8 that could each require a different management policy. The next step is to reduce the number, although R. G. Brown argues that this is not necessary when the computer can keep track of any number of policies. However, we are concerned about having a number with which people can cope. A simple mechanical procedure is used to combine classifications to provide three initial categories of items. These categories, AA, BB, and CC provide a starting point for management to reassess the item's classifications. The procedure simply assigns every item in A-I (see Figure 4.8), A-II, and B-I to AA; every item in A-III, C-I, and B-II to BB; and every item in B-III, C-II, and C-III to CC. This results in 15 AA items, 22 BB items, and 91 CC items. We then ask management to review each item's classification.

Multiple-Criteria ABC Management Policies

The final step is to define specific policies for managing each category. In fact, it is helpful to develop tentative policies first. These can be a guideline in reviewing each item's classification. With the policies in mind, the question to ask when reviewing each item is, should it be managed with the procedures that apply to its classification? Figure 4.9 shows the manager's reclassification of the items. There were changes from the mechanical assignments in each category. Managers even cre-

FIGURE 4.7

Distributions of Dollar Usage and Criticality for a Sample of Maintenance Inventory Items

	Dollar usage				Criticality		
Category	Number of items	Percentage of items	Percentage of dollar usage	Category	Number of items	Percentage of items	Percentage of dollar usage
A	15	11%	84%	I	5	4%	40%
B	25	15	15	II	48	39	56
C	88	74	1	III	75	57	4
Total	128	100	100		128	100	100

Source: B. E. Flores and D. C. Whybark, "Implementing Multiple Criteria ABC Analysis," *Journal of Operations Management* 7, no. 1 (Fall 1987).

FIGURE 4.8
Number of Items Classified by Dollar Usage and Criticality

Dollar Usage	Criticality			
	I	*II*	*III*	*Total*
A	2	12	1	15
B	1	19	5	25
C	2	17	69	88
Total	5	48	75	128

Source: B. E. Flores and D. C. Whybark, "Implementing Multiple Criteria ABC Analysis," *Journal of Operations Management* 7, no. 1 (Fall 1987).

ated a fourth category, although we have not shown it. In evaluating the items, they found that nearly half should not be carried in inventory at all. This demonstrates our observation that it is hard to enhance a system that does not have sound basics.

Specific inventory management policies are needed for each category to bring meaning to phrases such as "closer management" or "more management attention." Policies are developed to cover four areas: inventory record verification, order quantity, safety stock, and classification of the item itself. The first area, verification, is to prevent the unpleasant surprises that often occur when the computer record does not agree with the physical count. To improve accuracy, more frequent counts should be made. This implies a higher frequency for the AA items than for the BB or CC items. Order quantity and safety stock levels are established for each item depending on both the economics and the criticality. Finally,

FIGURE 4.9
Multiple-Criteria Distributions

Combined category	Number of items	Percentage of items	Percentage of dollar usage
AA	14	11%	78%
BB	16	13	12
CC	98	76	10
Total	128	100	100

Source: B. E. Flores and D. C. Whybark, "Implementing Multiple Criteria ABC Analysis," *Journal of Operations Management* 7, no. 1 (Fall 1987).

because it is a changing world, a specific period for reconsidering the item's classification is established.

Figure 4.10 shows the specific values chosen for each area. The frequency of counting was established using an average counting rate of 40 items per labor-hour, and taking into account past difficulties with the inventory records and transaction reporting system. The order quantities were roughly based on the EOQ values, whereas safety stock was based on the item's criticality. For both order quantity and safety stock, each part was considered individually. Finally, in order not to leave the impression that the item's category was "frozen," a specific frequency of review of each item's classification was established.

The multiple-criteria ABC categories take into account many factors not normally considered in classifying inventory items for management purposes. When combined with clear, specific policies for each category, they can substantially improve the use of scarce talent in managing the inventories.

Figure 4.11 illustrates the use of software to support multiple-criteria ABC analysis. The block labeled "Value Class Rules" contains the different criteria reported here: lead time, unit cost, and annual value (annual usage value). In this example, the various criteria have not been combined into a single category, but are kept separate by their individual A, B, C, and D classifications. Thus, for example, the first part, AA-O5,

FIGURE 4.10
Inventory Management Policy Parameters for Multiple-Criteria ABC Items

	Category		
	AA	*BB*	*CC*
Counting frequency	Monthly	Every six months	Yearly
Order quantity	Small for costly items	Medium: EOQ-based	Large quantities
Safety stock	Large for critical items	Large for critical items	Low or none
Reclassify review	Every six months	Every six months	Yearly

Source: B. E. Flores and D. C. Whybark, "Implementing Multiple Criteria ABC Analysis," *Journal of Operations Management* 7, no. 1 (Fall 1987).

FIGURE 4.11
Multiple-Criteria ABC Analysis Software

ABC INVENTORY CLASSIFICATION

VALUE CLASS RULES ①

VALUE CLASS	LEAD TIME	UNIT COST	ANNUAL VALUE
A	20	100.00	100,000
B	15	50.00	50,000
C	10	5.00	5,000
D	0	0	0

USAGE WEIGHT FACTORS ②: YTD 50, GROSS 50
POST VALUE CLASS: N

PART NO/ DESC	CODES TY AC	PART COUNT	PERCT TOTAL COUNT	ANNUAL USAGE	LEAD TIME DAYS	CURRENT UNIT COST	ANNUAL USAGE VALUE	PERCT VALUE	CUMM USAGE VALUE	PERCT TOTAL VALUE	VALUE CLASS CURR PREV ③
AA-05 CENTER MEMBER	1 3	1	14.3	11,000	15 B	10.00 C	110,000 A	25	110,000	24.5 A	A A
AA-09 RAW MATERIAL	3 4	2	28.6	12,500	30 A	7.50 C	93,750 B	50	203,750	45.4 B	A A
AA-11 KNOB & LOCK	1 3	3	42.8	20,000	15 B	4.50 D	90,000 B	80	293,750	65.5 C	B B
AA-10 GLUE	3 4	4	57.1	15,000	10 C	5.00 C	75,000 B	100	368,750	82.2 D	B C
AA-13 HINGE	1 3	5	71.4	240,000	10 C	.25 D	60,000 B		428,750	95.6 D	B B
AA-12 LOCK CATCH	1 3	6	85.7	30,000	10 C	.50 D	15,000 C		443,750	98.9 D	C C
AA-14 SCREW	1 3	7	100.0	480,000	5 D	.01 D	4,800 D		448,550	100.0 D	D D

① User-specified ABC parameters for lead time, unit cost, annual dollar value, and percent total value determine value class rules

② Annual usage can be weighted by year-to-date and/or planned usage percentages for more effective ranking

③ Value class ranking based on highest value in accordance with specified parameters

Source: MAC-PAC Manufacturing Planning and Control System General Description Manual (Chicago: Arthur Anderson & Co., 1980), p. 11.

is classified as B in terms of lead time, C in unit cost, and A in annual usage value. Note that it represents almost 25 percent of the annual usage value ("Perct Total Value").

CONCLUDING PRINCIPLES

A firm's investment in inventory is influenced by strategic and operational decisions in many different functional areas of the business. It is important to understand the reasons that inventory investment is required and to be able to relate this investment to the strategic and operational decisions that affect it. The theory of independent demand inventory management presented in this chapter is useful in developing this understanding. Despite the material's technical nature, several management principles emerge:

- The difference between dependent and independent demand must serve as the first basis for determining appropriate inventory management procedures.
- Organizational criteria must be clearly established before we set safety stock levels and measure performance.
- A sound basic independent demand system must be in place before we attempt to implement advanced techniques.
- All criteria should be taken into account in classifying inventory items for management priorities.
- The policies developed for each ABC classification should be used to guide the classification of each item as well as to manage its inventories.

INTEGRATED RESOURCE LINKAGES

The primary linkage of independent demand inventory management concepts is with logistics, because logistics is usually dealing with independent demand—that is, demand from customers. The basic trade-offs noted in this chapter are seen in several places in logistics. The "setup," "ordering," or fixed costs in logistics often include transportation, which may not vary as a function of order size. For example, in many situations a truck has to be sent to a distribution center, and it does not matter how much is sent because it will always be less than a full truck load.

Order timing decisions are also seen in logistics, based on the time it takes to process the order in manufacturing (which may or may not have finished-goods inventory), and the time required for delivery. Safety stocks, safety lead times, and order-filling performance measures are a central consideration in logistics; the basic trade-off and concepts are described here in Chapter 4.

Joint ordering procedures are important in both logistics and purchasing decisions. For example, if a truck load is to be ordered, or an order of a certain dollar amount is to be made, then the lot-sizing decision is based on total demand for the items to be purchased. However, the approach to this problem uses the same basic techniques as described here.

Purchasing decisions also need to include quantity discount data for determining the size of orders to be placed. These decisions are made by minor modification of the basic economic order quantity model. Essentially, the total cost of various order quantities is evaluated—those for EOQ values and those for quantities at price breaks. The quantity that provides the lowest overall cost is selected.

Accounting and finance has a linkage to independent demand inventory management in that the cost of carrying inventory is basically a financial issue. What return do we require for having our money tied up in inventory? Other cost estimates are also required, including the cost to place an order and the cost associated with being out of stock. Accounting and finance can help make those estimates.

Sales and marketing are also linked to independent demand inventory management. The primary linkage is in the specification of service levels for inventory management. Do we *need* 99 percent service levels? For which products? For which customers? What are the alternatives that will provide at least as good service in the eyes of the customer?

Process engineering has an interesting linkage with independent demand inventory management. The EOQ model is based on a trade-off between the costs of ordering and the costs of holding inventories. To the extent that process engineering can reduce setup times, manufacturing will be able to produce in smaller batches. That is a cornerstone of just-in-time manufacturing.

Field service uses independent demand inventory management principles for its inventory systems. Most of these systems are based on the order quantity/order point methods presented here. The more sophisticated systems almost always use techniques that are classified as independent demand inventory management techniques.

Quality plays a role in all areas of manufacturing. If quality is poor, then "unexpected" conditions arise, giving rise to the need for more safety stock. Poor quality makes routine operation of PIM systems more difficult. Conversely, if all quality problems can be eliminated, then greatly simplified PIM systems can be designed and implemented.

There is an important linkage with management information systems. In every inventory system it is essential to have computer-based systems—to do the routine things routinely and to separate the vital few from the trivial many.

REFERENCES

Brown, R. G. *Decision Rules for Inventory Management*. New York: Holt, Rinehart and Winston, 1967.

Davis, E. W., and D. C. Whybark. "Inventory Management." *Small Business Bibliography* 75. Washington, D.C.: Small Business Administration, 1980.

Flores, B. E., and D. C. Whybark. "Multiple Criteria ABC Analysis." *International Journal of Operations and Production Management* 6, no. 3 (Fall 1986).

Inventory Management Reprints. Falls Church, Va.: American Production and Inventory Control Society, 1989.

Krupp, James A. "Inventory Turn Rates as a Management Control Tool." *Inventories and Production* 6, no. 4 (September–October 1989).

MAC-PAC Manufacturing Planning and Control System General Description Manual. Chicago: Arthur Andersen & Co., 1980.

Porteus, E. L. "Investing in Reduced Setups in the EOQ Model." *Management Science* 31, no. 8 (August 1985).

Service Parts Management Reprints. Falls Church, Va.: American Production and Inventory Control Society, 1982.

Silver, E. A., and R. Peterson. *Decision Systems for Inventory Management and Production Planning*. 2nd ed. New York: Wiley, 1985.

SECTION 3

MASTER PLANNING

This section contains two chapters covering the elements of planning the overall production and inventory activities of the firm. The first chapter deals with the aggregate planning needed to integrate production into the rest of the company's functional plans. The second chapter treats master production scheduling, a key communication with the detailed material planning activity.

Production and Inventory Management

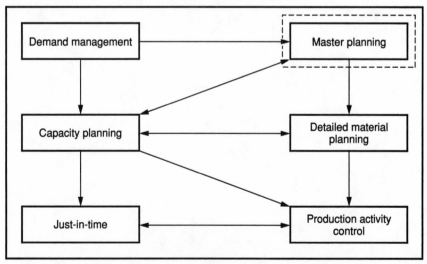

In Chapter 5 we cover the process of production planning, one of the least understood processes in the modern manufacturing firm. It is production planning that links the other company activities to manufacturing, and it is the production plan that states how production will support the company game plan. It has been referred to as management's handle on the business. Production plans are the communication media for integrating all functional areas of the company with manufacturing activities.

Master production scheduling, which is described in Chapter 6, is the communication link between the business and the factory floor. An effective master production schedule integrates the production plan (expressed in top management terms) into the actual production of products (expressed in manufacturing terms). Without this linkage in place, priorities, utilization of capacity, and customer satisfaction will all suffer. Master production scheduling is a major activity of integrated production and inventory management.

CHAPTER 5

PRODUCTION PLANNING

The production plan is a vital link between PIM and the planning decisions in other functional areas of the business. Sales, financial, and engineering plans are integrated with those of manufacturing through the production plan. The production plan is, therefore, a key factor in coordinating planning decisions in a company.

The production plan determines the manufacturing resource requirements necessary to achieve top management's strategic plans for the business. Several types of information shape the production plan. It reflects top management's intuition concerning direction of the business as well as its judgments regarding the likely impact of macroeconomic influences. The production plan is also affected by marketing research, which indicates customer needs, competitor actions, and so forth, and the financial and budgetary planning activities of the company. In fact, the production plan enables the business to translate manufacturing activities into monetary terms so that its financial impact can be understood.

Production planning is probably the least understood aspect of PIM. The objective is to develop an integrated game plan for the company in which the manufacturing portion is the production plan. If the production plan is not integrated, manufacturing managers cannot be held responsible for meeting the plan, and informal approaches will develop to overcome inconsistencies.

Our discussion of production planning is organized around four topics:

- Production planning in the firm: What is production planning and how does it link with strategic management and other MPC modules?
- The production-planning process: What are the fundamental activities in production planning?

- Operating production-planning systems: How is production planning carried out in practice?
- The new management obligations: What are the key responsibilities for ensuring an effective production-planning system?

PRODUCTION PLANNING IN THE FIRM

The production plan provides key communication links from top management to manufacturing. It determines the basis for focusing the detailed production resources to achieve the firm's strategic objectives. By providing the framework within which the master production schedule (MPS) is developed, we can plan and control subsequent MPS decisions, material resources, and plant capacities on a basis consistent with these objectives. We now describe the production plan in terms of its role in top management, necessary conditions for effective production-planning linkages to other PIM activities, and payoffs from effective production planning.

Production Planning and Management

The production plan provides a direct and consistent dialogue between manufacturing and top management, as well as between manufacturing and the other functions. As Figure 5.1 shows, many key linkages of production planning are *outside* the production and inventory management (PIM) system. As such, the plan necessarily must be in terms that are meaningful to the firm's nonmanufacturing executives. Only in this way can the top-management game plan in Figure 5.1 become consistent for each basic functional area. Moreover, the production plan has to be stated in terms that PIM professionals can use, so detailed manufacturing decisions are kept in concert with the overall strategic objectives reflected in the game plan.

The basis for consistency of the functional plans is resolution of broad trade-offs at the top-management level. Suppose, for example, that there is an opportunity to expand into a new market, and marketing requests additional production to do so. With a specified production plan, this could only be accomplished by decreasing production for some other product group. If this is seen as undesirable (i.e., the new market is to be a direct add-on), by definition a new game plan is required—with an updated and consistent set of plans in marketing, finance, and production.

FIGURE 5.1
Key Linkages of Production Planning

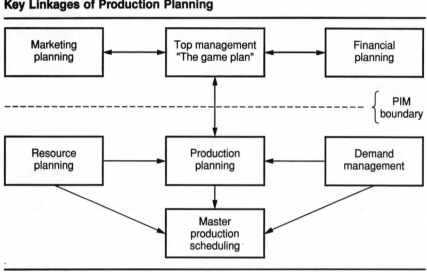

The feasibility of the added volume must be determined and agreed upon before detailed execution steps are taken.

The production plan states the mission that manufacturing must accomplish if the firm's overall objectives are to be met. How to accomplish the production plan in terms of detailed manufacturing and procurement decisions is a problem for manufacturing management. With an agreed-upon game plan, the job in manufacturing is to "hit the production plan." Similar job definitions should also exist in marketing and finance.

An interesting chicken-and-egg question sometimes arises about the production plan and detailed plans that result from the PIM system. Conceptually, production planning should precede and direct PIM decision making. Production planning provides the basis for making the more detailed set of PIM decisions. In some firms, however, it is only after the other PIM systems are in place that resultant production-planning decisions are clearly defined. In these cases, the first production plans are no more than a summation of the individual detailed plans. They are the *result* of other detailed decisions, rather than an input to those decisions. Even so, they provide the basis for management review.

The planning performed in other PIM activities is necessarily detailed, and the language is quite different from that required for production planning. The production plan might be stated in dollars or aggregate units of output per month, whereas the master production schedule (MPS) is usually more detailed, such as in end product units per week. The MPS might be stated in units that use special bills of materials to manage complicated options, and might not correspond to the units used to communicate with top management.

To perform the necessary communication role, the production plan must be stated in commonly understood, aggregated terms. In some companies, the production plan is stated as the dollar value of total monthly or quarterly output. Other firms break this total output down by individual factories or by product families or major product lines. Still other firms state the production plan in terms of total units for each product line. Measures that relate to capacity (such as direct labor-hours and tons of product) are also used by some firms. The key requirement is that the production plan be stated in some commonly understood homogeneous unit that thereafter can be kept in concert with other plans.

The production plan needs to be expressed in meaningful units, but it also needs to be expressed in a manageable number of units. Experience indicates that 5 to 15 family groups seem to be about right for a top-management group to handle. Each has to be considered in terms of expectations on sales, manufacturing, and resultant inventories and backlogs. The cumulative result, expressed in monetary units, also has to be examined and weighed against overarching business plans.

The overall context within which trade-offs are made and the production plan is developed is increasingly called *game planning*. The game plan reflects the strategy (e.g., increased market share) and tactics (e.g., increased inventory for improved service) that are *doable by* the firm. It is not a set of uncoordinated wishes that some people would like to see realized. The manufacturing part of the game plan is the production plan.

The production plan is *not* a forecast of demand! It is the planned production, stated on an aggregate basis, for which manufacturing management is to be held responsible. The production plan is not necessarily equal to a forecast of aggregate demand. For example, it may not be profitable to satisfy all demands, in which case production would be less than forecast. Conversely, a strategic objective of improved customer service could result in aggregate production in excess of aggregate demand. These are important management trade-offs.

The production plan for manufacturing is a result of the production-planning process. Inputs to the process include sales forecasts, but these need to be stated on the basis of shipments (not bookings) so that inventory projections match physical inventories and so demands on manufacturing are expressed correctly with respect to time.

Production Planning and PIM Systems

Up to this point, we have emphasized production planning's linkages to activities outside PIM system boundaries. Because of these linkages, the production plan is often called "top management's handle on the business." To provide execution support for the production plan, we need linkages to the PIM systems. The most fundamental linkage is to the master production schedule, which is a disaggregation of the production plan. The result drives the detailed scheduling through detailed material planning and other PIM activities.

The MPS must be kept in concert with the production plan. As the individual daily scheduling decisions to produce specific mixes of actual end items and/or options are made, we must maintain parity between the sum of the MPS quantities and the production plan. If the relationship is maintained, then "hitting the schedule" (MPS) means that the agreed-upon production plan will be met as well.

Another critical linkage shown in Figure 5.1 is the link with demand management. Demand management encompasses order entry, order promising, and physical distribution coordination as well as forecasting. This module must capture every source of demand against manufacturing capacity, such as interplant transfers, international requirements, and service parts. In some firms, one or more of these demand sources may be of more consequence than others. For the firm with distribution warehouses, for example, replenishing those warehouses may create quite a different set of demands on manufacturing than is true for other firms. The contribution of demand management, insofar as production planning is concerned, is to ensure that the influence of all aspects of demand is included and that property is coordinated.

As a tangential activity, the match between actual and forecast demand is monitored in the demand management module. As actual demand conditions depart from forecast, the necessity for revising the production plan increases. Thus, the assessment of changes' impact on the production plan and the desirability of making a change depends on this linkage. It is critical for top management to change the plans, rather than let the forecast errors per se change the aggregate production output level.

The other direct PIM linkage to production planning shown in Figure 5.1 is with resource planning. This activity encompasses long-range planning of facilities, and involves the translation of extended production plans into capacity requirements, usually on a gross or aggregate basis. In some firms, the unit of measure might be constant dollar output rates; in others, it might be labor-hours, head counts, machine-hours, key-facility-hours, tons of output, or some other output measure. The need is to plan capacity, at least in aggregate terms, for a horizon at least as long as it takes to make major changes.

Resource planning is directly related to production planning, because, in the short term, the resources available provide a set of constraints to production planning. In the longer run, to the extent that production plans call for more resources than available, financial appropriations are indicated. A key goal of the linkage between production planning and resource planning is to answer what-if questions. Maintaining current resource-planning factors, related to the product groupings used for planning, is the basis for performing this analysis.

Much of the very near-term production plan is constrained by available material supplies. Current levels of raw material, parts, and subassemblies limit what can be produced in the short run, even if other resources are available. This is often hard to assess unless information links from the detailed material planning and shop status data bases are effective.

Links through the MPS to material planning and other PIM activities provide the basic data to perform what-if simulations of alternative plans. Being able to quickly evaluate alternatives can facilitate the game-planning process. This is *not* an argument to always change the production plan. On the contrary, having the ability to demonstrate the impact of proposed changes may reduce the number of instances in which production "loses" in these negotiations.

The value of the production-planning activity is certainly questionable if there is no monitoring of performance. This requires linkages to the data on shipments and sales, aggregated into the production-planning groupings. Measuring performance is an important input to the planning process itself. Insofar as deviations in output are occurring, they must be taken into account. If the plan cannot be realized, the entire value of the production-planning process is called into question.

One final performance aspect in which effort must be expended is the reconciliation of the MPS with the production plan. As day-to-day

MPS decisions are made, it is possible to move away from the production plan unless constant vigilance is applied. Like other performance monitoring, it requires frequent evaluation of status and comparison to plan.

Payoffs

Game planning is top management's handle on the business. It provides important visibility of the critical interactions among marketing, production, and finance. If marketing wants higher inventories, but top management decides there is not sufficient capital to support the inventories, the production plan will be so designed. Once such critical trade-off decisions are made, the production plan provides the basis for monitoring and controlling manufacturing performance in a way that provides a much clearer division of responsibilities than is true under conventional budgetary controls.

Under production planning, manufacturing's job is to hit the schedule. This can eliminate the battle over "ownership" of finished-goods inventory. If actual inventory levels do not agree with planned inventory levels, it is basically not a manufacturing problem, *if* they hit the schedule. It is either a marketing problem (they did not sell according to plan) or a problem of product mix management in the demand management activity (the wrong individual items were made).

The production plan also provides the basis for day-to-day, tough-minded trade-off decisions. If marketing wants more of some items, it must be asked, "Of what do you want less?" There is no other response, because additional production without a corresponding reduction would violate the agreed-upon production plan. In the absence of a new, expanded production plan, production and marketing must work to allocate the scarce capacity to the competing needs (via the master production schedule).

The reverse situation is also true. If the production plan calls for more than marketing currently needs, detailed decisions should be reached about which items will go into inventory. Manufacturing commits people, capacities, and materials to reach company objectives. The issue is only how best to convert these resources into particular end products.

Better integration between functional areas is one of the major payoffs from production planning. Once a consistent game plan between top levels of the functional areas is developed, it can be translated into detailed plans that are in concert with top-level agreements. This results in a set of common goals, improved communication, and transparent systems.

Without a production plan, the expectation is that somehow the job will get done—and in fact, it does get done, but at a price. That price is organizational slack: extra inventories, poor customer service, excess capacity, long lead times, panic operations, and poor response to new opportunities. Informal systems will, of necessity, come into being. Detailed decisions will be made by clerical-level personnel with no guiding policy except "get it out the door as best we can." The annual budget cycle will not be tied in with detailed plans and will probably be inconsistent and out of date before it is one month old. Marketing requests for products will not be made so as to keep the sum of the detailed end products in line with the budget. In many cases, detailed requests for the first month are double the average monthly volume. Only at the end of the year does the reconciliation between requests and budget take place; in the meantime it has been up to manufacturing to decide what is really needed.

We have seen many companies with these symptoms. Where are these costs reflected? There is no special place in the chart of accounts for them, but they will be paid in the bottom-line profit results. More and more firms are finding that a well-structured monthly production-planning meeting allows the various functional areas to operate in a more coordinated fashion and to better respond to vagaries of the marketplace. The result is a dynamic overall plan for the company, one that changes as needed and fosters the necessary adaptation in each function.

THE PRODUCTION-PLANNING PROCESS

This section views aids to managing the production-planning process. Specifically, we will be concerned with routinizing the process and the game-planning output. We examine these issues with an example.

The game- and production-planning process typically begins with an updated sales forecast covering the next year or more. Any desired increases or decreases in inventory or backlog levels are added or subtracted, and the result is the production plan. The most immediate portion of this plan will not be changeable, because commitments to labor, equipment, and materials already will have been made. An effective production-planning process will typically have explicit time fences for when the aggregate plan can be increased or decreased; there may also be tight constraints on the amounts of increase or decrease. An example might be no changes during the most immediate month, up to +10 percent or −20 percent in the next month, and so on. Effective production planning also implies periodicity; that is, it is useful to perform the production- and game-planning process on a regular, routine cycle.

Performing the game-planning function on a regular basis has several benefits. It tends to institutionalize the process and force a consideration (which might otherwise be postponed) of changed conditions and trade-offs. The routine also keeps information channels open for forecast changes, different conditions, and new opportunities. Performing the task routinely helps to ensure a separation between forecasts and the plan.

The cycle's frequency varies from firm to firm, depending on the firm's stability, cost of planning, and ability to monitor performance. The trade-off is difficult. There is a high cost to planning that involves data gathering, meetings, what-if analysis, and other staff support activities. On the other hand, delaying the planning process increases the chance of significant departures of reality from plan, creating the opportunity for informal systems to take over. Ironically, the more successful firms can use a less frequent cycle because of their formal systems' ability to keep the firm on plan and warn of impending problems. A common schedule among successful firms is to review plans monthly and revise them quarterly or when necessary. Figure 5.2 shows a monthly cycle at Ethan Allen.

Ethan Allen is a make-to-stock furniture manufacturer, so much of its demand forecasting is based on routine extrapolation of historical data. The first event in Figure 5.2, "Determine (manual forecast)," is to forecast the nonroutine items. These include large contract sales (such as to a motel chain), new items for which there are no historical data, and market specials.

The second event in the figure is the "End of month." Following immediately is a "6-month economic review," a process that attempts to summarize opinions as to future economic conditions in the furniture industry. At the same time, the sales screening report is prepared. It is a review of the actual sales in light of the forecast, and suggests changes before the preparation of the new routine statistical forecast.

FIGURE 5.2
Example of a Monthly Cycle for Production Planning

Day of the week

Event	M	T	W	Th	F	M	T	W	Th	F	M	T	W	Th	F	M	T
Determine (manual forecast)																	
End of month																	
6-month economic review																	
Sales screening report																	
Review sales screening																	
Set output level for next 6 months																	
Prepare statistical forecast																	
Production-planning report																	
Production planning for individual factories																	
Computer-generated MPS																	
Plants modify as necessary																	
Final MPS published																	

Source: W. L. Berry, T. E. Vollman, and D. C. Whybark, *Master Production Scheduling: Principles and Practice* (Falls Church, Va.: American Production and Inventory Control Society, 1979), p. 45.

The sixth event in Figure 5.2 ("Set output level for next 6 months") is the production plan. The senior executives review the economic outlook, present inventory levels, statistical forecasts, and other factors. The net result is a rate of output in total dollars for Ethan Allen production. Subsequent activities involve preparing reports based on this production plan, allocating the total to individual factories, and preparing the detailed MPS that supports the production plan.

Discipline is required in routinizing the production- and game-planning process to replan when conditions indicate that it is necessary. If information from demand management indicates that differences between the forecast and actual have exceeded reasonable error limits, replanning may be necessary. Similarly, if conditions change in manufacturing, a new market opportunity arises, or the capital market shifts, replanning may be needed. So, although regularizing has its advantages, slavishly following a timetable and ignoring actual conditions is not wise management practice.

Because the purpose of the planning process is to arrive at a coordinated set of plans for each function (a game plan), mechanisms for getting support for the plans are important. Clearly, a minimum step here is to involve the top functional officers in the process. This does more than legitimize the plan; it involves the people who can resolve issues in the trade-off stage. A second step used by some firms is to virtually write contracts between functions on what the agreements are. The contracts serve to underscore the importance of each function performing to plan, rather than returning to informal practices.

OPERATING PRODUCTION-PLANNING SYSTEMS

In this section, we present the entire process for the Mohawk Electric Company. The Mohawk Electric Company (a disguised name for an actual Midwest firm) manufactures electrical switches, controls, and measurement instruments for industrial applications. Three main product lines (energy management devices, tachographs, and data systems) represent annual sales of $25 to $30 million, with a price range of $15 to $50,000 per unit. About 40,000 units are sold each year, involving some 5,000 unique final product catalog numbers. Approximately 70 percent of sales volume is shipped directly from the firm's finished-goods inventory.

The production plan and master production schedule are established quarterly as a part of the firm's regular budgetary planning activities. For most of Mohawk's business, the master production schedule is stated in terms of the number of units to be produced for each end product (catalog number) during the next four quarters.

Overall production lead time (covering the purchasing, fabrication, and assembly operations) generally exceeds the delivery time quoted to customers. Thus, the production plan and master production schedule are primarily based on sales forecasts and financial plans—instead of on actual customer orders. Figure 5.3 depicts the budgetary planning process. Once every quarter, the company's sales, finance, and manufacturing executives prepare an overall business game plan covering the next four quarters, including (a) a sales forecast for each of the firm's three product lines and (b) a detailed financial operating plan specifying a forecast of plant shipments (Mohawk calls this the "delivery plan"; in fact, it is the production plan), inventory level targets (the inventory plan), and a capacity plan (covering budgets for manpower and materials). Once these

FIGURE 5.3
Mohawk Company's Quarterly Budgeting Cycle Activities

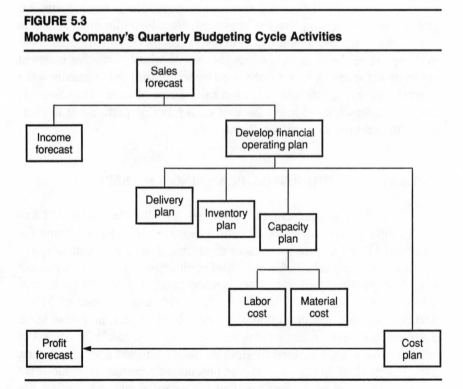

plans are prepared to produce an overall profit forecast for the firm, work can begin on preparing (revising) the master production schedule, which also covers the next four quarters.

The budgeting cycle, performed at each quarter's midpoint, begins with the preparation of a sales forecast for each of the firm's three product lines. Sales forecasting is the responsibility of a general manager, who has the profit responsibility for a particular product line. In preparing the sales forecast, the general manager, financial staff, and marketing organization work closely with a separate field sales organization. The initial sales forecast is for one year in the future. This forecast (stated in terms of both dollar sales and unit sales) corresponds to the product groupings that the financial staff uses to value inventory and measure gross profit levels.

As an example, the energy management product line (with annual sales of $15 to $18 million) includes some 75 individual product categories, each representing annual sales of $25,000 to $2.5 million. Although a separate forecast is prepared for each product category, some of these sales forecasts are combined to reduce the number of product categories considered in the budgeting cycle. In fact, only 21 product groupings are considered in the energy management product line budgeting cycle. They are shown in Figure 5.4, for which the sales forecast was prepared at the midpoint of the second quarter in year 1. In the figure, the sales forecast is expressed in dollars for each product grouping on a monthly basis for the next quarter, and on a quarterly basis for the following three quarters. In producing the data in Figure 5.4, sales for the second quarter of year 1 are treated as actual, even though the quarter is not yet finished. As a result, the monthly forecasts are for the third quarter of year 1 and the quarterly forecasts have been prepared through the second quarter of year 2.

Once the sales forecast is made, financial and manufacturing representatives become involved in the cycle to prepare a game plan for the product line. One of the first steps is to translate the sales forecast into a delivery plan (production plan) for manufacturing and an income forecast for finance. The company uses a tabular presentation form for preparing these plans.

The delivery plan is a statement of the total planned factory deliveries to customers, to finished-goods inventory, and to other company locations. Representatives from manufacturing, finance, and sales develop the delivery plan. The sales forecast, desired changes to inventory,

FIGURE 5.4

Mohawk Company's Summary Sales Forecast, Energy Management Products ($000)*

Product Grouping	History					Year 1				Year 2 1 Qtr.	Year 2 2d Qtr.
	Year 2	Year 1	Year 0	1st Qtr.	2d Qtr.	July	Aug.	Sept.	4th Qtr.		
Singlephase	886	700	265	51	23	13	14	14	41	41	39
Polyphase	4059	1699	349	46	32	20	20	20	60	60	50
Con-Ed	402	108	—								
Lincoln Billing	1609	1354	1412	451	351	102	161	146	409	527	435
Meter Timeswitch	331	224	188	63	76	20	30	27	77	78	69
Sockets	41	57	84	13	14	2	2	2	6	6	10
	7328	4142	2298	624	496	157	227	209	593	712	603
Lincoln Nonbilling	2301	2721	1837	725	560	149	176	204	529	528	586
Line Controls	615	698	358	97	120	15	21	22	58	83	90
Timeswitch	882	1107	708	186	185	43	55	76	174	262	202
	3798	4526	2903	1008	865	207	252	302	761	873	878
Transformers 600V	2767	3139	2248	666	559	193	254	281	728	756	677
Transformers 15KV	383	528	410	232	110	45	50	60	155	201	175
D. C. Meters	143	200	102	70	59	7	18	18	43	53	56
	3293	3867	2760	968	728	245	322	359	926	1010	908

FIGURE 5.4
Mohawk Company's Summary Sales Forecast, Energy Management Products ($000)* (continued)

Product Grouping	History					Year 1				Year 2 1 Qtr.	Year 2 2d Qtr.
	Year 2	Year 1	Year 0	1st Qtr.	2d Qtr.	July	Aug.	Sept.	4th Qtr.		
Survey Recorders	695	826	901	321	355	99	162	132	373	398	367
S.R. Systems				8	95	—	178	45	223	237	141
Digital Pulse Rec.	460	436	225	119	174	43	48	50	141	126	140
C.M.E.	663	448	407	153	168	6	31	57	94	145	145
Parts—Winchester & Memphis	1818	1710	1533	601	792	148	419	284	851	906	788
	1348	1466	1027	405	413	75	135	135	345	395	390
Misc.	407	307	276	224	82	24	32	33	89	120	129
Repairs (Replacement Parts)	37	46	53	16	10	3	3	4	10	10	12
	444	353	329	240	92	27	35	37	99	130	141
Resale: Demand Control	—	2	151	64	56	42	52	53	147	172	110
Sigma-form	482	443	—								
	482	445	151	64	56	42	52	53	147	172	110
Total	18511	16509	11001	3910	3442	901	1442	1379	3722	4198	3818

*Prepared at the midpoint of the second quarter of year 1.

Source: W. L. Berry, R. A. Mohrman, and T. R. Callarman, "Master Scheduling and Capacity Planning: A Case Study" (Bloomington: Indiana University Graduate School of Business, Discussion Paper No. 73, 1977).

potential capacity constraints, vendor deliveries, cash requirements, personnel available, and so on, are considered; adjustments to the sales forecasts (plan) and/or inventory plan are negotiated if necessary. If, for example, manufacturing cannot produce the volume necessary to satisfy both the sales plan and an increase in inventory, the cycle stops and a new sales and/or inventory plan is agreed upon. This production plan, therefore, is an integral part of the entire process; subsequent planning does *not* proceed until there is complete agreement among the sales, finance, and manufacturing representatives.

The next step in the cycle is converting the delivery plan into a capacity plan for each product line and for the plant in total. Figure 5.5 illustrates the development of the capacity plan for the energy management product line considering the sales forecast's labor content, the forecast labor content of the two inventories (finished-goods and work-in-process), and the labor content of the forecast interplant transfers both to and from this plant. The bottom line in the energy management section of Figure 5.5 ("Total labor input") indicates plant capacity requirements for this product line for the periods in which capacity is stated in terms of direct labor dollars. For example, $199,000 of direct labor input is planned for January, year 1. This represents about two-thirds of the total direct labor input (capacity) for the Mohawk plant in January ($290,000), which is shown on the next line of Figure 5.5. Because January has 21 working days, this means an average of $13,800 of direct labor input per day. This translates into a total manpower level for the plant, using planning factors for the number of dollars of direct labor per person per day.

Mohawk considers three factors in arriving at the capacity plan. First, it determines the sales forecasts' direct labor content using standard cost system data. Figure 5.5 shows the sales forecasts' direct labor content for the energy management product line (labeled "Labor in sales forecast"). Note that $176,000 of direct labor is required to support the sales forecast for January of year 1. Next, labor-dollars in the sales forecasts are modified to account for any inventory buildup or depletion planned for the coming year. Figure 5.5 indicates desired levels over the next year, including both finished-goods and work-in-process inventories. The levels (also measured in terms of direct labor-dollars) indicate cash requirements to finance the inventory during the next year as well. Note that a $41,000 inventory reduction is planned for the fourth quarter

FIGURE 5.5
Mohawk Company's Aggregate Production and Inventory Plan ($000)*

Labor forecast	Year 0		Year 1						Year 2	Year 3
	8/31 Actual	12/31 4th Qtr.	1/31 Jan.	2/29 Feb.	3/31 Mar.	6/30 2d Qtr.	9/31 3d Qtr.	12/31 4th Qtr.	12/31 1977	12/31 1978
Energy management:										
Finished goods inventory	$ 224	$ 240	$ 250	$ 270	$ 275	$ 310	$ 300	$ 300	$ 300	$ 300
Work-in-process inventory	862	825	825	805	800	800	800	800	800	800
Subtotal	$1,106	$1,065	$1,075	$1,075	$1,075	$1,110	$1,110	$1,110	$1,110	$1,100
Net change		(41)	10	—	—	35	(10)	—	—	—
Labor in sales forecast		599	176	168	210	540	531	542	2,196	2,146
Transfer from Memphis		(54)	(12)	(12)	(12)	(36)	(36)	(36)	(144)	(144)
Transfer to Memphis		72	25	25	15	13	13	13	52	52
Total labor input		$ 576	$ 199	$ 181	$ 213	$ 552	$ 498	$ 519	$2,104	$2,054
Plant total:										
Labor input	$ 210	$ 829	$ 290	$ 273	$ 342	$ 847	$ 745	$ 830	$3,243	$3,706
Days per period	20	61	21	20	25	62	52	57	236	236
Average labor per day	$ 10.5	$ 13.6	$ 13.8	$ 13.6	$ 13.7	$ 13.7	$ 14.3	$ 14.6	$ 13.7	$ 15.7

*Measured in direct labor-dollars.

Source: W. L. Berry, R. A. Mohrman, and T. R. Callarman, "Master Scheduling and Capacity Planning: A Case Study" (Bloomington: Indiana University Graduate School of Business, Discussion Paper No. 73, 1977).

of year 0, while an increase of $10,000 is planned for January, year 1. These changes must be considered in planning the direct labor input for the energy management product line. Thus, the $10,000 increase in January means that $186,000 of direct labor is needed in this month, instead of $176,000. The third factor in determining plant capacity is interplant sales of equipment. Figure 5.5 shows that in January the Memphis plant will expend $12,000 of labor for products it sells. An additional $25,000 in labor will be expended here for products sold by Memphis. Thus, there is a net addition of $13,000 in direct labor required above and beyond sales by this plant. When added to the $10,000 inventory increase and the $176,000 of labor in the sales forecast, total labor input for January, year 1, is $199,000.

After all negotiations are complete, the budgeting cycle produces an overall game plan for the business that includes an approved sales plan, a delivery plan, an inventory plan, and a capacity plan. Additional steps are performed in the budgeting cycle. They involve preparing a direct material budget of the purchasing dollars required to support the delivery plan, and a cost plan specifying a budget of indirect manufacturing and administration expenses. Engineering and marketing are also included in the budgeting cycle. All plans are then combined by the finance staff to produce a profit forecast for each product line (profit center).

THE NEW MANAGEMENT OBLIGATIONS

Implementing production planning requires major changes in management, particularly in top-management coordination of functional activities. If the production plan is to be the game plan for running a manufacturing company, it follows that top management needs to provide the necessary direction.

Top-Management Role

Top management's first obligation is to commit to the production-planning process. This means a major change in many firms. The change involves the routine aspects of establishing the framework for game planning: getting forecasts, setting meetings, preparing plans, and so on. The change may also imply modifications of performance measurement and reward structures to align them with the plan. We should expect at the outset that many existing goals and performance measures will be in conflict with the integration provided by a working production-planning system. These should be rooted out and explicitly changed. Enforcing changes implies a need to abide by and provide an example of the discipline required to manage with the planning system. This implies that even top management must act within the planned flexibility range for individual actions and must evaluate possible changes that lie outside the limits.

As part of the commitment to the planning process, top management *must force* the resolution of trade-offs between functions prior to approving plans. The production plan provides a transparent basis for resolving these conflicts. It should provide basic implications of alternative choices even if it does not make decisions any easier. If trade-offs are not made at this level, they will be forced into the mix of day-to-day activities of operating people who will have to resolve them—perhaps unfavorably. If, for example, manufacturing continues long runs of products in the face of declining demand, the mismatch between production and the market will lead to increased inventories.

Game-planning activities must encompass *all* formal plans in an integrated fashion. If budgeting is a separate activity, it will not relate to the game plan and operating managers will need to make a choice. Similarly, if the profit forecast is based solely on the sales forecast (revenue) and accounting data (standard costs), and does not take into account implications for production, its value is doubtful. The intention of the production-planning process is to produce complete and integrated plans, budgets, objectives, and goals that are used by managers to make decisions and provide the basis for evaluating performance. If other planning activities or evaluation documents are in place, the end result will be poor execution. An unfortunate but frequent approach is to invest management time in the production-planning activity, but thereafter allow the company to be run by a separate performance measurement system or budget.

Some firms find the term *game planning* more acceptable than *production planning,* which connotes a functional focus that is not accurate. Lately, the term *sales and operation planning* is being used to describe the interfunctional nature of the process. Whatever the term, the production-planning process is interfunctional and needs to be coordinated at the top-management level.

Functional Roles

The primary obligation under game planning is to "hit the plan" for all functions involved: manufacturing, sales, engineering, finance, and so on. A secondary obligation is the need to communicate when something will prevent hitting the plan. The sooner a problem can be evaluated in terms of other functional plans, the better. The obligation for communication provides the basis for keeping *all* groups' plans consistent when changes are necessary.

The process of budgeting usually needs to change and to be integrated with game planning and subsequent departmental plans. In many firms, budgeting is done on an annual basis, using data that are not part of the production and inventory management system. Manufacturing budgets are often based on historical cost relationships and a separation of fixed and variable expenses. These data are not as precise as data obtained by utilizing the PIM system data base. By using the data base, we can evaluate tentative master production schedules in terms of component part needs, capacities, and expected costs. We can then analyze the resultant budgets for the effect of product mix changes, as well as for performance against standards.

Another important aspect of relating budgeting to the game-planning activity and underlying PIM systems and data base is that the cycle can be done more frequently. We will not need to collect data—they always exist in up-to-date form. Moreover, inconsistencies are substantially cut. The budget should always agree with the production plan, which, in turn, is in concert with the disaggregated end item and component plans that support the production plan. As a result, an operating manager should have to choose between a budget and satisfying the production plan far less often.

With budgeting and production planning done on the same basis, with the same underlying dynamic data base, it is natural to incorporate cost accounting. This enables us to perform detailed variance accounting and to cross-check transaction accuracy.

The most obvious need for integrated planning and control is between marketing and production, but this is often the most difficult to accomplish. Firms must ensure product availability for special promotions, match customer orders with specific production lots, coordinate distribution activities with production, and deal with a host of other cross-functional problems.

The marketing job under integrated game planning is to sell what is in the sales plan. We must instill the feeling that overselling is just as bad as underselling. In either case, there will be a mismatch with manufacturing output, financial requirements, and inventory/backlog levels. If an opportunity arises to sell more than the plan, it needs to be formally evaluated via a change in the game plan. By going through this process, we can time this increase so it can be properly supported by both manufacturing and finance. And once the formal plan has been changed, it is again each function's job to achieve its specified objectives—no more and no less.

Similarly, it is manufacturing's job to achieve the plan exactly. Overproduction may well mean that too much capacity and resources are being utilized. Underproduction possibly means the reverse (not enough resources), or means poor performance; in either case, performance against the plan is poor. This can be the fault of either the standard-setting process or inadequate performance. Both problems require corrective action.

When manufacturing is hitting the schedule, it is a straightforward job for marketing to provide good customer order promises and other forms of customer service. It is also a straightforward job for finance to plan cash flows and anticipate financial performance.

If the production-planning results cannot be achieved, those who cannot meet their plan must be clearly responsible for reporting this condition promptly. If, for example, a major supplier cannot meet its commitments, the impact on the detailed marketing and production plans must be quickly ascertained.

Integrating Strategic Planning

An important direction-setting activity, strategic planning, can be done in different ways. Some companies approach it primarily as an extension of budgeting. These firms typically use a bottom-up process, which is largely an extrapolation of the departmental budgets based on growth assumptions and cost-volume analysis. One key aspect of these firms' strategic plans is integrating these bottom-up extrapolations into a coherent whole. Another is to critically evaluate the overall outcome from a corporate point of view.

A more recent approach to strategic planning is to base the plan more on products and less on organizational units. The company's products are typically grouped into strategic business units (SBUs), with each SBU evaluated in terms of its strengths and weaknesses vis-a-vis competitors' similar business units. The budgetary process in this case is done on an SBU basis rather than an organizational unit basis. Business units are evaluated in terms of their competitive strengths, relative advantages (sometimes based on learning curve models), life cycles, and cash flow patterns (e.g., when does an SBU need cash and when is it a cash provider?). From a strategic point of view, the objective is to carefully manage a portfolio of SBUs to the firm's overall advantage.

Game planning and departmental plans to support these strategic planning efforts can be important. In the case of the production plan, the overall data base and systems must ensure that game plans will be in concert with disaggregated decision making. In other words, the MPS and related functions ensure that strategic planning decisions are executed.

The advantages of integrating production planning with budgeting also apply when the SBU focus is taken. It makes sense to state the production plan in the same SBU units; that is, rather than using dollar outputs per time unit, the production plan should be stated in SBU terminology.

Controlling the Production Plan

A special responsibility involves control of performance against the plan. As a prerequisite to control, the game-planning process should be widely understood in the firm. The seriousness with which it is regarded should be communicated as well as the exact planned results that pertain to each of the organization's functional units. In other words, the planning process must be transparent, with clear communication of expectations, to control actual results. For the production plan, this means wide dissemination of the plan and its implications for managers.

Another dimension of control is periodic reporting. Performance against the production plan should also be widely disseminated. When actual results differ from plans, we must analyze and communicate the source of these deviations.

The Tennant Company provides an example of this communication. Here are some of its more important measures of performance and reporting frequency:

Measure	*Reporting*
Conformity of the master production schedule to the production plan	Weekly
Capacity utilization	Weekly
Delivery performance	Daily
Actual production to master production schedule performance	Weekly
Inventory/backlog performance	Weekly

At a key point in its history, Tennant had not missed a quarterly production plan for the previous 2.5 years. Moreover, it had met the monthly production plan in 10 out of 12 months for each of the previous years. These results are well known inside the company, and widely disseminated outside as well. All levels of the firm understand the production plan's importance.

Key issues in production planning are when to change the plan, how often to replan, and how stable to keep the plan from period to period. No doubt, a stable production plan results in far fewer execution problems in the detailed master production scheduling, material planning, and other execution activities. Stability also fosters achievement in some steady-state operations, where capacity can be more effectively utilized.

At Tennant, production plan changes are batched until the next review unless they are required to prevent major problems. In other companies, stability in the plan is maintained by providing time fences for changes and permissible ranges of deviation from plan. Tennant provides flexibility in the plan by planning adequate inventories or other forms of capacity to absorb deviations within an agreed-upon range.

Increasingly, companies are using just-in-time (JIT) concepts, with many aspects of the system based on manual controls. One key to making JIT work in many cases is a stable production plan. The output rate is held constant for long time periods and is only modified after extensive analysis. This means that the production rate at each step of the manufacturing process can be held to very constant levels, providing stability and predictability.

We can see the other side of this coin by reviewing one U.S. auto manufacturer's approach. In the face of diminishing sales, the company continued to produce in excess of sales. This led to a buildup of finished-goods inventory exceeding 100 days of sales. The results on the financial statements were significant; adjustments in manufacturing were even more severe. Finished-goods inventories and order backlogs can buffer manufacturing from day-to-day shocks, but long-run changes have to be reflected in the basic production plan itself.

CONCLUDING PRINCIPLES

The production plan plays a key role in integrating the planning activities of the various functions in a business. In this chapter we have illustrated the importance of the production plan in coordinating the marketing, financial, engineering, and manufacturing efforts of a company. Likewise, production and game planning are vital inputs to PIM in a company. They represent top management's handle on the business, and link manufacturing activities to the strategic plans for the business. We have also emphasized the key relationships of top management and functional management in developing and maintaining an effective production plan. The following important principles summarize our discussion:

- The production plan is not a forecast; it must be a managerial statement of agreed upon production output.
- The production plan should be a part of the game-planning process so it will be in complete agreement with the other functional plans (sales plan, budget, and so on) that make up the game plan.
- The trade-offs required to frame the production plan must be made *prior* to final approval of the plan.
- There must be top-management involvement in the game-planning process, which should be directly related to strategic planning.
- The PIM systems should be used to perform routine activities and provide routine data so that management time can be devoted to important tasks.
- Reviews of performance against manufacturing plans and sales forecasts are needed to prompt replanning when necessary.
- The production plan should provide the MPS parameters, and flexibility should be specifically defined. The sum of the detailed MPS must always equal the production plan.
- The production plan should tie the company's strategic activities directly through the MPS to PIM execution activities.

INTEGRATED RESOURCE LINKAGES

Production planning is the most strategic aspect of PIM decisions. This means that the primary linkages with other resource areas are of a strategic nature. The production plan is manufacturing's version of the overall company game plan, and important trade-offs exist with sales and marketing. How much inventory will we hold? In which production family? What is the rate of production for the next few months in each of these families? What are the corresponding estimates of demand? How will we jointly plan for a major marketing campaign? What will be our response to variations in the effectiveness of the campaign?

Related linkages to finance and accounting consider the financial implications of production rates, sales rates, inventory additions and depletions, and unplanned variations in all of these. When is an inventory of some product family too high? What are the resultant sets of decisions in marketing and manufacturing? Should production be curtailed? Should sales be stimulated through price discounts or other means?

The linkages of PIM with sales, marketing, finance, and accounting also help to define the basic manufacturing strategy itself. What is the required degree of flexibility and responsiveness? To what extent can we focus particular production units on particular product families, technologies, or groups of customers?

Design engineering also has a linkage to production planning. The introduction of new products has to be evaluated on an overall basis as well as in terms of the requirements for sales, marketing, manufacturing, logistics, and accounting and finance. It is also usually important to plan carefully for the impact on other products. Typically, new products make certain existing products obsolete—or at least obsolete in certain markets. These inputs need to be clearly defined so that inventory can be reduced on these products. It is also important to understand whether the new products will have the same requirements for materials, equipment, and personnel. For example, if the new products are to be built in a different factory, the impact on existing operations needs to be carefully planned.

A related linkage is with human resource management (HRM). Changes in production plans directly determine changes in HRM requirements, so it is critical to continually assess these requirements. For companies in high technology, there is a particular phenomenon here that needs to be understood. Computer manufacturers, such as Digital Equipment, need to expand their sales by 20 to 25 percent each year—just to *maintain* employment levels. The direct labor-hours per dollar of product is continually reduced; the boxes are smaller and smaller and the power is greater and greater. This is because the integrated circuits are ever more powerful and encompassing.

The production plan is linked to logistics in that the output from manufacturing necessarily feeds logistics—and constrains the actions that can be taken in logistics. The overall inventories in logistics need to be considered when making production-planning decisions, as well as the ways in which subsequent production quantities will be distributed through the logistics systems.

The management information system linkages with production planning are more complex and strategic than is true for other aspects of PIM. It is essential that data elements be defined so that one set of numbers is used in game planning. We have seen many companies that produce multiple answers to a question as routine as what was last month's shipments of product X? This leads to great confusion. Moreover, the results of game planning *must* be linked directly to other PIM systems—as well as to operational systems in the other business functions.

REFERENCES

Berry, W. L.; R. A. Mohrman; and T. Callarman. "Master Scheduling and Capacity Planning: A Case Study." Bloomington: Indiana University Graduate School of Business, Discussion Paper no. 73, 1977.

Bitran, Gabriel R.; Elizabeth A. Haas; and Arnoldo C. Hax. "Hierarchical Production Planning: A Single Stage System." *Operations Research* 29, no. 4 (July–August 1981), pp. 717–43.

Dougherty, John R. "Getting Started with Production Planning." *Readings in Production and Inventory Control and Planning,* APICS 27th Annual Conference, 1984, pp. 176–79.

Goldratt, Eliyanu. "The Unbalanced Plant." *APICS 24th Annual Conference Proceedings,* 1981, pp. 195–99.

Hall, Robert. "Driving the Productivity Machine: Production Planning and Control in Japan." Falls Church, Va.: APICS, 1981.

Hayes, R. H., and S. C. Wheelright. *Restoring Our Competitive Edge.* New York: Wiley, 1984.

Hill, Terry. *Manufacturing Strategy.* London: MacMillan Education Ltd., 1985.

Hodgson, T. J.; R. E. King; and C. U. King. "Development of a Production Planning System: A Case History." *Production and Inventory Management* 31, no. 4 (4th quarter 1990), pp. 18–24.

Holt, C. C.; F. Modigliani; J. F. Muth; and H. A. Simon. *Planning Production, Inventories, and Workforce*. New York: Prentice Hall, 1960.

Ling, R. C., and W. E. Goddard. *Orchestrating Success*. Essex Junction, Vt.: Oliver Wight Ltd., 1988.

Leong, G. K.; M. D. Oliff; and R. E. Markland. "Improved Hierarchical Production Planning." *Journal of Operations Management* 8, no. 2 (April 1989), pp. 90–114.

Peterson, Rein, and Edward A. Silver. *Decision Systems for Inventory Management and Production Planning*, 2nd ed. New York: Wiley, 1985.

Sari, John F. "Why Don't We Call It Sales and Operations Planning, Not Production Planning?" *APICS 29th Annual Conference Proceedings*, 1986, pp. 22–24.

Shirley, G. V., and R. Jaikumar. "Production Planning in Flexible Transfer Lines." *Journal of Manufacturing and Operations Management* 2, no. 4 (1989), pp. 249–67.

Singhal, K., and V. Adlakha. "Cost and Shortage Trade-Offs in Aggregate Production Planning." *Decision Sciences Journal* 20, no. 1 (Winter 1989), pp. 158–65.

Skinner, C. W. *Manufacturing in the Corporate Strategy*. New York: Wiley, 1978.

Vollmann, T. E. "Capacity Planning: The Missing Link." *Production and Inventory Management*, 1st quarter 1973, pp. 61–74.

CHAPTER 6

MASTER PRODUCTION
SCHEDULING

The master production schedule plays a critical role in coordinating and integrating operational decisions in all of the business functions, including marketing, engineering, finance, manufacturing, and human resources. For example, the master production schedule is used to match customer orders with manufacturing schedules for individual products, to link customer delivery requirements with manufacturing resources and cash flows, to indicate the required timing of engineering design activities, and to determine capacity limitations for critical human resources. As a result, the master production schedule provides the necessary detail to translate the production plan into an integrated operational plan for the business.

The design of the master production schedule (MPS) also reflects the marketing strategy of a company. If, for example, products of standard design are required in short lead times by customers, a make-to-stock approach may be taken in the design of the master production schedule. In this case, the close coordination of the MPS with sales forecasting, distribution planning, and transportation activities is required. However, if a wide variety of custom-designed products is sold in low volume, a make-to-order master production scheduling approach may be taken and the MPS would be closely coordinated with the order entry, customer order promising, and engineering design functions. In designing the master production scheduling system, it is important to consider the way in which the MPS supports the company strategy in the marketplace, and the level of service offered to customers.

Construction and management of the master production schedule is a critical activity in production and inventory management. The master production schedule provides the basis for making customer order delivery promises, utilizing plant capacity effectively, attaining the firm's strategic objectives as reflected in the production plan, resolving tradeoffs between manufacturing and marketing, and sending the right overall set of directives to the detailed PIM systems. The prerequisites are to define the master scheduling task in the organization and to provide the master production schedule with the supporting concepts described in this chapter.

This chapter is organized around five topics:

- The master production scheduling activity: What is the role of master production scheduling in production and inventory management, and what is its relation to other business activities?
- The Ethan Allen master production schedule example: How does an actual MPS system work in practice?
- The master production scheduler: What does a master production scheduler do and what are the key organizational relationships?
- Master production schedule stability: How can a stable MPS be developed and maintained?
- Managing the MPS: How can MPS performance be monitored and controlled?

THE MASTER PRODUCTION SCHEDULING ACTIVITY

We begin with a brief overview of the master production scheduling process. What is the MPS activity, and how does it relate to other production and inventory management (PIM) system functions and other company activities? What is the sequence of tasks performed by the master production scheduler?

At an operational level, the most basic decisions concern how to construct and update the MPS. This involves processing MPS transactions, maintaining MPS records and reports, having a periodic review and update cycle (we call this "rolling through time"), processing and responding to exception conditions, and measuring MPS effectiveness on a routine basis.

On a day-to-day basis, marketing and production are coordinated through the MPS in terms of *order promising*. This is the activity by which customer order requests receive shipment dates. The MPS provides the basis for making these decisions effectively, as long as manufacturing executes the MPS according to plan. When customer orders create a backlog and require promise dates that are unacceptable from a marketing viewpoint, trade-off conditions are established for making changes.

The Anticipated Build Schedule

The master production schedule is an anticipated build schedule for manufacturing end products (or product options). As such, it is a statement of production, not a statement of market demand. That is, the MPS is *not* a forecast. The sales forecast is a critical input into the planning process that is used for determining the MPS, but the MPS differs from the forecast in significant ways. The MPS takes into account capacity limitations, and attempts to utilize capacity effectively. This means that some items may be built before they are needed for sale, and other items may not be built even though the marketplace could consume them.

The master production schedule forms the basic communication link with manufacturing. It is stated in product specifications—in part numbers for which bills of material exist. Because it is a build schedule, it must be stated in terms that can be used to determine component-part needs and other requirements. The MPS cannot, therefore, be stated in overall dollars or some other global unit of measure. Specific products in the MPS can be end item production designations, or they may be groups of items, such as models. For example, a General Motors assembly plant might state the MPS as so many thousand J-body cars per week, with exact product mix (e.g., Chevrolet, four-door, four-cylinder) determined with a *final assembly schedule* (FAS), which is not ascertained until the latest possible moment. If the MPS is to be stated in terms of product groups (e.g., J-body cars), we must create special bills of material (planning bills) for these groups (e.g., an average J-body car planning bill).

Linkages to Other Company Activities

Figure 6.1 presents a schematic that depicts the linkages of master production scheduling to other key PIM activities.

The demand management block in Figure 6.1 represents a company's forecasting, order entry, order promising, and physical distri-

FIGURE 6.1
Key Linkages of Master Production Scheduling

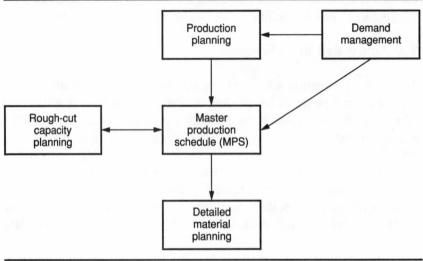

bution activities. This includes all activities that place demand (requirements) on manufacturing capacities. These demands may be actual and forecast customer orders, branch warehouse requirements, interplant requirements, international requirements, and service part demands. The resultant capacity needs must be coordinated with the MPS on an ongoing basis.

The production plan represents production's role in the company's strategic business plan. It reflects the desired aggregate output from manufacturing that is necessary to support the company game plan. In some firms, the production plan is simply stated in terms of the monthly or quarterly sales dollar output for the company as a whole, or for individual plants or businesses. In other firms, the production plan is stated in terms of the number of units to be produced in each major product line each month for the next year. This aggregate plan constrains the MPS, as the sum of the detailed MPS quantities must always equal the whole dictated by the production plan.

Rough-cut capacity planning involves an analysis of the master production schedule to determine the existence of manufacturing facilities that represent potential bottlenecks in production flow; that is, the linkage provides a rough evaluation of potential capacity problems from a particular MPS.

The MPS is the basis for key interfunctional trade-offs. The most profound of these is between production and marketing in terms of exact product definition in the MPS. A request to increase production for any item usually results in the need to reduce production on some other item. If production for no item can be reduced, then by definition the production plan and resultant budget for production must be changed.

Because the MPS becomes the basis for the manufacturing budget, it follows that financial budgets should be integrated with production planning and MPS activities. When the MPS is extended over a time horizon sufficient to make capital equipment purchases, a better basis is provided for capital budgets. On a day-to-day basis, both cash flow and profits can be better forecast by basing these forecasts on the planned production output specified in the MPS. The linkage with detailed material planning is based on the MPS providing overall direction (e.g., end items). Detailed material planning explodes the MPS plans into plans for all the purchased and fabricated components and subassemblies.

The Business Environment for the MPS

The business environment, as it relates to master production scheduling, encompasses the production approach used, the variety of products produced, and the markets served by the company. Three classic types of MPS approaches have been identified: make-to-stock, make-to-order, and assemble-to-order. The choice among these alternatives concerns the unit to be used for the MPS; that is, is the MPS to be based on end items, specific customer orders, or some group of end items and product options?

The *make-to-stock* company produces in batches, carrying finished-goods inventories for most, if not all, of its end items. The MPS is the production statement of how much of and when each end item is to be produced. Firms that make to stock frequently produce consumer products as opposed to industrial goods, but many industrial goods, such as supply items, are also made to stock.

The choice of MPS unit for the make-to-stock company is fairly straightforward. All use end item catalog numbers, but many tend to group these end items into model groupings until the latest possible time in the final assembly schedule. Thus, the Ethan Allen Furniture Company uses a *consolidated item number* for items that are identical except for the finish color, running a separate system to allocate a lot size in the MPS to specific finishes at the last possible moment. Similarly, the Black & Decker tool manufacturing firm groups models in a series, such as sanders, which are similar except for horsepower, attachments, and private brand labels. All products so grouped are run together in batches to achieve economical runs for component parts, and to exploit the learning curve in the final assembly areas.

The *make-to-order* company, in general, carries no finished-goods inventory and builds each customer order as needed. This form of production is often used when there is a very large number of possible production configurations, and thus a small probability of anticipating a customer's exact needs. In this business environment, customers expect to wait for a large portion of the entire design and manufacturing lead time. Examples include a tugboat manufacturer or refinery builder.

In the make-to-order company, the MPS unit is typically defined as the particular end item or set of items comprising a customer order. The definition is difficult because part of the job is to define the product; that is, design often takes place as manufacturing occurs. Production often starts before a complete product definition and bill of materials have been determined.

The *assemble-to-order* firm is typified by an almost limitless number of possible end item configurations, all made from combinations of basic components and subassemblies. Customer delivery time requirements are often shorter than total manufacturing lead times, so production must be started in anticipation of customer orders. The large number of end item possibilities makes forecasting exact end item configurations extremely difficult, and stocking end items very risky. As a result, the assemble-to-order firm tries to maintain flexibility, starting basic components and subassemblies into production, but generally not starting final assembly until a customer order is received.

Examples of assemble-to-order firms include General Motors, with its endless automobile end product combinations; the Hyster Company, which makes forklift trucks with such options as engine type, lift height, cab design, speed, type of lift mechanism, and safety equipment; and Tennant Company, which makes industrial sweeping machines with many user-designated options.

The assemble-to-order firm typically does not master production schedule end items. The MPS unit is stated in *planning bills of material,* such as an average lift truck of some model series. The MPS unit (planning bill) has as its components a set of common parts and options. The option usages are based on percentage estimates, and their planning in the MPS incorporates buffering or hedging techniques to maximize the response flexibility for actual customer orders.

A key difference between make-to-stock, make-to-order, and assemble-to-order firms is in the definition of the MPS unit. However, many master production scheduling techniques are useful for any kind of MPS unit definition. Moreover, choice of MPS unit is somewhat open to definition by the firm. Thus, some firms may produce end items that are held in inventory, yet still use assemble-to-order approaches. Also, some firms use more than one of these approaches at the same time, so common systems are important.

THE ETHAN ALLEN MASTER PRODUCTION SCHEDULE EXAMPLE

We turn now to an actual MPS example, Ethan Allen's approach to master production scheduling. The approach uses time-phased planning information. We will see how standard software for material requirements planning (MRP) can be usefully applied, and highlight aspects of the master production scheduler's job.

The Ethan Allen Furniture Company produces case goods (wood furniture) in 14 geographically dispersed factories. Its total product line is 980 consolidated item numbers. (Different finishes for the same item make the number of end items about 50 percent larger.) Each consolidated item number is uniquely assigned to a particular assembly line or building station in one of the 14 factories. For each assembly line in each factory, a capacity is established in hours such that, if the hours of capacity are fully utilized on all lines, the overall company objectives as stated in its production plan will be met.

A forecast of demand is made for each consolidated item number, using statistical forecasting methods. A lot size for each item is also determined, based on economic order quantity concepts. For each assembly lot size, hours required on the assembly line are estimated. For each product, expected weekly priorities are established by dividing the expected beginning inventory by the weekly forecast. In weeks after the first, expected beginning inventory takes account of production and expected sales. The assembly line is loaded to capacity in priority sequence, smallest to largest. Figure 6.2 provides a simplified example

---

FIGURE 6.2
Simplified Ethan Allen MPS Example

Basic data:

Product	Beginning inventory	Weekly forecast	Lot size	Hours per lot size
A	20	5	50	20
B	50	40	250	80
C	−30	35	150	60
D	25	10	100	30

Priorities:

Product	P_1	P_2	P_3	P_4	P_5	P_6	P_7	P_8
A	4	3			0		−2	4.5
B	1.25	.25			3.5		1.5	.5
C	−.86	.64			−.57		.29	.71
D	2.5	1.5			−1.5		6.5	5.5

Schedule:

for an assembly line with 35 hours of weekly capacity. The simplified example is based on only four products, though actual lines typically manufacture from 15 to 100 different items.

The top section of Figure 6.2 provides the basic data for each of the four products: the beginning inventory, weekly forecast of sales, lot size, and estimated hours to assemble one lot. Note that for product C, there is a beginning back order or oversold condition.

The middle portion of Figure 6.2 is the set of time-phased priority data. For product A in week 1, the beginning inventory of 20 is divided by the weekly forecast of 5, yielding a priority of 4; that is, at the beginning of week 1 there are four weeks of inventory for product A. Similar priority calculations are made for products B, C, and D in week 1.

The rule for assigning products to the assembly line is to take that product with the smallest priority—the most urgent need. Thus, product C is scheduled for production first. The assignment of product C to the assembly line in week 1 consumes all of the 35 hours of capacity in that week, plus 25 hours in week 2, because it takes 60 hours to assemble a batch of 150 of product C.

Moving to week 2, we see that the expected beginning inventory for product A is 15, as forecast sales for week 1 is 5. Divide 15 by the weekly forecast (5) to get the expected priority for week 2 (15/5 = 3). Alternatively, if four weeks of sales are in inventory at the beginning of week 1, we would expect to have three weeks of sales at the beginning of week 2 if no production of product A takes place. This means that, for each product not produced, its priority number in the succeeding week is reduced by 1. The expected priority for product C at the start of week 2 can be computed by finding 35/60 of 150, adding this to the beginning inventory of −30, subtracting 35 units of forecast demand for week 1, and dividing the result by the forecast of 35 to give a value of 0.64.

The lowest-priority product for week 2 is B (.25). Because a lot size of the product takes 80 hours, capacity is fully utilized until the end of week 4. This is why no priority data are given for weeks 3 and 4. A similar situation is true for week 6 when product C, started in week 5, uses the full week's capacity. By loading each line to its weekly capacity, no more and no less, the match between the production plan dictated for each assembly line and detailed MPS decision making is maintained. Calculations in subsequent weeks involve adding in any production and reducing inventories by expected sales. For example, product C's priority in week 5 can be calculated as follows:

$$
\begin{array}{rr}
\text{Beginning inventory} = & -\ 30 \\
\text{Production} = & 150 \\
\hline
& 120 \\
-4 \text{ weeks' sales at } 35 = & 140 \\
\hline
& -\ 20 \\
-20/35 = & -.57
\end{array}
$$

Figure 6.3 shows another way to create the Ethan Allen MPS. Here, the same four products are used to illustrate the application of a standard MRP approach to planning. For each, a *time-phased order point* (TPOP) record is developed. The same schedule shown in the bottom portion of Figure 6.2 is achieved when the line is loaded to capacity in the sequence of the planned orders in the TPOP records; that is, product C has the first planned order, then B, then D, and so on. Of course, the planned order for D in week 3 is not placed in week 3 because capacity is not available until week 5. There is also a tie shown in week 8. Both products B and C have planned orders in that week. The tie-breaking decision could produce a schedule that differs slightly from that shown in Figure 6.2.

The great advantage to using TPOP approaches in developing the MPS is that specialized MPS software development is reduced. TPOP records are produced with standard MRP logic using the forecast quantities as gross requirements. Using product A in Figure 6.2 as an example, the forecast of 5 per week is shown as "a requirement" in each week. The beginning on-hand balance or "available" quantity is 20 units. At the end of week 1, it will be 15, and the firm expects to run out at the end of week 4. Thus, receipt of an order for 50 is planned in week 5.

The master production scheduler's job is to convert these planned orders to "firm planned orders," so that capacity is properly utilized. At Ethan Allen, conversion of TPOP planned orders to firm planned orders is largely an automatic activity, so it has been computerized. Note, however, that the objective is to load the assembly stations to their absolute

FIGURE 6.3
Ethan Allen MPS Example Using Time-Phased Order Point

Week	1	2	3	4	5	6	7	8	
Gross requirements	5	5	5	5	5	5	5	5	
Scheduled receipts									A
Available 20	15	10	5	0	45	40	35	30	
Planned orders					50				

Week	1	2	3	4	5	6	7	8	
Gross requirements	40	40	40	40	40	40	40	40	
Scheduled receipts									B
Available 50	10	220	180	140	100	60	20	230	
Planned orders		250						250	

Week	1	2	3	4	5	6	7	8	
Gross requirements	35	35	35	35	35	35	35	35	
Scheduled receipts									C
Available −30	85	50	15	130	95	60	25	140	
Planned orders	150			150				150	

Week	1	2	3	4	5	6	7	8	
Gross requirements	10	10	10	10	10	10	10	10	
Scheduled receipts									D
Available 25	15	5	95	85	75	65	55	45	
Planned orders			100						

capacity, in priority sequence. Other firms might use other criteria, such as favoring those jobs with high profitability, favoring certain customers, or allowing flexibility in the definition of capacity. If so, the master production scheduler's detailed decisions would be different.

THE MASTER PRODUCTION SCHEDULER

We turn now to the role of the master production schedulers. Who is the master production scheduler, what does he or she do, and what is the appropriate job description? First, we briefly examine the use of firm planned orders.

The MPS as a Set of Firm Planned Orders

An interesting advantage of using the time-phased order point approach shown in Figure 6.3 to manage the master production schedule derives from the firm planned order concept. The firm planned order is similar to any planned order in that it explodes through product structures. However, it is *not* changed in either timing or amount as a result of processing the MRP record. It is firm, and it can only be changed as the result of an action taken by a responsible person.

It is useful to think of the MPS as a set of firm planned orders. Thereafter, the master production scheduler's job is to convert planned orders to firm planned orders, and to *manage* the timing and amounts of the firm planned orders. The "available" row in the time-phased record provides the primary signal for performing this task. The MRP exception codes can provide indications of when and to what extent firm planned orders might not meet the needs.

Managing the timing and amounts of the firm planned orders means that any changes to the MPS have to be carefully evaluated in terms of their impact on material and capacity plans. The key need is to clearly understand trade-offs between customer needs and other PIM objectives.

The Job

The master production scheduler has the primary responsibility for making any additions or changes to MPS records. He or she also has the primary responsibility for disaggregating the production plan to create the MPS and for ensuring that the sum of the detailed MPS production decisions matches the production plans. This involves analyzing trade-offs and telling top management about situations that require decisions beyond the scheduler's authority level.

As part of the general feedback process, the master production scheduler should monitor actual performance against the MPS and production plan and distill operating results for higher management. The master production scheduler can also help in the analysis of what-if questions by analyzing the impact on the MPS of changes in plans.

The master production scheduler is often responsible for launching the final assembly schedule. This schedule represents the final commitment, made as late as possible, to exact end items; that is, the final assembly schedule has to be based on specific finished-good items. Other master production scheduler activities include interface with order entry, and an ongoing relationship with production control to evaluate the feasibility of suggested changes.

Much of this activity involves resolving competing demands for limited capacity. Clearly, if several master production schedule records show a negative available at the end of the planning horizon, some trade-offs must be made, because not everything can be scheduled at once. Management of the firm planned orders must be done within capacity constraints. The available column now indicates the priority for making those trade-offs. The lower the number of periods of supply or the larger the number of periods of backlog at the end of the planning horizon, the more urgent the need. If too many are urgent, feedback to marketing may be necessary to change budgets.

Figure 6.4 shows the job description for the master production scheduler at Hyster-Portland. This formal job description makes it clear that the master production scheduler needs to constantly balance conflicting objectives and make trade-offs. The position requires maturity, an understanding of both marketing and finance, and an ability to communicate. Computer software can greatly aid the master production scheduler, but judgments will always be required.

Managing the MPS Data Base
For the master production scheduler to operate effectively, it is also critical that there be one single unified data base for the MPS, that it link to the production plan and to detailed material planning systems, and that clear responsibilities for all transactions be established. This involves not only the usual data integrity issues, but also some organizational issues.

In the case of the MPS, many transactions occur in different functional areas. For example, receipts into finished goods may come from completed assemblies (production), shipments from order closing (marketing), or bills of lading (finance). It is critical that exact responsibilities

FIGURE 6.4
Hyster-Portland Master Production Scheduler Job Description

NAME		JOB TITLE
		MASTER SCHEDULER
DEPARTMENT NAME CAPACITY AND MATERIAL PLANNING		DATE ASSIGNED TO PRESENT POSITION
LOCATION NAME PORTLAND PLANT	LOC. CODE 02	DATE OF LAST EVALUATION

PREPARED BY: Roger B. Brooks **JOB DESCRIPTION** 8-23

RATING				
INADEQUATE	MARGINAL	SATISFACTORY	GOOD	SUPERIOR

BASIC FUNCTION:

Responsible for planning, organizing, and controlling the activities of the Master Scheduling Section within the Material and Capacity Planning Department.

REPORTS TO: Capacity and Material Planning Manager

SUPERVISES: Order Entry Administrator, Assembly Schedulers, Master Scheduling Planners

RESPONSIBILITIES:

1. Responsible for creating and maintaining a realistic and valid Master Schedule for all Portland Products. The Master Schedule should reflect requirements for Customer Orders, Stock Orders, the Depot, Product Availability Plan and Option Forecast, Interplant and Export Orders with economic and time consideration for Plant Inventory, Manufacturing Efficiencies, Customer Service and Plant Capacity. Proper Master Scheduling will allow the plant to operate at a steady state during periods of oversold order bookings without a build up of past due job orders and inventories, while simultaneously experiencing no idle capacity on bottleneck work centers.

2. Responsible for accurate, timely and organized order entry of Sales Orders, including IMT's and Export Orders, for all Portland manufactured lift trucks, carriers, winches, sold alones and production parts. Responsible for maintaining communications with the Industrial Truck and Tractor Attachment Sales Order desks to provide accurate and timely customer sales order shipping commitments.

3. Responsible for obtaining shipping instructions for all customers orders via communications with the Industrial Truck and Tractor Attachment Sales Order desks to prevent shipping delays.

4. Responsible for scheduling industrial truck, carrier, sold alone and winch assembly to support customer commitments within the constraints of the Master Schedule, Assembly Department and Parts Bank. Responsible for scheduling major weldments and front ends to support the assembly schedule.

5. Responsible for publishing the Daily Production Report and Final Unit Shipment Report in an accurate and timely manner.

6. Select, develop, and evaluate employees so they, as a group, accomplish the foregoing tasks in a businesslike, efficient, and professional manner.

Source: W. L. Berry, T. E. Vollman, and D. C. Whybark, *Master Production Scheduling: Principles and Practice* (Falls Church, Va: American Production and Inventory Control Society, 1979), p. 142.

be established for transaction processing, and that data linkages to MPS systems and files be rigorously defined and maintained.

Another critical data base requirement for the MPS is proper control over both engineering and nonengineering changes to the bill of material data base. The MPS is often stated in planning bill units that may not be buildable (e.g., an average J-body car). This requires a more complex bill of material or product structure data base. The result is a greater need to procedurally control all changes to the bill of material and to evaluate the impact of changes both from an engineering point of view and in terms of the effect on nonengineering bills of material.

To support the master production scheduler, effective MPS software systems provide time-phased MPS records, maintaining the data base, linkages with other critical systems, MPS monitoring and exception messages, and MPS transaction procedures. Included are entering of order quantities into the MPS, firm planned order treatment, removing MPS order quantities, changing the latter's timing or amount, converting MPS quantities to final assembly schedule (FAS) quantities, launching final assemblies, monitoring FAS scheduled receipts for timing or quantity changes, closing out FAS receipts into finished-goods inventory, and providing for all customer order entry and promising activities.

MASTER PRODUCTION SCHEDULE STABILITY

A stable master production schedule translates into stable detailed material planning schedules, which mean improved performance in plant operations. Too many changes in the MPS are costly in terms of reduced productivity. However, too few changes can lead to poor customer service levels and increased inventory.

The objective is to strike a balance whereby stability is monitored and managed. The techniques most used to achieve MPS stability are firm planned order treatment for the MPS quantities, frozen time periods for the MPS, and time fencing to establish clear guidelines for the kinds of changes that can be made in various periods.

Ethan Allen Stability

Construction of the Ethan Allen MPS is based on TPOP records, with assembly lines loaded up to exact capacities, and the sequence of MPS items determined by the date sequence of planned orders. This process might seem to lead to a great deal of repositioning of MPS quantities; that is, as actual sales occur, forecast errors will tend to rearrange the MPS. In fact, this does not occur because planned orders from TPOP records are "frozen," or firm planned, under certain conditions.

Ethan Allen uses three types of firm planned orders for the MPS, as Figure 6.5 shows. In essence, any firm planned order is frozen in that it will not be automatically repositioned by any computer logic. All MPS quantities for the next eight weeks are considered to be frozen or firm planned at Ethan Allen. In addition, any MPS quantity used to make a customer promise (i.e., a customer order is specifically tied to that MPS batch) is also a firm planned order. The third type of firm planned order used in Ethan Allen's MPS is for what they call the *manual forecast*. Included are contract sales (e.g., items to a motel chain), market specials (i.e., items to go on special promotion), and new items (MPS here being when the product is to be introduced). Finally, all blank space in Figure

FIGURE 6.5
Ethan Allen Firm Planned Order Approach

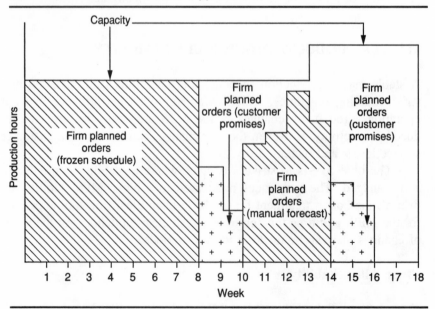

Source: W. L. Berry, T. E. Vollmann, and D. C. Whybark, *Master Production Scheduling: Principles and Practice* (Falls Church, Va: American Production and Inventory Control Society, 1979), p. 51.

6.5 is filled with the TPOP-based scheduling technique discussed earlier. Computerized MPS logic fills in the holes up to the capacity limit without disturbing any firm planned order.

Freezing and Time Fencing

Figure 6.5 shows the first eight weeks in the Ethan Allen MPS as *frozen*. This means that *no* changes inside of eight weeks are possible. In reality, "no" may be a bit extreme. If the president dictates a change, it will probably happen, but such occurrences are rare at Ethan Allen.

Many firms do not like to use the term *frozen,* saying that anything is negotiable—but negotiations get tougher as we approach the present time. However, a frozen period provides a stable target for manufacturing to hit. It also removes most alibis for missing the schedule!

Time fencing is an extension of the freeze concept. Many firms set time fences that specify periods in which various types of change can be handled. For example, at Black & Decker three time fences are used: 26, 13, and 8 weeks. The implication is that beyond 26 weeks the marketing and logistics people can make any change, as long as the sum of all MPS records is synchronized with the production plan. From weeks 13 to 25, substitutions of one end item for another are permitted, provided that required component parts will be available and the production plan is not violated. From weeks 8 to 13, the MPS is quite rigid; but minor changes within a model series can be made if component parts are available. The eight-week time fence at Black & Decker is basically a freeze period similar to that at Ethan Allen, but occasional changes are made within this timing. In fact, assembly lines have been shut down to make changes—but it is so rare that everyone in the factory remembers when this happens! To achieve the productivity necessary to remain competitive, stability in short-range manufacturing plans is essential.

Two common fences are the *demand fence* and the *planning fence*. The demand fence is the shorter of the two. Inside the demand fence, forecasts of demand are ignored on the assumption that it is only customer orders—not the forecast—that matter in the very near term. The planning fence indicates the time at which the master production scheduler should be planning more MPS quantities. Within the demand fence it is very difficult to change the MPS. Between the demand fence and the planning fence, management trade-offs must be considered in making changes; outside the planning fence, changes can be made by the master production scheduler. Some firms refer to these as the ice, slush, and water zones.

MANAGING THE MPS

We turn now to managing the MPS: How do we measure, monitor, and control detailed day-to-day performance against the MPS? The first pre-requisite for control is to have a realistic MPS. Most basic management textbooks say that it is critical to only hold people accountable for performance levels that are attainable. This means the MPS cannot be a wish list, and it should not have any significant portion that is past due. In fact, we claim that significant past due in the MPS is a major indication of a sick PIM system.

Stability and proper buffering are also important, because the objective is to remove all alibis and excuses for not attaining the performance for which the proper budget has been provided. Successful companies hit the production plan every month, and they do the best job possible in disaggregating the plan to reflect actual product mix in the MPS.

The Overstated MPS

Most authorities have warned that the MPS must not be overstated; to do so destroys the relative priorities developed by detailed planning and execution on the shop floor. More importantly, the overstated MPS erodes belief in the *formal system,* thereby reinstituting the informal system of hot lists and black books. Walter Goddard, a well-known MPS expert, no longer tells companies not to overstate the MPS, because at some point the temptation is overwhelming; he now tells them to learn from the experience so they will not do it again! A key to not overstating the MPS is to always force the sum of the MPS to equal the production plan. Then when someone wants to add something, the question is, "Of what do you want less?" The company must give up what is referred to as *the standard manufacturing answer.* The standard manufacturing answer to whether more output of some product is possible is,"We do not know, but we will try!"

The company *must* know. There should be an overall output budget for manufacturing. Capacity should be in place, and should match (not be more or less than) the budget. Manufacturing and marketing should work diligently to respond to product mix changes, but within the overall budgetary constraint. The correct response to whether more output of some product is possible is, "What else can be reduced?" If nothing, then the answer is either "No" or "The output budget and concomitant resources will have to be changed to increase capacities."

MPS Measures

There is an old Vermont story about the fellow who was asked, "How is your wife?" His answer: "Compared to what?" Likewise, measuring MPS has to be in concrete terms that reflect the firm's fundamental goals. This is not as easy as it might seem. At one time, Ethan Allen evaluated each factory on the basis of dollar output per week. At one plant, an assembly line produced both plastic-topped tables and all-wood tables. Plastic-topped tables sold for more and could be assembled in roughly half the time, because the top was purchased as a completed subassembly. Obviously, the factory favored plastic-topped tables, even when inventories were high on those items and low on wood tables.

Ethan Allen had to change the measure for evaluating plant performance. Each line in each plant is now scheduled by the techniques we have described, and performance is based upon hitting the schedule.

Another important measure of MPS and other PIM system functions is customer service. In virtually every company, customer service is an area of concern. However, in many firms, a tight definition of precisely how the measure is to be made is lacking. Measurement is a critical step in control, and each firm will need to express how this important aspect of its operation is to be measured.

It is to be expected that whatever measure for customer service is chosen, the firm may have problems similar to those of Ethan Allen when evaluating plants using dollar output. However, the way to find the problems and thereafter eliminate them is, in fact, to start with *some* measure, no matter how crude, and evolve.

Appropriate measures vary a great deal from firm to firm, reflecting the type of market response typical in the industry and the particular company. Ethan Allen measures customer service in terms of hitting the order acknowledgment or promise dates. At another company, Jet Spray, manufacturing performance is measured against the MPS, as is monthly performance in "equivalent units" of output versus the budget. The goal is a cumulative performance of at least 95 percent. At Black & Decker, management measures its customer service in distribution in terms of a 95 percent ability to deliver any customer order from inventory. Some assemble-to-order firms evaluate production against the production plan, which is to deliver a specific number of each model to marketing in the agreed-upon time frame. They also evaluate customer service in terms of how long customers have to wait until they can get a specific end item. This indicates how well the production plan is being disaggregated.

Monitoring the MPS at Ethan Allen

Figure 6.5 shows Ethan Allen's firm planned order approach to its MPS. We also know that each plant is evaluated on hitting the MPS, so it should be useful to see how detailed monitoring takes place and how overall company operations have been affected.

Every Tuesday morning, Ethan Allen's vice president of manufacturing gets a report detailing each factory's performance in the prior week. Figure 6.6 shows this overall performance report. Figure 6.7 is the detail for one factory at Beecher Falls, Vermont.

Figure 6.6 shows one plant, Boonville, as having had poor performance. The last two comments about packed production and outside suppliers show total production achieved in these two categories.

The "STATIONS" in Figure 6.7 are the assembly lines; their capacities are stated in hours. The "PRIORITY" data reflect expected operating conditions 18 weeks in the future. If each priority number were the same, each line would have the same average weeks of anticipated supply for its items. As it is, some lines will be seriously behind in terms of meeting anticipated customer demands for some items. This is a question of capacity that is reflected in the comments about each station. For example, for the 06 station, the detail indicates that additional capacity is required to catch up, while 08 should reduce capacity. Note, however, that lack of capacity does not mean the plant is not meeting its schedule. All eight lines are reported as "no misses." This means that in the week covered by this report, the plant met its schedule exactly. Jobs in the schedule are being run. The schedule is loaded up to capacity—not in excess of capacity. Lack of adequate capacity means longer delivery times to customers, but not missed schedules.

By evaluating the reports in Figures 6.6 and 6.7, it is clear which plants are performing according to expectations. Life in the factories

---

FIGURE 6.6
Ethan Allen Summary MPS Performance

April 5,

To: Bill Morrissey

From: Marty Stern

Production schedule review
4/1

Summary:

Nine of the 14 factories operating hit their schedules
100 percent.

Performance against schedule was poor this week at
one of the factories: Boonville---75 percent

Packed production was 196 million over total scheduled.
11 of the factories reporting met or exceeded their schedule.

The outside suppliers produced 171 million under their schedule
bringing total production to 25 million over scheduled goal.

cc: Marshall Ames
Barney Kvingedal
Ray Dinkel
Walter Blisky
Andy Boscoe
Steve Kammerer
Tom Ericson
Bob Schneble
Hank Walker

Source: W. L. Berry, T. E. Vollmann, and D. C. Whybark, *Master Production Scheduling: Principles and Practice* (Falls Church, Va.: American Production and Inventory Control Society, 1979), p. 54.

---

is much more calm with performance more clearly defined. No longer do salespeople, customers, marketing people, and executives call the factories. The interface between functions is reflected in the master production schedule, and each factory's job is to hit its MPS. In a sense, the entire master scheduling effort has enabled Ethan Allen to achieve centralized management of decentralized operations. Factory operations are geographically dispersed over wide areas, but those operations are

FIGURE 6.7
Ethan Allen Detailed MPS Performance (for one factory)

SUMMARY OF SCHEDULE REVIEW

PLANT: BEECHER FALLS

FROM: MARTY STERN

SCHEDULE DATE ____3/27____

THRU WEEK OF ____8/28____

STATION	CAPACITY	PRIORITY	PROD. SCHED. DOLLARS	PRODUCTION GOAL
06-Cases	175.0	1	$240.1	232.0
07-C/Hutch	10.0	11	10.0	9.0
08-Hutch	15.0	14	17.9	19.0
20-Beds	60.0	1	85.7	84.0
21-Misc.	3.0	11	3.7	4.0
22-Bookstack	70.0	3	33.0	31.0
24-Desks	10.0	8	8.8	10.0
26-Mirrors	25.0	12	23.0	19.0
PLANT TOTAL			$422.2	408.0

Station 06 — Cases: Other than misses caused by reporting date change (Canbury closed Good Friday) no misses. Items such as 10-4017, 4066, 4512P, 4522P, 11-5215, 5223 delayed 1 to 4 weeks. Nine items' service position improved. Some jobs outside frozen schedule should have been made "A" jobs and shifting would not have occurred. Priority down to 1 from 2. To schedule through priority 18 requires 10 weeks capacity, slightly higher than last months' 9 3/4 weeks.

Station 07 — C/Hutch: No misses. Delayed 3 of 5 items on this line. Priority down to 11 from 14. 7 weeks capacity will schedule thru priority 18, up from 5 weeks.

Station 08 — Hutch: No misses. Delayed 2 items, pulled 3 ahead. (Plant comments base the shift on purchase parts). Priority up to 14 from 3. To schedule thru priority 18 requires 3 weeks capacity, down from 6 weeks.

Station 20 — No misses. Delayed the 11-5632-5. Pulled a number of beds ahead. Priority unchanged at 1. 8 weeks capacity, down from 10 3/4 weeks will schedule thru priority 18.

Station 21 — Misc.: No misses. Some shifting but orders are O.K. Priority up from 10 to 11. 3 weeks capacity, same as last month, will schedule thru priority 18.

Station 22 — Bookstack: No misses. Built 1 assembly ahead. Priority up to 3 from 2. To schedule thru priority 18 requires 4 1/2 weeks capacity down from 6 weeks.

Station 24 — Desks: No misses. Built 1 assembly ahead. Some shifting, no delays. Priority up to 8 from 4. 3 1/2 weeks capacity, down from 5 1/2 weeks, will schedule thru priority 18.

Station 26 — No misses. Some shifting but ahead only. Priority up to 12 from 1. 2 3/4 weeks capacity, down from 8 weeks will schedule thru priority 18.

Source: W. L. Berry, T. E. Vollmann, and D. C. Whybark, *Master Production Scheduling: Principles and Practice* (Falls Church, Va.: American Production and Inventory Control Society, 1979), p. 55.

carefully evaluated in the corporate offices. Execution responsibility and criteria are unambiguously defined for each plant.

One of the master production scheduling system's most important benefits for Ethan Allen is its upward compatibility; that is, the system is transparent and will work with 5 factories or 25 factories, with new ones easily added. Centralized coordination is maintained and performance is very clear, with the result being an important tool to support orderly growth for the company. The company roughly tripled in size since the start of the master production scheduling effort.

CONCLUDING PRINCIPLES

The master production schedule provides a means of integrating the operational plans of the sales, marketing, engineering, and manufacturing functions. It includes the necessary detail to link specific customer orders and product requirements to manufacturing plans and schedules, and facilitates discussion of changes in these schedules among the different areas of the business. Furthermore, it is important to note that the MPS function can be designed in different ways to provide strategic support for a company's markets.

In this chapter we have addressed what the MPS is, how it is done, and who does it. The following general principles emerge from this discussion:

- The MPS unit should reflect the company's approach to the business environment in which it operates.
- The MPS is one part of a PIM system—the other parts need to be in place as well for a fully effective MPS activity.
- Time-phased MPS records should incorporate useful features of MRP planning approaches.
- The master production scheduler must keep the sum of the parts (MPS) equal to the whole (production plan).
- The MPS activity must be clearly defined organizationally.
- The MPS can be usefully considered as a set of firm planned orders.
- Stability must be designed into the MPS and managed.
- The MPS should be evaluated with a formal performance measurement system.

INTEGRATED RESOURCE LINKAGES

The primary linkage of master production scheduling is with the sales and marketing area. The master production schedule is the disaggregation of the production plan—it is the detailed individual end items or product options that collectively make up the families planned in the production plan. The sum of the parts equals the whole. The detailed MPS quantities need to be matched up with detailed customer orders. Thus, the MPS is intimately connected to order entry, to customer order date promising, and to the process by which sales forecasts are "consumed" by actual order entry.

In practice, the master production scheduler plays a key role between sales and manufacturing. As actual customer orders are booked, the master production scheduler continually tries to adjust manufacturing orders to maximize the responsiveness and flexibility for new orders. If orders are requested that cannot be fulfilled within the present MPS parameters, he or she tries to find ways to accomodate the requests, or at least to minimize the discrepancy between the request and the delivery. Moreover, when the inevitable problem comes up in manufacturing, it is the master production scheduler who determines which customer orders will be effected, how to minimize the effect, and how to help the sales and marketing activities describe the bad news (and the response) to the customers.

The MPS is also closely linked with logistics, because the output of the MPS flows through logistics to the customers. In the case of make-to-stock situations with distribution centers, the master production scheduler often determines how the DCs are to be replenished. He or she often uses distribution requirements planning (DRP) for this purpose. DRP allows the master production scheduler to see the impact of trade-offs on all interested parties. The goal is to best serve *all* the customers and create an overall level of optimization, rather than allow individual DCs to serve their own markets at the expense of service from other DCs. The master scheduler is also closely involved with transportation planning—again with an overall framework. For example, if a large batch of product A has been produced, and a truck is going to DC X, the master scheduler must consider the trade-off between filling the truck and shipping more product A than DC X needs at the moment.

There is a fundamental philosophical issue here. Rather than having DCs order *from* manufacturing, the master scheduler, with an overall view of both manufacturing and distribution, *sends* materials to the DCs. This is only possible with an information system in which all demands on the DCs (as well as inventories) are completely visible to master production scheduling.

There are several important linkages of the MPS to performance measurement. Execution of the MPS represents both a performance measure of manufacturing and a measure of strategy—to the extent that the sum of the MPS quantities matches the production plan. MPS execution is also often monitored by the accounting and finance activities, as the results directly affect cash flows and financial performance.

There are many issues associated with MPS data base design and maintenance. The MPS system has to match the approach taken to manufacturing (make-to-stock, make-to-order, assemble-to-order). The system also has to have the capability of freezing order quantities (the firm planned order concept), and the system needs to maintain all the associated data elements and their linkages (such as pegging). Whenever possible, comprehensive software packages should be used to support master production scheduling.

REFERENCES

Berry, W. L.; T. E. Vollmann; and D. C. Whybark. *Master Production Scheduling: Principles and Practice*. Falls Church, Va.: American Production and Inventory Control Society, 1979.

Blevins, Preston. "MPS—What It Is and Why You Need It—Without the Jargon and Buzz Words." *APICS Master Planning Seminar Proceedings*, Las Vegas, March 1982, pp. 69–76.

Brongiel, Bob. "A Manual/Mechanical Approach to Master Scheduling and Operations Planning." *Production and Inventory Management*, 1st quarter 1979, pp. 66–75.

Dougherty, J. R., and J. F. Proud. "From Master Schedules to Finishing Schedules in the 1990s." *American Production and Inventory Control Society 1990 Annual Conference Proceedings*, pp. 368–70.

Ford, Q. "Secrets of the 5 Percent that Make MPS Work." *American Production and Inventory Control Society 1990 Annual Conference Proceedings*, pp. 360–63.

Funk, P. N. "The Master Scheduler's Job Revisited." *American Production and Inventory Control Society 1990 Annual Conference Proceedings*, pp. 374–77.

Garwood, R. D. "The Making and Remaking of a Master Schedule—Parts 1, 2, and 3." *Hot List,* January–February and March–June 1978.

Gessnez, R. *Master Production Schedule Planning.* New York: Society of Manufacturing Engineers, 1986.

Hoelscher, D. R. "Executing the Manufacturing Plans." *1975 APICS Conference Proceedings,* pp. 447–57.

Kinsey, John W. "Master Production Planning—The Key to Successful Master Scheduling." *APICS 24th Annual Conference Proceedings,* 1981, pp. 81–85.

Ling, R. C., and K. Widmer. "Master Scheduling in a Make-to-Order Plant." *1974 APICS Conference Proceedings,* pp. 304–19.

Proud, John F. "Controlling the Master Schedule." *APICS 23rd Annual Conference Proceedings,* 1980, pp. 413–16.

———. "Master Scheduling Requires Time Fences." *APICS 24th Annual Conference Proceedings,* 1981. pp. 61–65.

Sulser, Samuel S. "Master Planning Simulation: Playing the 'What-lf' Game." *APICS Annual Conference Proceedings,* 1986, pp. 91–93.

Tincher, Michael G. "Master Scheduling and Final Assembly Scheduling: What's the Difference?" *APICS Annual Conference Proceedings,* 1986, pp. 94–96.

Vollmann, Thomas E. *Master Planning Reprints.* Falls Church, Va.: American Production and Inventory Control Society, 1986.

Ware, N., and D. Fogarty. "Master Schedule/Master Production Schedule: The Same or Different?" *Production and Inventory Management* 31, no. 1 (1st quarter 1990), pp. 34–38.

SECTION 4

CAPACITY PLANNING

Chapter 7 is the only one in this section. It covers both capacity planning and control. The establishment of capacity and managing its utilization is critical to both efficiency and effectiveness. Efficiency can be mea-

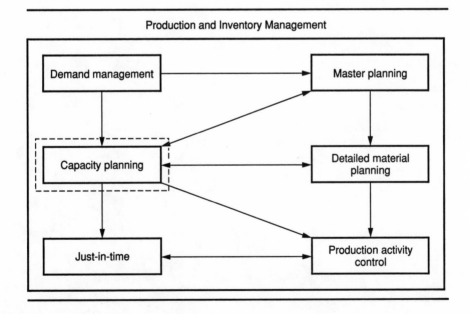

Production and Inventory Management

sured in terms of the resources used in producing the products, and effectiveness in terms of meeting the company's market requirements. Both require increased management attention as the pressures of global competition and standards of customer satisfaction mount.

CHAPTER 7

CAPACITY PLANNING

Throughout this book we have emphasized that effective integration of business and manufacturing plans is critical to achieving close coordination among the sales, marketing, financial, engineering, and manufacturing functions. In most areas of a company, business plans are normally expressed in monetary terms (e.g., sales forecasts, budgets, inventory projections, and so on). In manufacturing, however, personnel, time, equipment, and materials are the key resources. Therefore, business plans also need to be expressed in terms of these manufacturing resource capacities.

As an example, the sales forecast projections for a company may indicate little change in the overall level of sales during the coming year. However, because of a subtle shift in the mix of customers being targeted or the types of products being promoted by marketing, dramatic shifts in the capacity requirements for individual work centers and departments may occur. Swings in capacity requirements of 200 percent or more can be attributed to shifts in product mix—even when the overall sales level does not change. Because of the need for different employee skills, these changes often need to be coordinated with the human resource planning.

Still another example of the integrated nature of capacity planning efforts in a company concerns a shift in marketing strategy. It might be necessary, for instance, to provide a 24-hour turnaround on filling orders for a key customer (instead of a previous four-week customer lead time) in order to retain the business. To provide this level of customer service, it may be essential to maintain slack capacity in key work centers. The shift in available capacity might make it necessary to evaluate the impact on other scheduled customer orders in order to determine the best way of meeting the changed requirements for the key customer. To perform these evaluations, an effective capacity planning system is needed in manufacturing.

This chapter discusses how manufacturing plans are developed in terms of capacity, and the issues of matching available capacity to the firm's business plans. We are primarily concerned with techniques for determining the capacity requirements implied by the production plan, master production schedule, or detailed material plans. The managerial objective in planning capacity is to ensure the match between capacity available in specific work centers and the capacity needed to achieve planned production.

The approaches described here enable a company to estimate needed capacity. If sufficient capacity cannot be made available either inside or outside the firm, the only managerial alternative is to change the plans to conform to available capacity. The chapter is organized around five topics:

- Capacity planning's role in production and inventory management systems: How does it fit and what role does it play?
- Examples of applications: How are capacity planning techniques applied and used for managing capacity?
- Controlling capacity: What techniques are useful for monitoring and controlling the use of capacity?
- Management and capacity planning: How can managers decide which technique(s) to use and how to use them?
- Data base requirements: How should data base be designed for a capacity planning system?

CAPACITY PLANNING'S ROLE IN PIM SYSTEMS

A critical activity that parallels developing material plans is developing capacity plans. Without our providing adequate capacity or recognizing excess capacity's existence, we cannot fully realize benefits of an otherwise effective PIM system. On the one hand, insufficient capacity quickly leads to deteriorating delivery performance, escalating work-in-process inventories, and frustrated manufacturing personnel. On the other hand, excess capacity might be a needless expense that we can reduce. Even firms with advanced material planning capability have found that their inability to provide appropriate work center capacities is a major stumbling block to achieving maximum benefits. This underscores the importance of developing the capacity planning system in concert with the rest of the production and inventory management system.

Hierarchy of Capacity Planning Decisions

Figure 7.1 relates capacity planning decisions to a PIM system's other modules. It shows the scope of capacity planning, starting from an overall plan of resources, proceeding to a rough-cut evaluation of a particular master production schedule's capacity implications, moving to a detailed evaluation of capacity requirements based on detailed material plans, then continuing to finite loading procedures, and ending with input/output techniques to help monitor the plans.

These five levels of capacity planning activities range from large aggregations of capacity for long time periods to very detailed machine scheduling for time intervals of an hour or less. This chapter's major focus is rough-cut capacity planning, which is central to establishing a correspondence between capacity plans and material plans in virtually every business, including companies using just-in-time (JIT) methods. We also discuss capacity requirements planning, a commonly used technique in companies that prepare detailed material plans using time-phased material requirements planning (MRP) records. Finally, we examine input/output analysis as a method to control capacity plans in companies using MRP.

Many authorities distinguish between long-, medium-, and short-range capacity planning and control horizons as indicated in Figure 7.1. This is a useful view, but the time dimension varies substantially from company to company. This chapter emphasizes capacity planning decisions involving a planning horizon that ranges from one week to a year or more in the future, depending on the firm's specific needs.

Links to Other MPC System Modules

System linkages for the capacity planning modules follow the basic hierarchy shown in Figure 7.1. *Resource planning* is directly linked to the production planning module and is the most highly aggregated and longest-range capacity planning decision. Resource planning typically involves converting monthly, quarterly, or even annual data from the production plan into aggregate resources such as gross labor-hours, floor

FIGURE 7.1
Key Linkages of Capacity Planning

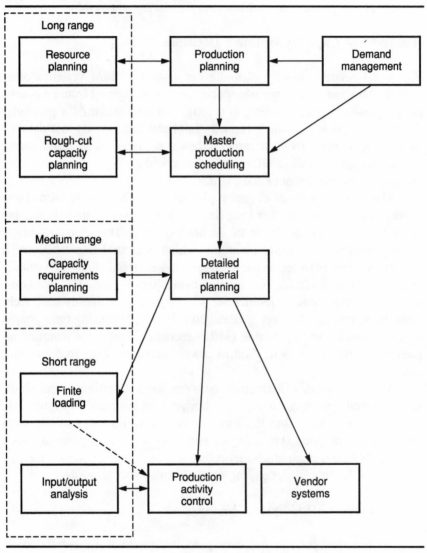

space, and machine-hours. This level of planning involves new capital expansion, bricks and mortar, machine tools, warehouse space, and so on, and requires a time horizon of months or even years.

The master production schedule is the primary information source for *rough-cut capacity planning*. A particular master schedule's rough-cut capacity requirements can be estimated by several techniques. In this chapter we discuss use of the *capacity bill* approach in two different companies. The capacity bill essentially creates a "bill of capacity," similar to a bill of materials, which estimates the capacity requirements in each department to make one unit of each item that can appear in the master production schedule.

For firms using material requirements planning to prepare detailed material plans, a much more detailed capacity plan is possible using the *capacity requirements planning (CRP)* technique. To provide this detail, time-phased material plans produced by the MRP system form the basis for calculating time-phased capacity requirements. Data files used by the CRP technique include work-in-process, routing, scheduled receipts, and planned orders. Information provided by the CRP technique can be used to determine capacity needs for both key machine centers and labor skills, typically covering a planning horizon from several weeks to a year. An example of this approach is also discussed.

Resource planning, rough-cut capacity planning, and capacity requirements planning link with the production plan, master production schedule, and detailed material planning systems, respectively. The linkages are shown as double-headed arrows in Figure 7.1 for a specific reason: There must be a correspondence between capacity required to execute a given material plan and capacity made available to execute the plan. Without this correspondence, the plan will be either impossible to execute or inefficiently executed. We do not claim that capacity must always be changed to meet material plans. In fact, whether this is worthwhile or whether *plans* should be changed to meet capacity is a managerial judgment. Capacity planning systems provide basic information to make that a *reasoned* judgment.

Input/output analysis provides a method for monitoring the actual consumption of capacity during execution of detailed material plans produced by time-phased MRP systems. It is necessarily linked to the shop-floor systems and data base for production activity control. Input/output analysis can indicate the need to update capacity plans as actual shop performance deviates from current plans, as well as the need to modify planning factors used in the capacity planning techniques.

This overview of capacity planning's scope sets the stage for the techniques this chapter discusses. The primary interaction among these techniques is hierarchical: long-range planning sets constraints on medium-range capacity planning, which in turn constrains detailed scheduling and execution on the shop floor.

EXAMPLES OF APPLICATIONS

Here are examples of capacity planning techniques in practice. Specifically, we look at the Twin Disc Company's use of capacity bills, Applicon's rough-cut capacity planning system for JIT operations, and the Black & Decker Company's use of CRP.

Capacity Planning at Twin Disc

The Twin Disc Company manufactures gears, transmissions, and other heavy components for the farm implement and heavy equipment industries. It is primarily a make-to-order firm. As part of its capacity planning system, Twin Disc uses capacity bills for rough-cut capacity planning. Figure 7.2 shows a sample output from this system. For each machine or work center, we see the percentage of available capacity required by each of the nine product lines that Twin Disc uses for master production scheduling purposes. For example, the MPS for product line A requires 22 percent of the 1,561 hours of weekly capacity at the 2AC Chucker. Total capacity requirements for all nine product lines indicate a total load of 95 percent of the 2AC Chucker capacity.

The most important aspect of this report may be the last column, where we see managerial actions taken to overcome capacity problems. For example, the present MPS loads the Maag gear grinder to 113 percent of rated capacity. One Reishauer gear grinder, however, is only loaded to 69 percent of its capacity. A decision has been made to shift some work, taking into account differences in the two grinders' capacitites (roughly a 3 : 1 ratio in machine-hours required). Other managerial actions in the report include moving an additional machine in from another factory and adding shift capacity. The point is that this is a working document used to make capacity management decisions.

Capacity Planning at Applicon

Applicon, a division of Schlumberger, designs and manufactures computer-aided engineering (CAE), computer-aided design (CAD), and computer-aided manufacturing (CAM) systems. Applicon has implemented numerous JIT concepts and replaced some of its detailed material planning system modules. Its dramatic results include a reduction in lead time (20 weeks to 4 days), inventory reduction of over 75 percent, virtual elimination of obsolescence costs, little or no inspection, and a decline in PIM personnel (86 to 14).

Figure 7.3 shows an Applicon "Capacity Status Report." Applicon has divided the factory into 17 capacity groupings (work centers) for planning purposes. It uses actual customer orders as a monthly MPS to drive capacity planning. Capacity bills are used to convert the MPS into the present "load" over the next month (20 working days) in standard hours (the second column in Figure 7.3). The capacities in column 3 are based on a total work force of 48 people (e.g., ALF-A has three workers who work 8 hours per day for 20 days in the month = 480 standard hours). Work center OLD-P's zero capacity indicates that no worker is presently assigned to this activity.

The fourth column reduces the capacity amounts by 30 percent (the desired rate of direct labor productivity for Applicon workers). The remaining time is used for other manufacturing activities. The last column provides a "maximum" capacity value based on 10 percent overtime.

This report was run on June 12 for the next 20 days. Differences between "load" and the three capacities represent Applicon's ability to take on additional work in the next month. Large orders can be included in a trial run of the MPS to examine the orders' impact in terms of existing capacity availabilities. Total load (3,634 hours) represents 47 percent of standard capacity, 68 percent of adjusted capacity, and 43 percent of maximum capacity. Management reviews these numbers carefully— particularly if possible large orders are under negotiation. It is relatively easy to make trial runs with those orders included to examine the impact of accepting the orders.

Of all the work centers in Figure 7.3, MVX-T appears to be in the most trouble. However, this can easily be fixed. MVX-T only has one-half person allocated to it (80 hours per month). Reducing MVX-A (or some other work center) by one-half person and increasing MVX-T's

FIGURE 7.2
Twin Disc Capacity Bill Report

Center 03-05	Type	Qty.	No. of shifts	Cap. (hrs/weks)	A	B	C	D	E	F	G	H	I	TOTAL	Remarks
	Work center description				Percent utilization of capacity by product line										
BD	2AC chucker	4	3	1561	22	22	16	3	8	11	11	2		95	
BR	3AC Warner & Swasey	8	3	2966	3	16	46	1	13	2	1	2	–	84	
CA	Reishauser gear grinder	2	3	900			38		22	–	12			72	
CAB	Reishauser gear grinder	2	3	950		10	43		13	2			1	69	
CD	P. & W. gear grinder	1	3	544			59		4					63	Off load to CAB 3:1 ratio
CEA	Maag gear grinder	4	3	3044		10	76		14	5			8	113	
CG	P. & W. gear grinder	4	3	1190			120		8					128	Off load to CA, CD
CI	Pfauter hobber	5	3	2374	6	22	41		9	2	4		2	86	
CJ	Barber colman hobber	1	3	620	27	39	50	1	29	25		8	1	180	Off load to CI, CW
CN	Gear shaver	3	2.5	700	14	37	15		8	9	4			87	
CQ	Gear pointer	1	1	22	13	56	–		12	3				84	
CS	Fellows shaper	1	3	549		37			8	–				45	
CW	Barber colman hobber	3	3	1530	7	12	26	2	8	9	6			70	Off load to CS
CX	Barber colman shaper	1	3	546	–	38	25	7	6	2	24			102	Off load to CS
CY	Fellows shaper	1	3	514	15	77	17		10	12			2	133	

FIGURE 7.2
Twin Disc Capacity Bill Report (continued)

Center 03-05	Type	Qty.	No. of shifts	Cap. (hrs/wks)	A	B	C	D	E	F	G	H	I	TOTAL	Remarks
	Work center description				Percent utilization of capacity by product line										Remarks
FD	Internal grinder	1	3	285	8	8	10	5	8	4	6			49	Relieve FI and
FI	Internal grinder	1	3	275	25	59	32	11	25	10	9			171	move machine from PLI2
FJ	Surface grinder	1	1	328	6	41	20	1	11	14				93	
FM	Vertical internal grinder	1	2	368		38	57	1	16	1			3	116	Add ½ shift
FY	Gear hone	2	2	528	19	28	11	12	9	5				84	
H	Engine lathe	1	3	427	26	42	29	–	15	8	6		–	126	Off load to HES
HES	W. & S. Lathe—Special	2	2	234	5	43	18	2	11	12				89	Add 1 shift
JA	Horizontal broach	1	1	90	14	3	53	2	12	3				87	
NH	Gear chamfer	1	3	307	18	42	10		12	11	5			98	
PC	Magnaflux	1	1	240	3	35	48		12	2	2		–	102	Add ½ shift

Source: E. S. Buffa and J. G. Miller, *Production-Inventory Systems: Planning and Control*, 3rd ed. (Homewood, Ill.; Richard D. Irwin, 1979), p. 598.

FIGURE 7.3
Applicon Capacity Status Report

0612

Work Center	Load (Std. Hours)	Capacity (Standard)	Capacity (Adj. Std.)	Capacity (Maximum)
******	*************	**********	***********	*********
ALF-A	70	480	336	528
ALF-T	5	80	56	88
HLT-A	438	800	560	880
HLT-T	85	160	112	176
MIS-A	270	800	560	880
MIS-T	14	80	56	88
MVX-A	399	1120	784	1232
MVX-T	106	80	56	88
OLD-P	81	0	0	0
PCB-A	52	160	112	176
PCB-H	44	160	112	176
PCB-I	124	320	224	352
PCB-M	441	480	336	520
PCB-P	408	960	672	1056
PCB-T	918	1680	1176	1848
PCB-V	123	160	112	176
PCB-W	56	160	112	176
TOTALS	3634	7680	5376	8440

20 TOTALS WORKDAYS INCLUDED

capacity to one person for the month solves the problem. OLD-P also needs to have a person allocated to it.

This rough-cut capacity planning system serves Applicon well. Problems can be anticipated, and JIT operations mean that results are very current, with little or no bias because of work-in-process inventories. Results of the capacity planning analyses are given to shop personnel, who make their own adjustments as they see fit, making allowances for absenteeism, particular workers' relative strengths, and other local conditions.

Capacity Planning at Black & Decker

The Black & Decker Company produces a broad line of consumer workshop, garden, and household products. Production is mostly make-to-stock, and capacity planning is largely based on CRP. Figure 7.4 shows

FIGURE 7.4
Black & Decker CPR Report

KMG WEEKLY LOADS, HAMPSTEAD

SEQ 1033 KMG 073 DEPT 8-01 CST/CN 063 KMG NAME BH GROUP MACH QTY 1 WEEKLY CAP 106.0

	WIP	741	742	743	744	745	746	747	748	749	750	751	752	753	754	755
MFG. WEEK	WIP	741	742	743	744	745	746	747	748	749	750	751	752	753	754	755
S/U HRS.	38	5	4	2	5	2	3	4	5	5	2	4	5	3	4	1
OP HRS.	314	104	102	105	95	94	107	111	84	92	41	101	128	100	72	87
TOTAL	352	109	106	107	100	96	110	117	88	97	43	105	133	103	76	88
% OF CAP		103	100	100	94	90	104	110	83	91	40	100	125	97	72	83

	756	757	758	759	760	761	762	763	764	765	766	767	768	769	770	771
MFG. WEEK	756	757	758	759	760	761	762	763	764	765	766	767	768	769	770	771
S/U HRS.	8	1	3	4	3	3	4	5	3	4	9	1	5	5	2	3
OP HRS.	91	92	107	151	65	96	140	86	68	97	117	62	93	98	83	132
TOTAL	99	93	110	155	68	99	144	91	71	101	126	63	98	103	85	135
% OF CAP	93	88	104	146	64	93	136	86	67	96	119	59	92	97	80	125

	772	773	774	775		AVERAGE FOR	
MFG. WEEK	772	773	774	775	1st 10 Wks	92%	
S/U HRS.	3	6	8	2	2nd 13 Wks	99%	
OP HRS.	91	121	134	104	3rd 12 Wks	98%	
TOTAL	94	127	142	106	Tot 35 Wks	97%	
% OF CAP	89	120	134	100			

NUMBER WKS OVER 80%   30

Source: R. W. Hall and T. E. Vollmann, "Black & Decker: Pioneers with MRP," *Case Studies in Materials Requirements Planning,* ed. by E. W. Davis (Falls Church, Va.: American Production and Inventory Control Society, 1978), p. 38.

the weekly CRP report for one key machine group (KMG 073) in department 8-01 of the Hampstead, Maryland, plant. It is called the BH "group" but contains a single critical machine. The time periods are weeks (from 741 through 775). For each week, the projection is based on the combined open shop orders (MRP scheduled receipts) and MRP planned orders. Times include setup hours ("S/U HRS.") and run-time hours ("OP HRS.").

This machine center's weekly capacity is 106 hours. Since there is only one machine, 18 hours per day, five days per week, plus 8 hours each on Saturday and Sunday account for all the capacity. The report shows the percent of capacity ("% OF CAP") required by the projected arrival of work in each week (planned input). This is shown in Figure 7.4, in which 30 of the 35 weeks shown are loaded to over 80 percent. Black & Decker keeps track of the number of weeks for which projected needs exceed 80 percent of capacity. This can indicate potentially serious capacity problems. Moreover, the average level for the total 35-week period is shown to be 97 percent.

The capacity problem may be significantly greater than the percentage of capacity indicates. The report shows that the current WIP (work-in-process), or backlog, is 352 standard hours. This work is presently at the machine, with 109 standard hours scheduled to arrive in the upcoming week. The work center is already more than three weeks behind schedule. Given projected load and present capacity, the backlog will not decrease for the foreseeable future.

To complete the capacity planning picture, Black & Decker uses the MRP data base to analyze capacity loads on a quarterly basis and to prepare a four-week, detailed day-by-day capacity report for each work center. The four-week report is the basis for daily capacity planning decisions. Figure 7.5 shows this daily load report for the next four weeks for the KMG 073 key machine group.

Total values for the weeks show the same capacity problem as in Figure 7.4. Figure 7.5 also provides last week's actual performance.

As useful as these capacity planning reports have been to Black & Decker over the years, they do not allow for the desirable level of what-if analysis. Subsequently, Black & Decker designed two new systems to support capacity planning. One, a capacity bill approach to rough-cut capacity planning, produces total dollar output levels by divisions and product groups, work center loadings, and critical machine group capacity requirements directly from the MPS.

FIGURE 7.5
Black & Decker Daily Machine Load Report

09/15/ Week 741-1   HAMPSTEAD MACHINE LOAD REPORT   DEPT. 8-01

COST CTR 002 KMG 073   BHG ROUTING MACH   1 MACH @ 18 HRS/DAY   18 HRS/DAY AVAIL

	TOT SCH	TOT AVAIL	PCT LOAD	CUM AVAIL HRS		TOT SCH	TOT AVAIL	PCT LOAD	CUM AVAIL HRS
741	109	106	103	-3	742	106	106	100	-3

SCHED OP HRS (741)
-1	-2	-3	-4	-5	-6	-7*
18	19	19	19	8	8	

SCHED OP HRS (742)
-1	-2	-3	-4	-5	-6	-7
18	18	18	18	16	8	10

	TOT SCH	TOT AVAIL	PCT LOAD	CUM AVAIL HRS		TOT SCH	TOT AVAIL	PCT LOAD	CUM AVAIL HRS
743	107	106	100	-4	744	100	106	94	2

SCHED OP HRS (743)
-1	-2	-3	-4	-5	-6	-7
19	19	19	18	17	7	8

SCHED OP HRS (744)
-1	-2	-3	-4	-5	-6	-7
20	16	18	19	17	7	4

HRS PRODUCED LAST WEEK

AHEAD	CURR BHND	TOTAL	BACKLOG
15	93	108	352

*Days of the week.

Source: R. W. Hall and T. E. Vollmann, "Black & Decker: Pioneers with MRP," *Case Studies in Materials Requirements Planning*, ed. by E. W. Davis (Falls Church, Va.: American Production and Inventory Control, 1978), p. 37.

The other aid to capacity planning is called *alternations planning*. This approach to what-if analysis allows use of the MRP data base to determine the effect of changing the timing or quantities of selected MPS values. Changes can be evaluated in terms of time-phased capacity requirements on particular machine centers without disturbing the operative data base. The report's output shows both the current plan and the revised plan in a format similar to Figure 7.4. This report permits a quick assessment of the effect of MPS changes.

CONTROLLING CAPACITY

Each capacity planning technique's basic intent is to project capacity needs implied by either the production plan, the MPS, or the detailed material plan so that timely actions can be taken to balance capacity needs with capacity available. Once decisions are made concerning additions to and deletions of capacity, or adjustments to the material plan, a workable capacity plan can be created. We must thereafter monitor this plan in terms of actual conditions, to see whether the actions were correct and sufficient. Monitoring also provides the basis for ongoing corrections of capacity planning data.

Input/Output Control

The basis for monitoring the capacity plan is *input/output control*, meaning that planned work input and output at a work center will be compared to the actual work input and output. The capacity planning technique used delineates the planned input. Planned output results from managerial decision making to specify the capacity level; that is, planned output is based on staffing levels, hours of work, and so forth. In capacity-constrained work centers, planned output is based on the rate of capacity established by management. In noncapacity-constrained work centers, planned output is equal to planned input (allowing for some lead time offset).

Capacity data in input/output control are usually expressed in hours. Input data are based on jobs' expected arrivals at a work center. For example, a CRP procedure would examine the status of all open shop orders (scheduled receipts), estimate how long they will take (setup, run, wait, and move) at particular work centers, and thereby derive when they will arrive at subsequent work centers. This would be repeated for all planned orders from the MRP data base. The resultant set of expected arrivals of exact quantities would be multiplied by run time per unit from the routing file, and this product would be added to setup time, also from the routing file. The sum is a planned input expressed in standard hours.

Actual input would use the same routing data, but for the *actual* arrivals of jobs in each time period as reported by the production activity control system. Actual output would again use the production activity control data for exact quantities completed in each time period, converted to standard hours with time data from the routing file.

The only time data not based on the routing file are those for planned output. In this case, management has to plan the labor-hours to be expended in the work center. For example, if two people work 9 hours per day for five days, the result is 90 labor-hours per week. This value has to be reduced or inflated by an estimate of the relation of actual hours to standard hours. In our example, if people in this work center typically work at 80 percent efficiency, then planned output is 72 hours.

A work center's actual output will deviate from planned output. Often deviations can be attributed to conditions at the work center itself, such as lower than expected productivity, breakdowns, absences, random variations, or poor product quality. But less than expected output can also occur for reasons outside the work center's control, such as insufficient output from a preceding work center or improper releasing of planned orders. Either problem can lead to insufficient input or a "starved" work center. Another reason for a variation between actual input and planned input can be data errors in any of the production activity control, capacity planning, or detailed material planning files.

Input/output analysis also monitors backlog. Backlog represents the cushion between input and output; it decouples input from output, allowing work center operations to be less affected by variations in requirements. Arithmetically, it equals prior backlog plus or minus the difference between input and output. The planned backlog calculation is based on planned input and planned output. Actual backlog uses actual input and output. The difference between planned backlog and actual backlog represents one measure of the total, or net, input/output deviations. Monitoring input, output, and backlog typically involves keeping track of cumulative deviations and comparing them with preset limits.

The input/output report in Figure 7.6 is based on "work center 200," shown in weekly time buckets measured in standard labor-hours. The

FIGURE 7.6
Sample Input/Output for Work Center 200* (as of End of Period 5)

		Week				
		1	2	3	4	5
Planned input		15	15	0	10	10
Actual input		14	13	5	9	17
Cumulative deviation		−1	−3	+2	+1	+8
Planned output		11	11	11	11	11
Actual output		8	10	9	11	9
Cumulative deviation		−3	−4	−6	−6	−8
Actual backlog	20	26	29	25	23	31

Desired backlog: 10 hours

*In standard labor-hours.

report was prepared at the end of period 5, so the actual values are current week-by-week variations in planned input. These could result from actual planned orders and scheduled receipts; that is, for example, if the input were planned by CRP, planned inputs would be based on timings for planned orders, the status of scheduled receipts, and routing data. The *actual* input that arrives at work center 200 can vary for any of the causes just discussed.

Work center 200's planned output has been smoothed; that is, management decided to staff this work center to achieve a constant output of 11 hours per week. The result should be to absorb input variations with changes in the backlog level. Cumulative planned output for the five weeks (55 hours) is 5 hours more than cumulative planned input. This reflects a management decision to reduce backlog from the original level of 20 hours. The process of increasing capacity to reduce backlog recognizes explicitly that flows must be controlled to change backlog; backlog cannot be changed in and of itself.

Figure 7.6 summarizes the results after five weeks of actual operation. At the end of week 5, the situation requires managerial attention. The cumulative input deviation (plus 8 hours), cumulative output deviation (minus 8 hours), current backlog (31 hours), or all three could have exceeded the desired limits of control. In this example, the increased backlog is a combination of more than expected input and less than expected output.

One other aspect of monitoring backlog is important. In general, there is little point in releasing orders to a work center that already has an excessive backlog, except when the order to be released is of higher priority than any in the backlog. In general, the idea is to not release work that cannot be done, but to wait and release what is really needed. Oliver Wight summed this up as one of the principles of input/output control: "Never put into a manufacturing facility or to a vendor's facility more than you believe can be produced. Hold backlogs in production and inventory control."

The Capacity "Bath Tub"

Figure 7.7 depicts a work center "bath tub" showing capacity in hydraulic terms. The input pipe's diameter represents the maximum flow (of work) into the tub. The valve represents PIM systems such as MPS, MRP, and JIT, which determine *planned input* (flow of work) into the tub. Actual input could vary because of problems (such as a corroded valve or problem at the water department) and can be monitored with input/output analysis. We can determine *required capacity* to accomplish the planned input to the work center with any of the capacity planning techniques. The output drain pipe takes completed work from the work center. Its diameter represents the work center's planned or *rated capacity*, which limits planned output. As with actual input, actual output may vary from plan as well. It too can be monitored with input/output analysis. Sometimes planned output cannot be achieved over time even when it is less than maximum capacity and there is a backlog to work on. When that occurs, realized output is called *demonstrated capacity*. The "water" in the tub is the *backlog* or *load*, which can also be monitored with input/output analysis.

MANAGEMENT AND CAPACITY PLANNING

In designing and using the capacity planning system, we must take several management considerations into account. Here we discuss designing

FIGURE 7.7
The Capacity Bath Tub

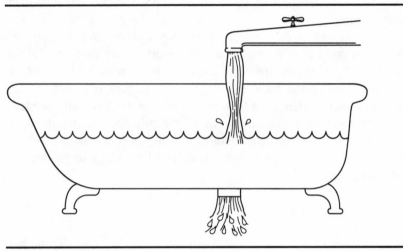

the systems from the perspective of PIM, consider the capacity measure, look at choices in tailoring the capacity planning system to a particular firm, and consider how to use capacity planning data. Key elements of management's commitment to the design and use of the system are emphasized.

Capacity Planning in PIM

Figure 7.1 shows the relationship between PIM and various capacity planning modules. The five modules range from long-range resource planning to day-to-day control of capacity utilization. There is a vertical relationship among the capacity planning modules, as well as the horizontal relationship with the material planning modules of PIM. These relationships can affect managerial choices for capacity planning systems' design and use in a specific firm.

To illustrate the importance of the interrelationships in designing and using the capacity planning system, let us consider the impact of production planning and resource planning decisions on shorter-term capacity planning decisions. To the extent that production planning and resource planning are done well, problems faced in capacity planning can be reduced, because appropriate resources have been provided. If, for example, the production plan specifies a very stable rate of output, then changes in the master production schedule (MPS) requiring capacity changes are minimal. If the detailed material planning functions effectively, the MPS will be converted into detailed component production plans with relatively few unexpected execution problems.

Toyota and several other Japanese auto manufacturers are good cases in point. These firms' production plans call for a stable rate of output (cars per day), and product mix variations are substantially less than for other auto companies because they carefully manage the number and timing of option combinations. Order backlogs and finished-goods inventories also separate factories from actual customer orders. The result is execution systems that are simple, effective, and easy to operate, with minimal inventories and fast throughput times. The careful resource and production planning, and resultant stability, means that these firms have little need for either rough-cut capacity planning procedures or CRP.

A quite different but equally important linkage that can affect capacity planning system design is the linkage with the shop-floor systems in production activity control. A key relationship exists in scheduling effective use of capacity. With sufficient capacity and efficient use of that capacity ensured by good shop-floor procedures, we will see few unpleasant surprises requiring capacity analysis and change. Effective shop-floor procedures utilize available capacity to process orders according to PIM system priorities, provide insight into potential capacity problems in the short range (a few hours to days), and respond to changes in material plans. Thus, effective shop-floor systems reduce the necessary degree of detail and intensity in use of the capacity planning system.

In providing effective control of capacity plans, the production activity control system again is key. Good shop-floor scheduling makes plans more likely to be met. The result is a better match between actual input/output and planned input/output. Again we see attention to the material planning side of PIM—in this case scheduling on the shop-floor—having an effect on the capacity planning side.

Choosing the Measure of Capacity

The choice of capacity measure is an important management issue. Alternatives run from machine-hours or labor-hours to physical or monetary units. The choice depends on the constraining resource and the firm's needs. In any manufacturing company, the "bundle of goods and services" provided to customers increasingly includes software, other knowl-edge work, after-sale service, and other customer services. In every case, providing these goods and services requires resources—"capacities" that must be planned, managed, and developed. Appropriate measures of ca-pacity must be established and changed as evolution in the bundle of goods and services occurs.

Several current trends in manufacturing have a significant bearing on the choice of capacity measures; each can have a major impact on what is important to measure in capacity. One important trend is consid-erable change in the concept of direct labor, which has been shrinking as a portion of overall manufacturing employment. Distinctions between direct and indirect labor are also shrinking. The ability to change labor capacity by hiring and firing (or even using overtime) has been reduced; notions of "lifetime employment" have further reduced this form of ca-pacity adjustment.

An increasingly important direct labor issue is the "whole person" concept of JIT, which has labor capacity changing qualitatively as more staff work is incorporated into their jobs. Because an objective in JIT systems is continued improvement, the basis for labor capacity planning is constantly changing. This mandates control procedures for identifying and changing the planning factors as improvements take place.

Another important trend is decreased internal fabrication and in-creased emphasis on outside purchasing. This trend can alter the concep-tion of which capacity requirements are important. Procurement analysis, incoming inspection, and engineering liaison may become the critical ca-pacities to be managed, as well as planning and scheduling the capacities in vendor firms.

For many firms engaged in fabrication, machine technology is changing rapidly. Flexible automation has greatly increased the range of parts that can be processed in a machine center. Future product mixes are likely to be much more variable than in the past, with a marked effect on the equipment capacity required. Moreover, as equipment becomes more expensive, it may be necessary to plan and control the capacity of key pieces of equipment at a detailed level.

To the extent that cellular technologies are adopted as part of man-ufacturing, the unit of capacity may need to change. Usually the entire cell is coupled and has only as much capacity as its limiting resource. Often, the cell is labor limited, so the unit of capacity is labor-hours (continually adjusted for learning). Sometimes, however, the capacity measure needs to be solely associated with a single aspect of the cell. Also, when dissimilar items are added to the cell for manufacture, it is necessary to estimate each new item's capacity requirements in terms of individual processing steps.

The first task in choosing a capacity measure is to creatively identify resources that are key and in short supply, because capacity planning and control is too complicated to apply to all resources. The next step is to define the unit of measure. If the key resource is people, then labor-hours may be appropriate. In other instances, such measures as tons, gallons, number of molds, number of ovens, hours of machine time, square yards, linear feet, lines of code, customer calls, and cell hours have been used. In some cases, these are converted to some "equivalent" measure to accommodate a wider variety of products or resources.

After the resources and unit of measure have been determined, the next concern is to estimate available capacity. The primary issue here is theory versus practice. The engineer can provide theoretical capacity from the design specifications for a machine or from time studies of people. A subissue is whether to use "full" capacity or some fraction thereof (often 75 percent to 85 percent). A further issue is "plasticity" in capacity. For almost any resource, if it is really important, more output can be achieved. We have seen many actual performances that fall short of or exceed capacity calculations.

Choice of capacity measure follows directly from the objective of providing capacity to meet production plans. The appropriate measure of capacity most directly affects meeting these plans. The measure, therefore, should be appropriate to the key limited resources and should be based on what is achievable, with allowances for maintenance and other necessary activities. It must be possible to convert the bundle of products and services into capacity measurement terms. The results must be understood by the people responsible, and they should be monitored.

Choice of a Specific Capacity Planning Technique

In this chapter's discussion, two popular capacity planning techniques for converting a material plan into capacity requirements were discussed: rough-cut capacity planning (capacity bills) and capacity requirements planning (CRP). The choice of method depends heavily on characteristics of the manufacturing process.

The rough-cut methods are the most general, being applicable even in companies using just-in-time methods on the shop floor. Rough-cut approaches can be useful in JIT operations to estimate the impact of changes in requirements called for by revisions to the master production schedule. For example, under level scheduling conditions, a change from a production rate of 480 units per day (one unit per minute) to 528 units per day (1.1 units per minute) might be needed. A rough-cut procedure could be used to examine the impact on each work center or manufacturing cell through which this volume would pass, and any indicated problems or bottleneck conditions could be addressed *before* the crisis hits. Similarly, a planned reduction in MPS could be evaluated to determine resources that might be freed to work on other tasks.

Rough-cut approaches do vary in accuracy, aggregation level, and ease of preparation. There is a general relationship between the amount of data and computational time required and the quality and detail of the capacity requirements estimated. The issue is whether additional costs of supporting more complex procedures are justified by improved decision making and subsequent plant operations.

Capacity requirements planning, however, is only applicable in companies using time-phased MRP records for detailed material planning and shop-order-based shop scheduling systems. CRP is unnecessary under JIT operations where minimal work-in-process levels mean that there is no need to estimate the impact on capacity requirements of partially processed work. If all orders start from "raw materials" with virtually no amount of "capacity" stored in component inventories, there is no need for formal shop-floor control procedures. If there are no work orders, there are no status data on work orders.

Input/output control is not usually an issue under JIT operations because attention has been shifted from planning to execution. As a result, actual input should equal actual output. Actual input becomes actual output with an insignificant delay, and the backlog is effectively a constant zero. However, planned input can indeed vary from actual input, and so can planned output vary from actual output. With high flexibility or "band width" of the JIT unit, these variations should be achievable without violating the equality between actual input and actual output—with backlog remaining at zero. To the extent that plan-to-actual variations are accommodated with a quick response system, the firm is better able to adapt to its marketplace.

Using the Capacity Plan

The techniques we have described provide data on which a manager can base a decision. The broad choices are clear—if there is a mismatch between available capacity and required capacity, either the capacity or the material plan should be changed. If capacity is to be changed, the choices include overtime/undertime authorization, hiring/layoff, and increasing/decreasing the number of machine tools or time in use. Capacity requirements can be changed by alternate routing, make or buy decisions, subcontracting, raw material changes, inventory changes, or changing customer promise dates.

The choice of capacity planning units can lead to more effective use of the system. Capacity units need not be work centers as defined for manufacturing, engineering, or routing purposes. They can be groupings of the key resources (human or capital) important in defining the factory's output levels. Many firms plan capacity solely for key machines (or work centers) and gateway operations. These key areas can be managed in detail, whereas other areas fall under resource planning and the production activity control system.

Capacity planning choices dictate the diameter of the manufacturing pipeline. Only as much material can be produced as there is capacity for its production, *regardless of the material plan*. Not understanding the critical nature of managing capacity can lead a firm into production chaos and serious customer service problems. In the same vein, the relationship between flexibility and capacity must be discussed. You cannot have perfectly balanced material and capacity plans *and* be able to easily produce emergency orders! We know one general manager who depicts his capacity as a pie. He has one slice for recurring business, one for spare parts production, one for down time and maintenance, and a final specific slice for opportunity business. He manages to pay for this excess capacity by winning lucrative contracts that require rapid responses. He *does not add* that opportunity business to a capacity plan fully committed to the other aspects of his business.

DATA BASE REQUIREMENTS

We have seen that each capacity planning technique requires different systems linkages. These linkages imply different data elements and data base considerations. Managers' use of the different capacity planning techniques and enhancements to improve their usefulness can have data base implications as well.

Data Base Design Considerations

Capacity bills and CRP procedures both use MPS data to develop capacity requirements. The capacity bill procedure uses bill of material and routing information to calculate capacity at work centers, and thus reflects the particular mix of end items shown in the MPS. The CRP procedure employs additional information from MRP and shop-floor systems to account for the exact timing, quantities, and status of component part and end item production orders.

We see that there is an increasing requirement for data. The capacity bills procedure requires MPS data and bills of capacity. The CRP techniques require increased amounts of production/inventory control, industrial engineering, and shop-floor control data. The latter procedure incurs increased computational cost as well. The specific data linkages with the PIM activities are shown in Figure 7.1.

Although data base size for capacity bills is much smaller than for CRP, the CRP data base already largely exists if the firm has a working MRP system. For this reason, many firms use CRP systems to answer questions that could be analyzed at far lower computational cost with rough-cut techniques. They do so because there are no additional data base requirements. All that is needed is the additional computer run time, which can be expensive but is usually available. However, they usually do not do what-if analysis. This would be exceedingly expensive. The result is only *one* capacity plan—the one associated with the current MRP-based material plan.

Several other factors influence the data base's design and maintenance. The level of detail appropriate for capacity management implies a corresponding level of detail in the data base and in data base maintenance. If capacity assessments are made in terms of sales dollars or average labor-hours, data may be extracted from the financial accounting data base. This reduces the PIM data base's complexity but requires some coordinating data base maintenance.

Input/output analysis requires a communication link with the production activity control system to gather data for analysis. A closely related issue affecting data base complexity is labor productivity. Many firms have standard time data that differ widely from actual practice, and this difference can vary between work centers. This fact can greatly complicate the data base design, and maintenance problem, because it is critical to keep track of actual production rates to make an accurate conversion of material plans into capacity needs.

Extended Capabilities and Data Base Design

We have discussed the desirability of incorporating a what-if capability into the capacity planning system. This capability can create severe demands on data base design. The consideration of computer time has already been raised, and the need to evaluate a number of alternative material plans means that the ability to easily change the MPS must be included in the design. Also, changes must be isolated from current actual MPS and MRP records, both for the sake of recovery and not to create false signals on the shop floor before appropriate analysis and approval have been accomplished.

Along with the capability of what-if testing runs a parallel set of questions on detailed implementation decisions. The choice of the level of aggregation for capacity planning, the size of the time period for analysis, the number of future periods to be analyzed, and the number and composition of machine centers all influence the data base's size, complexity, and maintenance. If capacity plans are based on one set of numbers and time periods, and another set is used to make implementation decisions, mismatches and other problems can occur. On the other hand, designing the system to support any kind of question and any kind of decision may be prohibitively expensive.

Perhaps the ultimate design objective for the data base and its use is to be able to identify and plan for the key work centers as they change over time. This would require careful attention to design of the input/output module and the tolerance limits used to trigger attention. It would also require flexibility in the data base to permit analysis of different possible groupings over time and of groupings that might not correspond to current work centers or labor categories.

CONCLUDING PRINCIPLES

This chapter indicates how business plans can be converted into capacity terms so that important changes in plans can be evaluated in terms of the manufacturing response. Without an effective capacity planning system it is difficult for a business to assess the dynamic nature of its markets. Moreover, changes in business plans may have capacity implications that require a response by another business function. That is, because of changed capacity requirements, the human resource group may need to initiate lengthy job change discussions with a union, or engineering may need to redesign a product to avoid a costly change in capacity.

Clearly, capacity planning is a key activity in integrating manufacturing operations with the efforts of other business functions. Important principles for the design and use of the capacity planning system emerge from this chapter:

- Capacity plans must be developed concurrently with material plans if the material plans are to be realized.
- The particular capacity planning technique(s) chosen must match the level of detail and actual company circumstances to permit making effective management decisions.
- Capacity planning can be simplified in a JIT environment.
- The better the resource and production planning process, the less difficult the capacity planning process.
- The better the shop-floor system, the less short-term capacity planning is required.
- The more detail in the capacity planning system, the more data and data base maintenance are required.
- It is not always capacity that should change when capacity availability does not equal need.
- Capacity must not only be planned, but use of that capacity must also be monitored and controlled.
- Capacity planning techniques can be applied to selected key resources (which need not correspond to production work centers).
- The capacity measure should reflect realizable output from the key resources.

INTEGRATED RESOURCE LINKAGES

Capacity planning has several key linkages with other integrated resource areas. The most immediate is human resource management, as a critical output from capacity planning is an anticipated set of human resource requirements. Many of the requirements—and their changes—can be met through relatively routine adjustments on the shop floor. But some capacity planning outputs indicate the need for either sharp increases in human resources or the need to think very seriously about a layoff of workers.

Marketing and sales are other areas that can have an important linkage with capacity planning. The sales forecast and marketing portion of the game plan provide one key input into the production plan—which drives capacity planning. To the extent that various marketing "what-if" scenarios are generated and evaluated, one part of the evaluation is based on the resultant capacity plans and requirements.

Facilities management also has a strong tie to capacity planning, because capacity plans dictate the needs for facilities. Also, one view holds that it is the job of facilities management to maintain the equipment and to ensure sufficient equipment capabilities during the right time periods. Another perspective is to include planned maintenance activities on all equipment as sources of "capacity requirements," to be planned and scheduled.

Manufacturing strategy has a linkage with capacity planning in that the desired production plan results in a set of capacity requirements— which, if not sufficient, calls for either provisions of more capacity or revisions of plans. Moreover, as manufacturing strategy shifts, there are almost always changes in the resultant set of capacity plans. For example, if individual plants are to be focused on particular product groups, there are major capacity implications. Sometimes the results are not easily foreseen. Recently a company made a decision to focus a group of factories on different products in a broad product line, only to learn that each would require an expensive heat-treating capability. Similarly, if a decision is made to pursue just-in-time manufacturing or time-based competition, the capacity requirements (and capacity utilizations) can change dramatically.

A related issue concerns quality. If the company decides to pursue statistical process control, it may well be necessary to change equipment—and the new equipment may have different capacity planning factors.

Capacity planning is linked with purchasing in that state-of-the-art PIM calls for managing vendor capacity with the same degree of care and enthusiasm as internal capacities.

Process engineering and design engineering both have linkages to capacity planning. Changes in the way products are produced almost always use resources in different ways, and this has to be planned. Cellular manufacturing is a good example. The focus is on material velocity, and the appropriate capacity measure is for the overall cell, not for the individual pieces of equipment within the cell. New product designs similarly can have a major impact on particular capacity requirements. The growing practice of "design for manufacturing" is focused directly on how to make the products with more efficient use of existing equipment and personnel.

Finally, there is the issue of the data base design for capacity planning and the computer systems to perform the analysis. Both are critical to achieving good capacity plans.

REFERENCES

Aherns, Roger. "Basics of Capacity Planning and Control." *APICS 24th Annual Conference Proceedings*, 1981, pp. 232–35.

Belt, Bill. "Integrating Capacity Planning and Capacity Control." *Production and Inventory Management*, 1st quarter 1976.

Berry, W. L.; T. Schmitt; and T. E. Vollmann. "Capacity Planning Techniques for Manufacturing Control Systems: Information Requirements and Operational Features." *Journal of Operations Management* 3, no. 1 (November 1982), pp. 13–26.

———. "An Analysis of Capacity Planning Procedures for a Material Requirements Planning System." *Decision Sciences* 15, no. 4 (Fall 1984).

Blackstone, J. H., Jr. *Capacity Management*. Cincinnati: Southwestern, 1989.

Bolander, Steven F. "Capacity Planning through Forward Scheduling." *APICS Master Planning Seminar Proceedings*, Las Vegas, April 1981, pp. 73–80.

Burlingame, L. J. "Extended Capacity Planning." *APICS Annual Conference Proceedings*, 1974, pp 83–91.

Capacity Planning Reprints. Falls Church, Va.: American Production and Inventory Control Society, 1986.

Chakravarty, A., and H. K. Jain. "Distributed Computer System Capacity Planning and Capacity Loading," *Decision Sciences Journal* 21, no. 2, (Spring 1990), pp. 253–62.

Hall, R. W., and T. E. Vollmann. "Black & Decker: Pioneers with MRP." *Case Studies in Materials Requirements Planning*. Falls Church, Va.: American Production and Inventory Control Society, 1978, p. 38.

Karmarkar, U. S. "Capacity Loading and Release Planning with Work-in-Progress (WIP) and Leadtimes." *Journal of Manufacturing and Operations Management* 2, no. 2 (1989), pp. 105–23.

Lankford, Ray. "Short-Term Planning of Manufacturing Capacity." *APICS 21st Annual Conference Proceedings*, 1978, pp. 37–68.

———."Input/Output Control: Making it Work." *1980 APICS Conference Proceedings*, pp. 419–420.

Solberg, James J. "Capacity Planning with a Stochastic Flow Model." *AIIE Transactions* 13, no. 2 (June 1981), pp. 116–22.

Wemmerlöv, Urban. "A Note on Capacity Planning." *Production and Inventory Management*, 3rd quarter 1980, pp. 85–89.

———.*Capacity Management Techniques for Manufacturing Companies with MRP Systems*. Falls Church, Va.: American Production and Inventory Control Society, 1984.

Wight, O. W. "Input-Output Control, A Real Handle on Lead Time." *Production and Inventory Management*, 3rd quarter 1970, pp. 9–31.

SECTION 5

DETAILED MATERIAL PLANNING

This section contains a description of one of the most important contributions to integrated production and inventory management in the last half century, material requirements planning. The insights that went into the

Production and Inventory Management

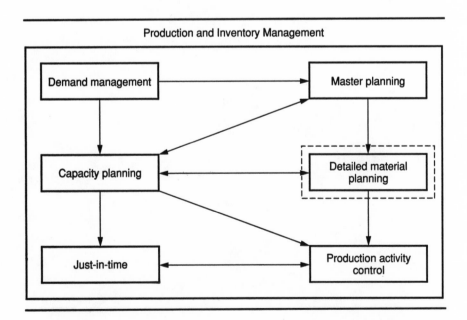

discovery and application of the material requirements planning (MRP) technique were truly revolutionary. Implementation of the technique became possible only because of the concurrent development of the high speed digital computer. MRP provided the capability for integration within manufacturing, between manufacturing and other business functions, and between firms. It also provided one foundation from which JIT has grown in the last few years.

Chapter 8 provides the basic background concepts of material planning. It has to do with fundamental MRP techniques and their application in industry. The chapter also describes how the integration of manufacturing activities is accomplished with MRP. This detailed material device is then linked to other PIM functions to extend the integration.

The basic material in Chapter 8 forms a background for the treatment of the way in which detailed material plans are kept in sync with a dynamic world in Chapter 9. The constantly changing environment and customer desires mean that the conditions to which MRP must respond are constantly changing. The implication is not only a need for a mechanism to respond to the changes, but also, a need for a current data base to support it. In addition, the changing conditions mean that the planners in all other activities must be kept up-to-date, implying data base integration.

CHAPTER 8

MATERIAL REQUIREMENTS PLANNING

Once the overall game plan for a company is agreed upon, the development of the MPS and resultant detailed material plans can proceed. Detailed material plans use engineering design information to convert the master production schedule into plans for the production of manufactured and purchased components.

The development of material plans requires substantial integration among several business functions, including engineering design, industrial engineering, information systems, manufacturing, and purchasing. Engineering design information is required for material planning purposes that specify not only the product components, but also how the product is to be manufactured. Computer approaches to developing material plans require the product design information to be organized into computer files for efficient processing. Finally, data from actual operations in manufacturing and suppliers must be analyzed and processed by manufacturing and purchasing in order to maintain up-to-date material plans that reflect actual operating conditions.

Detailed material planning is an integrative activity that involves the coordination of efforts in several areas of a company. It is critical in linking the plans of manufacturing, purchasing, and suppliers with the customer requirements placed on the business by sales and distribution. Changes in customer requirements, alterations in product design, and unplanned events in manufacturing and supplies all need to be reflected in the detailed material plans, and in the manufacturing priorities.

The material in this chapter shows how detailed material planning can be accomplished on a routine basis using material requirements planning (MRP). MRP is a basic tool for performing the detailed material planning function in the manufacture of component parts and their assembly into finished items. It is used by many companies that have invested in batch manufacturing processes. MRP's managerial objective is to provide "the right part at the right time" to meet the schedules for completed products. To do this, MRP provides formal plans for each part number, whether raw material, component, or finished good. Accomplishing these plans without excess inventory, overtime, labor, or other resources is the goal.

Chapter 8 is organized around the following six topics:

- Material requirements planning in production and inventory management: Where does MRP fit into the overall PIM system framework and how does it work?
- MRP system examples: How is MRP used in actual firms?
- System dynamics: How does MRP reflect changing conditions, and why must transactions be processed properly?
- Using the MRP system: Who uses the system, how is it used, and how is the exact match between MRP plans and physical reality maintained?

MATERIAL REQUIREMENTS PLANNING IN PIM

Joe Orlicky, whom many authorities regard as the father of modern MRP, called it a "Copernican revolution." MRP is as different from the traditional approaches to manufacturing planning and control as the Copernican model of the earth rotating around the sun was to the older model of the sun rotating around the earth. For companies assembling end items from components produced in batch manufacturing processes, MRP is central to the development of detailed plans for part needs. It is often where companies start in developing their PIM systems. Facility with time-phased planning and the associated time-phased records is basic to understanding many other aspects of PIM. Finally, although introduction of JIT and investments in repetitive manufacturing processes have brought about fundamental changes in detailed material planning for some firms, companies continue to adopt the MRP approach to enhance their existing systems.

For firms using MRP, the key linkages depicted in Figure 8.1 show that detailed material planning is characterized by the use of time-phased (period-by-period) requirement records. Several other supporting activities are shown as well. The master production schedule (MPS) drives detailed material planning. Material and capacity plans in turn drive the execution systems, shop-floor scheduling of the factory, and managing materials coming from vendor plants.

FIGURE 8.1
Key Linkages of Material Requirements Planning

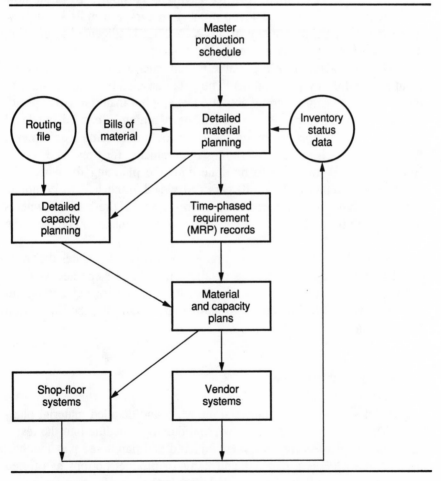

The detailed material planning function represents a central system in PIM. Figure 8.1 shows the key linkages of MRP with other PIM activities. For firms preparing detailed material plans using MRP, this means producing a time-phased set of master production schedule requirements and a resultant time-phased set of component part and raw material requirements.

In addition to master production schedule inputs, MRP requires two other basic inputs. A *bill of material* shows, for each part number, what other part numbers are required as direct components. For example, it could show five wheels required for a car (four plus the spare) and for each wheel the bill of materials could be a hub, tire, valve stem, and so on. The second basic input to MRP is *inventory status*. To know how many wheels to make for a given number of cars, we must know how many are on hand, how many of those are already allocated to existing needs, and how many have already been ordered.

The MRP data make it possible to construct a time-phased requirement record for any part number. The data can also be used as input to the detailed capacity planning activity. Developing material and capacity plans is an iterative process in which the planning is carried out level by level. For example, planning for a car could determine requirements for wheels, which in turn determines requirements for tires, and so on. But planning for tires has to be done *after* the planning for wheels; if the company wants to build 10 cars (50 wheels) and has 15 complete wheels on hand, it only needs 35 more—and 35 tires. If 20 wheels have already been ordered, only 15 more must be made to complete the 10 cars.

An MRP system serves a central role in PIM. It translates the overall plans for production into the detailed, individual steps necessary to accomplish those plans. It also provides information for developing capacity plans, and it links to the systems that actually get the production accomplished.

MRP AND MRPII

Figure 8.1 shows the link between the MPS and detailed material planning. This disaggregation of a master production schedule into the resultant detailed plans is for each manufactured and purchased part number. That is, the MPS is a plan for end items or product options as offered to the customers. MRP is the detailed planning process for components to support the MPS. The box labeled "Detailed material planning" in this section represents the system that does the disaggregation. MRP was a major breakthrough in PIM, made feasible by random access computers and data base management systems. Later, it was realized that due dates for shop orders could be updated by MRP replanning. This resulted in recasting MRP as more than a disaggregation technique for planning; it was now also seen as a dynamic priority-setting scheme so that shop-floor and vendor operations could do a better job of execution.

When execution on the shop floor was improved, attention naturally turned to better master production scheduling, production planning, and demand management. The question was how to establish and maintain a viable master production schedule—one that could be executed. When better master production scheduling was incorporated into MRP-based PIM systems, people began to describe them as *closed loop MRP systems*.

Additional enhancements included better capacity planning procedures at several levels. As this occurred, users of these systems began to consider them less as PIM systems and more as companywide systems. It was now possible to include financial plans based on the detailed PIM planning process. Because execution was improved, the resultant plans became more and more believable. Simulation possibilities were added, along with various ways to examine "what-if" scenarios. This overall vision of an MRP system for planning and controlling company operations was so fundamentally different from the original concepts of MRP that a new term seemed appropriate. Oliver Wight coined the term *MRPII*. In this case, MRP did not stand for material requirements planning; MRPII means *manufacturing resource planning*. The old term MRP is now sometimes referred to as "mrp" or "little MRP." These terms are now widely accepted, and most PIM professionals clearly understand the distinction between MRP, mrp, and MRPII.

At the heart of PIM is a universal representation of the status and plans for any single item (part number), whether raw material, component part, or finished good. This universal representation is the MRP time-phased record. Figure 8.2 provides an illustration, displaying the following information:

- The anticipated future usage of or demand for the item during the period (gross requirements).
- Existing replenishment orders for the item due to be received at the beginning of the period shown (scheduled receipts).

FIGURE 8.2
The Basic MRP Record

Period		1	2	3	4	5
Gross requirements			10		40	10
Scheduled receipts		50				
Projected available balance	4	54	44	44	4	44
Planned order release					50	
Lead time = 1 period Lot size = 50						

- The current and projected inventory status for the item at the end of the period shown (projected available balance).
- Planned replenishment orders for the item that must be released at the beginning of the period shown (planned order releases).

The top row in Figure 8.2 indicates periods which can vary in length from a day to a quarter or even longer. This period is also called a time bucket. The most widely used time bucket or period is one week. A timing convention for developing the MRP record is that the current time is the beginning of the first period. The initial available balance of four units is shown prior to period 1. The number of periods in the record is called the planning horizon, which indicates the number of future periods for which plans are made. In the simplified example shown as Figure 8.2, the planning horizon is five periods.

The second row, gross requirements, is a statement of the anticipated future usage of, or demand for, the item. The gross requirements are time phased, which means they are stated on a unique period-by-period basis rather than aggregated or averaged. That is, the gross requirements are stated as 10 in period 2, 40 in period 4, and 10 in period 5, rather than as a total requirement of 60 or as an average requirement of 12 per period. This method of presentation allows for special orders, seasonality, and periods of no anticipated usage to be explicitly taken into account.

A gross requirement in a particular period signifies that a demand is anticipated during that period which will be unsatisfied unless the item is available during that period. Availability is achieved by having the item in inventory, or by receiving either an existing replenishment order or a planned replenishment order in time to satisfy the gross requirement.

Another timing convention comes from the question of availability. The convention we use is that the item must be available at the beginning of the time bucket in which it is required. That means that plans must be made so that any replenishment order will be in inventory at the beginning of the period in which the gross requirement for that order occurs.

The scheduled receipt row describes the status of any open orders (work in process or existing replenishment orders) for the item. This row shows the quantities that have already been ordered and when we expect them to be completed. Scheduled receipts result from previously made ordering decisions and represent a source of the item to meet gross requirements. For example, the gross requirements of 10 in period 2 cannot be satisfied by the 4 units presently available. The scheduled receipt of 50, due in period 1, will be used to satisfy the gross requirement in period 2 if things go according to plan. Scheduled receipts represent a commitment. For an order in the factory, necessary materials have been committed to the order, and capacity at work centers will be required to complete it. For a purchased item, similar commitments have been made to a vendor. The timing convention used for showing scheduled receipts is also at the beginning of the period. That is, the order is shown in the period during which the item must be available to satisfy a gross requirement.

The next row in Figure 8.2 is called projected available balance. The timing convention in this row is the end of the period. That is, the row is the projected balance after replenishment orders have been received and gross requirements have been satisfied. For this reason, the projected available balance row has an extra time bucket shown at the beginning. This bucket shows the balance at the present time. That is, in Figure 8.2, the beginning available balance is four units. The quantity shown in period 1 is the projected balance at the end of period 1. This means that the projected available balance shown at the end of a period is available to meet gross requirements in the next (and succeeding) periods. For example, the 54 units shown as the projected available balance at the end of period 1 result from the addition of the 50 units scheduled to be received in period 1 to the beginning balance of 4 units. The gross requirement of 10 units in period 2 reduces the projected balance to 44 units at the end of period 2. The term "projected available balance" is used instead of "projected on-hand balance" for a very specific reason. Units of the item might be on hand physically, but not be available to meet gross requirements because they are already promised or allocated for some other purpose.

The planned order release row is determined directly from the projected available balance row. Whenever the projected available balance shows a quantity insufficient to satisfy gross requirements (a negative quantity), additional material must be planned for. This is done by creating a planned order release in time to keep the projected available balance from becoming negative. For example, in Figure 8.2, the projected available balance at the end of period 4 is four units. This is not sufficient to meet the gross requirement of 10 units in period 5. Because the lead time is one week, the MRP system creates a planned order at the beginning of week 4, providing a lead time offset of one week. As we have used a lot size of 50 units, the projected available balance at the end of week 5 is 44 units. Another way this logic is explained is to note that the balance for the end of period 4 (4 units) is the beginning inventory for period 5, during which there is a gross requirement of 10 units. The difference between the available inventory of 4 and the gross requirement of 10 is a net requirement of 6 units in period 5. Thus, an order for at least six units must be planned for period 4 to avoid a shortage in period 5.

The MRP system produces the planned order release data in response to the gross requirement, scheduled receipt, and projected available data. When a planned order is created for the most immediate or current period, it is in the "action bucket." A quantity in the action bucket means that some action is needed to avoid a future problem. The action is to release the order, which converts it to a scheduled receipt.

The planned order releases are not shown in the scheduled receipt row because they have not yet been released for production or purchasing. No material has been committed to their manufacture. The planned order is analogous to an entry on a Christmas list; it is comprised of plans. A scheduled receipt is like an order that has been mailed to a catalog firm to send someone on the list a particular gift for Christmas; a commitment has been made. Like Christmas lists versus mailed orders, planned orders are much easier to change than scheduled receipts. There are many advantages to not converting planned orders into scheduled receipts any earlier than necessary.

The basic MRP record just described provides the correct information on each part in the system. Linking these single part records together is essential to managing the flow of parts needed for a single product or customer. Key elements for linking the records are the bill of materials, the explosion process (using inventory and scheduled receipt information), and lead time offsetting.

MRP SYSTEM EXAMPLES

We turn now to two examples of actual MRP systems. The first example shows the detailed material plans developed from the MRP information. The second is a fully integrated system illustration.

An MRP System Output

The Hill-Rom Company uses MRP to prepare detailed material plans for some 13,000 part number items at its Batesville, Indiana plant. Figure 8.3 provides an example of a time-phased material plan for one of the component parts manufactured at Batesville.

Figure 8.3 shows a sample time-phased MRP record that includes three types of information. The header information shown in the upper portion of Figure 8.3 provides descriptive information for the component part used in developing the material plan, which includes the date the report (material plan) was run, the part number and item description, planner code number, buyer code number (for purchased parts), unit of measure for this part number (pieces, pounds, and so on), rejected parts that have yet to receive disposition by quality control, safety stocks, shrinkage allowance for anticipated scrap loss, lead time, family data (what other parts are similar to this one), year-to-date scrap, usage last year, year-to-date usage, and order policy/lot size data. The policy code of 3 for this part means that the order policy is a "*period order quantity* (POQ)." In this case, "periods to comb. = 04" means that each order should combine four periods of requirements (after on-hand inventory and open shop orders have been taken into account).

FIGURE 8.3
Example MRP Record

```
                                         MATERIAL STATUS-
          DATE- 01/21
* * * * PART NUMBER * * *
NONJEK OPTY  SSV LAM PP UPHL           DESCRIPTION

USTR040                      3/16x7/8 MR P & C STL STRAP
                                * * * * * * * * * *
 YTD         * * * USAGE * *       POLICY        STANDARD
SCRAP       LAST YR      YTD        CODE          QUANTITY
                                     3
```

	PAST DUE	563 01/22	564 01/29	565 02/05
REQUIREMENTS	495			483
SCHEDULED RECEIPTS				
PLANNED RECEIPTS				
AVAILABLE ON-HAND	1,500	508	508	25
PLANNED ORDERS	491			337

	574 04/09	575 04/16	576 04/23	577 04/30
REQUIREMENTS	337			
SCHEDULED RECEIPTS				
PLANNED RECEIPTS				334
AVAILABLE				334
PLANNED ORDERS				

	VACATION	586 07/16	587 07/23	588 07/30
REQUIREMENTS				
SCHEDULED RECEIPTS				
PLANNED RECEIPTS				
AVAILABLE				
PLANNED ORDERS				

```
* * * * EXCEPTION MESSAGES  * * *
PLANNED ORDER OF  491 FOR M-WK  568     OFFSET INTO A PAST
* * *  PEGGING DATA (ALLOC) * * *
790116  455 JN25220
* * *  PEGGING DATA (REQMT) * * *
790205  483 F 17144                              790305
790507  334 F 19938
```

PRODUCTION SCHEDULE

PLNR CODE	BYR COE	U/M	REJECT QUANTITY	SAFETY STOCK	SHRINKG ALLOWNE	LEAD TIME	FAMILY DATA
01	9	LFT		497	1	08	

ORDER POLICY AND LOT SIZE DATA* * * * * * * * * * * * * * * * * * *

PERIODS TO COMB.	MINIMUM QTY	MAXIMUM QTY	MULTIPLE QTY	MIN ORD POINT
04				

566 02/12	567 02/19	568 02/26	569 03/05	570 03/12	571 03/19	572 03/26	573 04/02
				516			
		491					337
25	25	516					337
				334			

578 05/07	579 05/14	580 05/21	581 05/28	582 06/04	583 06/11	584 06/18	585 06/25
334							

589-592 08/06	593-596 09/03	597-600 10/01	601-604 10/29	605-608 11/26	609-612 12/24

PERIOD BY 03 PERIODS

516 F 19938   790409 337 F 17144

The middle portion of Figure 8.3 displays the detailed material plan for this item for the coming year. The first time period in the material plan is called the "past due bucket." After that, weekly time buckets are presented for the first 28 weeks of data; thereafter, 24 weeks of data are lumped into 4-week buckets. In the computer itself a bucketless system is used, with all data kept in exact days and printouts prepared in summary format for one- and four-week buckets. The company maintains a manufacturing calendar; in this example, the first week is 563 (also shown as 1/22), and the last week is 612.

In this report, safety stock is subtracted from the on-hand balance (except in the past-due bucket). Thus, the exception message indicating that a planned order for 491 should have been issued three periods ago creates no major problem, because the planner noted that this amount is less than the safety stock. The report also shows the use of "safety lead time." *Planned* receipts are given a specific row in the report, and are scheduled one week ahead of the actual need date. For example, the 337-unit planned order of week 565 is a planned receipt in week 573, although it is not needed until week 574.

The lower portion of Figure 8.3 shows the "pegging data" section, which relates specific requirements to the part numbers from which those requirements came. For example, in week 565 (shop order no. 790205) the requirement for 483 derives from part number F17144.

Jet Spray—An Intergrated On-Line Example

Jet Spray Corporation manufactures and sells dispensers for noncarbonated cold beverages (e.g., lemonade) and hot beverages (e.g., coffee). Jet Spray uses a software package called Data 3 for manufacturing planning and control. The package is an integrated on-line system encompassing MRP, capacity planning, shop-floor control, master production scheduling, inventory management, and other functions.

One part at Jet Spray, 3273, is a beverage bowl used for the TJ3 model cold drink dispenser. It is also sold as a replacement or service part, as part number S3273. Figure 8.4 is a portion of a detailed material planning (inquiry) record for the S3273, where the time-phased record is displayed in vertical format. There are 11 units on hand, and a series of customer orders marked C/O. The record begins with the oldest date for a past-due customer order (8/4); all of these past-due orders are on credit hold. The projected balance goes negative at 9/25. A work order (W/O

FIGURE 8.4
Jet Spray MRP System Inquiry (part S3273)

9/29/ 8:17:23   MRP INQUIRY FOR PART: S3273   C/N 1 RNMRP001

DESCRIPTION: BOWL PINCH TYPE

QTY ON HAND:	11	LEADTIME DAYS : 3
SAFETY-STCK:	0	BUYER/PLANNER : 030

TYP	ORDER #	REQUIRED QUANTITY	RECEIVABLE QUANTITY	MESSAGE	PROJECTED BALANCE	DUE DATE	OPT
C/O	9007987	1			10	8/04/	
C/O	9009239	1			9	9/08/	
C/O	9009314	1			8	9/10/	
C/O	9009344	1			7	9/11/	
C/O	0201038	3			4	9/19/	
C/O	9009811	1			3	9/24/	
C/O	9009830	1			2	9/24/	
C/O	9009875	2			5-	9/25/	
C/O	9009879	5			6-	9/25/	
C/O	9009917	1			8-	9/26/	
C/O	9009944	2			8-	9/26/	
W/O	0078450		96	RSI 09/26/	88	9/29/	
F/C					78	9/29/	
W/O	0078450	10	96		174	10/03/	
C/O	0201118	50			124	10/03/	
C/O	0201129	5			119	10/03/	
PLO			96	OPEN SCH REC	215	10/06/	
F/C		65			150	10/06/	
F/C		65			85	10/13/	
PLO			96	OPEN SCH REC	161	10/20/	
F/C		65			116	10/20/	

78450) for 96 pieces is due on 9/29, but it has a reschedule-in (RSI) message to expedite the work order completion to 9/26. Other exception messages are given to help the planner manage the item.

Figure 8.5 shows the portion of the report that extracts the exception code in formation from the individual MRP records (such as that shown in Figure 8.4) into one overall report for items made in the plastic finishing department. This is where plastic parts sold as service parts are packaged. Item S3273 is shown with the information from Figure 8.4. By looking at the overall report shown as Figure 8.5, work can be efficiently released to the plastic finishing department on a daily basis.

Figure 8.6 presents the inquiry record for part 3273 (not the service part S3273). It contains information derived from the service part record (e.g., the 96 units of WOA 78450 shown as 23 and 73 that have not yet been picked) and from records for the end item on which this part is used. Figure 8.6 combines the service part requirements and the requirements for building TJ3 drink dispensers. It tells us that we have sufficient inventory to meet all requirements until 10/29.

Figure 8.7 shows the daily exception message report for the plastic molding department. It is used to help schedule the extensive changeovers of the molding machines. The exception message for 3273 indicated in Figure 8.6 can be seen in Figure 8.7.

FIGURE 8.5
Jet Spray MRP System Exception Messages (part S3273)

```
001   9/26/   20.56.49              JET SPRAY CORPORATION
                                    MRP EXCEPTION MESSAGE REPORT
                        FOR BUYER/PLANNER: 030 - J.CAPPADONA--

PART NUMBER --RT DESCRIPTION ------------------*  ACTION MESSAGES--

S3170           BOWL GASKET                       OPEN A SCHEDULED
                                                  OPEN A SCHEDULED
                                                  OPEN A SCHEDULED
                                                  OPEN A SCHEDULED

S3273           BOWL  PINCH TYPE                  RESCHEDULE IN
                                                  OPEN A SCHEDULED
                                                  OPEN A SCHEDULED
                                                  OPEN A SCHEDULED

S3338           BOWL COVER                        RESCHEDULE IN
                                                  OPEN A SCHEDULED
                                                  OPEN A SCHEDULED
```

Figures 8.4 through 8.7 show an integrated set of real time MRP records, which are used on a daily basis at Jet Spray. Many MRP reports are rarely, if ever, printed; they are replaced with a "paperless" system. Each day the planners, using video screens, take the actions required for that day. This results in lead time and inventory reductions, but it comes at the cost of all procedures and support activities, such as stockrooms executing instructions in a more timely mode. There are pressures for high levels of data integrity and performance, and one of Jet Spray's goals is to pick orders from stock on the same day that they are created by MRP planners.

SYSTEM DYNAMICS

Murphy's law states that if anything can go wrong, it will. Things are constantly going wrong, so it is essential that the MRP system mirror actual shop conditions, that is, both the physical system and the information system have to cope with scrap, incorrect counts, changes in customer needs, incorrect bills of material, engineering design changes, poor vendor performance, and a myriad of other mishaps.

```
MOSUPVSR          RNMRPPO2                              PAGE    17
SEQUENCED BY MAKE/BUY
PLASTIC FINISHING
                                                        MAKE/BUY
---------------------------------------------------------* CODE

   RECEIPT DUE  9/26/   FOR QTY OF     1,000                IF
   RECEIPT DUE 10/03/   FOR QTY OF     1,000
   RECEIPT DUE 10/13/   FOR QTY OF     1,000
   RECEIPT DUE 10/27/   FOR QTY OF     1,000

W/O NO. 0078430 TO  9/26/   FROM  9/29/  . QTY IS      96   IF
   RECEIPT DUE 10/06/   FOR QTY OF        96
   RECEIPT DUE 10/20/   FOR QTY OF        96
   RECEIPT DUE 10/27/   FOR QTY OF        96

W/O NO. 0079380 TO  9/26/   FROM 10/03/  . QTY IS      50   IF
   RECEIPT DUE 10/06/   FOR QTY OF       100
   RECEIPT DUE 10/27/   FOR QTY OF       100
```

FIGURE 8.6
Jet Spray MRP System Inquiry (part 3273)

```
9/29/            MRP INQUIRY FOR PART: 3273
DESCRIPTION: BOWL TJ3
QTY ON HAND: 1,034                        LEADTIME DAYS :    6
SAFETY-STCK:     0                        BUYER/PLANNER : 020
MISC. SHORT:     0
                REQUIRED                PROJECTED
TYP  ORDER #    QUANTITY    MESSAGE     BALANCE   DUE DATE
WOA  0078450        23                    1011     9/23/
WOA  0078450        73                     938     9/23/
DEP                 96                     842     9/24/
DEP                 20                     822     9/26/
DEP                126                     696    10/01/
DEP                113                     583    10/06/
DEP                 96                     487    10/07/
DEP                 96                     391    10/15/
DEP                145                     246    10/22/
DEP                150                      96    10/24/
PLO                        500 OPEN SCH REC 596   10/29/
DEP                120                     476    10/29/
DEP                 96                     380    10/29/
DEP                150                     230    10/30/
DEP                 96                     134    11/04/
```

FIGURE 8.7
Jet Spray MRP System Exception Messages (part S3273)

```
001   9/26/                          JET SPRAY CORPORATION
                                     MRP EXCEPTION MESSAGE REPORT
                     FOR BUYER/PLANNER: 020

PART NUMBER --RT DESCRIPTION ------------------* ACTION MESSAGES--

  3223            SPACER/JT JS EVAP              OPEN A SCHEDULED

  3273            BOWL TJ3                       OPEN A SCHEDULED

  3715            FUNNEL COVER HC2 HCL           RESCHEDULE IN
```

In this section, we look at the need for quick and accurate transaction processing and review the MRP planner's replanning activities in coping with change. We discuss sources of problems occurring as a result of data base changes and actions to ensure that the system is telling the truth, even if the truth hurts.

Transactions during a Period

To illustrate transaction processing issues, we use a simple example for one part. Figure 8.8 shows an MRP record (for part 1234) produced over the weekend preceding week 1. The planner for part 1234 would receive this MRP record on Monday of week 1.

The planner's first action would be to try to launch the planned order for 50 units in period 1; that is, the PIM system would first check availability of the raw materials for this part and then issue an order to the shop to make 50, if sufficient raw material is available. Launching would require allocating the necessary raw materials to the shop order, removing the 50 from the "Planned order releases" row for part 1234, and creating a scheduled receipt for 50 in week 3, when they are needed. Thereafter, a pick ticket would be sent to the raw material area and work could begin.

Let us assume that during week 1 the following changes occurred, and the transactions were processed:

- Actual disbursements from stock for item 1234 during week 1 were only 20 instead of the planned 30.

```
PLASTIC MOLDING

----------------------------------------------------------* CODE

 RECEIPT DUE 10/24/   FOR QTY OF        5,000               IF

 RECEIPT DUE 10/29/   FOR QTY OF         500               IF

W/O NO. 0078990 TO  9/26/   FROM 10/02/86. QTY IS      2,000    IF
```

FIGURE 8.8
MRP Record for Part 1234 as of Week 1

		1	2	3	4	5
Gross requirements		30	20	20	0	45
Scheduled receipts		50				
Projected available balance	10	30	10	40	40	45
Planned order release		50		50		

Lead time = 2
Lot size = 50

- The scheduled receipt for 50 due in week 1 was received on Tuesday, but 10 units were rejected, so only 40 were actually received into inventory.
- The inventory was counted on Thursday and 20 additional pieces were found.
- The requirement date for the 45 pieces in week 5 was changed to week 4.
- Marketing requested an additional five pieces for samples in week 2.
- The requirement for week 6 has been set at 25.

The resultant MRP record produced over the weekend preceding week 2 is presented as Figure 8.9.

Rescheduling

The MRP record shown in Figure 8.9 illustrates two important activities for MRP planners: (1) indicating the sources of problems that will occur as a result of data base changes, and (2) suggesting actions to ensure that the system is telling the truth. Note that the scheduled receipt presently due in week 3 is not needed until week 4. The net result of all the changes to the data base is that it is now scheduled with the wrong due

FIGURE 8.9
MRP Record for Part 1234 as of Week 2

Lead time = 2
Lot size = 50

		2	3	4	5	6
Gross requirements		25	20	45	0	25
Scheduled receipts			50			
Projected available balance	50	25	55	10	10	35
Planned order release				50		

date, and the due date should be changed to week 4. If this change is not made, this job may be worked on ahead of some other job that is really needed earlier, thereby causing problems. The condition shown in Figure 8.9 would be highlighted by an MRP exception message, such as "reschedule the receipt currently due in week 3 to week 4."

Complex Transaction Processing

So far, we have illustrated system dynamics by using a single MRP record. However, an action required on the part of an MRP planner may have been caused by a very complex set of data base transactions, involving several levels in the bill of materials. As an example, consider the MRP records shown in Figure 8.10, which include three levels in the product structure. Part C is used as a component in parts A and B as well as being sold as a service part. Part C, in turn, is made from parts X and Y. The arrows in Figure 8.10 depict the pegging data (which show the relationships between planned orders and gross requirements).

The part C MRP record is correctly stated at the beginning of week 1. That is, no exception messages would be produced at this time. In particular, the two scheduled receipts of 95 and 91, respectively, are scheduled correctly, as delaying either by one week would cause a

FIGURE 8.10
MRP Record Relationships for SeveralParts

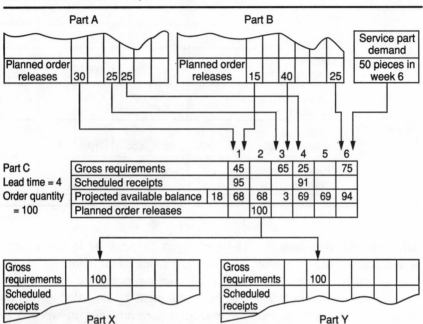

Part C Lead time = 4 Order quantity = 100		1	2	3	4	5	6
Gross requirements		45		65	25		75
Scheduled receipts		95		91			
Projected available balance	18	68	68	3	69	69	94
Planned order releases			100				

Note: This example is based on one originally developed by Joseph Orlicky, *Material Requirements Planning* (New York: McGraw-Hill, 1975), chap. 3, pp. 44–64.

shortage, and neither has to be expedited to cover any projected shortage.

Although the two scheduled receipts for part C are currently scheduled correctly, transactions involving parts A and B can have an impact on the proper due dates for these open orders. For example, suppose an inventory count adjustment for part A resulted in a change in the 30-unit planned order release from week 1 to week 3. In this case, the 95 units of part C would not be needed until week 3, necessitating a reschedule. Similarly, any change in timing for the planned order release of 25 units of part A in week 4 would call for a reschedule of the due date for 91 units of part C. Finally, suppose a transaction requiring 5 additional units of part B in week 5 were processed. This would result in an immediate release of an order for 100 units of part C, which might necessitate rescheduling for parts X and Y. The point here is that actions required by an MRP planner can result from a complex set of data base transactions involving many different parts. They may not necessarily directly involve the particular part being given attention by the MRP planner.

Procedural Inadequacies

MRP replanning and transaction processing activities are two essential aspects of ensuring that the PIM data base remains accurate. However, although these activities are necessary, they are not sufficient to maintain accurate records.

Some of the procedures used to process transactions may simply be inadequate to the task. To illustrate inadequate transaction procedures, let us return to the example in Figure 8.10. Note that if 4 or more pieces are scrapped on the shop order for 95, there will be a shortage in week 3, necessitating a rescheduling of the order for 91 one week earlier.

It is even more interesting to see what would happen if 4 pieces were scrapped on the order for 95 and this scrap transaction were not processed. If the scrap is not reported, MRP records would appear as shown in Figure 8.10, indicating no required rescheduling, when in fact that is not true. If the shortage were discovered by the person in charge of the stockroom when he or she puts away this order, then only one week would be lost before the next MRP report shows the problem. If, however, the stockroom person does not count, or if the person who made the scrap puts the defective parts at the bottom of the box where they go undetected by quality control, then the problem will only be discovered when the assembly lines are trying to build As and Bs in week 3. Such a discovery comes under the category of unpleasant surprises. An interesting footnote to this problem is that the cure will be to rush down to the shop to get at least 1 piece from the batch of 91. The very person who failed to report the earlier scrap may now be screaming, "Why don't those idiots know what they need!"

Still another aspect of the scrap reporting issue can be seen by noting that the 95 and 91 were originally issued as lot sizes of 100. This probably means that 5 and 9 pieces of scrap have occurred already, and the appropriate adjustments have been made in the scheduled receipt data. Note that if these adjustments had *not* been made, the two scheduled receipts would show as 100 each. The resultant 14 (or 5 + 9) pieces (that do not, in fact, exist) would be reflected in the MRP arithmetic. Thus, the projected available balance at the end of period 5 would be 83 (or 69 + 14); this is more than enough to cover the gross requirement of

75 in period 6, so the planned order release for 100 in period 2 would not exist and the error would cascade throughout the product structure. Further, even if shop orders are carefully counted as they are put into storage, the five-piece shortage in period 1 is not enough to cause the MRP arithmetic to plan an order. Only after period 4 (the beginning of period 5) will the additional nine pieces of scrap be incorporated into the MRP record showing a projected shortage in period 6. This will result in an immediate order to be completed in one week instead of four! What may be obvious is that if accurate counting is not done, the shortage is discovered in week 6, when the assembly line goes down. This means that procedures for issuing scrap tickets when scrap occurs and procedures for ensuring that good parts are accurately counted into inventory must be in place. If not, all the PIM systems will suffer.

The long and the short of all this is that we have to believe the numbers, and an error of as little as *one* piece can cause severe problems. We have to know the truth. We have to tightly control transactions. Moreover, we have to develop ironclad procedures for processing PIM data base transactions.

USING THE MRP SYSTEM

In this section, we discuss critical aspects of using the MRP system to ensure that MRP system records are exactly synchronized with physical flows of material.

The MRP Planner

The persons most directly involved with the MRP system outputs are planners. They are typically in the production scheduling, inventory control, and purchasing departments. Planners have the responsibility for making detailed decisions that keep the material moving through the plant. Their range of discretion is carefully limited (e.g., without higher authorization, they cannot change plans for end items destined for customers). Their actions, however, are reflected in the MRP records. Well-trained MRP planners are essential to effective use of the MRP system.

Computerized MRP systems often encompass tens of thousands of part numbers. To handle this volume, planners are generally organized around logical groupings of parts (such as metal parts, wood parts, purchased electronic parts, or the West Coast distribution center). Even so, reviewing each record every time the records are processed would not be an effective use of the planners' time. At any time, many records require no action, so the planner only wants to review and interpret those that do require action. The primary actions taken by an MRP planner are the following:

1. Release orders (i.e.,launch purchase or shop orders when indicated by the system).
2. Reschedule due dates of existing open orders when desirable.
3. Analyze and update system planning factors for the part numbers under his or her control. This would involve changes in lot sizes, lead times, scrap allowances, or safety stocks.
4. Reconcile errors or inconsistencies and try to eliminate root causes of these errors.
5. Find key problem areas requiring action now to prevent future crises.
6. Use the system to solve critical material shortage problems so that actions can be captured in the records for the next processing. This means that the planner works within formal MRP rules, not by informal methods.
7. Indicate where further system enhancements (outputs, diagnostics, and so forth) would make the planner's job easier.

Order Launching

Order launching is the process of releasing orders to the shop or to vendors (purchase orders). This process is prompted by MRP when a planned order release is in the current time period, the action bucket. Order launching converts the planned order into a scheduled receipt reflecting the lead time offset. It is the opening of shop and purchase orders; closing these orders occurs when scheduled receipts are received into stockrooms. At that time, a transaction must be processed to increase the on-hand inventory and eliminate the schedule receipt. Procedures for opening and closing shop orders have to be carefully defined so that all transactions are properly processed.

The orders indicated by MRP as ready for launching are a function of lot-sizing procedures and safety stock as well as timing. A key responsibility of the planner is to manage with awareness of the implications of these effects. For example, not all of a fixed lot may be necessary to cover a requirement, or a planned order that is solely for replenishment of safety stock may be in the action bucket.

When an order is launched, it is sometimes necessary to include a shrinkage allowance for scrap and other process yield situations. The typical approach allows some percentage for yield losses that will increase the shop order quantity above the net amount required. To effect good control over open orders the total amount, including the allowance, should be shown on the shop order, and the scheduled receipt should be reduced as actual yield losses occur during production.

Component Availability Checking and Allocation

A concept closely related to order launching is allocation, a step prior to order launching that involves an availability check for the necessary component or components. For example, if we want to assemble 20 wheels, the availability check would be whether 20 tires, hubs, valve stems, and so on are available. If not, the shop order for 20 wheels should not be launched, because it cannot be executed without component parts. The planner role is key here, as well. The best course of action might be to release a partial order, and the planner should evaluate that possibility.

Most MRP systems first check component availability for any order that a planner desires to launch. If sufficient quantities of each component are available, the shop order can be created. If the order is created, then the system allocates the necessary quantities to the particular shop order. (Shop orders are assigned by the computer in numerical sequence.) The word *allocation* means that this amount of a component part is mortgaged to the particular shop order and is, therefore, not available for any other shop order. Thus, the amounts shown as projected available balances in MRP records may not be the same as the physical inventory balances. The physical inventory balances could be larger, with the differences representing allocations to specific shop orders that have been released without the component parts having been removed from inventory.

After availability checking and allocation, *picking tickets* are typically created and sent to the stockroom. The picking ticket calls for a specified amount of some part number to be removed from some inventory location, on some shop order, to be delivered to a particular department or location. When the picking ticket has been satisfied (inventory moved), the allocation is removed and the on-hand balance is reduced accordingly.

Availability checking, allocation, and physical stock picking are a type of double-entry bookkeeping. The result is that the quantity physically on hand should match what the records indicate is available, plus what is allocated. If they do not match, corrective action must be taken. The resulting accuracy facilitates inventory counting and other procedures for maintaining data integrity.

Exception Codes

Exception codes in MRP systems are used "to separate the vital few from the trivial many." If the manufacturing process is under control and the MRP system is functioning correctly, exception coding typically means that only 10 to 20 percent of the part numbers will require planner review at each processing cycle. Exception codes are in two general categories. The first, checking the input data accuracy, includes checks for dates beyond the planning horizon, quantities larger or smaller than check figures, nonvalid part numbers, or any other desired check for incongruity. The second category of exception codes directly supports the MRP planning activity. Included are the following kinds of exception (action) messages or diagnostics:

1. Part numbers for which a planned order is now in the most immediate time period (the action bucket). It is also possible to report any planned orders two to three periods out to check lead times, on-hand balances, and other factors while there is some time to respond, if necessary.

2. Open order diagnostics when the present timing and/or amount for a scheduled receipt is not satisfactory. Such a message might indicate that an open order exists that is not necessary to cover any of the requirements in the planning horizon. This message might suggest order cancellation caused by an engineering change that substituted some new part for the one in question. The most common type of open order diagnostic shows scheduled receipts that are timed to arrive either too late or too early and should, therefore, have their due dates revised to reflect proper factory priorities. Another open order exception code is to flag past-due scheduled receipt (scheduled to have been received in previous periods, but for which no receipt transaction has been processed). MRP systems assume that a past-due scheduled receipt will be received in the immediate time bucket.

3. A third general type of exception message indicates problem areas for management; in essence, situations in which end item production quantities cannot be satisfied unless the present planning factors used in MRP are changed. One such exception code indicates that a requirement has been offset into the past period and subsequently added to any requirement in the first or most immediate time bucket. The presence of this condition means that an order should have been placed in the past. Because it was not lead times through the various production item levels must be compressed to meet the end item schedule. A similar diagnostic indicates that the allocations exceed the on-hand inventory—a condition directly analogous to overdrawing a checking account. Unless more inventory is received soon, the firm will not be able to honor all pick tickets issued, and there will be a material shortage in the factory.

CONCLUDING PRINCIPLES

This chapter describes how an MRP system can be used to prepare and maintain detailed material plans for manufactured and purchased components. It also illustrates the integrative nature of this function in coordinating the development of manufacturing and procurement plans with other business functions such as engineering design, information processing, purchasing, marketing and sales, and industrial engineering. Information inputs from all of these areas are critical in maintaining effective detailed material plans for the business, thereby enabling manufacturing schedules to be visible to all areas of the business.

In this chapter we have described some of the basic data used by MRP in material planning, and how MRP systems are used in practice. MRP, with its time-phased approach to planning, is a basic building block concept for materials planning and control systems. There are also many other applications of the time-phased record. We see the most important concepts or principles of this chapter as follows:

- Effective use of an MRP system allows the development of a forward-looking (planning) approach to managing material flows.

- The MRP system provides a coordinated set of linked product relationships, thereby permitting decentralized decision making on individual part numbers.
- All decisions made to solve problems must be done within the system, and transactions must be processed to reflect the resultant changes.
- Effective use of exception messages allows focusing attention on the "vital few," not on the "trivial many."
- System records must be accurate and reflect the factory's physical reality if they are to be useful.
- Procedural inadequacies in processing MRP transactions need to be identified and corrected to ensure that material plans are accurate.

INTEGRATED RESOURCE LINKAGES

Material requirements planning is linked to many other resource areas. In order for MRP to be technically feasible, it was first necessary to have computers with random access memory. In the early days of MRP, the most difficult aspect of the job was getting a computer to perform the necessary calculations. Today, there are scores of packaged computer systems for MRP, but certain aspects of the management information system design still remain.

There is a linkage to design engineering in that this group establishes the basic product design and the resultant bills of material. Design engineering is also typically responsible for bill of material maintenance and for engineering changes. The procedures for both of these need to be tightly defined and followed so that this aspect of the MRP data base is maintained at a very high level.

A similar connection exists for process engineering and the routing data base. It is the routing file which specifies each conversion step required to transform one or more MRP part numbers into another. Data integrity is critical, and any changes or improvements in process technology need to be accurately reflected in the MRP data base.

Quality has an interesting linkage with both process engineering and MRP. If the processes are not under good control, poor quality output is often the result. This in turn causes problems in executing PIM overall plans, and rush orders are put through the factory to replace defective material. We have audited several firms in which we were told that MRP was not working correctly—only to find that in almost every case the cause was *not* poor MRP planning, but poor quality, resulting in subsequent rush orders.

Field service has an important link with MRP, in that service part demands represent a source of "independent demand" for parts that are mostly subject to "dependent demand." Service parts demand needs to be forecasted (typically with a short-term forecasting model) and this forecast needs to be included in the gross requirements for the respective part numbers. Pegging data are particularly useful here so that the source of the gross requirements is transparent.

Purchasing has a particularly important linkage to MRP. The jobs in purchasing are fundamentally different under MRP than they were before companies implemented routine MRP planning. Before, it was necessary for production people to tell purchasing people what was *really* needed— usually on a very short-term basis, and for purchasing to follow up by telephone with vendors, making plans and threats and using a great deal of air transport. Now, the MRP record tells purchasing *precisely* what the needs are—in both the near term and further out. Purchasing's job is to hit *its* schedule; it does not need to get confirmation from manufacturing.

Moreover, purchasing in many companies has been divided into two activities, procurement and order release. The former involves the establishment of partnerships and general conditions—a job for professionals. The latter is a clerical activity that can be routinely done by clerical people and/or electronic data interchange (EDI).

An important linkage is that between MRP and cost accounting. The data base of MRP transactions provide the means to accumulate actual cost and performance data with a very fine level of detail. Job order costing is one possible output from processing these data. Others include the detailed tracking of times, materials, and the determination of variances.

REFERENCES

Davis, E. W. *Case Studies in Material Requirements Planning*. Falls Church, Va.: American Production and Inventory Control Society, 1978.

Gray, C. D. *The Right Choice*. Essex Junction, Vt.: Oliver Wight Ltd., 1987.

Miller, J. G., and L. G. Sprague. "Behind the Growth in Materials Requirements Planning." *Harvard Business Review,* September–October 1975.

Orlicky, J. *Material Requirements Planning*. New York: McGraw-Hill, 1975.

Steinberg, E.; W. B. Lee; and B. M. Khumawala. "MRP Applications in the Space Program." *Journal of Operations Management* 1, no. 2 (1981).

Wight, Oliver. *Manufacturing Resource Planning: MRPII*. Essex Junction, Vt.: Oliver Wight Ltd., 1984.

CHAPTER 9

INFORMATION REQUIREMENTS
FOR DETAILED
MATERIAL PLANNING

This chapter describes the data base used by a material requirements planning (MRP) system to develop detailed material plans. It also discusses a number of technical issues related to the design of the information system that is required to support the time-phased MRP approach to detailed material planning. This background is important in understanding the way that the introduction of just-in-time methods are changing the nature of the detailed material planning function in some companies.

The introduction of just-in-time manufacturing has led to major changes in the way that detailed material plans are developed in some companies. These changes are largely due to changes in the design of the production process which enable much shorter manufacturing lead times to be achieved. These shifts in the design of the process further illustrate the integrated nature of production and inventory management decisions. They demonstrate the impact that design engineering and industrial engineering have on the design of products and processes, as well as on the information systems used by manufacturing for operational control.

An example of this impact will be presented in this chapter. This example illustrates the nature of the improvements that can be made in the manufacturing infrastructure by implementing just-in-time methods in the design of the manufacturing process. The improvements have to do with eliminating much of the cost of the "hidden factory," that is, the data base transactions required to support the development of time-phased material plans.

Chapter 9 is organized around the following four topics:

- The MRP data base: What is the nature of the information required by MRP to develop detailed material plans?
- Technical issues: What are some of the important technical features and supporting systems for producing time-phased MRP material plans?
- Information requirements under JIT: What are the changes in information requirements when detailed material planning is carried out under just-in-time manufacturing?
- The hidden factory: What are the nature of the improvements in transaction processing that can be obtained under JIT?

THE MRP DATA BASE

To install and derive maximum benefit from a detailed material planning system, a large integrated data base is usually required. The computer hardware and software design aspects of common data bases are beyond the scope of this book. However, their importance in PIM systems compels us to briefly identify the required primary files and communication links. In this section, we treat the data files that would usually be required to support basic MRP processing. We make no claim that the following approach is optimal, or that you might not group the data in different ways, with different data base management systems. Rather, our objective is to illustrate the different types of data, the elements needed, and how they are updated and maintained. The enormity of the overall data base even for small firms is awesome, but data needs exist *even if there is no formal system*, as long as products are being manufactured.

The Item Master File

The data on an individual part are often contained in two files. The information that remains the same (or nearly so) from period to period is found in the *item master file*, whereas information on part status is found in the subordinate file. The item master file typically contains all the data needed to completely describe each part number. These data are used for MRP, purchasing, cost accounting, and other company functions. The objective is to hold, in one file, all of the static data describing the attributes of individual part numbers. Included are part number, name, unit of measure, engineering change number, drawing reference, release date, planner code, order policy code, lead time, safety stock, standard costs, and linkages to other data files, such as routing, where used, and bill of material.

The Subordinate Item Master File

A *subordinate item master file* is often used for changing or dynamic data about individual part numbers. Included are current allocations and the shop order number to which each allocation is tied, time-phased scheduled receipts and associated order numbers, time-phased gross requirements, planned orders, firm planned orders, pegging data, and linkages to the item master file.

The Bill of Material File

The bill of material file is typically established on a *single-level basis*, with each part number linked only to the part numbers of the immediate components required to produce it; that is, the linkages are to one level further down in the product structure only. By successively linking the part numbers, a full bill of material for each product can be developed from the individual single-level linkings. Data elements held in this file usually include component part numbers required to make each individual part, number of each required, units of measure, engineering change numbers, effectivity dates, active/inactive coding, and where-used information.

The Location File

The *location file* keeps track of the set of exact physical storage locations for each part number. This can be a highly dynamic file, with frequent updating, because the data elements include departments, rows, bays, tiers, quantities, units of measure, in dates, original quantities, date of last activity, and so on.

The Calendar File

The *calendar file* converts the shop day calendar used by the firm to a day/date/year calendar. The file also provides for phenomena such as annual vacations and holidays. This file can differ for each plant or location. It can also include information on particular shifts of operation in various work centers.

Open Order Files

An entire set of files is maintained to support the scheduled receipts (open orders) in the MRP system. These involve both purchase orders and shop orders. For the purchase orders, we need to keep track of open purchase orders, open quotations, a vendor master file, vendor performance data, alternate sources, price, and quantity information. Another set of records needs to be maintained to support shop orders in the factory. Included are data files describing open orders, the source of requirements for those orders, routings, work centers, employees, shifts, tooling, labor, and performance reporting. Data from the open order files also need to be converted into "history" files when the orders have been completed (closed).

Other File Linkages

In addition to the data files needed for MRP, many other data files are necessary to flesh out the entire PIM system. Among them are files for forecasting, capacity planning, production scheduling, cost accounting, budgeting, order entry, production activity control, distribution, invoicing, payroll, job standards, and engineering. One particularly large set of files is the detailed routing data base, which describes each of the conversion steps necessary for each part number.

MRP Data Base Maintenance

Each of the data base files to support routine MRP processing has to be maintained if the detailed plans are to be believed. The item master file will have to be updated as costs change, as engineering designs are revised, as new parts are added or substituted, as lead time quotations from vendors change, and as any of the other data elements are modified.

Similar maintenance requirements exist for all of the other MRP data base elements. As transactions are processed, errors are an inevitable result. Therefore, transaction procedures must be tightly defined, and control over the details is essential. For most MRP-based systems, maintenance of the data base requires a significant investment in time and money.

TECHNICAL ISSUES

In this section, we briefly introduce some technical information processing issues in designing MRP systems.

Processing Frequency

A fundamental aspect of developing material plans with MRP is the detailed construction of individual records and linking the individual records together. As conditions change and new information is received, the MRP records must be brought up to date so that plans can be adjusted. This means processing the MRP records anew, incorporating current information. Two issues are involved in the processing decision: how frequently the records should be processed and whether all the records should be processed at the same time.

Processing all of the records in one computer run is called *regeneration*. This signifies that *all* part number records are completely restructured each time the records are processed. An alternative is *net change* processing, in which only those records affected by the new or changed information are reconstructed. The key issue raised by contrasting regeneration and net change is the frequency of processing.

The appropriate frequency for processing the MRP time-phased records depends on the firm, its products, and its operations. Historically, the most common practice has been weekly processing using regeneration. But some firms regenerate only every two weeks or even monthly, whereas others process all the MRP time-phased records twice per week or daily.

The prime motivation for less frequent processing is the computational cost. This can be especially high with regeneration, because a new record is created for every active part number in the product structure file at each processing. But the computational time required varies considerably from company to company, depending on the computer approach used, the number of part numbers, the complexity of product structure, and other factors. For companies using regeneration, 8 to 24 hours of central processing unit (CPU) time are often required. For example, at one time at the Hill-Rom Company in Batesville, Indiana, regeneration for approximately 13,000 active part numbers was done over each weekend, requiring approximately 16 hours of CPU time on a mid-range main frame computer.

The problem with processing less frequently is that the portrayal of component status and needs expressed in the records becomes increasingly out of date and inaccurate over time. This decrease in accuracy has both anticipated and unanticipated results. As the anticipated scheduled receipts are received and requirements are satisfied, the inventory balances change. If unanticipated scrap, requirement changes, stock corrections, or other such transactions are not reflected in all the time-phased records influenced by the transactions, they cause inaccuracies. Changes in one record are linked to other time-phased records as planned order releases become gross requirements for lower-level components. Thus, some change transactions may cascade throughout the product structure. If these transactions are not reflected in the time-phased records early enough, the result can be poor planning.

More frequent processing of the MRP records increases computer costs, but results in fewer unpleasant surprises. When the records reflecting the changes are produced, appropriate actions will be indicated to compensate for the changes. Increasingly, more frequent processing is favored as more firms drive toward lower inventories, face decreased costs of computation, use improved software packages, and hire more professional PIM personnel. Daily processing, and in some cases on-line processing, are becoming the norm.

A logical response to the pressure for more frequent processing is to reduce the required amount of calculation by processing only those records affected by the changes. This net change approach creates a new part number record only when a transaction makes the present component plan inaccurate. Although this could be done as the transaction occurs, typically all transactions are accumulated daily and then processed overnight.

The argument for the net change approach is that it can reduce computer time enough to make daily or more frequent processing possible. Companies in which this can be done have the added advantage of smoothing the computational requirements over the week. On the other hand, daily processing of part of the records could lead to even greater overall computational cost than weekly regeneration. As only some of the records are reviewed at each processing, there is a need for very accurate computer records and transaction processing procedures. Some net change users do an occasional regeneration to clean up all records.

As computers get faster, firms are increasingly adopting daily processing of records, either through regeneration or through net change. The state of the art in hardware and software technology now supports on-line systems with a daily updating cycle.

Bucketless Systems

The original approach to MRP employed the concept of *time buckets*. This divided a year or more into weekly time periods for perhaps the most immediate 3 or 4 months, with the latter planning done in monthly periods or buckets. Within a time bucket, all activity is assumed to take place at one point in time. To some extent, the problems of timing are tied to the use of time buckets. When the buckets are small enough, the problems are reduced significantly. Another way to visualize this planning is as a spreadsheet or matrix.

However, smaller buckets mean more buckets, which increases review, storage, and computation costs. A bucketless MRP system specifies the exact release and due dates for each requirement, scheduled receipt, and planned order. The structure is like a list, rather than a spreadsheet. The managerial reports are printed out on whatever basis is required, including by exact dates.

Bucketless MRP systems are a better way to use the computer. Above and beyond that, the approach allows better maintenance of lead time offset data and provides more precise time-phased information. The approach is consistent with state-of-the-art software, and many firms now use bucketless systems. The major addition is that the planning cycle itself is bucketless. That is, plans are revised as necessary, not on a periodic schedule, and the entire execution cycle is shortened.

Lot Sizing

MRP systems rarely use the economic lot size model to determine the size of orders. The time-phased record permits us to develop *discrete lot sizes* that will exactly satisfy the net requirements for one or more periods. Several formal procedures have been developed for lot sizing the time-phased requirements. The basic trade-off usually involves elimination of one or more setups at the expense of carrying inventory longer. In many cases, the discrete lot sizes possible with MRP are more appealing than fixed lot sizes.

One discrete lot-size model is simply to order only what is required for each requirement. This approach is called "lot-for-lot." At first glance the lot-for-lot technique seems a bit too simple-minded because it does not consider any of the economic trade-offs or physical factors. However, batching planned orders at one level will increase gross requirements at the next level in the product structure, so that larger lot sizing near the end item level of the bill of materials cascades down through all levels. Thus, it turns out that lot-for-lot is better than we might expect in actual practice, particularly at the intermediate levels in the bill of materials. This is especially the case when a product structure has many levels, and the cascading effect becomes greatly magnified. This cascading effect can be mitigated to some extent for components and raw materials that are very common. When this is the case, again lot sizing may be appropriate. As a consequence, many firms employ lot sizing primarily at the end item and basic component levels, whereas intermediate subassemblies are planned on a lot-for-lot basis.

Safety Stock and Safety Lead Time

Carrying out detailed component plans is sometimes facilitated by including *safety stocks* and/or *safety lead times* in the MRP records. Safety stock is a buffer of stock above and beyond that needed to satisfy the gross requirements. Safety lead time is a procedure whereby shop orders or purchase orders are released and scheduled to arrive one or more periods before necessary to satisfy the gross requirements.

Safety stocks can be incorporated into MRP time-phased records. The result is that the projected available balance does not fall below the safety stock level instead of reaching zero. To incorporate safety lead time, orders are issued (planned) earlier and are scheduled (planned) to be received into inventory before the time that the MRP logic would indicate as necessary. Figure 9.1 shows an item being planned with a one-week safety lead time. Notice that both the planned release and planned receipt dates are changed. Safety lead time is not just inflated lead time.

Both safety stock and safety lead time are used in practice and can be used simultaneously. However, both indicate that orders should be released (launched) or that they need to be received when, in fact, this is not strictly true. To use safety stocks and safety lead times effectively,

FIGURE 9.1
MRP Record with Safety Lead Time

		1	2	3	4	5	6	7	8	9	10
	Gross requirements			3		35	10				
Lead time = 1	Scheduled receipts										
Lot-for-lot	Projected available balance 15	15	15	12	35	10	0	0	0	0	0
Safety lead time = 1	Planned order releases			23	10						

we must understand the techniques' influence on plans. If they are not well understood, wrong orders can be sent to the factory, meaning that workers will try to get out part A because of safety lead time or safety stock when, in fact, part B will be required to meet a customer order.

Safety stock tends to be used in MRP systems in which uncertainty about quantities is the problem (e.g., where some small amount of scrap, spare part demand, or other unplanned usage is a frequent occurence). Safety lead time, on the other hand, tends to be used when the major uncertainty is the timing rather than the quantity. For example, if a firm buys from a vendor who often misses delivery dates, safety lead time may provide better results than safety stock.

Pegging

Pegging relates all the gross requirements for a part to all the planned order releases or other sources of demand that created the requirements. The pegging records contain the specific part number or numbers of the sources of all gross requirements. At the finished item lead, for example, pegging records might contain the specific customer orders to be satisfied by the gross requirements in the end item time-phased records. For lower-level part numbers, the gross requirements are most often pegged to planned orders of higher-level items, but might also be pegged to customer orders if the part is sold as a service part.

Pegging information can be used to go up through the MRP records from a raw material gross requirement to some future customer order. In this sense, it is the reverse of the explosion process. Pegging is sometimes compared to *where-used data*. Where-used data indicate, for each part number, the part numbers of all items on which the part is used. Pegging, on the other hand, is a *selective* where-used file, and shows only the specific part numbers that produce the specific gross requirements in each time period. Thus, pegging information can trace the impact of a material problem all the way up to the customer order it would affect.

Firm Planned Orders

The logic used to illustrate the construction of an MRP record for an individual part number is automatically applied for every processed part number. The result is a series of planned order releases for each part number. If changes have taken place since the last time the record was processed, planned order releases can be very different from one record-processing cycle to the next. Because planned orders are passed down as gross requirements to the next level, the differences can cascade throughout the product structure.

One device for preventing this cascade is the creation of a *firm planned order* (FPO). FPO, as the name implies, is a planned order that the MRP system *does not* automatically change when conditions change. To change either the quantity or timing of a firm planned order, managerial action is required. This means that the trade-offs in making the change can be evaluated before authorization.

The FPO provides a means for temporarily overriding the system to provide stability or to solve problems. For example, if changes are coming about because of scrap losses on open orders, the possibility of absorbing those variations with safety stock can be evaluated. If more rapid delivery of raw material than usual is requested (say, by using air freight) to meet a special need, lead time can be reduced for that one order. An FPO means that the system will not use the normal lead time offset from the net requirement for that order.

Service Parts

Service part demand must be included in the MRP record if the material requirements are not to be understated. The service part demand is typically based on a forecast, and is added directly into the gross requirements for the part. From the MRP system point of view, the service part demand is simply another source of gross requirements for a part, and the sources of all gross requirements are maintained through pegging records. The low-level code for a part used exclusively for service would be zero, indicating that it goes directly to a customer. If it is used as a component part as well, the low-level code would be determined on the basis of on what parts it was used, and where they are in the bill of materials.

As actual service part needs occur, it is to be expected that demand variations will arise. These can be partially buffered by safety stocks (inventories specifically allocated to service part usage) or by creative use of the MRP system. By careful examination of pegging records, expected shortage conditions for manufacturing part requirements can sometimes be satisfied from available service parts. Conversely, critical service part requirements can perhaps be met with orders destined for higher-level items. Only one safety stock inventory is needed to buffer uncertainties from both sources, however.

Scheduled Receipts versus Planned Order Releases

A true understanding of MRP requires knowledge of certain key differences between a scheduled receipt and a planned order. The scheduled receipt represents a commitment, whereas the planned order is only a plan—the former is much more difficult to change than the latter. A scheduled receipt for a purchased item means that a purchase order, which is a formal commitment, has been prepared. Similarly, a scheduled receipt for a manufactured item means that there is an open shop order. Raw materials and component parts have *already* been specifically committed to that order and are no longer available for other needs.

Living with the Technical Requirements

Using an MRP based system for detailed material planning usually produces dramatic results, but *only* when the system is used correctly. We occasionally run into people that tell us that MRP does not work. Our usual response is that your calculator does not work either if you push the wrong buttons. MRP *does* work, but it is not easy. All of the systems need to be in place, the data base elements must be maintained religiously, transaction processing must be tight, error detection and correction has to be very timely, and the technical issues need to be resolved for each situation. Moreover, this set of requirements is not a one-time fix that can subsequently be ignored. Eternal vigilance is the price of a working MRP system!

The total of all these requirements is daunting, but the payoffs are almost always well worth it. Reductions of 25 percent in inventory, productivity increases of 20 percent, vastly improved customer service, and a host of other benefits are routinely achieved. But more and more manufacturing companies are beginning to question the need for *all* of the requirements. In particular, leading edge firms are finding that *speed* is the answer. If products can be produced faster—much faster—it is possible to reduce the data base requirements, to eliminate transactions, and to use much less sophisticated planning tools. Just-in-time manufacturing is the approach most frequently used to achieve these benefits.

INFORMATION REQUIREMENTS UNDER JIT

Just-in-time (JIT) systems are playing an increasing role in PIM, as the prerequisites for successful JIT implementation are becoming better understood. Companies implementing JIT find that many previous beliefs about inventories, data bases, transactions, and controls are no longer valid. Instead of using inventory as a buffer to decouple successive stages in the product creation/distribution/consumption chain, JIT deliberately makes the linkages more closely integrated and the stages less independent. A primary objective in JIT is "material velocity." Anything that can be done to increase the speed at which materials move through the stages is desirable. Inventories decouple the stages and increase throughput times, and thus require vastly larger data bases, transaction processing, and control mechanisms. However, JIT is not a panacea for all company environments, and achievement of successful JIT requires many changes in company operations.

Impact on Inventories

Just-in-time approaches usually plan manufacturing activities at the level of end items, rather than at the piece part or operation and routing level. This means a reduction in detail and transaction processing of two to three orders of magnitude (i.e., one-hundredth to one-thousandth). Inventories are essentially only either in raw materials or in finished goods.

The information requirements to support detailed material planning under just-in-time manufacturing are quite different than under MRP planning. The major difference comes from the absence of formal shop orders with JIT. Because materials move through the factory so quickly, there is no need for detailed tracking to know where they are, or to know their status. In essence, one can assume that there are either raw materials or finished goods; there is virtually no work-in-process inventory worth keeping track of.

The item master file concept is still valid under JIT. Part numbers need to be maintained, as do engineering change number status, units of measure, and most of the other static data. What is changed, however, is the emphasis given to intermediate part numbers and their planning. Under JIT, formal "orders" are only issued for end items (or major assemblies), with very limited formal planning for component parts. These are rapidly "pulled" through manufacturing stages by JIT execution.

The bill of material under JIT reflects the lack of formal planning for component parts. The actual bill of material kept in the computer may be the same as for MRP planning except for two important differences. First, the lead times for all nonpurchased components is set to zero and the lot size is established as lot-for-lot. The second difference is called "phantom" coding, which means that there is never any intention for these parts to be kept in inventory. If by chance some do enter inventory, they will be used up at the earliest possible opportunity. This means that although the bill of materials may *appear* to have many levels, in essence there is only one level. Purchase parts are pulled from inventory, and only finished goods are returned to inventory.

The impact of JIT on information requirements is most clearly seen in the subordinate item master file. Whereas this file is very large and requires a great deal of updating (many transactions) under MRP planning, with JIT this is not the case. Allocations are largely unnecessary; there are no scheduled receipts except for purchase orders; and pegging is just not important within the factory. Inventory transactions for component materials are not done as they move out of inventory. Instead they are made through "backflushing" as finished goods enter inventory. That is, inventories for components are decremented as finished goods are incremented—on the assumption that if a finished good enters inventory, then it should contain the associated components.

Overhead Reductions

The impact that this process has on overhead costs is significant. Transaction costs can be reduced by orders of magnitude. This is nicely seen in the practice of some JIT companies in their partnerships with suppliers. If the suppliers deliver at least daily, and the firm only receives its immediate needs, there again is so little work-in-process inventory that neither company needs to be concerned with it. The supplier can be paid once per week or month, based on the actual production of finished goods. There is no need for shipping papers, receiving procedures, scrap reporting, and debit memos (send any bad ones back!), or many accounting procedures in both firms.

It needs to be pointed out, however, that backflushing carries certain risks and places severe demands on production process reliability. Quality levels have to be high, and bill of material usage numbers have to be *right*, or the backflushing will yield erroneous information. JIT implies both very high quality levels and processes that are working as they should.

Processing frequency becomes an interesting issue under JIT as well. MRP is still required, but only for component parts. Many firms find that the frequency of replanning under JIT goes down. There just is not the need for frequent replanning of the basic purchased part inputs. JIT by its nature is more or less continually planning—with execution following so rapidly that replanning is just not an issue.

Other Changes

Some of the other technical issues of MRP planning become less critical as well. Whether or not one needs bucketless systems is strongly influenced by the relative importance of component part costs. Very expensive component parts that must be ordered from companies that are not in a partnership arrangement may dictate the use of careful planning at the detailed level. On the other hand, if the component costs are not a major item, *or* if a partnership can be established, then the supplier can deliver whatever is required—within the limits of flexibility established in the partnership.

Lot sizes under JIT are essentially lot-for-lot, with the exception of nonpartner supplier lot sizes. When JIT is running right, there are very minor safety stocks, and safety lead times are only for unreliable vendors. Not having any buffers to speak of means that there is no margin for error, but it also means that there is no need to interpret problems in terms of their influence on the buffers. The planning work is completely straightforward, and can be done as part of the basic manufacturing infrastructure—with very limited need for planning staff personnel.

Finally, data base maintenance and transaction processing procedures are vastly different under JIT. If the process itself is right, the emphasis is on routine execution, the planning of requirements is part of the basic system, workers concentrate on execution, and they also take on the lion's share of the detailed material planning as a part of their day-to-day activities.

THE HIDDEN FACTORY

A manufacturing firm can be thought of as comprising two "factories." One makes products and the other (the hidden factory) largely consists of overhead personnel who process transactions on papers and computer systems. Over time, the former factory has been decreasing in relative cost compared with the latter. Hidden factory reduction is a foundation to JIT. The annual survey of manufacturing firms in North America by the Boston University Manufacturing Roundtable has consistently found rising overhead costs to be an important concern of manufacturing managers. A major driver for these costs is transactions.

Transactions

Logistical transactions include ordering, execution, and confirmation of materials moving from one location to another, along with the costs of personnel in receiving, shipping, expediting, data entry, data processing, accounting, and error follow-up. Under JIT, the goal is to eliminate the vast majority of this work and the associated costs. The fundamental concept is that if the flow can be simplified, fast, and guaranteed, then there is no need for paperwork. Of course, achieving this desired state requires a great deal of change in the company and its culture.

A second category, *balancing transactions*, is largely associated with the planning that generates the logistical transactions. Included are production control, purchasing, master production scheduling, forecasting, customer order processing, and data maintenance. In most companies, balancing costs are 10 to 20 percent of the total manufacturing overhead costs. JIT again offers a significant opportunity to sharply reduce these costs, but achieving the savings requires fundamental changes in manufacturing. For example, JIT processes mean that MRP planning can be cut by perhaps 75 to 90 percent in complexity. The concepts can also be extended into vendor scheduling and paperwork systems; vendor firms will no longer have to process their sets of transactions that are paid for in hidden factory costs.

A third category, *quality transactions*, extends far beyond what one normally thinks of as quality control. Included are transactions associated with identification and communication of specifications, certification that other transactions have indeed taken place, and recording of required backup data. Many of the costs of quality identified by Juran and others are largely associated with transactions. Successful JIT, with closer coupling of production and consumption, can provide faster quality monitoring and response capability. But at the same time, it is important to point out that these benefits are only attained after JIT has been successfully implemented.

The term "quality control" itself is a problem. In well-run JIT companies, controls of all kinds are seen as "coping mechanisms" which are there to cope with problems that should not exist. If quality is guaranteed through process design, poka-yoke, and other means, then traditional quality control becomes unnecessary.

Still another category is *change transactions*. This category includes engineering changes and all changes that update planning and control systems, such as routings, bills of material, and material specifications. Engineering change transactions are some of the most expensive of any in the company. A typical engineering change, for example, might require a meeting of people from production control, line management, design engineering, manufacturing engineering, and purchasing. The change has to be approved, scheduled, and monitored for execution. JIT again reduces this source of hidden factory costs. By having only minor amounts of work-in-process, the timing for changes is much easier to coordinate. The workers themselves often take over the details for implementing changes, with minimal need for overhead staff support.

Fundamental Changes

Achieving a significant reduction in the hidden factory requires fundamental changes in the underlying processes used for manufacturing, design of the products themselves, new job or work designs, and new systems for planning and control. We thus see once again the need for an integrated view: PIM is only one part of the solution.

CONCLUDING PRINCIPLES

This chapter describes the nature of the information system design that is required to support the detailed preparation and maintenance of material plans for manufactured and purchased components. It also illustrates the improvements in transaction processing and overhead costs that can be obtained from a just-in-time manufacturing process. Major reductions in manufacturing lead time, improvements in the flow of materials, a decrease in work-in-process inventory, and more highly aggregated material plans all lead to important improvements in the information requirements for control of manufacturing, and the associated costs.

Most importantly, this chapter demonstrates the value of taking an integrated view of product design, manufacturing process design, and the design of information systems for PIM activities. We see the following major concepts or principles coming from this chapter:

- The MRP system for detailed material planning requires a significant investment in information system support to enable realistic detailed material plans to be developed and maintained.
- The development of time-phased MRP material plans requires the close control of shop and inventory transaction processing, and a high level of information accuracy.
- Under just-in-time-based material planning, shop and inventory transactions are dramatically reduced because of the nature of the production process.
- JIT-based material planning requires far less information system support to develop detailed material plans for manufactured and purchased items than does time-phased MRP material planning.
- JIT-based material planning requires an investment in product and process design.

INTEGRATED RESOURCE LINKAGES

The most obvious linkage of the information requirements for detailed material planning is with management information systems, as a primary focus of the chapter is on maintaining the necessary data base to make MRP systems operate effectively. All of the transactions must be understood, and processed correctly, and all errors must be found and corrected quickly. The underlying concept in MRP is to substitute information for inventory; this only works if we have high-quality information.

Information requirements for detailed material planning are also related to the resource area called "manufacturing." The shift from MRP-based planning to JIT approaches for detailed material planning involves the fundamental nature of manufacturing. It is necessary to empower workers, to change attitudes, and to effectively develop a new paradigm for manufacturing. First, one needs to adopt many of the techniques that are collectively called "world-class manufacturing." Increasingly, however, we see firms going beyond these techniques. Many of them are yesterday's game. Tomorrow's game requires world-class manufacturing as the ante to play; winning demands flexibility, responsiveness, and value chain partnerships. One underlying support for these capabilities is very good routine planning for the detailed material requirements.

Efforts in both design engineering and process engineering are required to achieve effective detailed material planning. These efforts include physical changes, such as work place design and product design, as well as information changes such as maintenance of the underlying data base elements.

Information requirements for detailed material planning extend to vendor companies. Purchasing needs to make significant changes in both its internal operations and its connections with supplier firms. Simplified transaction processing is in everyone's interest, because transactions do not add value to the products. Companies that have made the transition from MRP to JIT often find that the next critical step is to develop vendor (or other supply chain) partnerships. In most cases, this involves education of the suppliers and cross-company project teams to find the best opportunities for mutual advantage.

A similar partnership linkage is with sales, marketing, and customers. Partnerships can and should be developed with customers. The issues are almost precisely the same as those in purchasing; the search for mutual advantage is critical, with overall customer benefits at lowest cost the objective. We have found it useful to make a detailed audit inside the company of the linkages with vendors and those with customers— and compare the results. In many cases, one finds new opportunities for improvement. How do the relationships match up? Are there true partnerships? What are the opportunities for improvement?

Links with suppliers and customers also lead to changes in logistics. The means of transportation are often found to be an area for improvement, particularly when JIT deliveries are involved. New approaches to the physical movement of goods are often required, as well as new exchanges of information. All of this has to be carefully integrated with the detailed material planning systems in *all* firms in the value-added chain.

REFERENCES

Green D.R. "Direct Pegging, MRP/JIT Bridge," *Production and Inventory Management Review*, April 1987.

Jenson, Andrew J. "Controlling Material Movement with an Automated Pick-list Subsystem," *Production and Inventory Management* 30, no. 3, (3rd quarter 1989), pp. 35–39.

Miller, J. G., and T. E. Vollmann. "The Hidden Factory." *Harvard Business Review,* September–October 1985, pp. 142–50.

Rao, Ashok, and David Scheraga. "Moving from Manufacturing Resource Planning to Just-In-Time Manufacturing," *Production and Inventory Management Journal* 29 no. 1 (1st quarter 1988), pp. 44–49.

Saunders, C. A., and C. E. Meyer. "MRPII + Repetitive = JIT," *Production and Inventory Management Review*, April 1989.

Sepehri, Mehran, and John Costanz. "MRP/JIT System at GTE,"*Production and Inventory Management Review*, December 1986.

SECTION 6

JUST-IN-TIME

Just-in-time has affected the conduct of manufacturing activities in firms all over the world. The JIT concept is very broad. It includes a philosopy that says that the road to manufacturing effectiveness involves the elimination of all waste in the production process. The JIT philosophy goes considerably beyond PIM with signifigant linkages to other activities in the organization. One cornerstone for JIT in many companies is a major

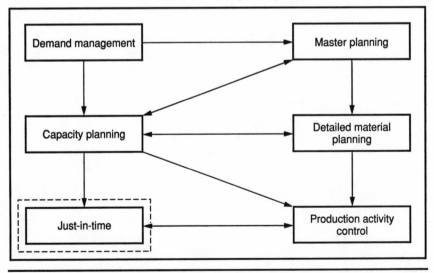

Production and Inventory Management

relayout of the factory. Others are changed jobs throughout the manufacturing organization, new designs, and processes, a host of activities that are beyond PIM. At the same time, JIT uses techniques that have increased the world's vocabulary, including Japanese terms such as *kanban* and *kaizen*.

Implementation of JIT in PIM requires a host of changes as well. Included are level scheduling, "pull systems," simplification, elimination of transaction processing, and a major reduction of the "hidden factory."

To cover the breadth of JIT is impossible in a book this size. Our two primary goals are reflected in the design of Chapters 10 and 11. Chapter 10 deals with the broad organizational and philosophical aspects of JIT, and the integration of JIT with other resource areas. Chapter 11 deals with the more detailed aspects of JIT in PIM.

CHAPTER 10

JUST-IN-TIME AS A COMPANY PHILOSOPHY

Just-in-time encompasses both a philosophy and a set of techniques. The philosophy incorporates a broad set of beliefs about the manner in which manufacturing should be managed, as well as the changes that are required in other company activities to achieve overall best practice. Some aspects of JIT are also embraced by other philosophies or approaches. For example, much of TQM (Total Quality Management) reflects JIT principles, and terms such as "world-class manufacturing" also reflect some of the same ideas.

Our intent in this chapter is not to define the exact "turf" of just-in-time, but to describe the underlying set of philosophical concepts and how they relate to other integrated resource issues.

The chapter is organized around the following seven topics:

- The JIT-based design option: What is the JIT alternative and how does it fit into the company's strategy?

- Building blocks: What are the underpinnings of a JIT program?

- JIT action programs: What are the specific action programs undertaken in various parts of the company to achieve JIT payoffs?

- Company examples: How have major JIT payoffs been achieved in specific company examples?

- JIT extensions: How has JIT been extended to other resource areas of the company?

- Nonrepetitive JIT: How are the concepts of just-in-time being applied in high-velocity production environments?

- Lessons for managers: What are the major issues associated with JIT that need to be understood by general managers?

THE JIT-BASED DESIGN OPTION

A beginning question for JIT-based systems, as is the case for any PIM system, is when is JIT most applicable? What are the market conditions and manufacturing approaches that best lend themselves to just-in-time methods? In the world of manufacturing, with component parts being assembled into subassemblies and end items, there are two fundamental approaches for detailed material planning of factory operations: *time-phased planning,* and *rate-based planning.* Time-phased planning is supported with material requirements planning (MRP) systems, and rate-based planning systems are increasingly using JIT methodologies. Rate-based material planning implementations include repetitive manufacturing, assembly lines, and other flow systems.

Market Requirements for Rate-Based System

Rate-based systems are usually adopted when the market requirements are for a relatively narrow range of standard products (or standard product options), with stable product designs, in high volumes. Rate-based planning implies that the materials move through the factory as a flow rather than in discrete batches that wait long times between successive processing steps. The equipment and layout of facilities are arranged with this flow in mind, where specialized work centers based on equipment commonality are dominant (Berry and Hill).

Strengths and Weaknesses

In general, JIT systems are much more limited than MRP systems in their ability to cope with changes in product mix, volume surges, design modifications, and complex manufacturing process stages. They also do not usually utilize equipment capacities as intensely. On the other hand, JIT-based systems have much lower inventories than MRP-based systems. JIT can sharply reduce detailed processing of transactions, and the underlying philosophy is based on mutual problem solving throughout the stages of procurement, manufacturing, distribution, and consumption.

The Strategic Fit

JIT has been most successfully applied when the products produced have high volumes, market demand without major fluctuations, relatively stable designs, limited variety (at least as far as building the products is concerned), a production process that is under statistical process control, and processing steps that are relatively simple without utilizing very expensive equipment. When these conditions do not hold, most firms find that systems based on material requirements planning provide a better strategic alternative. That is, for example, if the set of products produced tends to be quite unique from one to the next, an MRP system with batch manufacturing is usually the best approach. If great seasonal, cyclical, or random changes in demand exist, a company often finds that it needs non-JIT approaches. If quality problems or other disturbances are a normal part of the manufacturing environment, JIT can make a firm more vulnerable. Similarly, firms with very expensive pieces of equipment often want utilization of that equipment to be high, even if it means building inventories. Having said all this, we will see that some clever firms are beginning to find ways to apply JIT concepts to some of these market areas that traditionally had to be approached with batch manufacturing and MRP planning approaches.

JIT is often adopted by firms that wish to respond to the marketplace with short lead times. In the most common implementations, an overall game plan is agreed upon among marketing, finance, and manufacturing that provides a smooth build rate for some family of end items. Thereafter, as actual customer orders are received, sales and manufacturing attempt to satisfy the customers requirements; they also make decisions as to the exact configuration of products that will be held in inventory in anticipation of future customer orders.

BUILDING BLOCKS

Many definitions of just-in-time have been put forward, and they have been evolving as JIT becomes more globally adopted. Several of the more popular current definitions focus on JIT as an approach to minimizing waste in manufacturing. This focus is so broad as to be of limited use. It helps to subdivide waste into time, energy, material, and errors. JIT foundation concepts all attempt to reduce time, energy, material, paperwork, overhead costs, and errors.

A useful common denominator running through most JIT definitions is a broad philosophy of pursuing zero inventories, zero transactions, and zero "disturbances"; *zero disturbances* means routine execution of schedules, day in and day out, without intervention of staff personnel or other "control" mechanisms. Obviously, this objective is more capable of being achieved in some environments than in others.

Figure 10.1 depicts JIT as having four detailed building blocks: product design, process design, human and organizational elements, and production and inventory management. JIT provides the connecting link for these four areas.

Product Design

Critical integration activities in product design include quality, design for cellular manufacture, and reducing the number of "real" levels in the bill of materials to as few as possible. Some firms say that there should

FIGURE 10.1
Building Blocks For Just-In-Time

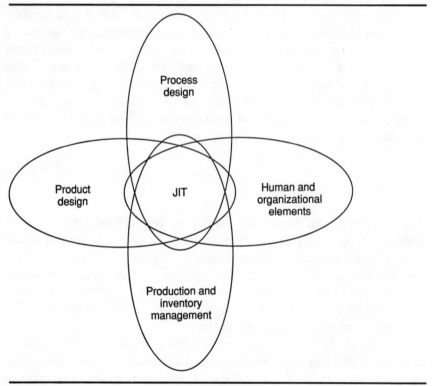

be no more than two or three levels that require MRP planning (levels that exist to depict the engineering design, but are not processed with formal inventory receipt and disbursement, should not be included in this count). By not having more than two or three levels in the bill of materials, materials only have to go into inventory and out again with MRP-based planning once or twice as end products are produced.

The implications for design engineering are significant. Products have to be designed with particular processes and PIM approaches in mind. Product and process design need to be integrated. The data base to support PIM needs to reflect the JIT approach to PIM. New product introduction and subsequent design enhancements are made easier, because there is essentially *no* work-in-process inventory to be considered.

Process Design

Reducing levels in the bill of materials and designing the manufacturing process are closely related. For fewer levels to be practical, the number of product conversion steps included in each processing stage must be increased through process design changes. A related concept in process design is cellular manufacturing. Equipment under cellular manufacturing is positioned to achieve in one pass what might originally have required many routing steps, or even part number changes (assemblies), under more conventional MRP planning and batch manufacturing processes.

An important notion in process design for JIT is expressed in the idea of *band width*. A wide band width process has an ability to take on an ever-greater product mix, as well as some surge capacity to tolerate variations in the overall demand for the products. To the extent that process band width can be widened, PIM becomes more flexible and customer service is enhanced; smaller finished-goods inventory levels can be maintained with the same levels of customer service, and efficiencies in manufacturing are achieved as well. The ultimate objective is to make any order desired by the customer—right behind any other—with minimal disruption and with no need to backlog any order.

Human and Organizational Elements

Human and organizational elements are the third building block for JIT. An aspect of this is the *whole person concept,* which will continually apply training, study, process improvement, and whatever else is needed to eliminate recurring problems. The objective is continual learning and improvement. Human and organizational elements recognize that workers' ranges of capabilities and level of knowledge are often more important assets to the firm than equipment and facilities. Education and cross training are continuing investments in the human asset base. As the asset base's capabilities grow, need for overhead support is reduced and overhead personnel can be redeployed to address other issues.

The whole person concept has an important linkage to band width. Under the whole person concept, workers on production lines do not produce more than the customers request. This implies "idle time," a practice that traditional approaches to manufacturing attempted to avoid. Under JIT, best practice calls for performance to be evaluated by *"maximizing* the idle time." If customer requests can be satisfied in ever-smaller amounts of time, the firm can increase band width—and integrate ever-larger amounts of work traditionally done by staff groups into the basic manufacturing infrastructure.

Linking human and organizational elements with the other building blocks has a significant impact on the operation of the production process and PIM systems. Band width rather than building inventories to utilize direct labor means that surge capacity must be available. Surge capacity in direct labor personnel means that these people will not be fully utilized in direct production activities. In fact, the whole person concept is based on the premise of hiring people, not just their muscles. As a consequence, direct workers are cross-trained to take on many tasks not usually associated with "direct labor." This includes equipment maintenance, education, process improvement, quality control, data entry, and scheduling. From a JIT standpoint, the human and organizational elements building block puts a greater emphasis on scheduling by workers and less on scheduling by a centralized staff function. The entire process is fostered by the inherent JIT push toward simplification. With no defects, zero inventories, no disturbances, and fast throughput, detailed scheduling is easier; moreover, any problems tend to be local in nature and amenable to solution on a decentralized basis.

Production and Inventory Management

The final building block in Figure 10.1 is production and inventory management and its link to JIT. The systems used for master production scheduling, detailed material planning, and execution all have to reflect the JIT approach. The master production schedule (MPS) is typically leveled and rate-based (so many units per day). Detailed material planning is usually only done to determine purchased part and raw material requirements; so little work-in-process inventory is in the system that level-by-level planning is usually unnecessary.

In execution, JIT is completely different than it is under time-phased MRP planning and batch manufacturing operations. There is no formal shop-floor control and no detailed tracking of manufacturing orders. JIT typically utilizes "pull systems" for detailed material flow that restrict work-in-process inventories to minimal levels. With these methods, a work center is only authorized to produce when it has been signaled that there is a need for more material in a downstream work center. In general, this means that no work center is allowed to produce parts just to keep workers or equipment busy. It also means that no work center is allowed to "push" material to a downstream work center. All movements and production are authorized by a signal from a downstream work center when it has a need for component parts. Frequently, it is believed that the pull system creates the benefits in JIT, but the primary payoffs actually come from process improvements and the discipline required to make the system work. The benefits include lot-size reductions, limited work-in-process, hidden factory reduction, fast throughput, and guaranteed quality. None of these is achieved without significant effort.

We see then that JIT has the potential for changing the entire nature of manufacturing planning and inventory control in a company. Figure 10.2 provides a more detailed listing of JIT's building blocks and objectives.

JIT ACTION PROGRAMS

The building blocks of JIT and the expanded list of activities shown in Figure 10.2 imply to many the need to undertake many specific action programs to change manufacturing practices. In this section several of these programs are presented. They primarily address issues in product, process, and human elements of the building blocks and those with a fundamental impact on integrated production and inventory management.

FIGURE 10.2
JIT Objectives and Building Blocks

Ultimate objectives:
- Zero inventory.
- Zero lead time.
- Zero failures.
- Flow process.
- Flexible manufacture.
- Eliminate waste.

Building blocks:
- Product design:
  Few bill of material levels.
  Manufacturability in production cells.
  Achievable quality.
  Appropriate quality.
  Standard parts.
  Modular design.
- Process design
  Setup/lot size reduction.
  Quality improvement.
  Manufacturing cells.
  Limited work-in-process.
  Production band width.
  No stockrooms.
  Service enhancements.
- Human and organizational elements:
  Whole person.
  Cross training/job rotation.
  Flexible labor.
  Continuous improvement.
  Limited direct/indirect distinction.
  Cost accounting/performance measurement.
  Information system changes.
  Leadership/project management.
- Production and inventory management.
  Pull systems.
  Rapid flow times.
  Small container sizes.
  Paperless systems.
  Visual systems.
  Level loading.
  MRP interface.
  Close purchasing/vendor relationships.
  JIT software.
  Reduced production reporting/inventory transaction processing.
  Hidden factory cost reductions.

Product Design

The JIT impact on product design has been remarkable. JIT practice requires that product designs be capable of routine, error-free production with simplified control systems. The development of concurrent engineering design (simultaneous engineering) has greatly enhanced the design of products from a manufacturing point of view. Concurrent engineering design is the process of simultaneously developing a product and the manufacturing process used to produce that product. The work is often undertaken by interdisciplinary teams of experts (including people with direct shop floor experience) in order to get as wide a view of the problems as possible.

One of the criteria used for the concurrent engineering of products is improved *design for manufacturability* (DFM). DFM searches constantly for ways to improve product manufacturing. DFM might involve use of sophisticated equipment, such as automated assembly design or robots, but also includes routine product (and process) simplification. In all DFM projects, an overarching goal is to simplify the process by improving the design, and then to simplify again.

Teams that work on product and process design often extend beyond the firm itself. In addition to technical equipment experts, many DFM teams extend into both vendor and customer factories and engineering staffs. There are often nonmanufacturing people involved, sometimes including focus groups of final customers.

Setup Time Reduction

Just-in-time manufacturing has a goal of achieving a lot size of one unit. That is, any item can be made efficiently behind any other; material velocity will not be slowed by making many items at a time in order to reduce changeover times. To make this a reality, firms have to establish programs to reduce setup times.

Setup time reduction is typically achieved through several physical system changes or projects. The trade-off expressed in the economic lot size (between setup cost and inventory holding cost) is correct; the way to achieve smaller batches is to drive the setup time (and attendant cost) down significantly. This is necessary to make all of the products constantly, rather than in large batches. It is also consistent with reducing inventory levels. Setup times are typically reduced by applying traditional industrial engineering techniques to analyzing the setup process itself. In some firms this activity is carried out by the industrial engineers; increasingly it is done by workers themselves using a video camera. Implied in this approach to setup time reduction is another change in the nature of work done. The emphasis necessarily shifts to continuous improvement.

The results of setup time reduction programs have been impressive. One consultant guarantees his clients a reduction of 75 percent—before "real money" has to be spent. These savings are achieved through simple rearrangements and better planning. The primary technique used to attain these setup time reductions is to turn a video camera on while the machine is being set up, and thereafter examine the tape. In most cases, one finds the machine standing idle for long time periods while workers search for one thing or another.

Changeovers of several hours have been reduced to less than 10 minutes in several reported cases. Examples include changing stamping dies for sheet metal body parts in automobile factories. The goal now being achieved by many firms is expressed by Shigeo Shingo: SMED (single-minute exchange of dies, meaning all changeovers in less than ten minutes).

Total Quality Management

A foundation of JIT has been pursuit of improved quality through process improvement. Most JIT firms have adopted total quality management (TQM) programs that include quality awareness, statistical process control, and many other techniques. In a repetitive manufacturing system, any quality problem will result in a stoppage of the entire flow line unless undesirable buffer inventories are held.

Quality improvement programs have taken many forms, and are largely beyond our present scope. But there is an important point of integration between quality improvement and JIT: Guaranteed quality is a prerequisite for effective JIT operations; JIT identifies and prioritizes quality improvement efforts. For the firm considering JIT, it is essential that quality problems be solved, and that an ongoing program be directed to continuing progress.

In many cases the achievement of the quality levels necessary to support JIT comes through more reliable manufacturing processes—ones that have quality as their underlying premise. Two of these that are critical for JIT are *TPM* and *poka-yoke*. TPM can mean total preventative maintenance and/or total productive maintenance. The underlying focus is to apply the same diligence of product quality approaches to equipment and process quality. Poka-yoke means foolproof operations. The intent is to guarantee quality by building checking operations into processes so that the quality of every part is evaluated as it is created. This also ensures low cost, because the cost of finding defects is lowest when they are found at the same time they are made. Achieving TPM and poka-yoke requires significant investments in process engineering, as well as in new maintenance systems and approaches.

Continuous Improvement

In a JIT program, most people now include continuous improvement as a foundation—and a maxim for day-to-day operations. Every day, each worker should get better in some dimension, such as fewer defects, more output, or fewer stoppages. Continuous improvement, as a cornerstone of JIT, means making thousands of small improvements in methods, processes, and products in a never-ceasing quest for excellence. Most JIT implementations include a strong degree of worker involvement and worker participation. All of this implies a new approach to human resource management, as well as new patterns of supervision on the shop floor. Some people now make a distinction between being a "boss" and being a "coach." Continuous improvement implies learning, and the company that learns faster than its competitors does not need to worry. Every worker needs to constantly seek improvement, linkages need to be improved between sources of knowledge within the company, and worker evaluation needs to reflect the ongoing quest for excellence.

Continuous improvement clearly can exist without JIT. However, it often seems to be more compatible with JIT than with other production and inventory management approaches. In JIT, the workers are more in control of their own working environment than is the case when a heavily centralized planning and control system is in place. Moreover, if the nonmanufacturing time that is inherent in JIT can be used for continuous improvement activities, the rate of improvement can be accelerated. Finally, under JIT, there are more activities undertaken as a basic part of the manufacturing infrastructure—which provides a larger set of targets for continuous improvement.

Cellular Manufacturing

JIT manufacturing is often based on equipment arranged for cellular manufacturing. In cellular manufacturing a dedicated set of machines and workers manufactures some group of parts, subassemblies, or final products. The equipment layout minimizes both travel distances and inventories between machines. Cells are typically U-shaped to increase worker interactions and reduce material handling. Workers are cross-trained to run several of the machines; they also need to be trained in the products to be produced so that minimal instructions are required to shift from one product to another in the cell. An extension of the cellular process is the plant within a plant, where a portion of a factory focuses entirely on one group of products.

In order to make cellular manufacturing a reality, new layouts of equipment are required, a team of workers has to be selected and trained, a "family" of units to be manufactured needs to be selected, equipment and tooling have to be modified so that all items in the family are easily made with minimal changeover times, and all of the equipment has to be well maintained because a breakdown of any machine is a breakdown of the entire cell. All of these changes imply significant efforts on the part of process engineers, and a very different working environment for the workers in the cell.

Transaction Processing

Execution under JIT is based on the premise that orders will move through the factory so quickly that it is not necessary to track their progress with complex control systems. A similar argument holds for purchased items. If they are converted into finished goods within hours or days of receipt, it is unnecessary to put them into stockrooms, pick them, and go through all the details normally associated with receipts from vendors. Instead, the JIT firm can simply pay the vendor for the purchased components in whatever finished products are completed each time period; there will be so little work-in-process that it is not worth either party keeping track of it for purposes of accrual payments.

The concept of updating component inventory records and determining component disbursements as finished goods are received into stock is called *backflushing*. Instead of creating detailed work-in-process accounting systems and paying for all of the associated transaction costs, many

JIT firms use backflushing to reduce component part inventory balances by exploding the bills of material for whatever has been delivered into finished goods.

The JIT approach in execution is focused on simplicity and speed. The intent is to design the manufacturing cells, products, and systems so that materials flow through very routinely. With problems of quality and disturbances largely eliminated, routine execution becomes just that— routine. Simple systems can be employed by shop people without detailed records or the need for extensive overhead staff support.

Implementing simplicity and speed requires high quality (minimal losses), rapid flows, and new mind-sets about "control." Accounting and other functions need to give up the detailed order tracking that produces job order costing; in JIT there are no "jobs." Flow manufacturing is just that—a continuous flow of products.

COMPANY EXAMPLES

In this section, two company examples illustrate the changes required in many company activities, not just those on the factory floor. The first example, IBM's Proprinter factory, illustrates the concurrent engineering design of product and process. The second, NeXT's "fingerless" factory, shows an extraordinary amount of attention to human resource issues.

IBM

IBM set very tough goals for the introduction of the Proprinter, its entry into the low-cost, dot-matrix printer business. Although IBM had a very secure position in the market for high speed, heavy duty printers for the main frames used in corporate data processing departments, its PCs were hooked to printers from other manufacturers in 1982. It was then that IBM decided to try to develop a printer for the PC line.

The market window was estimated to be 30 months, which would require reducing approximately 18 months from the usual development time. The other parameters of the project were equally demanding. The printer had to meet stringent cost objectives, it required reliability standards that would mean that no field service would be necessary, and it needed to be rugged enough to be distributed through new distribution channels. Artemis March reports on how these objectives were achieved.

IBM achieved its goals for the Proprinter project, producing an award-winning design in the process. The printer was brought to market on time, within the cost parameters, and had less than 50 percent of the parts of comparable printers. The success of the effort demanded the use of many JIT principles, primarily those that stem from the product and process design building blocks.

Some of the early decisions were based on design for manufacturability (DFM) concepts. Each major component (print head, power supply, electronics, and so on) was given to a cross-functional design team made up of experts from several functions (product engineering, manufacturing, robotics, and so on). Their task was to ensure that the component could be manufactured within the cost parameters required.

Early in the concurrent engineering activities, the teams concluded that manual assembly would be too costly in the United States. This led them to adopt a design for automated assembly approach to the printer. They also adopted a "no fasteners" ground rule, as robots have inherent problems with screws and other metal fasteners. Competitive products contained 150 to 200 parts, mostly fasteners and parts that move things around. By using plastic and multifunction parts, the total number of parts was reduced to 60 for the Proprinter. The design-to-cost process is illustrated in Figure 10.3.

By decreasing the number of parts, there were many spillover benefits in the reduction of hidden factory costs. Not only were the costs of materials reduced, but also the costs of sourcing, qualification, inspection, storage, production control, scheduling, inventory control, materials handling, and record keeping.

Concurrent engineering had other implications in addition to the design of the product and process; the need for rapidly testing and approving performance led to changes in procedures. The same occurred in the tooling and parts procurement process. The overlapping of functions and increased responsibility at the team level meant a great deal of increased communication, including visits to the vendors' facilities for on-the-spot negotiations and decision making.

The increased risk of the revised and speeded-up procedures was diffused through the use of cross-functional "swat" teams. These teams brought ownership of the design, process, and procedures to the level at which decisions were being made. The key customer-to-company linking

FIGURE 10.3
The Design-To-Cost Process For The IBM Proprinter

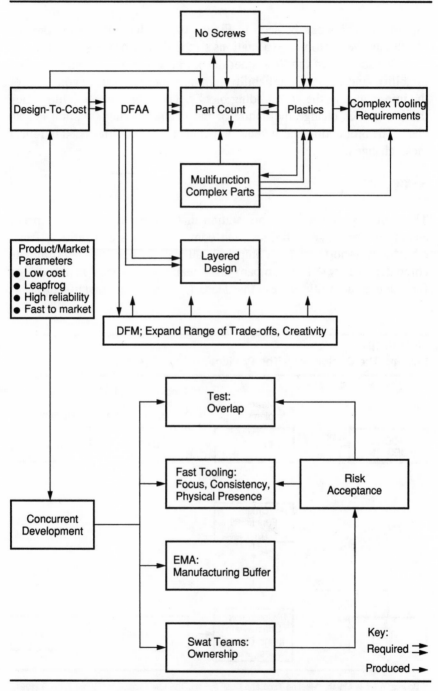

Source: Artemis March, "Meeting Time and Cost Targets: The IBM Proprinter," *Target* 7, no. 3 (1991), pp. 18–24.

role of the teams can be seen in Figure 10.4, which shows the process of relating the customer expectations to the design process.

The success of the Proprinter design in meeting the cost, manufacturability, and customer reliability requirements is a clear indication of the importance of the JIT building blocks. The extensiveness with which these activities change the nature of the manufacturing situation is also clear. The production and inventory management activities need to reflect these changes.

NeXT

The NeXT computer is a work station that combines processing speed, advanced graphics capabilities, and communications capabilities. Patricia Moody reports on the company's attempt to become the "ultimate computer factory." The company uses teams extensively in the design for manufacturability process that leads to "fingerless" manufacturing.

FIGURE 10.4
Relating The Customer To The Product/Process Design Activity

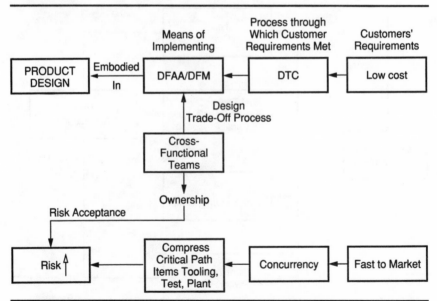

Source: Artemis March, "Meeting Time and Cost Targets: The IBM Proprinter," *Target* 7, no. 3 (1991), pp. 18–24.

The design teams at NeXT are interdisciplinary (purchasing, materials, engineering, and so on) and meet on a weekly schedule to continually improve product and process. The focus on education is high; college degrees are common for production technicians and there are also a high number of advanced degrees in the company.

The functioning of these teams has led to some remarkable performance statistics. Some of the company "benchmarks" are shown in Figure 10.5. The company stresses time to market in the design process and has mounted an effort to reduce the nonproduction times in their order-to-delivery cycle.

According to Moody, at NeXT you will not see any of the following: tubs of integrated circuits waiting for insertion by rows of bench workers; racks of completed boards; piles of rework boards; warehouses; paper shortage lists, reject tags, work orders; expediters; or fingers. Perhaps the most impressive achievement of all, though, is that Sony buys monitor boards from NeXT for less than it can from its Japanese subcontractor.

FIGURE 10.5
Some Performance Statistics From The NeXT Factory

Benchmarks

New product design to rollout:	nine months
Board redesign to production:	one week
Part count:	220
Suppliers:	60
Yields:	
Complete systems, first time power-up	80–95 percent
Surface mount solder joint failures	4–6 parts per million
First-time turn-on board yields in test	90–95 percent
Cycle times:	
Complete system	1 hour
Board assembly	20 minutes
Scrap	$70–80 per month
Lot size	1
Employee turnover	2 percent
Total employees	480
Manufacturing only	55 (11 percent)

Source: P.E. Moody, "NeXT Computer, the Ultimate Computer Factory," *Target* 7, no. 1 (Spring 1991), pps. 25–31.

JIT EXTENSIONS

As JIT is adopted in more and more companies, the applications of JIT concepts are extended to an increasing number of situations. JIT is best seen as an integrated approach to achieving continuing manufacturing excellence. A holistic view of JIT encompasses a set of programs, as well as a process in which human resources are continually redeployed in better ways to serve company objectives in the marketplace. In this section, we consider some additional implications of JIT in terms of linkages with other integrated resource management areas.

Purchasing

JIT has been applied and misapplied in purchasing. Some firms simply demand JIT deliveries in a way that can only be satisfied by the suppliers holding buffer inventories. On the other hand, when done well, a joint approach can lead to greater bottom-line results for both firms and increased competitiveness in the marketplace.

The first prerequisite to JIT in purchasing is a scheduling system that produces requirements that are reasonably certain. Without predictability, JIT for vendors is merely a case of customers exporting their problems to their vendors. Although this may work in the short run, in the long run it cannot. We have seen a factory in which JIT virtues were extolled, only to find a new paving project—for vendors' trucks! Inventory had been effectively moved from the warehouse to trailer trucks. Similar war stories abound about warehousing firms in Detroit that are there to buffer suppliers from demands made on them by auto companies as they implement JIT.

JIT requires an integrated production and inventory management system that supports execution in short time frames. Because this will also be needed in the vendor factories, it makes sense that the basics of JIT first be implemented in the customer factories. It is only by having the firsthand experiences that customers know how to properly communicate with vendors. As a firm becomes used to JIT operations itself, it will produce the right set of signals for implementation with vendors. The firm will also pick up the language and understanding of how to solve problems. When people in the firm can truly view inventory as covering up problems, understand the whole person concept, adopt a true zero defects mentality and know what that implies, and adopt a fanatical drive toward continually improved performance, they can be much more effective in extending JIT into vendor firms.

With this understanding, communications with vendor firms will be fundamentally different than without it. Vendors can learn by observing JIT firsthand in their customer's factory. Talking to counterparts at a detailed level is critically important. Instead of exporting problems, with an internally functional JIT program, the customer now accepts joint responsibility for problem solving. Vendor and customer learn together; both are willing to change ways they do business in order to achieve the overall benefits that JIT offers.

Another requirement of JIT for purchasing is to achieve, to whatever extent possible, a stable schedule. This is consistent with level schedules for the repetitive manufacturer. To the extent that the firm makes the same products every day in the same quantities, without defects and without missing the schedule, a supplier firm's schedule is extremely simple. For the nonrepetitive manufacturer, the issue is not leveling as much as it is no surprises. The level schedule may be violated in nonrepetitive environments, but the cost is a greater need for coordinated information flows and *perhaps* for larger buffer inventories. However, there is a big difference between a *stable* (albeit nonlevel) schedule and one that is simply uncertain. The only cure for the latter case is buffer inventories.

Certainty is a relative commodity. A vendor might be able to live fairly well with a schedule that is unpredictable on a daily basis but very predictable on a weekly basis. A weekly MRP-based total, with some kind of daily call-off of exact requirements, could be reasonably effective. In fact, some firms have developed "electronic kanbans" for this purpose.

Other "basics" for JIT in purchasing include the objectives and building blocks discussed earlier in the chapter. These are necessary both inside the customer plant and for the vendors. Setup time reduction, error-free production, statistical process control, no work-in-process tracking, worker involvement, cellular manufacturing, cross training of workers, and all the issues associated with product design, process design, human and organizational elements, and production and inventory management systems must be actively pursued. Pursuing them on a joint basis and sharing experiences will only improve the speed at which true JIT gets implemented.

A JIT "basic" uniquely associated with purchasing relates to pruning the number of vendors. It follows that, if the customer firm is to work closely with supplier firms, it is important to limit the number of suppliers. Many companies have reduced their vendor base by more than 90 percent to achieve an environment in which it is possible to work on a truly cooperative basis with the remaining vendors.

Hidden factory issues have to be considered in vendor relations as well. Some successful JIT firms use blanket orders for their vendors, with MRP to provide weekly quantities and agreed-upon safety stocks. Thereafter, a daily phone call or electric kanban to the supplier for the next day's in-shipment is all that is needed. All of this could be done without intervention of indirect labor personnel.

A computer disk drive manufacturer has a system in which, each day at about 4 P.M., an assembly line worker calls a key vendor and tells them how many of a particular expensive item to deliver the day after tomorrow. The units are delivered directly to the line, without passing through a stockroom or being fed into any inventory records. They are not inspected, and are assembled into finished products the same day they are received. The vendor is paid based on receipts of finished goods into inventory (backflushing). Stability is supported by the customer providing the vendor with weekly MRP records indicating the expected quantities well into the future, with time fences that define guarantees to the vendor.

Another issue relating to frequent deliveries is the cost of transportation. Some firms have approached this by asking vendors to build factories in near proximity. Although this is possible for very large companies, where a plant's output is largely dedicated to one customer, this clearly is not possible for most vendors.

A different solution is for the customer to pick up goods from vendors on some prearranged schedule. This is done for several reasons. The most obvious is the potential savings in transportation costs over having each vendor deliver independently. A second reason relates to stability and predictability. If the customer picks up the material, some of the uncertainty inherent in vendor deliveries can be eliminated. Finally, pickup offers more chances to directly attack hidden factory costs. The customer can, for example, provide containers that hold the desired amounts and that will flow as kanbans through the plant. Savings in packaging materials, costs of unpacking, and disposal costs for packing materials are also avoided. Items can also be placed on special racks in the customer trucks to minimize damage. Defective items can be returned easily for replacement without the usual costly return-to-vendor procedures and paperwork. Other paperwork can similarly be simplified when third parties are not involved and when the loop is closed between problem and action in a short time frame.

Pickup can also be done in geographic areas beyond the factory. A Hewlett-Packard factory in Boise, Idaho, has shipments from its suppliers in Silicon Valley (about 600 miles away) pooled by a trucking firm, and thereafter moved to Boise on a daily basis. New United Motor Manufacturing Inc. (NUMMI) in Freemont, California, does the same thing with its Midwest suppliers; a Chicago-based trucking company collects loads for daily piggyback shipments to California, about 2,000 miles away. NUMMI started off holding a three-day safety stock of these parts, with plans to reduce it to one day after experience had been gained.

The primary lesson to be learned in JIT purchasing is to not shift the burden for holding inventory from the customer to the supplier. At an early point in its JIT efforts, Xerox made this error. When the consequences became known, emphasis shifted to joint problem identification and solution, a need for stabilized schedules, a true partnership, and help for Xerox suppliers to implement JIT in *their* suppliers. The results for Xerox have been most impressive: overcoming a 40 percent cost disadvantage, reducing its worldwide vendor base from 5,000 to 300, and winning several awards for excellence in manufacturing.

Another lesson is to keep the relationship with the vendors simple, and to strive for even greater simplicity and transparency. Harley-Davidson made the mistake of attempting to tie up its vendors with complex legal documents in an environment where schedules were always being expedited and deexpedited. Again, joint problem solving was implemented, simple agreements were put in place, and a spirit of mutual trust was developed. Harley-Davidson has also achieved extraordinary results. The same company that was being forced out of business by Japanese competition has now come back to be a strong competitor, known for high-quality products and widely recognized as a great turnaround example.

Accounting and Performance Measurement

The firm adopting JIT in its fullest context will need to think very carefully about reward systems and managerial scorekeeping. Traditional measurement systems tend to focus attention on costs associated with producing the products, using cost accounting systems that have changed little since the industrial revolution. These systems were instituted in an era when direct labor was the products' major cost source. Now in many companies, material costs dominate and direct labor cost is continually decreasing.

More and more firms are providing a bundle of "service-enhanced" goods and services, including logistical support, fast response, rapid design changes, and hidden factory reductions. In most cases, these services are provided with knowledge work, rather than by the usual definitions of direct labor work.

JIT focuses on material velocity, which is consistent with inventory reduction and lead time compression. Achieving these objectives incurs "costs"; but we need to be very careful about how these costs are measured and the resultant implications for decision making. The values of band width, flexibility, responsiveness, and worker skill enhancement are not incorporated into traditional cost accounting systems.

The implementation of JIT creates many problems and opportunities in terms of its interactions with cost accounting. In an MRP system, the process of opening, monitoring, and closing shop orders can provide extremely accurate information for a job order cost accounting system, as well as inventory data so accurate that physical inventory no longer needs to be taken. The cost of this accuracy is all the detailed transaction processing that is borne as a cost of running a company with MRP.

In just-in-time systems, these transactions are eliminated. The result at first appears to be a degradation of cost accounting at the expense of JIT, but this does not have to be the case. In a well-run JIT company, inventories of work-in-process should be considered to be either zero or some relatively small constant. The relative importance of any error in this assumption will be insignificant. Furthermore, the cost of materials used is simply the cost of goods purchased—if JIT purchasing is in place. This assumption is true for almost any accounting period one wishes to consider, but the magnitude of the error is potentially greater for very short time periods (e.g., days).

A similar redefinition of traditional accounting occurs when the "whole person" concept is considered. To what account does the accountant charge the time of "direct labor" workers when they are not producing products? Does it make sense to keep track of their time in traditional ways? Hewlett-Packard has given up the category of direct labor in some of its factories, and so have some other leading edge firms. The companies just employ *people*—sometimes they make products and sometimes they do other things. If the people do the right things, the company will be successful.

The potential implications for cost accounting are profound. Those accountants who hold to traditional definitions of product costs and period cost determination will find their jobs difficult and frustrating. On the other hand, those who see their role as helping the firm to isolate the key activities or drivers of costs—to help make decisions that are directionally correct, and that understand how the financial stewardship position can be accurate without being precise—will be able to accomplish the usual accounting tasks with much less effort; their talents can be used for in-depth analysis of what *really* matters to the long-term health of the organization.

Information Systems

Because JIT requires changes in the ways manufacturing is managed and executed, changes are also required in how computer-based systems are designed to support manufacturing. The changes run counter to many existing approaches to the use of computers, and present new opportunities for integrated problem solving.

JIT calls for reducing the number of transactions and the size of the hidden factory. This means that large centralized computer systems will tend to be used less than local systems to work on particular problems seen at that time by the particular user groups. To the extent that JIT is used for nonrepetitive manufacturing, personal computers—perhaps with MRP-based software—may be used by people on the shop floor to provide whatever detailed scheduling information is required. Increased band width in product mix can be supported by being able to plan and control more complex product structures on the shop floor.

The whole person concept also supports this trend. Shop people can and will learn how to use spreadsheet programs and other user-friendly computer software. Moreover, if we accept the goal of continuous improvement, much of the improvement will come from more creative uses of computer power—with the needs determined by shop floor users.

A fundamental change in this use of computer systems is the *discarding* of existing systems. Under traditional practices, systems tend to be designed, implemented, and used in perpetuity. But under the concept of continuous improvement, if a detailed statistical process control

(SPC) program were needed to solve a quality problem, it would be constructed and implemented by the users. Later, perhaps the process is improved so much that quality is not a problem. At that point, the SPC program should be abandoned and the users should go on to the next set of problems.

The implications of this change in computer usage are profound for computer specialists. Their role needs to shift from providing software in response to user requests to empowering the users to make ever-greater use of computer power. Additionally, they need to continually "prospect" for new computer packages that the users might be able to apply, determine the minimal set of information that has to be maintained on a centralized basis, and encourage the users to concentrate on problems rather than esoteric solutions—the answer is not another computer department in every user group!

Human Resource Management

The whole person concept can only be achieved when the human resource management (HRM) philosophy is consistent with its basic tenants. The HRM function needs to see the employees as the most important asset in the company, and development of their talents as critical to the future prosperity of the organization. Constant education and training, new performance metrics, better teamwork on improvement projects, elimination of hidden factory and other nonvalue-adding activities, and an air of constant ferment need to be supported by the human resource activity. Just-in-time methods of manufacture and the JIT philosophy are consistent with these needs; the visual successes achieved through JIT go a long way toward fostering commitment to a more enlightened HRM activity.

Distribution

The extensions of just-in-time manufacturing to distribution are considerable. As JIT reduces lead time and the company becomes more responsive to the vagaries of the marketplace, distribution needs to serve less as a buffer and more as an information conduit. As JIT moves manufacturing more toward a make-to-order environment, the demands on distribution change. As increased band width is developed, the company must learn to deal routinely with changing customer demands and conditions. Distribution systems, including customer support functions, need to be changed in order to capitalize on this capability. Fewer people, less routine transaction processing, and more direct linkages with customers and suppliers, based on an atmosphere of joint problem identification and solution, should be the results.

NONREPETITIVE JIT

Many JIT principles that we have described for high-volume repetitive manufacturing apply in high-variety production environments as well. However, most of these manufacturers have balked at two basic problems presented by the "classical" approaches to JIT: (1) the requirement of setting up high-volume flow lines dedicated to a few products, and (2) level loading. A merging may be taking place because, even for the classical repetitive manufacturer, it is increasingly important to respond to customer pressures for greater flexibility in volume, product mix, and other service features. High-volume repetitive manufacturers are necessarily learning to cope with greater product variety; the lower-volume high-variety manufacturers are in turn learning to adapt JIT to their batch manufacturing environments.

A Service-Enhanced View of Manufacturing

An examination of service operations can provide insights that are particularly germane to producing products with greater service enhancements. By service enhancements, we mean the additional items that make up the "bundle of goods and services" that customers purchase to solve their problems. Included are customization, special packaging, software, field service, joint engineering, and any other attributes that can be provided to better satisfy the customers. Service operations have limited ability to buffer customer demand with inventories, because the customer is typically more closely involved in the actual service creation process. Rapid response is critical, and the number of possible product and service combinations continues to grow, so end item forecasting is more difficult and large buffer inventories are not acceptable. Customers are more actively involved in product and service definition, particularly when we take into account logistical coupling of firms as vendor and customer.

All of this argues for a JIT mode of manufacture in which the factory is able to accept any customer order and turn it out right behind any other, and can have the flexibility to handle surges in volume or mix changes. But this has to be done on a routine basis. Once again, service operations provide an example. McDonald's can handle two unexpected bus loads of Boy Scouts or an unexpected shift from Big Macs to fish sandwiches without resorting to a "panic mode" of operation. Manufacturing firms, however, tend to call in the indirect labor "shock troops" and overpower the formal system whenever a significant unexpected event comes along.

Fast-food operations also provide another good service example. Most successful chains have seen an evolution toward a broader product line (one of the two greater band width attributes). McDonald's now serves chicken salad and other food items, for example. The objective is to increase market appeal while maintaining maximum responsiveness, minimal inventories, small lot sizes, and short lead times.

The traditional JIT view of level loading also changes in adapting to nonrepetitive situations. Responsiveness to fickle demand requires a larger band width in terms of surge capacity. For example, no one wants the fire department to be operated at high capacity utilization; immediate response is essential. Surge capacity must be in place in both equipment and labor. When carrying these ideas into nonrepetitive manufacturing, a different view of asset management and labor utilization is required. Fixed assets (both capital and labor) will be less intensely utilized to increase material velocity and overall system responsiveness. This necessitates a new view of human resource management, as well as changes in traditional uses of financial metrics for evaluating manufacturing performance.

Labor capacity has to be available to handle surges. To the extent that the whole person concept is achieved, cross training and other investments in personnel development can be focused on better ability to handle surges and more useful application of "excess" time to other enterprise objectives. More and more work now handled by staff personnel can and should be handled by people traditionally considered to be direct labor. In fact, the distinction between "direct/blue collars" and "indirect/white collars" is being abandoned in leading edge companies.

Capital utilization has to be reexamined in light of overall objectives. An example is found in a large electronics firm with two factories making similar products. In one factory, automatic insertion equipment was purchased that operated close to its capacity. The other plant purchased considerably more insertion capacity relative to expected needs. The first plant initially thought it had done a superior job because it was using capital assets more intensely. After several months, however, plant managers changed their minds. They now see the equipment as relatively inexpensive, compared with an ability to respond to surges brought on by changes in requirements. By having "excess" capacity in equipment and people, changes in schedules and design are more easily handled; that is, the increased band width was well worth any extra cost. Routine execution is achieved without leveling, inventories, or use of complex systems in a rapidly changing manufacturing environment.

Flexible Systems

Leading edge firms are coming to understand requirements for volume and product flexibility. Some have had experience in repetitive manufacturing applications of JIT and are now moving into nonrepetitive applications. An example is a telecommunications equipment manufacturer that began JIT in its high-volume telephone handset operations. The firm only made six models; in two years its inventory turns were tripled, work-in-process was reduced by 75 percent, failure rates in manufacturing were cut in half, and setup times fell 50 percent. Thereafter the firm turned to its low-volume CBX plant, where more than 150 basic circuit boards were manufactured and every end item was somewhat of a custom order. The company learned that it must go back to the basics of JIT—product engineering, process engineering, and the whole person—to successfully implement JIT for its nonrepetitive products.

The firm developed cellular product designs, began cellular manufacturing with great flexibility, and cross-trained people with an emphasis on being able to handle volume surges in the CBX plant. MRP was still used for overall planning, but fewer transactions were processed by the hidden factory of indirect labor. In the first six months, first-pass yields on circuit boards improved 27 percent, work-in-process fell 31 percent, manufacturing cells under JIT hit 100 percent of schedule, and the people helped other parts of the company that were behind schedule.

Simplified Systems and Routine Execution

A major issue in any JIT firm, repetitive or nonrepetitive, is flow times. Work must flow through the factory so quickly that detailed tracking is not required. A related idea is the system's responsiveness. In several JIT systems we have seen in nonrepetitive environments, the firm installed what might be called a *weekly wash*. In its simplest form, weekly wash means that this week's sales orders become next week's production schedule.

As an example, Stanley Hardware in New Britain, Connecticut, is a make-to-stock firm for most of its items, but some are unique to a particular customer. It has applied JIT with the weekly wash concept to three different production areas. In each case, weekly sales (withdrawals from inventory) for a particular week were determined on Friday, and the resultant quantities were manufactured the next week within some change parameters. In one case, the week-to-week variation in production could be plus or minus 20 percent. For a second product group, the swing was plus or minus 35 percent, and for a third group of products any adjustment could be handled. Because response times have been shortened, customer service has been enhanced and finished-goods inventory levels have been significantly reduced.

Products must be manufacturable in this time frame, and manufacturing processes must have the necessary band width to take on required volume and mix changes for this approach to work. At Stanley this was easier for some product lines than for others. We noted differences among the three production area's ability to take week-to-week output variations; this is the band width concept applied to volume. Band width as applied to product diversity was also different across the three lines. In one case, there were fewer than a dozen end items. For another, end item possibilities were about two dozen. However, the third product group encompassed several hundred items. Moreover, the mix among end items varied significantly from week to week, making this the most difficult line to design for product mix band width.

Sometimes required flexibility in volume and mix was provided by product design; other times it was provided by the processing unit's inherent flexibility. Creative use of people also supported the weekly wash at Stanley Hardware. For example, when they are not required to make products, personnel in one department are utilized in packaging some other items. A large amount of hardware packaging is done at Stanley, and required equipment is not expensive. Having extra equipment available for these workers enhances flexibility.

The weekly wash approach to JIT for nonrepetitive manufacturing shifts the emphasis from scheduling material to scheduling time blocks.

The focus is on what is required in the next time frame rather than on when we will make product X. This focus is driven by the actual requirements, rather than a forecast of needs. It is as though we were scheduling a set of trains or buses. We do not hold the train until it is full and we can always cram a few more people into a car, within reason. By scheduling trains on a relatively frequent basis, attempting to keep capacity as flexible as possible, and only assigning "passengers" to a time frame, responsiveness to actual demand can be increased and detailed scheduling can be made more simple.

LESSONS FOR MANAGERS

In this section, we recap some of the ideas presented in the chapter in the form of lessons for managers. In particular, we present the most important ideas that the nonspecialist in production and inventory management should try to retain. That is, in the last analysis, we address the reader's question: "So what?"

JIT Is Not for Everyone

Too often in the press one gets the impression that JIT is a logical progression, that one logically arrives at JIT after first implementing other approaches, and that the result is always wonderful: inventories and lead times reduced by 90 percent, dramatic improvements in customer service, and so on. This is just not the case. There are many manufacturing companies that are well advised to *not* pursue JIT. If the products are complex, if they tend to be unique, if the equipment is very expensive, if quality problems are endemic, if seasonality of demand is strong—all of these conditions call for non-JIT approaches. Many Japanese companies are now actively implementing not JIT, but MRP. Why? Because the companies are moving into more complex products, such as machine tools and earth-moving equipment, instead of large-volume consumer electronics. The market-place increasingly dictates that Japanese firms move to products with higher value added, giving up commodity products to countries with lower wage costs. The systems for production and inventory management *must* reflect the new marketplace requirements.

Continuous Improvement—In What?

Just-in-time is founded on the principle of continuous improvement. But as evolution takes place, the improvement can and should shift to new horizons. The first cut at continuous improvement is in terms of factory operations. Improvements in cost, quality, and inventory performance are seen as important. The second cut often focuses on service to markets. Improved customer service is followed by shifting to "solving customer problems" as the basic objective in manufacturing. A final cut is in the deployment of the overhead personnel. All nonvalue-adding work is highlighted and reduced. New jobs are defined and created. The culture in the company is changed dramatically. The key point is that evolution needs to be evaluated with an ever-changing and more critical yardstick.

Implementation Requirements

JIT requires a change in mind-sets throughout the organization. On the factory floor, JIT typically requires a redeployment of overhead personnel from staff groups in offices to employees dedicated to a particular cell or line. Many firms find that making an industrial engineer part of a work team provides an excellent focus for continuous improvement. Other staff personnel also work more closely with the line, with a resultant blurring of responsibilities. Included are scheduling and inventory control activities, purchasing and order release for vendors, preventative maintenance, and any clerical activities that support manufacturing.

Achieving these changes requires development of a new culture in manufacturing. Overhead redeployment and new job definitions throughout the company are required. This type of change can be difficult, particularly if some people see it as a diminution of their status. It is particularly helpful if the results achieved through the changes are widely disseminated, with appropriate kudos for those who have made it a reality.

As JIT applications increase in the company, and as the basic philosophy becomes widely adopted, it is critical for top management to strongly identify with it. This is particulary true in supporting the linkages that cross traditional organizational boundaries. A strong commitment from the top of the company makes all the difference in the speed with which continuous improvement takes place.

CONCLUDING PRINCIPLES

This chapter describes the basic philosophical underpinnings of JIT. Included are the ways in which JIT needs to support a company's approach to the marketplace, the basic building blocks for JIT, the action programs that are needed to achieve JIT, examples of JIT, the links to other functions of the company, applying JIT principles to the nonrepetitive manufacturing situation, and some lessons for managers. In summarizing this chapter, we see the following principles as important:

- JIT systems are particularly useful for firms that need to respond to the marketplace with short lead times.
- JIT production is most compatible with high volume, stable demand, and limited product variety.
- JIT manufacturing attempts to institute a "zero disturbances" approach, with minimal transaction processing.
- Concurrent design and process engineering facilitate JIT.
- JIT manufacturing supports important improvements in nonmanufacturing functions of the business.
- To achieve JIT benefits in nonrepetitive applications, some basic features of repetitive-based JIT must be modified.
- JIT is *not* for everyone.

INTEGRATED RESOURCE LINKAGES

Several major linkages were described at length in the chapter, and will not be reexamined here. Perhaps the most fundamental linkage of JIT is with manufacturing strategy. Just-in-time manufacturing requires many changes in operation and, more importantly, in mind-sets. So JIT adoption is most compatible with a manufacturing strategy that focuses on time-based competition, very fast material velocity, and continued development of working skills as the keys to the marketplace. It is less compatible with companies in which large investments in equipment dictate their use at high utilization rates, labor costs are a high percentage of total costs, or product obsolescence is not a major factor.

JIT is also consistent with a philosophy of total quality management. The "no disturbance" feature of just-in-time mandates very high levels of quality. There is simply no "slack" in the system to allow for poor quality.

Just-in-time manufacturing is best achieved when the products and processes are designed for JIT in the first place. It is much harder to implant JIT for existing products with existing processes.

In the last analysis JIT is a philosophy that has a profound inpact on human resource management. The basic principle is that workers can learn—continuously—and that this learning will represent a very significant asset to the business.

REFERENCES

Berry, W. L., and T. J. Hill, "Linking Systems to Strategy," *International Journal of Operations and Production Management* 12, no. 10, 1992.

Brooks, Roger. "Backflush with Caution." *Oliver Wight Newsletter.* Essex Junction, Vt.: Oliver Wight Companies, 1986.

Chapman, S. N. "Schedule Stability and the Implementation of Just-in-Time." *Production and Inventory Management* 31, no. 3 (3rd quarter 1990), pp. 66–70.

Gelb, Tom. "Harley-Davidson: A Company That's Taking a Different Route." *Target* 9 (October 1985).

Goddard, Walter. *Just-in-Time: Surviving by Breaking Tradition.* Essex Junction. Oliver Wight, Ltd., 1986.

Hall, R. W. *Driving the Productivity Machine.* Falls Church, Va.: American Production and Inventory Control Society, 1981.

———. *Zero Inventories.* Homewood, Ill.: Dow Jones-Irwin, 1983.

Hall, R. W.; H.T. Johnson; and P.B.B. Turney. *Measuring Up: Charting Pathways to Manufacturing Excellence.* Homewood, Ill.: Business One Irwin, 1990.

Karmarkar, Uday S. "Getting Control of Just-in-Time." *Harvard Business Review,* September–October 1989, pp. 122–31.

March, A. "Meeting Time and Cost Targets : The IBM Proprinter," *Target* 7, no. 3 (Special Issue, 1991), pp. 18–24.

Miller, J. G., and T. E. Vollmann. "The Hidden Factory." *Harvard Business Review,* September–October 1985, pp. 141–50.

Moody, P.E. "NeXt Computer, the Ultimate Computer Factory," *Target* 7, no. 1 (Spring 1991), pp. 25–31.

Shingo, Shigeo. *A Revolution in Manufacturing: The SMED System*. Cambridge, Mass.: Productivity Press, 1985.

Suzaki, Kiroshi. *The New Manufacturing Challenge: Techniques for Continuous Improvement*. New York: Free Press, 1987.

Voss, C. A., and L. Okazaki-Ward. "The Transfer and Adaptation of JIT-Manufacturing Practices by Japanese Companies in the U.K." *Operations Management Review* 7, nos. 3 and 4 (1990).

CHAPTER 11

JUST-IN-TIME AND PRODUCTION & INVENTORY MANAGEMENT

In this chapter the aspects of JIT that are most closely associated with integrated production and inventory management are discussed. Several basic techniques of JIT will be described, including level scheduling, pull systems, and kanbans as well as examples of practice. The broad nature of JIT as a philosophy and the action programs needed in various areas of the company serve as the background within which these issues are discussed.

The chapter is organized around the following four topics:

- Basic JIT techniques: How do level scheduling and pull systems work?

- JIT applications: How does JIT work in practice and how is it tailored to meet different needs?

- Implementation: What does it take to get just-in-time into a company on a sustainable basis?

- A comprehensive JIT perspective: What is the role of JIT as a philosophy, as a set of techniques, and as a linking mechanism?

BASIC JIT TECHNIQUES

In this section, two fundamental techniques for material flow under JIT are described: level scheduling and pull inventory systems. These two techniques have a profound impact on the way that PIM activities are carried out.

Level Scheduling

Level scheduling in the extreme means that the same models are made in the same quantities every day, and perhaps even every hour. This concept is consistent with viewing JIT manufacturing as a flow rather than as a set of discrete steps with waiting between those steps. For level scheduling to be most effective, the rate of demand for final products also needs to be relatively level.

Complicating the issue is the question of product mix. That is, a JIT line often makes several different end products on the same line. This requires a "mixed model" schedule. The most common approach to mixed model scheduling is to try, as much as possible, to make every product every day. In this way the workers are always familiar with the products being produced, without major learning or other changeover costs.

In some firms—for example, those selling seasonal products such as lawn mowers—a level schedule over the entire year would result in very high finished-goods inventories. Moreover, if there is a large number of end items (made from a significant number of common parts), the finished-goods inventories are highly likely to be in the wrong product configurations. For this reason, many of these firms establish different level schedules for various times in the year. This approach has major implications for the rest of the factory and for other PIM activities. In some cases, the entire plant is scheduled at different output levels during different parts of the year. In other situations, high-cost equipment is utilized more uniformly, building inventories of certain components which are thereafter assembled at different rates during the year. Similar coordination problems often have to be worked out with suppliers.

However level scheduling is finally established, it is usually a result of strong integrative efforts among manufacturing, marketing, and finance. A balance needs to be struck among utilization of fixed assets, marketplace requirements, and inventory holding costs. Because the trends are toward increasing levels of uncertainty in demand, the balance has been shifting away from fixed asset utilization toward developing an ever more responsive manufacturing activity.

Pull Systems

A second material flow technique in JIT is "pull-based" systems. The fundamental idea is that there is a finite inventory allowed between successive steps in manufacturing, and no one is allowed to build components if the inventory downstream from their work place is at the maximum level. This is called a pull system because the work at each step is initiated by the removal of inventory from a downstream location. That is, the flow of work in the factory is pulled from the final product end, not pushed from the raw material/component beginning.

A variety of signals for starting production have been developed— all of which are triggered by downstream actions. What is interesting about these techniques for implementing a pull system is that workers will not always be fully utilized in making products. If the downstream inventory area is full, the workers cannot make more product. They have to either do nothing or do something else in lieu of making products.

And what do the workers *do* when they have no authorization to produce? This "idle time" is a source of debate in many companies. The answer is found in the whole person concept. Workers give first priority to filling downstream material requests, but at other times engage in quality control, maintenance, scheduling, training, or whatever will enhance the long-run effectiveness of the manufacturing system.

Making pull systems a reality almost always requires a new physical layout of facilities, including carefully designated areas for work-in-process inventories. Most importantly, however, new mind-sets for job design and performance evaluation are required. A major goal in JIT is material velocity; moving materials through manufacturing is more important than achieving high worker utilization in the classic definition of direct labor utilization. Under JIT, the task of workers is to build products and build them quickly, not to "absorb overhead."

The signals for communicating downstream work center demand vary widely. They include rolling a colored golf ball from a downstream work center to its supplying work center when it wants parts; yelling, "Hey, we need some more"; sending an empty container back to be filled; and using cards (kanbans) to say that more components are needed. A widely used technique is to paint a space on the floor between the two work centers that holds a specified amount of parts. When the space is empty, the producing work center is authorized to produce materials to fill it. The consuming work center takes material out of the space as they need it; this typically occurs when the space authorizing its output is empty.

What all of these approaches have in common is a limitation on when and how much can be produced. If special containers are used, it is only possible to produce when a container has been emptied. If a space on the floor holds four boxes of parts, more can only be made when less than four boxes are in the space. If kanban cards are used, the production is similarly restricted by the number of cards. The greater the size of the space on the floor, number of containers, or kanban cards, the greater the autonomy that is achieved between the work centers. But in good JIT practice, the attempt is always to *reduce* the buffers between work centers so that inherent problems of balance and other issues become very visible.

The use of kanbans is worthy of further explanation. Although cellular manufacturing is often used in JIT, this is not always the case. Some JIT companies, such as automobile factories, have very complex flows between work centers that are arranged as one would expect in batch manufacturing; that is, all the punch presses together. In these cases, the flows of materials are often coordinated through kanban systems.

A single-card kanban system is illustrated in Figure 11.1 in which three work centers (A,B,and C) produce component parts that are consumed by three assembly work centers (X,Y,and Z). Also shown in Figure 11.1 is an intermediate storage area for component parts. A single component (part 101) is fabricated in work center C and used by work centers Y and Z. To illustrate how the system works, suppose that work center Z wishes to assemble a product requiring component 101. A box of part 101 would be moved from the storage area to work center Z. As the box was removed from storage, the accompanying kanban card would be removed from the box; shortly thereafter, the card would be placed in the card rack at work center C. The cards in the rack at any one time represent the authorized production for that work center.

JIT APPLICATIONS

Toyota is the classic JIT company in that it has gone further than any other discrete manufacturing firm in terms of truly making the production process into a continuous flow. Much of the basic terminology and philosophy of JIT have their origins at Toyota. A key issue in JIT at Toyota is understanding that automobile manufacturing is done in large factories. They use relatively simple systems based on visual control of parts movements, but there are greater complexities than in our simplified examples.

FIGURE 11.1
Single Kanban System

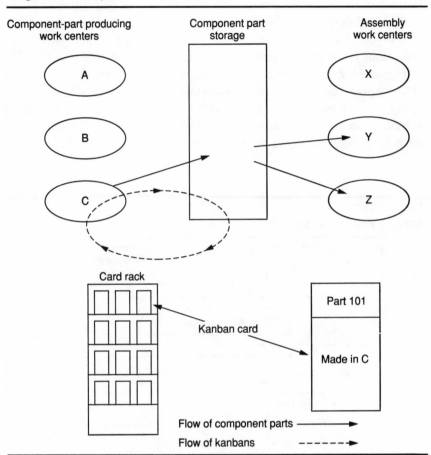

If Toyota is the classic Japanese example of JIT application, Hewlett-Packard is probably the U.S. company best known for their use of JIT. Let us now turn to these two examples.

Toyota

The benefits of the Toyota production system are seen on the highways of the world. By virtually any yardstick, Toyota is truly a great manufacturing company. For example, Toyota turns its inventories 10 times as fast as U.S. and European car manufacturers, and about 50 percent faster than its Japanese competitors. It is also very competitive in price, quality, and delivery performance.

Figure 11.2 shows the Toyota production system and where JIT fits within the overall approach. To some extent, the role given to JIT in Figure 11.2 may appear less encompassing than just described. For example, the "elimination of unnecessaries" is seen as fundamental. All of the fundamentals and building blocks for JIT listed in Figure 10.2 are in basic agreement with those in Figure 11.2, and the box for production methods is basically the same as process design in Figure 10.2. A linkage

FIGURE 11.2
Toyota's Production System

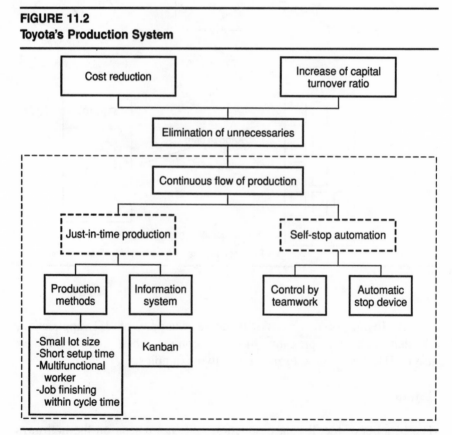

Source: European Working Group for Production Planning and Inventory Control, Lausanne, Switzerland, July, 1982

included under this heading is the multifunction worker, which matches several aspects of the human and organizational element building block. Also included is "job finishing within cycle time"; this is consistent with the dominance of material flow velocity and the subservient goal of direct labor utilization.

The Toyota view of just-in-time production shown in Figure 11.2 includes "information system," with "Kanban" below it. The information system encompasses the production and inventory management activities necessary to support JIT execution. Kanban is the Toyota technique for controlling material flows. The situation at Toyota is much more complex than that illustrated in the single-card kanban system example. Toyota has intermediate storage after production of components and additional intermediate storage in front of assembly work centers. This means that the materials flow from a producing work center into an inventory, then to another inventory, and then to the next work center.

Toyota uses a two-card kanban system to manage this complexity. The first is a transport or conveyance card, which moves containers of parts from one stock location to another. The second is a production card, which authorizes production. An example of the two cards, both for the same part number, is shown in Figure 11.3. Figure 11.4 shows the flow of the kanban cards and the resultant "pull" approach to authorizing production. The two-card system is more complicated than the one-card kanban system in Figure 11.1 because there are many more inventory locations and parts, and more work centers where parts are produced and consumed.

Starting at the right side of Figure 11.4, work center K123 decides to make one container (50 pieces) of some part number that requires part 33311-3501 as a component part. (It did so because a production kanban has been received in the K123 Box). Someone at work center K123 then removed a container of part number 33311-3501 from stock location A-12. When this container is removed from stock location A-12, a conveyance kanban is taken from the container (the top half of Figure 11.3) and placed in the A-12 Box. It authorizes someone to go to stock location A-07 and get a replacement container of part 33311-3501 to put in inventory at stock location A-12 (with the conveyance card). This container, while at stock location A-07, would have a production kanban attached (the lower half of Figure 11.3). This production kanban is removed before the container is moved to stock location A-12, and is placed in the A-07 Box. It then flows to the Y321 Box, where it becomes the authorization for work center Y321 to remove the two containers of

FIGURE 11.3
Kanban Cards

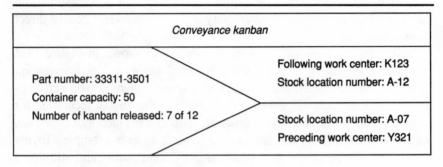

Conveyance kanban

Part number: 33311-3501
Container capacity: 50
Number of kanban released: 7 of 12

Following work center: K123
Stock location number: A-12

Stock location number: A-07
Preceding work center: Y321

Production kanban

Work center number: Y321
Part number to be produced: 33311-3501
Container capacity: 50 units
Stock capacity at which to store: A-07
Materials required:
Material number 33311-3504
Stock location: A-05
Part number 33825-2474
Stock location: B-03

Source: R. W. Hall, *Driving the Productivity Machine: Production Plans and Control in Japan* (Falls Church, Va: American Production and Inventory Control Society, 1981) p. 37. Reprinted with permission, American Production and Inventory Control Society, Inc.

indicated components from their respective input stock locations. These locations are not shown in Figure 11.4, but the production kanban tells us that, to make 50 units of part number 33311-3501, work center Y321 needs material 33311-3504 (location A-05) and part number 33825-2474 (location B-03). In each of these locations, we would find containers with exactly enough material to make 50 pieces of part 33311-3501.

The kanban cards replace all work orders, move tickets, and other shop floor paperwork. To the extent that work-in-process is significantly reduced, the problem of sequencing jobs at work centers is also diminished. The system is visual and manual in execution, and the chain of dual kanban cards can extend all the way to the suppliers. Several of Toyota's suppliers receive their authorizations to produce via kanban cards. In some cases, the "kanbans" are delivered electronically.

FIGURE 11.4
Flow of Kanban Cards

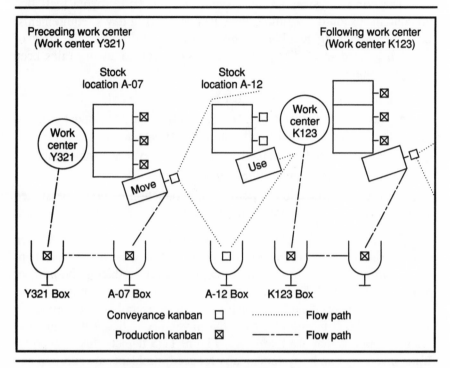

Source: R. W. Hall, *Driving the Productivity Machine: Production Planning and Control in Japan* (Falls Church, Va.: American Production and Inventory Control Society, 1981), p. 38.

The kanban system is a pull system because the work centers are only authorized to produce when they have a production kanban. They only get one when a downstream work center pulls a completed container of work from the producing work center's output storage area. No work center is allowed to process input to output merely to keep workers busy, nor is a work center allowed to transport (push) work to a downstream work center. All movements are pulled, and workers are paced by the flow of kanban cards.

The number of kanban card sets in the system directly determines the level of work-in-process inventory. The more cards, the more containers to be filled and waiting to be used at a work center. Note that the conveyance kanban in Figure 11.3 is numbered the seventh of 12 conveyance kanbans for that particular part and conveyance sequence. More kanbans allow greater independence between work centers, at the expense of higher inventories and less visibility in seeing inherent coordination problems between work centers.

The container sizes are kept small and standard; Toyota feels that no container should hold more than 10 percent of a day's requirements. Because everything revolves around these containers and the flow of cards, a great deal of discipline is necessary. The following rules keep the system operating:

- Each container of parts must have a kanban card.
- The parts are always pulled. The using department must come to the producing department, and not vice versa.
- No parts may be obtained without a conveyance kanban card.
- All containers contain their standard quantities.
- No extra production is permitted. Production can only be started upon receipt of a production kanban card.

These rules keep the factory floor under control. The execution effort is directed toward flawless following of the rules, and toward continuous improvement. In kanban terms, this means reducing the number of kanban cards and thereby reducing the work-in-process inventory. Reducing the number of cards is consistent with an overall view of inventory as undesirable. It is said at Toyota that inventory is like water that covers up problems that are like rocks. Figure 11.5 depicts this viewpoint. If the inventory can be systematically reduced, problems are exposed and

FIGURE 11.5
Toyota's View of Inventory

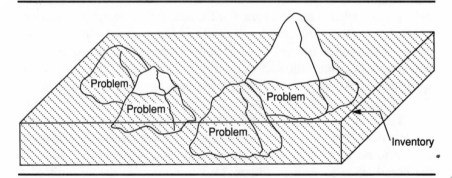

attention can be directed toward their solution. Problems obscured by inventory still remain.

Exposing the rocks is consistent with continuous improvement. The overriding objective is always to find new sources of improvement. When a problem is exposed, actions are taken to eliminate the problem and its underlying causes. The quality maxim of "a defect is a gem" is also operative. Whenever any anomaly occurs, the *major* issue is not to solve the immediate problem, but to discover how this anomaly was possible and find the means to eliminate its recurrence. The "whole person" concept provides the wherewithal for continuous improvement. When no pull signal exists, the workers are "idle," but this time is spent on continuous improvement. Thoughts are also directed to continuous improvement during actual production. No one is allowed to park a brain at the door!

Figure 11.2 shows "continuous flow of production" as hierarchically above just-in-time production. At Toyota, a great deal of care is put into achieving level production rates. Production is planned with a one-year horizon, and is updated monthly. The final assembly schedule is frozen for one month, and the daily schedule is identical for each day in the month in terms of basic models. Such stability is critical to using the kanban system with minimal inventory levels.

The stabilized schedule is also very useful for capacity planning purposes, both for Toyota and for its vendors. The plant is run as much as possible as a continuous flow. Cycle times are easily determined, and problem areas from a capacity point of view can be isolated.

Not everything at Toyota is controlled via kanban cards. Engines, for example, are planned somewhat differently because there are too many varieties. If done with the standard kanban card approach, it would be necessary to have at least one engine of every variety at both the final assembly station and at the engine assembly output storage area. The number of engine possibilities, as well as their physical size, make this unwieldy. Instead, the final assembly schedule is transmitted to the engine assembly area for its own scheduling. The schedule only needs to be frozen for several hours, because the engine assembly line can assemble the exact engine in a short time. The sequence of cars on the line is determined several hours before the engines are put into the cars.

The same approach, often called *broadcasting* of the final assembly sequence, is used to schedule all items having many options. In some cases, such as for seats, this schedule is electronically transmitted to vendors as the cars are started down the line; the vendors respond within hours, delivering seats in the exact sequence needed before the cars reach the seat assembly point. At the Nissan plant in Tennessee, for example, vendor trucks are loaded in the right sequence for final assembly, based on approximately four deliveries per hour. Neither Nissan nor the vendor retains inventories of seats; there is no extra movement of seats, and damage is minimized.

It is useful to note that this broadcasting approach is not a "pull" system with highly visible signals, as described above. But that does not mean that it is not JIT. The key determinants of a just-in-time system are whether individual work centers are forbidden to utilize capacity ("to keep busy") without being driven by a specific end item schedule, the elimination of the hidden factory, the speed with which material moves through the factory, and the focus on continuous improvement.

Hewlett-Packard

Hewlett-Packard (HP) was an early adopter of JIT manufacturing in the United States, and is regarded by many authorities as a leading edge JIT company. JIT has been implemented in many of its factories, including the Medical Instruments Division in Waltham, Massachusetts. JIT is being used for assembling two major patient monitoring products, which are internally called Pogo and Clover. Figure 11.6 shows the assembly area layout for these products. Clover is the older, more expensive product, with a larger number of customer-specified options. Pogo was designed as a lower-cost alternative with JIT manufacturing in mind. The Clover assembly process consists of four feeder subassemblies (A to D) and a final assembly and test area (E). Pogo is designed to be built in four successive assembly stations in a U shape, with a test performed in each. A final test is performed at station V. Both Clover and Pogo go into a heat test area, shown at the top of Figure 11.6. The series of tests performed on Pogo at each station (I through IV) has allowed HP to reduce the failure rate in heat testing more rapidly than is the case for Clover.

Both Clover and Pogo are supported by dedicated component stock areas. Each is also supported with a printed circuit board stock. In Pogo's case, 12 types of circuit boards are maintained with a single-card kanban approach. They are supplied in lot sizes of four, with a coded clothespin acting as the single-card kanban. On the other hand, the printed circuit

FIGURE 11.6
Hewlett-Packard Waltham Division Pogo/Clover Production "U"s

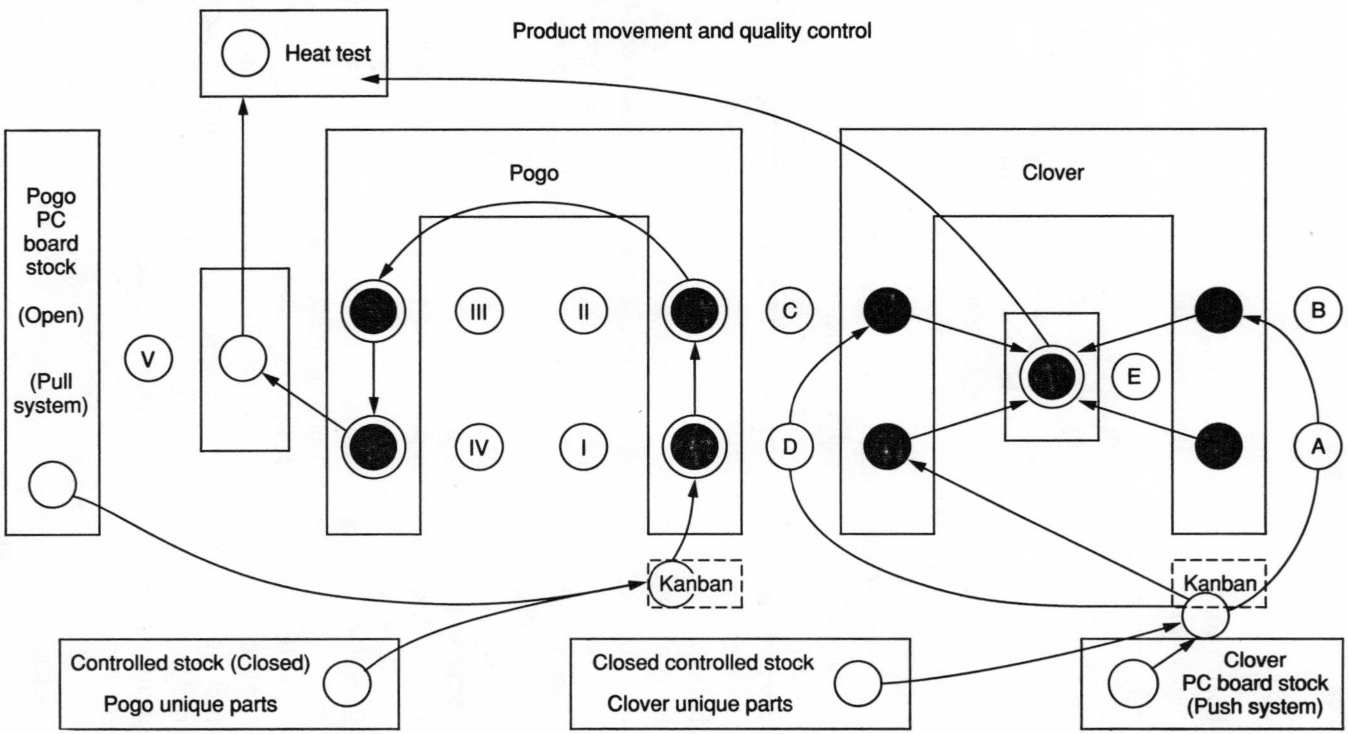

boards for Clover are maintained with traditional MRP approaches and much larger lot sizes. Both Pogo and Clover use a single-card kanban approach to pull kits of parts from the controlled stock areas.

The overall JIT philosophy at HP Waltham has been to concentrate on stability, predictability, and continuous improvement. In Pogo, for example, the original goal was to make 10 perfect units every day. Once this goal was achieved, the team went on to make 10 perfect units between 8 A.M. and 1:30 P.M. on most days. The last three hours of the day were thereafter devoted to continuous improvement and whole person activities.

Initially, the uniform output rate was buffered with finished-goods inventory levels, and defective materials were buffered with extra component stocks. But "lowering the water level" has taken place, and the assembly area can now produce 15 flawless units on a particular day if necessary. The result is a reduced need for finished-goods inventory buffers. Determining the causes for component part failures naturally leads to increased yields, and a reduction in component stock buffers.

As productivity rises, new alternatives are presented. For example, perhaps a rebalance of the Pogo line tasks can free up the first worker so that stock picking can be done by the line rather than by separate stockroom personnel. Increased cross training reduces the impact of absenteeism and fosters job rotation. JIT results at HP Waltham are impressive: Total plant inventory fell from $56 million to $40 million in 15 months. Work-in-process for the Pogo line was reduced from 40 units to 4, and the assembly floor space decreased by 65 percent. Quality increased substantially as well. But there is always more to be done, and the spirit of continuous improvement prevails.

HP Waltham manufacturing has been supported by several corporatewide computer systems, primarily for component-part planning. As time goes by, however, these systems are being replaced because semimonthly MRP explosions, weekly allocation quantities, and daily release against these allocation quantities are not compatible with JIT time frames for execution.

Hewlett-Packard now has a just-in-time manufacturing software package which they use internally as well as market with their HP computer systems. Figure 11.7 depicts key blocks of HP's JIT-based manufacturing system. Rate-based production scheduling is used for the master production schedule. A monthly plan is converted into a daily build schedule with a spreadsheet program and a personal computer

FIGURE 11.7
Block Diagram of HP's JIT Software

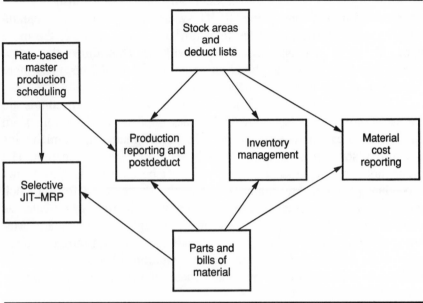

(PC). The resultant schedule is matched against backlogs of customer orders and forecasted sales, and problems highlighted by the program can lead a master scheduler to make changes to the daily build schedule. The software is designed so that data from the PC can be directly transferred to the HP JIT programs.

Stock area and deduct lists define the manufacturing process. A *stock area* is where any part is to be found; a *deduct list* is the set of parts (and quantities) to be decremented from their respective stock areas when a particular stage of product assembly (a deduct point) has been achieved. "Achievement" is transmitted to the system by production reporting. Deduct points in the process are those steps at which parts are to be associated with a higher-level assembly and no longer as individual parts. When production at a deduct point has been realized, backflushing of the component inventories (according to the deduct list) is done. In the HP software, this can occur at more than one stage in the assembly process. A deduct list is associated with each assembly for which a deduct point backflush is specified. The list also specifies from which stock areas deductions are to be made. The sum of all deducts has to equal the overall bill of material for the end item. By allowing deducts to occur at several stages, rather than only once when finished goods are received into inventory, the HP JIT system allows for an incremental adoption of JIT. The longer the total time for manufacturing, the more appealing more than one deduct point will be. This allows the actual inventories to be closer to the book inventories. As JIT becomes more pervasive, deduct points can be selectively eliminated.

Production reporting and postdeduct (backflushing) procedures are the subsystem shown in Figure 11.7 to accomplish the deductions from each stock area's inventory balance. Inventory management maintains the current status of inventories in each designated storage location. The numbers, however, are not precisely correct because of the postdeduct procedure's timing. Any material that is already removed from a stock area but has not yet reached a deduct point will incorrectly be treated as on hand at the location by the inventory management subsystem. Material costs reporting summarizes materials consumption during defined accounting periods, subject to the same limitations of postdeduct. These errors are small (and constant) when material velocity is high and the schedules are fairly level.

Selective JIT-MRP means that the HP JIT software can be integrated with an HP MRP package. Shared data bases can be used in both systems, and bills of material can be linked. Parts common to both systems are integrated in the HP MRP package, with the JIT-driven requirements treated as independent demand. Some products can be planned fully with MRP, whereas others can utilize JIT approaches. This means that JIT can be a steady evolution from MRP.

We can see how this works by returning to the example depicted in Figure 11.6. Concentrating on the Pogo example, let us suppose that this product was originally built as five separate subassembly and test steps (I to V), going into inventory at each step, and was planned and controlled with MRP at each stage of assembly or test. For each discrete step the prior assembly would be picked from inventory, along with the unique components associated with each particular subassembly stage. Withdrawals of subassemblies and component parts would be deducted from on-hand inventory balances as they occurred, as required for MRP record accuracy.

Under HP JIT, the entire flow might be considered one step from I to V; that is, the deduct point would be when step V is completed. This is the only step that needs to be reported through production reporting.

When this occurs, a deduct list would have all of the components required from steps I through V; all would be deducted at that point from the on-hand balance data associated with the Pogo printed circuit board stock and the controlled stock area for unique Pogo parts. We also noted that the printed circuit boards for Pogo were controlled with a JIT system. This means that receipt of boards into this area would also be a deduct point. When production reporting reports that particular circuit boards have reached the Pogo printed circuit board stock area, the deduct lists for the board components will decrement the respective parts and their appropriate locations.

If the inventory of printed circuit boards is reduced to some very small amount, it may make sense to then eliminate production reporting for circuit boards. The deduct list for Pogos at stage V can then include the circuit board components as well. The key point here is material velocity and predictability. If board components are flawlessly put into finished units in short time frames, there is no need to keep track of boards as a separate entity.

Parts and bills of material in HP JIT are the equivalent of the usual product structure files in MRP, but they are defined according to deduct points. The JIT-based product structures have only a few "real" levels, where each level corresponds to a deduct point and the components are the deduct list. Standard cost data are associated with the product structures in this JIT format. As products are converted to JIT from MRP, it is necessary to reformat the data according to the deduct points.

IMPLEMENTATION

Descriptions of JIT tend either to sound too good to be true or to cause wonder that anyone would ever do it otherwise. Both views are shortsighted. JIT will only work for certain kinds of manufacturing/marketplace combinations, and JIT requires many *fundamental* changes in the company—both within manufacturing and in linkage areas. In this section, we describe in more detail how JIT is carried out, and some of the major changes required.

Orchestration

Implementation of JIT almost always requires someone at a fairly high level in the company to become its champion. When this is not the case—that is, when implementation is started in a specialty area of the company—before long the basic philosophical issues come up. For example, implementation of JIT in one area of a factory will always lead to a certain amount of idle time for the workers in that area. This in turn often leads to a confrontation with systems based on the premise that workers should be kept busy at all times. Resolution of the conflict usually requires a high-level understanding of the inherent benefits, and an increased level of commitment from the top.

Most successful JIT implementations have been led by a group of individuals who can see the overall benefit potential, who understand why the fundamentals and building block concepts are required, who appreciate the necessary cultural changes required, and who have the determination to successfully implement the program. This group or project team in turn needs to be supported by senior managers who will provide the necessary resources and the rewards for success.

Progress toward implementation, both for JIT action plans and the JIT philosophy, needs to be monitored—in fact, to be orchestrated. Best-practice companies are never satisfied with their results. Any given level of success is only a platform for undertaking the next step in the ongoing quest for excellence. Orchestration requires monitoring, benchmarking against other efforts, seeking new directions and ideas, and continual striving for greater learning.

Commitment

JIT implementation requires more than leadership. The entire company needs to buy into the concepts, the philosophy, the techniques, and the changes in mind-sets. Just-in-time is based on empowerment of workers to constantly seek continuous improvement. It also embraces a continuous evolution in the work performed. Static definitions of jobs and job content need to be deliberately discarded. The classic relations of "bosses" and "underlings" needs to be replaced with one of cooperation. Those most capable at all levels become "coaches."

A COMPREHENSIVE JIT PERSPECTIVE

Just-in-time encompasses a great deal more than PIM. We have stressed two major aspects of JIT, as a philosophy for fundamental improvement and as a detailed set of PIM techniques. In the last analysis, JIT is both—and it provides a key linking mechanism for many other integrated resource efforts.

JIT as a Philosophy

The philosophical dimension of JIT leads to a vision of continuous improvement and the learning organization. There is a significant reduction in hierarchical relationships, and the cellular groups are empowered to move forward at a much faster pace than is the case under traditional work organizational forms (the job shop). The distinction between white collars and blue is diminished. The manufacturing infrastructure on the shop floor is much better able to deal with ongoing problems (and new ones!). The focus of attention is on reducing waste in all its forms and in solving fundamental problems, rather than wrestling with problem symptoms.

The concept of inventory covering up problems, as water covers rocks, is another philosophical underpinning to JIT; rather than hiding problems, they are to be exposed and eliminated. The hidden factory of paperwork and transactions is a *major* issue in JIT; it is the middle part of the iceberg, of which the tip is inventory reduction. The *base* of the iceberg is new models for how a manufacturing organization should function and a culture to support these new models.

JIT as a Set of Techniques

JIT requires many changes in manufacturing methods. Included are new arrangements of physical facilities, new equipment, methods for level scheduling, modifications to reduce changeover times, kanban and other methods to control the physical flow of materials through the factory, determination of "product families" that can be manufactured in cells, new performance metrics to evaluate operations under JIT, computer software systems that support JIT, and integration with suppliers. Many JIT implementation programs are represented by projects for achieving each of these activities.

The amount of work involved should not be underestimated. JIT is much more than a set of ideas; in order to achieve state-of-the-art JIT status in manufacturing, a significant investment in time and money is often required.

CONCLUDING PRINCIPLES

This chapter is devoted to the PIM techniques associated with JIT. Included are level scheduling, pull systems, kanban cards, continuous improvement using the whole person concept, JIT software, and the essential features of implementation. The following principles emerge from the chapter:

- Stabilizing and in some cases leveling the production schedules are prerequisites to effective JIT systems.
- Workers should be focused on building products quickly, not be kept busy by building inventories.
- Kanban is only one part of an effective system.
- Implementing the whole person concept reduces distinctions between white- and blue-collar workers.
- When material velocity is high, backflushing can be used to minimize transactions, with minimal reductions in inventory accuracy.
- JIT implementation requires top management commitment and a change in company mind-sets.

INTEGRATED RESOURCE LINKAGES

Just-in-time operations in a manufacturing company require many important linkages with activities traditionally performed in other functions. At the same time, JIT enables and invigorates these activities. The physical changes in manufacturing require significant efforts on the part of the manufacturing engineering group. But the work of manufacturing engineers becomes more appreciated, and the results are seen as critical in achieving critical company objectives.

A similar linkage takes place with marketing; competitive pressures and customer dictates are often the impetus for adopting JIT, and JIT operations provide a competitive weapon for capturing markets and winning orders. A very similar connection can be seen with vendors. JIT allows the customer to respond to its marketplace requirements, but requires closer integration with vendor operations. The connection with quality is more straightforward: flawless quality is required for JIT, and defects under JIT highlight necessary quality remediations.

Another critical linkage of just-in-time is with process engineering. Setup times must be reduced, processes must be capable of flawless execution, and workers must be able to operate the processes—typically, each worker can perform several operations. Moreover, the PIM aspects of JIT must be transparent, easily comprehensible, and foolproof.

Facilities maintenance also plays a big role in JIT manufacturing. The equipment must *not* be subject to breakdown except under very rare circumstances. This means that the processes themselves must be of a robust design, and the maintenance of equipment must be well designed and executed. Most successful JIT operations are not run on a 24 hour, 7-day week basis. At least one time period is usually set aside for preventive maintenance. The maintenance activity itself is also carefully designed; the term TPM is often used. Sometimes it refers to "total preventive maintenance," and other times it means "total productive maintenance."

Detailed execution of just-in-time systems still requires a change in mind-sets and attention to a different approach to human resource management. Continuous improvement does not happen by itself; workers must be encouraged to *never* be satisfied with the status quo. This attitude has to come from the top of the organization and not be a passing fad.

REFERENCES

Boccard, R. R. "A Paperless Manufacturing Environment is Possible." *APICS* 1, no. 6 (Dec. 1991), pp. 34–37.

Crosby, Philip B. *Quality Is Free: The Art of Making Quality Certain*. New York: McGraw-Hill, 1979.

Goddard, Walter. "Just-in-Time Needs Shop Floor Control." *Modern Materials Handling,* May 7, 1984.

Krajewski, L. J.; B. E. King; L. P. Ritzman; and D. S. Wong. "Kanban, MRP and Shaping the Manufacturing Environment." *Management Science* 33, no. 1 (January 1987), pp. 39–57.

Labach, E. J. "Faster, Better, and Cheaper," *Target* 7, no. 5 (Winter 1991), pp. 42–44.

Monden, Y. *Toyota Production System*. Norcross, Ga.: Institute of Industrial Engineers Press, 1983.

Monden, Yasuhiro. "Adaptable Kanban System Helps Toyota Maintain Just-in-Time Production." *Journal of Industrial Engineering,* May 1981, pp. 29–46.

Nakane, J., and R. W. Hall. "Management Specs for Stockless Production." *Harvard Business Review,* May–June 1983, pp. 84–91.

Ohno, Taiichi. *Toyota Production System: Beyond Large-Scale Production.* Cambridge, Mass.: Productivity Press, 1988.

Schonberger, Richard J. *Japanese Manufacturing Techniques: Nine Hidden Lessons in Simplicity.* New York: Free Press, 1982.

SECTION 7

PRODUCTION ACTIVITY CONTROL

Production activity control (PAC) addresses the most detailed aspects of manufacturing, managing the step by step manufacture of each component, subassembly, and product through manufacturing. This requires a great deal of information so that manufacturing people know where the

Production and Inventory Management

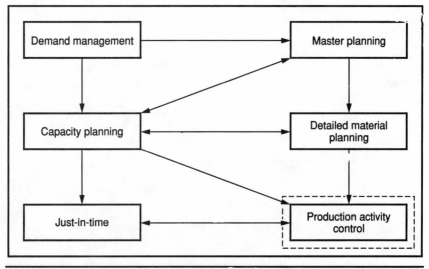

product is, where it is go to next, what steps are to be performed, when they should be performed, and the priorities for parts at different steps in manufacturing. In addition, PAC needs to provide status information to other production and inventory management activities, as well as to other parts of the company, such as customer order servicing.

Chapter 12, the only chapter in this section, presents the basic concepts required for effective production activity control in batch manufacturing, with emphasis on establishing basic priorities for jobs on the shop floor. These priorities indicate the order in which the jobs will be processed. There are a number of criteria involved in making the priority decision, including concern for equipment utilization, customer service, and overtime or other manufacturing costs. Many of these criteria are conflicting. Therefore, management needs a basic understanding of the trade-offs and implications of the choices to make informed decisions. Chapter 12 also presents the analogs to shop-floor scheduling that take place in vendor scheduling systems.

CHAPTER 12

PRODUCTION ACTIVITY CONTROL BASICS

Production activity control is concerned with the management of all the individual steps of the manufacturing process. Production activity control (PAC) addresses detailed scheduling and control of individual jobs at work centers on the shop floor, and vendor scheduling. This is where execution of the detailed plans takes place. The chapter describes basic concepts of production activity control, for batch manufacturing, from the planning and release of individual orders to closing out their completion. It is concerned with monitoring and controlling orders in the factory and with outside vendors.

This chapter will examine the aspects of PAC that are concerned with scheduling, monitoring, and managing shop orders for batches of material. Some of these topics are known as *shop-floor control*. Other aspects of PAC relate to JIT and recent developments in technology, but our emphasis here will be on shop-floor scheduling activities.

An effective production activity control system can ensure meeting the company's customer service goals. A PAC system can also reduce work-in-process inventories and lead times as well as improve vendor performance. A key element of an effective PAC system is feedback on shop and supplier performance against plan. This loop-closing aspect of PAC provides signals for revising plans if necessary.

The chapter is composed of five topics:

- The production activity control framework: Where does PAC fit into integrated production and inventory management and what is the perspective of this chapter?
- Basic production activity control concepts: What are the basic concepts of PAC?

- Production activity control examples: What basic concepts and approaches are used for shop-floor and vendor scheduling and control?
- Production activity control linkages: How does PAC relate to other activities in PIM, and other company activities?
- Lessons for managers: How does a modern PAC system differ from current practices, and where are we going?

THE PRODUCTION ACTIVITY CONTROL
FRAMEWORK

Production activity control (PAC) is the most detailed of production and inventory management processes. It is concerned with the execution of the plans made in the other PIM processes. PAC activities take place within the capacity established by capacity planning and operate on the plans produced by the detailed material planning activity. PAC is connected to each of these, as seen in Figure 12.1.

The relationships in Figure 12.1 are important to understanding the basic material presented in this chapter. The perspective of the chapter is that of a batch manufacturing company that releases orders to the shop floor from a material requirements planning (MRP) based detailed material planning process, presuming *infinite capacity*. The capacity levels are planned and managed through the capacity planning function. The PAC concepts described here relate to setting the priorities for the shop orders that will use that capacity, and the purchase orders that use vendor capacities.

Some details of the PIM system relationships are shown in Figure 12.1. The detailed material planning process produces time-phased MRP records, and the capacity planning process produces the capacity plans for shop scheduling. The MRP records are converted to shop orders and released within the plant and, through purchasing, into released purchase orders to vendors.

The orders are managed on the shop floor in the shop scheduling system. The vendor scheduling and follow-up systems similarly monitor progress of the purchase orders. Both of these systems provide order status of information back to detailed material planning in order to keep material plans current.

FIGURE 12.1
Key Linkages of Production Activity Control

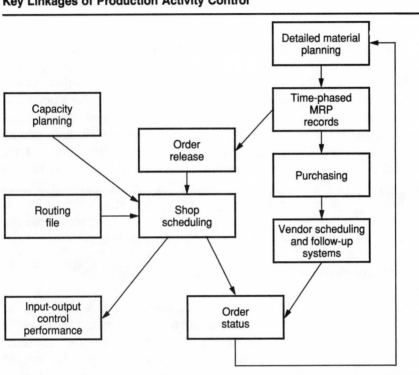

Capacity planning provides input to shop scheduling according to the expected requirements for each work center. Input-output control monitors actual results achieved in shop scheduling.

Vendor scheduling and follow-up is also an activity within production activity control. Here, the emphasis is on scheduling "the outside shop." In purchasing, *procurement* is seen as a professional activity by which information networks, relationships, terms, and conditions are established with vendor companies outside of PAC, whereas release of individual orders and follow-up activities are a part of PAC.

The extension of production activity control to vendor scheduling and follow-up is accentuated by the growing use of computers on the shop floor and *electronic data interchange (EDI)* with vendors. As more and more traditional staff work is integrated into the basic manufacturing infrastructure, it will expand PAC as well.

BASIC PRODUCTION ACTIVITY CONTROL CONCEPTS

This section begins by describing basic concepts of production activity control for batch manufacturing with an MRP system. It covers priorities, loading of a particular job onto a machine center, elements of lead time, and data inputs. It then examines two approaches to shop-floor control (SFC). The first, *Gantt charts,* provide graphic understanding of the shop-floor scheduling problem; moreover, Gantt chart models can be used in manual shop-floor scheduling systems. The second approach is based on *priority sequencing rules* for jobs at a work center. We next look at vendor scheduling, where the concepts are applied to supplier operations. To close the section, we comment on lead time management.

Basic Shop-Floor Scheduling Concepts

Figure 12.2, an example product structure for end item A, demonstrates basic concepts underlying shop-floor control techniques. One essential input to the SFC system is the routing and lead time data for each item. Figure 12.3 presents this for parts D and E of the example. The routing

---

FIGURE 12.2
Example Product Structure Diagram

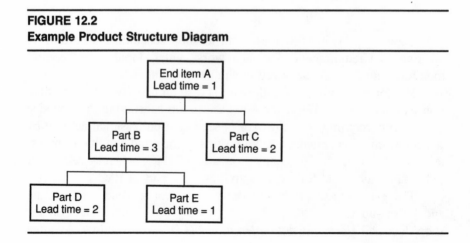

FIGURE 12.3
Routing Data and Operation Setback Chart

Part D Routing

Operation	Work center	Run time	Setup time	Move time	Queue time	Total time	Rounded time
1	101	1.4	.4	.3	2.0	4.1	4.0
2	109	1.5	.5	.3	2.5	4.8	5.0
3	103	.1	.1	.2	.5	.9	1.0

Total lead time (days) 10.0

Part E Routing

Operation	Work center	Run time	Setup time	Move time	Queue time	Total time	Rounded time
1	101	.3	.1	.2	.5	1.1	1.0
2	107	.2	.1	.3	.5	1.1	1.0
3	103	.3	.2	.1	1.5	2.1	2.0
4	109	.1	.1	.1	.5	.9	1.0

Total lead time (days) 5.0

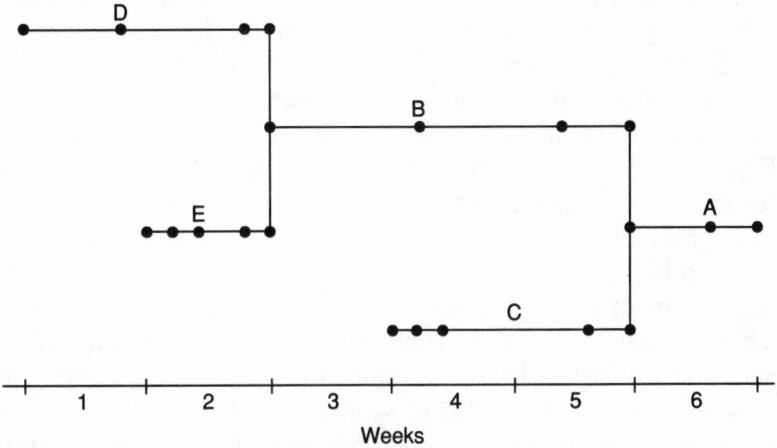

specifies each operation to be performed to make the part and which work center will perform the operation.

Production of part D, for example, requires three operations of 4, 5, and 1 days, respectively, for a total of 10 days, or two weeks. Part E requires four operations of 1, 1, 2, and 1 days, respectively, for a total of 5 days, or one week. The remaining lead times in Figure 12.2 are all derived the same way. Lead times used for MRP should match those in the routing file. If the MRP time for part E was set at two weeks instead of one week, orders would constantly be released one week early.

Lead times are typically made up of four elements:

- Setup time (time to prepare the work center—independent of lot size).
- Run time (operation or machine run time per piece × lot size).
- Move time (from one work center to the next).
- Queue time (time spent waiting to be processed at a work center, which depends on workload *and* schedule).

Queue time (the critical element) frequently accounts for 80 percent or more of total lead time; it is the element most capable of being managed. Reducing queue time means shorter lead time and, therefore, reduced work-in-process inventory. This reduction requires better scheduling.

The bottom of Figure 12.3 shows an *operation setback chart* based on each part's lead times. Here we clearly see the implications of incorrect MRP lead time. If the MRP lead time for part E is not the one week calculated from the routing data, the part will be released either early or late to the shop. Neither of these is a desirable outcome. Note that Figure 12.3 shows both parts D and E going through work center 101 for their first operation. The top of Figure 12.4 shows the partial schedule for work center 101, with parts D and E scheduled according to the timing in Figure 12.3.

The bottom of Figure 12.4 shows two alternative detailed schedules for part D in week 1 at work center 101. The cross-hatched portion represents the 1.8 days of lead time required for setup and run time. The early schedule has part D loaded as soon as possible in the four days. The late schedule loads part D into the latest possible time at work center 101.

The key differences between the top and bottom of Figure 12.4 are in lead times. The top half includes queue time. Queue time represents slack that permits the choice of alternative schedules—a form of flexibility. This slack can be removed by good shop scheduling practice; that is, this schedule allows 4 full days to complete part D, when actual time on the machine is only 1.8 days. For the remaining 2.2 days, the part waits in a queue or is moving between work centers.

The detailed schedules at the bottom of Figure 12.4 contain no queue time. These schedules represent loading a particular job onto a particular

---

FIGURE 12.4
Work Center 101 Schedules

Parts D and E with MRP lead times

Week 1					Week 2					Week 3				
M	T	W	T	F	M	T	W	T	F	M	T	W	T	F

Part D

E

Alternative detailed schedules for Part D
(Setup and run time only)

Monday	Tuesday	Wednesday	Thursday	
Part D				Early schedule
		Part D		Late schedule

---

work center for a particular time period. The two alternatives in the bottom of Figure 12.4 are different loadings. Typically the choice between alternative loadings is made to utilize the machine center effectively.

Gantt Charts

Gantt or *bar charts,* like those in Figure 12.4, show a schedule. The operation setback chart in Figure 12.3 is very similar. It too is a schedule for when to make each of the five parts based on lead times that include move and queue times.

One form of shop-floor scheduling is to prepare operation setback charts similar to Figure 12.3 for each job, and use them with the kind of data in Figure 12.3 to prepare Gantt charts, such as those in Figure 12.4. The objective is to prepare a schedule for each machine center. This schedule can be based on the assumptions in either the top or bottom of Figure 12.4; that is, the schedule may or may not use lead times that include queue and move times.

The more usual practice is to prepare the detailed work center schedule *without* move and queue times. Many firms' systems do this. The typical approach is a *schedule board* with racks to hold pieces of paper. Each paper is a job, and its length represents the time required.

The primary problem with this kind of system is updating. Actual data must be captured and integrated into an ongoing replanning cycle. Moreover, a means to communicate with the shop floor is usually required because schedule boards typically reside in planning offices. However, with personal computers on the shop floor, some firms have in essence created a fairly dynamic version of the "schedule board".

Priority Sequencing Rules

Priority sequencing rules concern which job to run next at a work center. To some extent, these rules can be seen as producing a loading of jobs onto individual machines, but usually only one job is committed at a time; that is, the job to run *next* is only determined near the time when the prior job has been completed. The priority (sequencing) rule is just what the name suggests: a *rule* for what job to process next.

Many different priority rules have been established. A fairly common one is to base priorities on the type of data in Figure 12.3. The lower half of that figure contains scheduled due dates for parts and operations which can be used as priorities. For example, a priority rule could be that the job to process next is the job with the earliest operation due date. An alternative is to next process the job with the earliest *part* due date. Four other commonly used sequencing rules are the following:

- *Order slack:* Sum the setup times and run times for all remaining operations, subtract this from the time remaining (now until the part due date), and call the remainder slack. The rule is to work on that job with the least slack. This rule addresses the problem of work remaining.

- *Slack per operation:* A variant of order slack is to divide the slack by the number of remaining operations, again taking next the job with the smallest value. The reasoning behind slack per operation is that it will be more difficult to complete jobs with more operations because they will have to be scheduled through more work centers.

- *Critical ratio:* A rule based on the following ratio:

$$\frac{\text{Time Remaining}}{\text{Work remaining}}$$

For calculation, the rule is expressed as

$$\frac{\text{Due date} \ - \ \text{Current date}}{\text{Lead time remaining (including setup, run, move, and queue)}}$$

If the ratio is 1.0, the job is on time. A ratio below 1.0 indicates a behind-schedule job, and a ratio above 1.0 indicates an ahead-of-schedule condition. The rule is to always process the job with the smallest critical ratio next.

- *Shortest operation next:* This rule ignores all due date information as well as all information about work remaining. It simply says, take as the next job the one that can be completed in the shortest time at the work center. This rule maximizes the number of shop orders that go through a work center, and minimizes the number waiting in queue.

In an MRP system, each shop order would be a scheduled receipt for the part. As such, the scheduled receipt has a due date. From this due date, operational due dates can be established by backing off expected operation times if these data are needed to establish priority sequence. The great advantage of this computer-based system is that, whenever the due date for a scheduled receipt changes, operation due dates can be changed accordingly. These changes, in turn, lead to priority changes for shop-floor scheduling, resulting in an execution system that works on the most-needed shop orders first. The objective is for high-priority jobs to move through the shop very quickly while low-priority jobs are set aside. In this way, the shop-floor scheduling system can indeed execute the dictates of the detailed material plan.

In recent times, many companies have developed a preference for sequencing rules that are easy to understand. One straightforward approach is to develop operation start and operation due dates, and use them for determining priority sequence decisions.

In a computer-based shop-floor scheduling system, due dates would not be printed on any shop paper that travels with the work-in-process inventory. The shop paper would show the routing or sequence of operations (static data), but no due dates. The changing (dynamic) due date information would be printed daily or displayed on-line in the form of a work center schedule or dispatch list. It is the dispatch list, not the traveling paper, that shows the priority sequence. The dispatch list can be updated as rapidly as transactions are processed to the MRP data base.

Vendor Scheduling and Follow-Up

The *vendor scheduling and follow-up* aspects of PAC are the direct analog of the shop-floor scheduling systems. There are some important differences, however. From the vendor's perspective, each customer is usually only one of a number of demand sources. Customer demands are managed in the vendor's plant with *its* PIM system. The PIM relationship is largely through information exchanged between vendor and customer, often from the shop scheduling activities of the customer directly to the vendor's PIM system.

From the customer's standpoint, the objectives of vendor scheduling are the same as those for internal work center scheduling: keep the orders lined up with the correct due dates from the material plan. This means that the vendor must have a continually updated set of relative priority data. A typical approach to providing this information is a weekly updated report reflecting the current set of circumstances in the customer's plant and, sometimes, the final customer requirements that dictate them. Increasingly, computer-to-computer communication is used to transmit this information.

Because the vendor follow-up system is often concerned with changes to the schedule and keeping priorities correct, there must be limits to the amount of change the vendor will be asked to accommodate. Contractual agreements with the vendor typically define the types and degree of changes that can be made, time frames for making changes, additional elements of flexibility required, and so on. In addition, the agreement specifies procedures for transmitting needs to the vendor and the units in which the vendor's capacity is planned and controlled. This sets the stage for vendor PAC, including order release, scheduling, and follow-up.

Lead Time Management

Many people think of *lead time* as a constant, such as pi. In fact, it is not as much a value to be measured as it is a parameter to be managed.

Of the four elements of lead time (setup, processing, move, and queue), the last two can be compressed with good PAC design and practice.

Lead time and work-in-process (WIP) are directly related, and some critical feedback linkages operate here. The longer the lead time is perceived to be, the longer the time between order launching date and due date. The longer this time, the more orders in the shop. The more orders in the shop, the longer the queue time (and WIP); we have a self-fulfilling prophecy.

Some WIP is needed at work centers in which high utilization is important. However, a basic principle of PIM is to *substitute information for inventory*. The firm does not need to have jobs physically in front of machines; orders can be held in a computer and converted to physical units as needed. For many plants, setup and run time only constitute 10 to 20 percent of total lead time. The rest is slack that can be substantially cut.

One interesting question is how to manage lead time. This means changing data base elements for both shop scheduling and MRP. One alternative is to go through the data base and systematically change all lead times. Reducing them could result in a transient condition of dry gateway work centers, but this might be a reasonable price to pay for the resulting WIP reduction.

Changing lead time data elements naturally leads to the question of how they are established in the first place. For most firms, lead time data are usually an input from some functional area, such as production control. An alternative is to *calculate* lead time. When we think about changing lead times as part of a management process, and when we remember that shop scheduling time must be in tune with MRP lead time offset data, this approach has increasing appeal. One firm calculated lead times as follows:

- Nonqueue time for each operation was set equal to setup plus run time (time per piece × lot size) plus move time.

- Nonqueue time was converted to days by dividing total hours by (7 × number of shifts per day), assuming seven productive hours per shift.

- Queue time was set equal to two days if the next work center in the routing was in another department, one day if it was in the same department but a different work center, and zero days if it was on the same machine.

- Lead time for the total order was the sum of queue and nonqueue times. This time was calculated with an average order quantity, rounded up to a weekly lead time, and used for MRP lead time offsetting.

Selecting queue time is the critical element in this formula. Values were chosen by taking a sample of 50 parts and using different queue time estimates to yield lead times consistent with production control personnel opinions. The initial estimates were padded, but the company was not very concerned. Once the system was in operation, estimates for queue times were systematically reduced a bit at a time. The results were a managed approach to shorter lead times and reduced work-in-process.

Before leaving this discussion, let us look at one firm's results. David A. Waliszowski says that a $25 million division of Hewlett-Packard reduced lead time 70 percent and increased customer service levels 80 percent. This amounted to a $1.7 million reduction in work-in-process inventory that was achieved in three months.

PRODUCTION ACTIVITY CONTROL EXAMPLES

This section applies production activity control techniques in examples covering both shop-floor control and vendor scheduling activities. The first example is the Twin Disc Company. Twin Disc has a large number of component parts, complex product structures, long lead times, complex part commonality, and expensive work centers that the firm wishes to utilize heavily. It has implemented a critical-ratio-based priority sequencing system and an analogous vendor scheduling system. The second example is vendor scheduling at Steelcase.

Critical Ratio Shop-Floor Control at Twin Disc

Twin Disc, Inc. is a manufacturer of small-lot, heavy-duty transmission equipment. Products are designed to customer specifications, produced in small lots, and range in unit price from several hundred dollars to over $10,000. Annual sales were approximately $200 million at the time of this study, with more than one half being to four large customers.

Data base size for shop-floor scheduling at Twin Disc is quite large. There are over 300 different machine centers. Open shop orders usually number about 3,500, and each part typically passes through 10 to 15 operations. The average product is made up ot approximately 200 parts, and the total part master data base includes about 60,000 separate part numbers.

Twin Disc installed the critical ratio priority system six years after implementing MRP. The MRP system was well understood at that time, and it provided the proper basis for updating priorities for individual shop orders. Now let us see how this shop-floor scheduling system works.

Figure 12.5 is the daily work center schedule. This report is printed during each night, so it is available to foremen at the beginning of every working day. The sample report in Figure 12.5 was printed for February 6, Wednesday of manufacturing week 446. (The manufacturing calendar is based on a five-day week.) It is for the BH machine center in plant 3, department 5. This machine center works two shifts and has a weekly rated capacity of 110.9 hours.

The report is divided into two parts. The top portion shows six orders presently at the BH work center; the lower portion shows orders that are one work center away from BH; that is, the shop orders at the bottom of the page are not now physically at BH, but their routings indicate that, when they are completed at their present work center location, they will be moved to BH for the next operation.

The first two columns on the report are the part number and part name. The third column is the shop order number for the part. The fourth and fifth columns are the operation number (its routing sequence) and a description of the operation. The priority numbers in columns 6 and 7 are more easily explained after we discuss the other data. Column 8 shows the quantity associated with the shop order, and column 9 shows the quantity physically at the work center. This distinction facilitates operation overlapping. Column 10 shows the hours each shop order is expected to take in the BH center. Notice that this column is totaled both for jobs in the machine center and for jobs one center away. Column 11 shows, for those jobs at BH, where each shop order will go when it leaves BH and where each order is for those jobs coming to BH.

Columns 12 and 13 show work remaining and time remaining for each shop order. In both cases, figures are stated in days. Time remaining is calculated by subtracting today's date from the due date shown for each shop order as a scheduled receipt in the appropriate MRP record. For example, if we go to the time-phased MRP record for part number 209335H, we find at least two scheduled receipt quantities (one for 142 pieces). Although the record might be printed in weekly time buckets,

FIGURE 12.5
Twin Disc Shop-Floor Control Report

DATE 02/06/   DAILY WORK CENTER JOB SCHEDULE   WEEK 446   DAY WEDNESDAY

PLANT 03   DEPT 05   MACH. CTR. BH   SHIFTS WORKED 2.0   CAPACITY 110.9

PART # (1)	PART NAME (2)	ORDER # (3)	OP # (4)	OPER DESC (5)	—PRIORITY— PO (6)	PI (7)	QTY OF OP (8)	QTY AT OP (9)	HOURS (10)	NEXT LOCATION (11)	WORK REM. (12)	TIME REM. (13)
209335H	IMP WHL	@ 438C34	020	FIN	.436		142	142	11.1	0316NB	18.3	8.0
216140A	SPINNER	445C22	010	TURN	1.236		88	88	6.4	0305BQ	18.6	23.0
20930BC	IMP WHL	445C67	020	FACE		.430	212	212	16.7	0316NB	18.5	8.0
A 4639A	CARRIER	445B45	010	TURN		2.675	54	54	5.4	**SAME**	8.5	23.0
A 4639A	CARRIER	445B45	020	FACE		2.675	54	54	5.4	0305YE	6.3	23.0
B 1640A	RETAINER	441B22	010	FACE		4.106	108	108	7.3	0305EG	10.4	43.0

TOTAL HOURS IN THIS MACHINE CENTER   52.3

PARTS IN PREVIOUS WORK CENTER   PREVIOUS

PART #	PART NAME	ORDER #	OP #	OPER DESC	PO	PI	QTY OF OP	QTY AT OP	HOURS	NEXT LOCATION	WORK REM.	TIME REM.
208346	IMP WHL	443C31	010	TURN	.437		27	27	4.7	0316NBR	18.2	8.0
203587E	FW PILOT	@ 444C98	010	SEMI-TURN	.462		28	28	4.3	0316NBR	17.3	8.0
208346G	IMP WHL	446A09	010	TURN	.742		250	250	15.4	0316NBR	24.2	18.0
208346A	IMP WHL	446A07	010	TURN	.907		1234	1234	62.2	0316NBR	36.3	33.0
209335H	IMP WHL	@ 446A10	010	TURN	1.388		141	141	11.1	0316NBR	20.1	28.0
B 5164	RETAINER	445C90	020	TURN		2.006	98	98	6.1	0305BQ	11.4	23.0
A 4639B	CARRIER	446B17	010	TURN		2.215	255	255	12.6	0316NBR	10.3	23.0
208457B	IMPELLER	444A44	010	TURN		3.632	10	10	4.1	0316NBR	10.4	36.0
208346C	IMP WHL	446A08	010	TURN		4.105	50	50	5.8	0316NBR	20.2	83.0

TOTAL HOURS FOR THIS MACHINE CENTER IN PREVIOUS CENTERS   126.3

Source: E. S. Buffa and J. G. Miller, Production-Inventory Systems: Planning and Control, 3rd ed. (Homewood, Ill: Richard D. Irwin, 1979), p. 597.

the convention would be to give it a due date of Friday in week 447. The five days of week 447 plus Wednesday, Thursday, and Friday of week 446 yield eight days remaining until this shop order is due to be closed out into inventory. This scheduled receipt for 142 pieces would be pegged to shop order 438C34. A second scheduled receipt for part 209335H would be for 141 pieces, due on Friday of week 451. This order (446A10) is shown as the fifth job in the list of orders one machine center away, with 28 days of time remaining. There could be other open shop orders for part number 209335H as well, but, they are not at BH or at one work center previous to BH.

The "Work remaining" column (12) represents lead time remaining to complete each order (18.3 days for the first order). This includes setup time, run time, move time, and queue time between operations. We can now define the critical ratio priorities shown as columns 6 and 7:

$$\text{Priority} = \frac{\text{Time remaining}}{\text{Work remaining}}$$

We see there that for the first shop order, 8.0/18.3 = .436. This means that this shop order will have to be completed in 43.6 percent of normal lead time. If this job is not run today, tomorrow's schedule will show a time remaining of 7 and a critical ratio of 7/18.3 = .383. Any order with a critical ratio priority greater than 1.0 is ahead of schedule; any priority less than 1.0 indicates a behind-schedule condition (based on total lead time values).

There is a distinction between columns 6 and 7, PO versus PI. PO is the case when the shop order is pegged all the way up through product structures, and an actual customer order depends on this particular shop order. It is a priority for *orders*. PI, on the other hand, is a priority for *inventory*. It means that at present, no customer order promise depends upon timely completion of this shop order. The order was issued based upon a forecast of customer orders that has not yet materialized.

The work remaining and associated priorities for orders one work center away are based on completing prior operations; that is, the priorities are those that would exist if the job were to arrive at BH today. This allows both sets of jobs to be evaluated on a common base.

Jobs are arranged on the daily work center schedule in priority sequence, PO before PI. This is the sequence that jobs should be run in, all other things being equal; that is, the company believes in running jobs to support customer orders before those to go into stock to support a forecast, and by running the smallest critical ratio job first, relative priorities are maintained.

In interpreting the shop-floor control report, a supervisor knows that a critical ratio of .436 is not a severe problem, providing that *all* the critical ratios are not less than 1.0. What will happen is that this order will be near the top of the list in each work center schedule as it passes through its routing steps. This means that it will be run shortly after arriving at the work center, or perhaps even be started *before* all parts are finished at the prior center (i.e., operation overlapping), so queue time will be small and the job should be completed on schedule.

The ability to see jobs that are coming enhances this ability to meet schedules. If the first job in the list of jobs one work center away (part 208346) had a priority of, say, .1, the BH supervisor could go to the supervisor in 0316NBR (the current location of the job) to see whether the job could be started in BH before all parts have been finished in 0316NBR, and perhaps try to overlap the operation following BH as well.

The report can also be used to sequence jobs to reduce setup times. If the order (446A10) for part number 209335H can be speeded up in 0316NBR, it can be combined on the same setup with order 438C34. Or perhaps running all (or most) of the impeller wheels in sequence makes sense. The report provides relative priority information to the supervisor but does not preclude intelligent decision making on his or her part. The extent to which supervisors can make decisions at variance with the shop-floor control report should be carefully defined. The key is to provide discretion—but not at the expense of missing due dates. We have already shown how priority data change on a daily basis, as the time remaining (numerator) grows smaller, and the lead time remaining (denominator) stays constant. If a job is not completed, its relative priority increases as it competes against other jobs for the available work center capacity.

Vendor Scheduling at Twin Disc

The vendor report in Figure 12.6 is analogous to the shop-floor control report for the Twin Disc Company; the firm calls it the "Open P.O. Buyer Fail-Safe Report." It lists all open purchase orders (scheduled receipts in MRP records), sorted by vendor.

In Figure 12.6 all purchase orders are for a single vendor. The first column of the report lists the buyer placing the purchase order. The second column is the vendor number (S52487); the third is the particular

FIGURE 12.6
Twin Disc Company's Open P.O. Buyer Fail-Safe Report

02/05		OPEN P.O.	BUYER FAIL-SAFE REPORT.				WEEK-343	
BUYER	VENDOR #	PART #	ORDER #	WEEK #	QTY.	FWEEK	FQTY.
D	52487	# 9670A	791930	345	5	345	1
D3	52487	# 9670B	819371	360	50		
D1	52487	# 9682	789410	344	50	338	19
D1	52487	# 9700B	808601	347	35	347	3
D3	52487	# 9753A	819380	352	100		
D3	52487	# 9791A	789561	345	25	348	25
D3	52487	# 9791A	810201	351	65	351	1
D1	52487	# 9813	810211	354	50		
D3	52487	# 9815B	788760	343	15		
D3	52487	# 9824	819390	350	25		
D3	52487	# 9825	793490	346	50	349	15
D1	52487	# 9841	793730	345	50		
D3	52487	# 9870A	758611	347	50		
D1	52487	# 9957	810220	348	25		
D1	52487	#201522	825880	352	1000		
D3	52487	#203717A	822100	354	250		
D1	52487	#205826	819330	349	100	349	38
D3	52487	#205896	826850	358	25		
D3	52487	#205896L	825890	357	50		
D3	52487	#206207	793770	348	200	346	108
D1	52487	#206331	791841	351	50	350	13

Source: E. S. Buffa and J. G. Miller, *Production-Inventory Systems: Planning and Control*, 3rd ed.
(Homewood, IL: Richard D. Irwin, 1979), p. 589.

part number on order. The fourth column is the purchase order number for the particular scheduled receipt quantity. Notice, for example, that the sixth and seventh orders are for the same part number, but these are on different purchase orders. The report is printed in part-number sequence by vendor, so *particular* orders can be identified. The fifth column on the report is the due date assigned to the purchase order when it was issued. Note that the report was printed at the beginning of week 343. The sixth column is the quantity on the purchase order. Columns 7 and 8 (the most important for vendor scheduling) are the fail-safe columns. Column 7 is the fail week (the date this order is needed to meet a higher-level assembly's planned start date). Column 8 (the fail quantity) is precisely how many are needed to keep from failing to meet this need.

The first order was issued for five units of part 9670A, with a due date of week 345. As of week 343, this due date is still valid. Failure occurs if it is not met. However, it is not essential that all five pieces be delivered. The company can get by if only one of the five is delivered.

"Getting by" has a definite meaning. The fail week and fail quantity are related to actual customer orders; that is, if we were to peg the scheduled receipt for five pieces under purchase order 791930, for part number 9670A, up through product structures, we would find a customer order depending upon one of the five parts being received in week 345. This concept is the direct analog of separating customer orders (priority PO) from inventory orders (priority PI) for jobs in the shop.

This means for example, that the ninth job on the list (part number 9815B) has a due date of the current week. Because there is no information in the "FWEEK" and "FQTY." columns, this order when pegged up will not be tied to a customer order. It will only go into Twin Disc's inventory.

Many of Twin Disc's vendors have been so well educated that this report can be sent directly to them. It provides a means for them to give priorities to all orders from Twin Disc, with continuous updating of their priorities. This information can then be integrated with data on other firms' competing needs in their own PIM systems.

Figure 12.6 indicates that the third order in the list (part number 9682) is now critical. It is not due until next week, but based on Twin Disc's present conditions, it was needed five weeks ago. Why this is true is not important. If we believe the records, this job is now very urgent. Twin Disc will have to shrink five weeks off the combined lead times for all assemblies above this part in the product structure to meet the customer promise date. Other purchase orders can be delayed if the vendor wishes to do so. However, Twin Disc is ready to accept the parts on the due dates even though they are not needed until later. This will fulfill its contractual obligations.

Vendor Scheduling at Steelcase

Steelcase is a large manufacturer of office furniture which made a fundamental change to its purchasing organization, separating procurement from the PAC activities of order release, vendor scheduling, and other clerical functions. An early user of MRP-based systems, Steelcase has since gone on to implement JIT manufacturing approaches. Figure 12.7

shows a vendor scheduling report for one of Steelcase's vendors, Cannon Mills, which supplies fabrics for upholstered furniture. In Figure 12.7 all orders through the week of 8/26 are asterisked, which means that they are firm commitments on Steelcase's part. Also shown are orders for the next four weeks out. With many vendors, Steelcase would commit to these to the extent of the vendor's investment in raw material.

In this example, the two firms agree on production of a particular cotton cloth, with a later decision on the color that it is to be dyed. The job of procurement is to negotiate the commitment's form, when and how these "time fences" (cotton versus color) are to be crossed, prices, lot sizes, and so on.

The report in Figure 12.7 can be sent directly to the vendor. Steelcase has eliminated formal purchase orders for all but occasional purchases. This saves on paperwork, cuts response time, and simplifies PAC. As actual orders come in for particular color fabrics, adjustments are made by clerical interactions between Steelcase and Cannon Mills.

PRODUCTION ACTIVITY CONTROL LINKAGES

In this section we look at how PAC links with some of the other production and inventory management processes and with other parts of the organization. We start by looking at the internal PIM linkages. We then turn to the accounting, human resource management, and other external links.

PIM System Linkages

The primary connections between PAC and the rest of the PIM processes shown in Figure 12.1 come from the boxes marked "Detailed material planning" and "Capacity planning." The capacity plan is especially critical to managing the detailed shop-floor flow of materials. In essence, the capacity provided represents resource availabilities for meeting material plans.

Capacity's importance for shop scheduling is illustrated by considering two extremes. If insufficient capacity is provided, no shop scheduling system will be able to decrease backlogs, improve delivery performance, or improve output. On the other hand, if more than enough capacity exists to meet peak loads, almost any shop scheduling system will achieve

---

FIGURE 12.7
Steelcase Requirements for Cannon Mills for the Week Ending 07/22

ALL TAGGED ORDERS (*) ARE FIRM
OTHER ORDERS ARE EXPECTED DATES AND QUANTITIES

						REQUIREMENTS	
PART	FINISH	DESCRIPTION			REC'D	CURRENT	
NUMBER	CODE				LAST	& PAST	
DIV		NO.	DATE	BUYER	WEEK	DUE	7/29
904550000	5350	RED COTTON					
4		9-0553 A	05/08/	010			
904550000	5351	RED RED ORANGE COTTON				800*	800*
4		9-0553 A	05/08/	010			
904550000	5352	RED ORANGE COTTON			415	785*	800*
4		9-0553 A	05/08/	010			
904550000	5353	YELLOW ORANGE COTTON				800*	400*
4		9-0553 A	05/08/	010		400*	
904550000	5355	YELLOW COTTON			402	331*	
4		9-0553 A	05/08/	010			
904550000	5356	YELLOW YELLOW GREEN COTTON					400*
4		9-0553 A	05/08/	010		200*	
904550000	5358	GREEN COTTON					
4		9-0553 A	05/08/	010			
904550000	5360	BLUE COTTON			416	384*	400*
4		9-0553 A	05/08/	010			
904550000	5368	TAN VALUE 1 COTTON			1445	1600*	800*
4		9-0553 A	05/08/	010		1600*	
904550000	5369	TAN VALUE 2 COTTON			725		
4		9-0553 A	05/08/	010		75*	

Source: P. L. Carter and R. M. Monczka, "Steelcase, Inc.: MRP in Purchasing," in *Case Studies in Materials Requirements Planning*, edited by E. W. Davis (Falls Church, Va.: American Production and Inventory Control Society, 1978), p. 215.

---

material flow objectives. It is in cases with bottleneck areas, and where effective utilization of capacity is important, that we see the utility of good shop scheduling systems.

A related issue is the extent to which good order release planning is done. If the order release activity in Figure 12.1 provides relatively

		REQUIREMENTS					
				NEXT 4	FOLLOW-ING 4		ISSUED LAST
8/05	8/12	8/19	8/26	WEEKS	WEEKS	ON-HAND	WEEK
400*		400*		400		442	
800*	800*	1200*	1200*	1200	1600	359	215
800*	400*	800*	800*	400	1200	415	
400*	1200*	800*	400*	800	1200	50	118
	400*		400*	400	400	1804	120
	400*		400*	400		237	
						237H	
400*	400*		400*	400	400	384	64
	400*	400*		400	400	416	
400*	800*	800*	800*	1600	1600	1502	234
	400*	400*	400	400	1305	197

level loading, shop scheduling is straightforward. On the other hand, if peaks and valleys in requirements are passed down to shop scheduling, execution becomes more complex and difficult. The same general issues apply to vendor follow-up systems: Vendor capacity must be carefully planned and loaded to ensure effective execution.

The detailed material plan provides information to shop scheduling and vendor follow-up systems and sets performance objectives. The essential objective of both execution systems is to achieve the material plan—to provide the right part at the right time. This will result in being able to hit the master production schedule and satisfy customer service objectives.

The shop and vendor scheduling activities begin when an order is released. A critical information service provided by MRP is appraising both scheduling systems of all changes in material plans. This means revising due dates and quantities for scheduled receipts so that correct priorities can be maintained. The job thereafter might be likened to a duck hunter following a moving target. Control and follow-up systems must keep each order lined up with its due date—one that is moving—so that overall PIM objectives are supported.

Linkages between PAC and detailed material planning are not all one-way. There is important feedback from the shop scheduling and vendor follow-up systems to material planning. Feedback is of two types: status information and warning signals. Status information includes where things are, notification of operational completions, count verifications, order closeout and disposition, and accounting data. The warning signals help to flag inadequacies in material and capacity plans; that is, will we be able to do what was planned?

Accounting Linkages

The PAC activities are a major source of information for the accounting department. The information on each order as it goes through the shop provides the basic information for job order costing, work-in-process inventory accounting, status reporting, and material consumption. The closing of orders into and out of inventory provide basic accounting information. The accuracy of raw material inventories depends on reports of order usage. The reporting of scrap, shortages, and other material-related statistics also comes from PAC transactions.

A fundamental source of accounting information coming from PAC is job costing. The time (labor and machine), material, and supplies consumed in the production process are collected and reported in PAC. The detailed information for costing products or bidding on future work comes from PAC records. This information linkage to accounting is consistent with, but sometimes separate from, that associated with linkages to PIM.

Human Resource Management Linkages

A closely related aspect of production activity control is labor cost reporting. The details of collecting labor-hours, associating them with jobs, and time accounting for payroll purposes are all performed on the factory floor, often within the PAC system. The accounting for time of the labor force (direct and indirect) and reporting that time is a key linkage with human resource management.

Another linkage between PAC and human resource management comes in the details of assigning labor to work centers, work orders, and other shop scheduling activities. It is through this dynamic process that the job priorities are maintained and adjusted. The assignment possibilities depend on the flexibility of the labor force, the work rules in place, and the needs of the moment. The human resource management area is key in changing the constraints that are imposed by the first two factors, and also provides input on how to match the labor resource to the current needs.

External Linkages

PAC maintains the detailed linkages with the supplier market in much the same way that demand management maintains the links to the sales markets. The relationships between vendors and customers are becoming ever closer and underscore the importance of this form of integration.

LESSONS FOR MANAGERS

Some important lessons come from this chapter. One of the major ones is that both the inside factory and outside factory can and must be managed in similar ways. In many firms, the responsibility for purchased material is assumed to rest with the supplier firm and the purchasing department. This is the "red phone" (hot line) approach to purchasing: Launch the order with the vendor and use the phone to keep changing things. In an effective PIM system, the vendor schedules and priorities must be managed in the same way that the shop floor is managed—through a carefully designed PAC system.

Another lesson that comes from this chapter is the need to provide feedback on material status and capacity consumption. Only with a feedback loop can the correct priorities be maintained and the plans changed if required. In the ultimate feedback, there are occasions when the customer must be told bad news. The sooner this can be done, the better able the customer is to react to the changes.

The world of the shop floor and purchasing is changing dramatically and quickly, but the basic lessons of maintaining priorities and using capacity intelligently will hold, even in world-class factories of the future. Understanding the relationship among shop-floor performance, the capacity plan, and the detailed material plans is essential to moving toward the standards of world-class excellence.

As integration inside the firms increases, the capability and need for external integration will increase as well. The lesson in this is that the firm can no longer look only internally for the linkages necessary to improve performance. The synergistic relationships must move outside the firm—to vendors and others as well.

CONCLUDING PRINCIPLES

This chapter has focused on the details of how a shop floor is scheduled inside a company using MRP systems, and how these approaches can be extended to scheduling of vendor capabilities—"the outside shop." The following principles summarize the key points for production activity control (PAC) :

- Lead times are made up of setup times, run times, move times, and queue times, with queue times (the most easily reduced) often accounting for more than 80 percent of the total.
- Reducing lead times reduces work-in-process inventory levels.
- Priority sequencing rules can be used to determine which job to run next at each work center when priorities are very dynamic.
- Vendor scheduling and follow-up systems can be used to continually update priorities with suppliers.
- Lead time can be *managed*—down !

INTEGRATED RESOURCE LINKAGES

The most critical linkages of PAC, both with other aspects of PIM and with other activities, are described in the chapter. The only major linkage not presented here is with management information systems. PAC requires a massive data base; for each part manufactured, all of the detailed steps must be identified, documented, and maintained. All changes to processes must be incorporated in the data base. Moreover, all actual operations must be in strict conformity with the specified process if statistical process control is to be a reality. All deviations from standard processes need to be carefully understood, both in terms of their reasons and in terms of the results. Continuous improvement is still a goal, but a shop floor needs to be run under tight conditions—not as an "art form." Experiments are worth trying, but only under experimental conditions.

REFERENCES

Berry, W.L., and V. Rao. "Critical Ratio Scheduling: An Experimental Analysis." *Management Science* 22, no. 2 (October 1975), pp. 192–201.

Bobrowski, Paul M., and Vincent A. Mabert. "Alternate Routing Strategies in Batch Manufacturing: An Evaluation." *Decision Sciences Journal* 19, no. 4 (Fall 1988) pp. 713–33

Melnyk, S. A.; S. K. Vickery; and P. L. Carter. "Scheduling, Sequencing, and Dispatching: Alternative Perspectives." *Production and Inventory Management,* 2nd quarter 1986, pp. 58–68.

Melnyk, S. A.; P. L. Carter; D. M. Dilts; and D. M. Lyth. *Production Activity Control,* Homewood, Ill.: Dow Jones-Irwin, 1987.

Philipoom, P.; R. E. Markland; and T. D. Fry. "Sequencing Rules, Progress Milestones and Product Structure in a Multistage Job Shop." *Journal of Operations Management* 8, no. 3,(August 1989), pp. 209–29.

Production Activity Control Reprints. Falls Church, VA.: American Production and Inventory Control Society, 1986.

Raffish, Norm. "Let's Help Shop Floor Control." *Production and Inventory Management Review* 1, no. 7 (July 1981), pp. 17–19.

Schonberger, Richard J. "Clearest-Road-Ahead Priorities for Shop Floor Control: Moderating Infinite Capacity Loading Unevenness." *Production and Inventory Management,* 2nd quarter 1979, pp. 17–27.

Schorr, J. E., and T. F. Wallace. *High Performance Purchasing.* Brattleboro, Vt.: Oliver Wight Ltd., 1986.

Wassweiler, W. L. "Fundamentals of Shop Floor Control." *1980 APICS Conference Proceedings,* pp. 352–54.

Williamson. R. F., and S. S. Dolan. "Distributed Intelligence in Factory Data Collection." *P and IM Review and APICS News,* February 1984.

SECTION 8

PIM AND MANUFACTURING STRATEGY

This section contains a chapter outlining our view of the competitive forces that drive integrated production and inventory management design. We view these forces as having two major dimensions, both related to integration. The first dimension is that of the integration of company strategy with manufacturing strategy and the implications for PIM system design. The second dimension of integration is that taking place on the shop floor itself as just-in-time concepts continue to be implemented in the work place. Both of these forces have profound impact on the relationships among PIM activities and their integration with other resource activities. We provide some insights into how these forces might change PIM in the future.

CHAPTER 13

LINKING PIM WITH MANUFACTURING STRATEGY

Throughout this book we have indicated the critical areas in which production and inventory management decisions need to be integrated and coordinated with other resource activities in a business. To be competitive, a company's marketing, sales, engineering, finance, and manufacturing plans need to be developed and executed in an integrated way so that people in all parts of the business can effectively work toward achieving company goals and objectives. Although the culture and the decision-making frameworks may vary among the business functions, the basic PIM system design provides critical linkages for these activities; it is essential that the design of PIM support the business strategy.

In this chapter we are concerned with the task of designing systems for production and inventory management (PIM) that support the strategic directions of the company. Our purpose is to integrate the strategic planning efforts of a company with the design of its PIM systems. This requires an understanding of the key market requirements placed on a company by its customers, and the role played by manufacturing in supporting these business requirements. It also requires an understanding of how different approaches to PIM can be used to support the tasks that are placed on manufacturing in different markets.

Two integrative issues are addressed in designing PIM systems. The first is linking the design of a firm's PIM system with its strategy for competing in the marketplace. As the investment in PIM systems is large and remains fixed over considerable time, getting it right is critical to short- and long-term prosperity. Many companies make costly mistakes when their PIM systems do not support their basic mission. The second issue concerns integrating material requirements planning (MRP) and just-in-time (JIT) in existing or new PIM systems. As markets change, the manufacturing strategy of a company also changes over time; it is often critical to shift from one PIM approach to another in an effective way.

The chapter centers around five topics:

- PIM design options: What are the critical alternatives in designing a PIM system?
- Choosing the options: How should the options be selected to best support corporate strategy and to fit with production process design?
- PIM option consistency: What are the consistency issues in PIM option choices?
- The choices in practice: How have manufacturing firms with different competitive missions gone about designing their PIM systems?
- Integrating MRP and JIT: How can these different approaches be linked in a company's PIM systems?

PIM DESIGN OPTIONS

A wide range of alternatives are available in designing PIM systems. These include MRP, MRPII, JIT, OPT (optimized production technology), periodic control systems, and finite scheduling systems. There are also a wide variety of options for designing the individual modules of the PIM system, as shown in Figure 13.1. The next three sections illustrate the variety of options for master production scheduling, detailed material planning, and production activity control.

Master Production Scheduling Options

Three major approaches can be taken in designing the master production schedule: *make-to-order* (MTO), *assemble-to-order* (ATO), and *make-to-stock* (MTS). Figure 13.2 shows the major differences between these alternatives. A *make-to-order* (MTO) approach to master production scheduling is typical when the product is custom-built to individual customer specifications. In this case, PIM needs to encompass preproduction engineering design activities as well as manufacturing and supplier operations. For MTO, the customer order represents the basic unit of

FIGURE 13.1
Basic PIM System

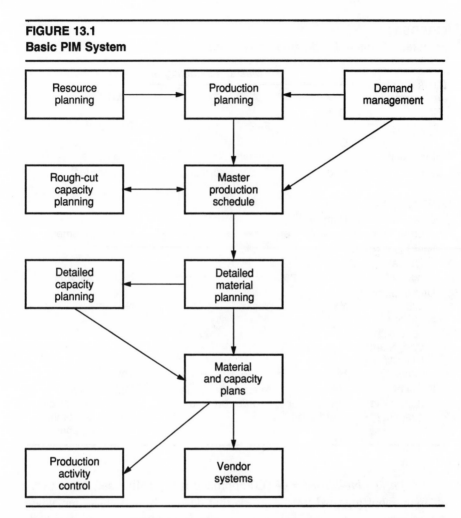

control in the MPS; the backlog of customer orders forms part of the overall lead time for the product. Overall, the order backlog is critical in estimating material and capacity requirements. Customer order promising is based on the backlog plus estimates for each design, procurement, and manufacturing step for a particular job. Planning bills of material are extensively utilized to estimate times and to prioritize design efforts on the "critical path." There is an inherently large degree of uncertainty associated with the time requirements, as each order requires a unique approach.

FIGURE 13.2
Features of Master Production Scheduling Approaches

Basis for planning and control	Master scheduling approach		
	MTO	*ATO*	*MTS*
Control point	Order backlog	FAS	Forecast
MPS unit	Customer orders	Options	End items
Product level	End product	End to intermediate product	End product
MPS features			
Customer order promising	High requirement ⟶		Low requirement
Need to monitor forecast accuracy	Low requirement ⟶		High requirement
Use of planning bills	Yes	Yes	No
Need to cope with design and process uncertainty	High ⟶		Low
Basis of delivery to customer	Make to customer order on time	Make to customer order on time	Make to stock replenishment order or to customer call-off schedule

---

An *assemble-to-order* (ATO) approach is typically used when over-all manufacturing lead time exceeds that desired by the customer, when the variety and cost of end products preclude investment in finished-goods inventory, and when engineering design has created modules or options that can be combined in many ways to satisfy unique customer requirements. Here component (or product option) inventory is held to reduce overall manufacturing lead time, and end products are assembled to meet the scheduled delivery dates for individual customer orders. As Figure 13.2 shows, a key control point is the final assembly schedule (FAS), which converts "average" products into unique products in response to actual customer orders. Planning bills of material are based on average products and on optional features. The planning bills reflect how the product is sold, rather than how it is manufactured. They are often used to simplify data requirements in preparing and maintaining the master production schedule. The uncertainty underlying an ATO business is fundamentally one of product mix, rather than one of product volume. The MPS and FAS are designed to hold off commitment to unique product configurations until the last possible moment and to offer a wide range of configuration choices to customers.

Under *make-to-stock* (MTS), the MPS is stated in end items, and these end products are produced to forecast demand; customer orders are filled directly from stock in order to provide short delivery lead times for standardized products. Although customer order promising records are not normally required, we must provide procedures for monitoring demand forecasts' accuracy, because manufacturing plans are mostly based on forecast information. This means that the type of uncertainty inherent in the MTS environment is one of forecasting errors; the manufacturing function needs to recognize errors on a timely basis and make corrective responses.

Detailed Material Planning Options

We can accomplish detailed material planning in several ways. The two basic alternatives are *time-phased* and *rate-based material planning*. Use of these approaches depends importantly on the production process's design characteristics. Figure 13.3 shows key differences between these approaches.

Time-phased planning for individual product components is typically carried out with material requirements planning approaches. The production process design is usually based on *batch manufacturing* and materials also purchased in batch orders. Preparation of time-phased plans requires a manufacturing data base that includes information on the following: MPS quantities stated in bill of material terminology to determine gross requirements; on-hand inventory balances and open shop (or purchase) orders to determine net requirements; production lead times, supplier lead times, and safety stocks to determine order release dates; and lot size formulas to determine order quantities. Under MRP, plans are typically updated on a periodic (daily or weekly) basis to develop priorities for scheduling manufacturing and supplier operations.

As Figure 13.3 indicates, time-phased material planning is based on explosion of requirements, where shop and purchase orders are created for batches of components. The schedule for any work center varies depending on the batches that arrive at that work center; work-in-process is

FIGURE 13.3
Features of Detailed Material Planning Approaches

Basis for planning and control	Material planning approach	
	Time-phased	Rate-based
Control point	Shop/purchase orders	Planning bills
Control unit	Batches	Kanbans
Product level	Material explosion of time-phased net requirements for product components	Material explosion of rate-based requirements for product components
Material planning features		
Level schedules	No	Yes
Use of WIP to aid planning	High	Low
Updating	Daily/weekly	Weekly/monthly
Inventory netting	Performed	None
Lead time offsetting	Performed	None
Lot sizing	Performed	None
Safety stock/safety lead time	Considered	Not considered
Container size	Not considered	Considered
Bill of material	Many levels	Single level

kept at high levels to effectively utilize work center capacities. Planning is carried out on a level-by-level basis corresponding to the levels in the bill of materials (BOM), with material going into and out of inventory at each level. Detailed planning is required for each level in the BOM, and lead time offsetting is utilized at each level.

A different approach is taken to detailed material planning under *rate-based planning*. Examples of firms using rate-based planning include repetitive manufacturing, assembly lines, just-in-time, and other flow systems. The primary intent in rate-based scheduling is to establish rates of production for each part in the factory. Realizing these rates allows the company to move material through the manufacturing system without stopping, in the shortest time possible. Typically, single-level planning bill of material information is used to convert rate-based master production schedules into material plans that specify the appropriate daily or hourly flow rates for individual component items. Planning of intermediate items in the bill of materials is not usually required, because the number of intermediate-level items is too small to be of concern. Because of MPS stability, high rates of material flow, negligible work-in-process inventory levels, short manufacturing lead times, and a relatively small variety of final products in the MPS, we do not need detailed status information on work-in-process items. This reduces the manufacturing data base's size, the number of transactions, and the number of material planning personnel in comparison with time-phased detailed material planning.

Production Activity Control: Shop-Floor Options

A wide variety of manual and computer-based production activity control (PAC) shop-floor scheduling systems exist. The detailed material planning approach used (driven by MRP or driven by JIT) depends greatly on the manufacturing process's characteristics. Figure 13.4 distinguishes between these approaches.

The MRP-based approach supports batch manufacturing operations in which shop orders are released against a schedule developed by the material planning function, based on lead times for component and subassembly items largely comprised of queue or waiting time. The shop-floor scheduling system's objective is to coordinate the sequencing of orders at individual work centers with customer delivery requirements. A large manufacturing data base requiring a substantial volume of shop transactions is needed to provide control reports for order tracking, dispatching, and work center monitoring.

In MRP-based shop-floor systems, one objective is to utilize each work center's capacity effectively. This form of manufacturing is based on relatively large batches of each component and significant work-in-process inventories to support independence among the work centers. This shop-floor approach is based on scheduling shop orders that dictate the set of detailed steps or operations necessary to make each component part. The flow of materials is controlled with dispatching rules establishing the order in which all jobs in a particular work center are to be processed. The primary criterion in establishing this order are the due dates for the parts, which are continually reestablished through MRP planning. Shop orders are tracked as they progress through the factory by processing detailed transactions of work at every work center. Shop

FIGURE 13.4
Features of Shop-Floor System Approaches

Basis for planning and control	Shop-floor system approach	
	MRP	JIT
Control basis	Work center capacity utilization	Overall product flow times
Unit of control	Shop orders	Kanban cards or containers
Product level	Individual operations scheduled at each work center	Production on an as-required basis to replenish down-stream stocks that support end item requirements
Shop-floor system features		
Control of material flow	Work center dispatching rules	Initiated by downstream kanban cards
Sequencing procedure	Due-date oriented dispatching rule	Not an issue
Order tracking	Shop-floor transactions by operation and stocking point	None (paperless system)
Monitoring and feedback	Input/output and shop load reports	Focus on overall result
Order completion	Shop order close-out in stockroom	None
Achieving delivery reliability	Batch order status reports	Through flow of material
Lot size	Large	Small
Work-in-process and safety stock	Large	Negligible

orders are opened as part of MRP planning, and they are closed out as components are received into a stockroom. Problems are highlighted through input/output analysis and shop load reports.

In JIT-based shop-floor scheduling systems, the approach is based on material velocity (minimal flow times for the entire product). That is, the emphasis is on end items, with the scheduling of individual operations and even component parts in a subservient position. Cellular manufacturing techniques are typically employed, and detailed scheduling is accomplished as part of the basic manufacturing task. Kanban cards, containers, and other signals of downstream need for components serve as the authorization to produce, typically in small lot sizes. The sequencing procedure is not an issue because work is only started on an as-needed basis, with little or no competition for work center capacity. Similarly, order tracking is nonexistent because work-in-process is minimal, and material moves through the factory quickly enough to negate the need for tracking. The only close-out is of finished items. Often the close-out transaction generates a computer-based "backflush" of the requisite component parts. The very short queue times, small lot sizes, and relatively narrow product range in JIT can result in a paperless shop-floor scheduling system. The manufacturing data base requirements, volume of shop transactions, and number of shop scheduling personnel are minimal.

Many authorities have attempted to use the terms *push* and *pull* to distinguish between MRP-based and JIT-based shop-floor systems. The argument is that under JIT, when a customer "pulls" some product out of inventory, it pulls some replacement inventory from the factory, which pulls some parts from the shops, which pulls some materials from the storerooms, and so on. On the other hand, MRP-based systems "push" components into the factory, then into inventory, then back into manufacturing, and so on. We find this terminology to be not very helpful. It has spawned debates over whether MRP is a push or pull system, whether kanbans are a part of a pull system when the company is make-to-stock with inventory, or if a JIT system is push-based when the need for an end item is exploded into raw materials that are then sent through the factory without any kanban type of replenishment. These debates simply are not very helpful. The distinction that we believe is useful pertains to whether individual work centers are allowed to utilize capacity ("to keep busy") without being driven by a specific end item schedule. Increasingly, JIT is being utilized in nonrepetitive environments, in which specific product configurations are moved through manufacturing in short lead times without tracking or other transactions, and in which capacity utilization is a result, not an objective.

The key distinction being made here is that these two approaches' characteristics must match the manufacturing process and infrastructure in which they operate. Activities in the MRP-based systems are triggered by paperwork authorizing production quantities, routings, due dates, and so forth. JIT-based systems produce in response to downstream use of the item, which may be work center by work center or may be in response to demand for the overall end item. For JIT systems installed to date, relatively constant demands are required for the approach to function.

CHOOSING THE OPTIONS

There is a temptation to view some PIM design options as a continuum in which movement toward JIT is "good." This is not the correct conclusion. We must match PIM system design with the ongoing needs of a company's market, the task in manufacturing, and the manufacturing process. A PIM system represents a major investment in a business, and as such it must be designed to support the firm's competitive strategy. One framework for accomplishing this was developed by Berry and Hill. Let us turn to how this matching takes place.

MARKET REQUIREMENTS

Figure 13.5 shows how PIM system design is influenced by a company's market requirements and the resultant manufacturing task. Figure 13.5 labels these last two factors "business specifications." The point is that these determine, from a business point of view, what has to be done in manufacturing to serve the chosen markets. Then technical requirements are defined. This involves the interaction of the manufacturing task, PIM system, and manufacturing process. Each of these three areas needs to be carefully considered before the choices can be made in the approaches to master production scheduling, detailed material planning, and shop-floor scheduling. Moreover, three areas must be seen as constantly changing: new customer requirements, new process technology, and new strategic goals in manufacturing. Any of these can mandate a change in the PIM system design.

Figure 13.5 also shows the PIM system design as influenced by the desired PIM system and existing PIM system. In some cases improvements can be made by investing in the evolution of the existing system design. In other cases, we need to start fresh.

FIGURE 13.5
PIM System Design Choices

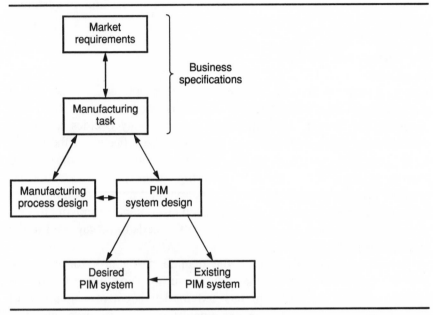

The first step in the development of market requirements is to review the customers and market segments targeted by the business, their present needs with regard to the company's products and services, competitors' products and services, and existing sales growth opportunities. Many companies face dynamic markets in which customer requirements and global competition are changing dramatically. We must continuously review market requirements and adapt marketing strategies to exploit opportunities. For example, many companies increasingly see the need to enhance their products with services to help their customers solve problems. *Market focus, customer prosperity*, and *delighting the customer* are common phrases that reflect this thrust. But if these phrases are to be more than hype, we must redefine the manufacturing task to create the desired results. Thereafter, we may well have to redesign the PIM system as well as the manufacturing process. To illustrate, the manufacturing organization in a packaging materials firm supplying the food industry suddenly had to deliver products in small quantities on a twice-weekly basis to support its major customer's new JIT program. However, neither the production process nor the PIM system was designed to support the changed business requirements. More fundamentally, the firm's manufacturing strategy had to be revised to support this kind of customer requirement.

The Manufacturing Task

The next step in choosing PIM system design options is to develop a statement of the manufacturing task that is consistent with (and that supports) the market requirements. If the company decides to satisfy customers on a just-in-time basis, this has to be reflected in the manufacturing task. Similarly, if quality is now the way to win orders, it too must be reflected in changed manufacturing values, process investments, improvements in the quality support function, and revised manufacturing performance measurements. If the targeted customers are moving toward more highly customized products, again this needs to be captured in the manufacturing task.

Hill points out that stating the manufacturing task for the business is critical to ensuring that manufacturing capabilities are developed to support the different targeted market segments, in terms of the requirements they place on manufacturing. Such requirements may, for example, include a particular volume level and delivery flexibility, low-cost production, critical product quality specifications, and other manufacturing-related capabilities—whatever is required to win orders in different market segments.

A clear statement of the manufacturing task enables management to recognize that major changes may be required in the design of both production processes and the PIM system. Figure 13.5 shows this by the two-headed arrows linking the manufacturing task to the design of both manufacturing processes and PIM systems.

Manufacturing Process Design

Most firms have large investments in production processes, employee capabilities, and other elements of infrastructure in manufacturing. As a consequence they tend to remain fixed over long periods of time. The arrow linking manufacturing process design and PIM design indicates the interdependency between PIM option choices and manufacturing process features. For example, installing a JIT process with cellular manufacturing and short production lead times means that rate-based detailed material planning approaches may be much more appropriate than time-phased approaches.

A more subtle example of manufacturing process design affecting PIM system design occurs in the case of quality improvement programs. Many companies use complex scheduling procedures because the firms suffer from poor quality and the resultant unpleasant surprises. Quality is usually improved through investments in better manufacturing processes. When quality is enhanced significantly, there are fewer surprises, the company is better able to execute routine plans, and PIM systems can be more straightforward.

Finally, in some cases there are simultaneous changes in marketplace requirements, manufacturing processes, and manufacturing task definitions. For example, Digital Equipment (DEC) and other computer manufacturers at one time faced a very long lead time to make a computer; they achieved customization by individual wiring and other hardware features. New computers were "announced" in the marketplace long before they were available for shipment, customers would place orders just to get their place in the line of orders, and the PIM system had to manage a fictitious backlog of orders. Moreover, each order's configuration would constantly change and delivery dates would be extended or canceled. The net result was a very complex set of requirements for the PIM system. Now computers are relatively easy to make, most customization is done with software, and orders are rapidly shipped. Moreover, computers per se are becoming a commodity; DEC and other companies increasingly view their manufacturing strategies as solving problems for their customers. The resultant changes in end "products"—and the processes that produce them—dictate a completely different set of design requirements for the PIM system.

PIM System Design

Because of the magnitude of the investment in PIM systems and the time required to implement PIM system changes, we must recognize differences between desired and existing PIM system options and features. Figure 13.5 shows this by the lines connecting PIM system design with desired and existing PIM systems. A company currently using time-phased detailed material planning records while installing a JIT process with cellular manufacturing might continue to use these records with some modifications until necessary investment funds and management time were available to make the PIM system changes required to implement rate-based material planning. Although the marketing strategy, manufacturing task, manufacturing process, and PIM system design specifications might have been agreed upon within the business, the opportunity to move to implementation might not yet have occurred.

PIM OPTION CONSISTENCY

A key strategic issue involves making internally consistent PIM option choices. We need to have the right choice (and consistency) in the MPS approach, the detailed material planning approach, and the shop-floor system approach. This issue frequently arises during JIT implementation in a company using MRP for detailed material planning. Here, batch and line production processes are appropriate for different parts of the business. Therefore, issues of how to link JIT and MRP options in PIM system design and how to maintain *one* PIM system are often difficult. Our experience indicates that attention paid to marketplace requirements and to how these requirements may be changing helps you to determine the dominant choices among the PIM options.

Master Production Scheduling Options

In Figure 13.6 the three MPS approaches are related to key aspects of marketplace requirements and to aspects of the manufacturing task and manufacturing process. A make-to-order (MTO) master scheduling approach supports products of wide variety and custom design, frequently involving the development of engineering specifications. They are typically produced in low unit volumes, where delivery speed is achieved through overlapping schedules for design and manufacture of the various elements comprising the customer order. Delivery reliability is somewhat difficult to guarantee, as products are customized to meet individual customer needs. This approach is frequently used to support markets characterized by high levels of product change and new product introductions, and where the firm's competitive advantage is in providing product technology requirements in line with the customer's delivery and quality requirements. Because the manufacturing task often involves providing a broad range of production capabilities, the process choice supports low-volume batch manufacturing. One key aspect of the manufacturing task is how to respond to fluctuations in sales volumes. These

FIGURE 13.6
Linking Market Requirements and Manufacturing Strategy to Design of the MPS Approach

Strategic variables			Master scheduling approach		
			MTO	*ATO*	*MTS*
Market requirements	Product	Design	Custom	———————————►	Standard
		Variety	Wide	———————————►	Predetermined and narrow
	Individual product volume per period		Low	———————————►	High
	Delivery	Speed	Through overlapping schedules	Through reducing process lead time	Through eliminating process lead time
		Reliability	Difficult	———————————►	Straight-forward
Manufacturing	Process choice		Low-volume batch	———————————►	High-volume batch/line
	Managing fluctuations in sales volume		Through order backlog	Through WIP or finished-goods inventory	Through finished-goods inventory

are typically managed through adjustments in the level of the customer order backlog.

An assemble-to-order (ATO) master scheduling approach represents an intermediate position. Products of both standard and special design are produced, and variety is accommodated by customer selection from a wide series of standardized product options. The unit production volumes are relatively high at the option level, and customer responsiveness in regard to delivery speed is enhanced by lead time reductions and short time frames for frozen final assembly schedules. Delivery reliability is well accommodated as long as overall volumes are kept within planning parameters. That is, the ATO environment is designed to be relatively accommodative of changes in product mix.

Typically, ATO manufacturing is done in batches, with more and more firms using cellular approaches for popular options and families of similar parts. Stocking components, intermediate subassemblies, or product option items can shorten customer lead time to that of the final assembly process, thereby improving delivery speed and reliability in markets in which fluctuations in sales volumes are hard to anticipate.

The make-to-stock (MTS) master scheduling approach supports products of standard design, produced in high unit volumes in narrow product variety, for which short customer delivery lead times are critical. Delivery speed is enhanced by reducing process lead times, frequently by adopting flow-based manufacturing methods. Reliability of production schedules is relatively straightforward.

The process choice is usually line manufacturing or high-volume batch manufacturing. An investment in finished-goods inventory can provide short, reliable delivery lead times to customers, and can buffer fluctuations in sales; it can also enable us to stabilize production levels, thereby permitting important cost improvements in manufacturing. Because products are often produced on high-volume batch or line processes, schedule stability is often critical, especially in price-sensitive markets.

Material Planning Options

Figure 13.7 relates the two detailed material planning approaches to key aspects of marketplace requirements and to aspects of the manufacturing task and manufacturing process. Time-phased detailed material planning is appropriate for custom products produced in wide variety and low volumes. It also facilitates schedule changes and revisions in customer delivery dates, as well as changes in product mix. Delivery speed is enhanced through better scheduling based on relative priorities. This approach can be applied in markets characterized by a high rate of new product introductions, rapid shifts in product technology, and custom-engineered products by using planning bill of material techniques.

Time-phased planning is often associated with batch manufacturing, and is supported by relatively high overhead and work-in-process inventory costs from the necessary planning staff and extensive transaction processing. This planning approach can result in higher capacity utilization and is often favored in manufacturing facilities employing expensive equipment.

Rate-based material planning is appropriate for a relatively narrow range of standard products, with stable product designs produced in high volume. Rate-based detailed material planning is much more limited in its ability to cope with changes in product mix. The limited product line

FIGURE 13.7

Linking Market Requirements and Manufacturing Strategy to the Design of the Detailed Material Planning Approach

Strategic variables			Detailed material planning approach	
			Time-phased	*Rate-based*
Market requirements	Product	Design	Custom	Standard
		Variety	Wide	Narrow
	Individual Product volume per period		Low	High
	Ability to cope with changes in product mix		High potential	Limited
	Delivery	Speed	Through scheduling/ excess capacity	Through inventory
		Schedule changes	Difficult	Straightforward
Manufacturing	Process choice		Batch	Line
	Source of cost reduction	Overhead	No	Yes
		Inventory	No	Yes
		Capacity utilization	Yes	No

permits straightforward changes in the schedule as long as they are within the product design specifications. Enhancements in customer delivery speed are typically accommodated with finished-goods inventories.

These marketplace requirements are normally best supported in manufacturing by production line processes. Use of rate-based material planning and line production processes yields an opportunity to cut work-in-process inventory and overhead costs, providing important support for price-sensitive markets. On the other hand, rate-based material planning does not support intensive utilization of capacities in the same way as time-phased approaches.

Shop-Floor System Options

In Figure 13.8 the two shop-floor system approaches are related to key aspects of marketplace requirements and to aspects of manufacturing task and manufacturing process. The MRP-based approach to shop-floor

FIGURE 13.8

Linking Market Requirements and Manufacturing Strategy to the Design of the Shop-Floor System Approach

Strategic variables			Shop-floor system approach	
			MRP-based	JIT-based
Market requirements	Product	Design	Custom	Standard
		Variety	Wide	Narrow
	Individual product volume per period		Low	High
	Accom-modating demand changes	Total volume	Easy/incremental	Difficult/stepped
		Product mix	High	Low
	Delivery	Speed	Achieved by schedule change	Achieved through finished-goods inventory
		Schedule changes	More difficult	Less difficult
Manufacturing	Process choice		Low-volume batch	High-volume batch/line
	Changeover cost		High	Low
	Organizational control		Centralized	Decentralized (shop-floor based)
	Work-in process		High	Low
	Source of cost reduc-tion	Overheads	Low	High
		Inventory	Low	High

scheduling is appropriate when a wide variety of custom products is produced in low unit volumes. Changes in demand are accommodated relatively easily; volume changes are supported by overtime operations in critical work centers, and product mix change is an inherent characteristic. This approach supports markets characterized by rapid changes in product technology, high rates of new product introduction, and substantial changes in product design.

Low-volume batch or jobbing processes involve use of the MRP-based shop-floor scheduling system approach. These processes have significant changeover costs and numerous manufacturing steps, requiring a complex shop-floor scheduling system that is centrally driven, thereby limiting the reduction of overhead and inventory-related costs.

JIT-based approaches to shop-floor scheduling provide important support for standard products produced in limited variety and high volume. Such products are best supported by high-volume batch or line production processes that are able to provide short customer lead times. Accommodation of changes in product volume is limited because of the cost of production schedule and capacity changes; this increases the need for schedule stability. Delivery speed is enhanced by short manufacturing throughput times and often by finished-goods inventories.

The emphasis on inventory reduction and the simplicity of shop-floor control procedures under the JIT approach provide the potential for significant cuts in overhead and inventory-related costs, providing important support for price-sensitive markets.

THE CHOICES IN PRACTICE

Achieving a close fit among marketplace requirements, the manufacturing task and process, and the PIM system design gives a firm important competitive advantages. In this section we briefly describe the marketing and manufacturing strategies of three companies (Moog, Inc., Space Products Division; Kawasaki, U.S.A.; and Applicon, Division of Shlumberger) and how they have designed their PIM systems. Figure 13.9 shows the three PIM systems' overall design. Moog uses MTO and ATO approaches to master production scheduling, a time-phased approach to detailed material planning, and an MRP-based shop-floor system. Kawasaki uses MTS master production scheduling, rate-based material planning, and JIT shop-floor scheduling. Applicon uses ATO master production scheduling, both MRP and rate-based scheduling for material planning, and a JIT-based shop-floor system.

Moog and Kawasaki provide examples of stable PIM system designs that support the requirements of a single market. Applicon, however, provides an example of a PIM system that changed in response to shifting market requirements and process design changes. Let us now see the overall pattern of decisions in each firm concerning the influence

---

FIGURE 13.9
Linking Business Characteristics to the Design of PIM Systems

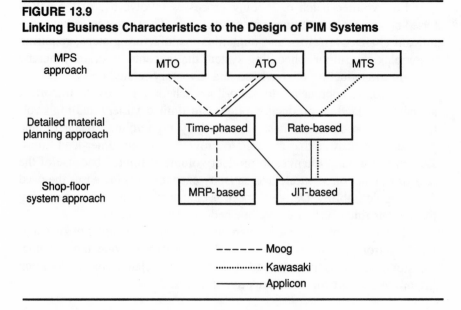

---

of marketing and manufacturing strategy on PIM system design, and see how the resultant systems support their businesses.

Moog, Inc., Space Products Division

This firm produces high-quality hydraulic systems of advanced design for the aerospace industry. These products cover a wide range of design types and represent a critical element in the overall production lead times for its aerospace customers. The company designs and produces the initial order for new products as well as follow-up orders. Thus, engineering design and advanced product features are key factors in obtaining sales. Other important factors that qualify the firm to compete in this market include delivery reliability, reputation for quality, and price. Figure 13.10 summarizes characteristics of the market served by Moog, along with key elements of its manufacturing strategy.

The manufacturing task involves providing a broad range of equipment and employee capabilities to make high-precision, custom-designed products in low unit volumes. Substantial uncertainty exists with regard to production process yields and time estimates to produce initial orders. In addition, design changes contribute to process uncertainty. Labor cost is a significant portion of product cost because highly skilled employees and a wide variety of precision equipment are characteristics of the production process. Major investments have been made in numerical control (NC) and computerized numerical control (CNC) equipment, as well as in machining centers in a batch manufacturing process.

All production and inventory management activities in Figure 13.1 are performed at Moog. Both make-to-order and assemble-to-order master production scheduling approaches are used. The MPS is stated in terms of actual, anticipated, and forecast customer orders with substantial emphasis on customer order promising and capacity planning activities. The master production schedule uses this information to determine requirements for component material. Time-phased material requirements planning records are used to coordinate scheduling of manufactured and purchased components, and these records are used to prepare shop load forecasts for individual departments and work centers.

At Moog the MRP-based approach is used for shop-floor scheduling and vendor scheduling. An advanced computer-based MRPII system provides priority scheduling information for sequencing and dispatching shop orders at individual work centers. The shop-floor system supports the batch manufacturing of products under high levels of process uncertainty. A variety of production reports assist supervisors in the detailed tracking of open shop orders, reporting order status, and evaluating work center performance.

Kawasaki, U.S.A.

Kawasaki produces six different types of motorcycles as well as motorized water skis at its U.S. plant. About 100 different end product items are manufactured for shipment to the firm's distribution centers. Although demand for products is highly seasonal, workload at the plant is stabilized by permitting fluctuations in the finished-goods inventory carried at the distribution centers. The company frequently introduces new product designs which represent styling changes in the product. The key elements in gaining sales are price, product styling, and product performance. Factors qualifying the firm to compete in the market are quality and delivery speed. Figure 13.11 summarizes characteristics of the market served by Kawasaki, along with key elements of its manufacturing strategy.

Manufacturing's task is to produce standardized products in high volume at low cost. Because material costs are significant, major emphasis is placed on reducing plant inventories using just-in-time manufacturing methods. The production process is characterized by short

FIGURE 13.10
Moog, Inc., Space Products Division

Market characteristics	Manufacturing strategy	
	Manufacturing	
	Task	Features
Customized products	Reducing process lead time	Batch manufacturing
Wide product range		Long process routings
Low volume per product	Manufacturing to engineering specifications and quality standards	High-precision work
Make-to-customer specifications		Accommodate delivery and design changes with reliable deliveries
Initial pilot orders		
Future repeat (blanket) orders	Deilvery reliability critical	Labor cost equals 60%
		Control of actual costs against budget
Key customer requirements: Design capability Delivery speed		Scrap and rework: First orders Repeat orders
Market qualifiers: Delivery reliability Quality Price		First order processing uncertainties (process unknown, time estimates)
		Process and product uncertainties

setup times and small production batches using production line and high-volume batch processes. Standardized assembly operations and repetitive employee tasks characterize the production process.

All the production and inventory management activities in Figure 13.1 are performed at Kawasaki; a make-to-stock master production scheduling approach is used. Customer orders for end products are filled from the finished-goods inventory held by the company's distribution division. The MPS is based on forecast information, and mixed model assembly is used in performing final assembly operations. Sub-

Manufacturing strategy		
Production and inventory management		
Master production scheduling	*Detailed material planning*	*Shop-floor systems*
Make-to-order/ assemble-to-order from: Customer orders Anticipated orders Forecast orders Used for rough-cut capacity planning due to long lead time impact on delivery Customer order promising	Time-phased material planning Material is particular to customer orders High obsolescence risk Extra materials needed for scrapped items Trade-off: shorter lead time versus raw material inventory	MRP-based systems Priority scheduling of shop orders System supported by dispatching and production control personnel Capacity requirements planning by work center Order tracking and status information

stantial emphasis is placed on leveling the master production schedule and freezing it over a three-month planning horizon.

A rate-based material planning approach utilizes a simple planning bill of materials to schedule the rates of flow for manufactured and purchased components. A JIT shop scheduling system using kanban containers controls the flow of material between work centers. The JIT system supports low-cost manufacturing with small plant inventory levels and high-volume material flows. Very few personnel and minimal transactions are required in planning and controlling production activities.

FIGURE 13.11
Kawasaki, U.S.A.

	Manufacturing strategy	
	Manufacturing	
Market characteristics	Task	Features
Narrow product range	Provide a low-cost manufacturing support capability	High-volume batch and line production process
Standard products		
High volume per product		Short setup times
Seasonal demand	Support the marketing activity with high delivery speed through finished-goods inventory	Small batch size
Sales from finished-goods inventory at distributors		Low-cost maufacturing
		Low labor cost
Introduction of new products		High material cost
Changing product mix		Low inventories (raw material, components, and WIP)
Key customer requirements: Price Delivery speed (through finished-goods inventory in distribution divisions)		Low overheads (low MPC costs)
Market qualifiers: Quality Deliver reliability Basic design and peripheral design		

Applicon

This firm designs and manufactures computer-aided engineering (CAE), design (CAD), and manufacturing (CAM) systems for the electronics and mechanical design markets. High-end products include systems for highly sophisticated customers in a variety of analytical engineering ap-

Manufacturing strategy		
Production and inventory management		
Master production scheduling	Detailed material planning	Shop-floor systems
Make-to-stock Manufacture to forecast Level production Three-month frozen planning horizon Manufacture to replenish distribution inventories	Rate-based material planning	JIT-based systems Kanban containers JIT flow of material Low raw material, component, and WIP inventory

plications. Low-end systems use Applicon software, Sun and Tektronics work stations, and DEC VAX processors for applications in robotics and numerical control machines.

The mechanical design market represents the firm's major growth area. In this market, unlike the electronics market, the price-to-performance ratio is a critical issue to price-sensitive CAD/CAM customers. In addition, the ability to respond rapidly to changes in technology and frequent design changes is also critical. Figure 13.12 summarizes characteristics of the market served by Applicon, along with key elements of the old manufacturing strategy (i.e., the one employed by the company before the process change).

FIGURE 13.12
Applicon's Old Manufacturing Strategy

	Manufacturing strategy	
	Manufacturing	
Market characteristics*	Task*	Features
Customized products	Low-cost manufacturing	Batch manufacturing
Wide product range	Short production lead times	General-purpose equipment
Major design changes occurring monthly	High product quality	Functional plant layout
Quick response required to changes in product technology	Rapid engineering change capability	4- to 5-month manufacturing lead time
Need to reflect both price sensitivity and the price/ performance ratio for a sophisticated customer base		Long design change cycle
		High rate of inventory obsolescence
High product quality requirements		85 percent plug and play rate in final inspection
Delivery responsiveness is critical		Excessive rework costs
		160 actual production operators in the manufacturing areas
		20 weeks of work-in-process inventory
		Product family mix change flexibility

*The market characteristics and manufacturing task are common to the old and new strategies.

The manufacturing task for the mechanical design market involves producing high-quality products that have a wide range of optional features in small volumes, at low cost, in short customer lead times, while accommodating rapid engineering changes. As Figure 13.12 shows, the previous manufacturing strategy was to produce products using a batch

Manufacturing strategy		
Production and inventory management		
Master production scheduling	*Detailed material planning*	*Shop-floor systems*
Make-to-stock MPS High levels of finished-goods inventory Monthly MPS is created for each end product, using an annual build plan	Conventional MRP system Stockroom kitting of assemblies prior to release of work orders at each stage in the process MPS is exploded into time-phased work orders for components and subassemblies using bill of materials, inventory data, and monthly time periods.	Large shop-floor order quantities typically representing one month's usage. Work is scheduled on the shop floor, using a priority control system for work orders. Large numbers of shop-floor and inventory transactions are processed to maintain data integrity in the MRP system. Large overhead costs are incurred to support the MPS system, as illustrated by 83 people employed in the materials management area.

manufacturing process in which the plant was organized into functional groupings of machines, and production was planned and controlled using an MRPII system to fill customer orders directly from finished-goods inventory. Long production lead times under this strategy led to poor competitive performance. Moreover, the inability to make changes in product designs did not allow the firm to keep up with major changes in product technology; large work-in-process and finished-goods inventories created substantial write-offs of obsolete inventory. Poor customer service in product delivery resulted, along with high manufacturing costs.

As a consequence the company changed its manufacturing strategy, and invested in a JIT production process having straight-line flows of material, with closely coupled manufacturing cells dedicated to individual product families and short changeover times. Four cells are dedicated to the final assembly of four different product model families, and the fifth cell produces printed circuit boards (PCBs) for the final assembly cells. Thanks to this process, overall manufacturing lead time fell from 75 to 5 days, work-in-process and finished-goods inventories declined significantly, and product quality improved greatly. Likewise, the PIM system design was changed to include an assemble-to-order MPS (because of the short manufacturing lead time), a new MRP material planning approach that takes into account JIT plant operations, and a JIT-based shop scheduling approach. Figure 13.13 describes the new manufacturing approach.

The Driver Is the Marketplace

It might be tempting to believe that evolution in PIM system design is always toward JIT-based systems. In fact, that is not the case. Several major Japanese companies that have used JIT approaches are now trying to integrate MRP into their PIM designs. Why? Because they are entering markets in which MRP approaches make sense. More and more Japanese firms are moving out of standardized product markets and into more customized areas, where MRP planning supports wider product variety. The resultant systems will almost surely be hybrids in which some JIT methodologies prevail, but the benefits of MRP planning are needed as well. The bottom line is that marketplace requirements should define the manufacturing task, the process, and PIM design.

INTEGRATING MRP AND JIT

As was clear with the Applicon example, there are many ways that MRP and JIT can be combined, and there is substantial need to do so. Here we discuss the needs to integrate these approaches, physical changes that support the integration, and techniques for integration.

The Need to Integrate

In the majority of cases, the need for integration arises in companies that have an installed MRP system and are in the process of implementing some aspect of JIT. The pressure of meeting world-class standards, the use of global benchmarking, and intimidating competition have all brought home the necessity of major changes in how manufacturing is done. The response to these concerns in the best of companies has been to implement aspects of JIT.

Often these JIT programs seem to be in conflict with the MRP system the firm may have in place. As lead times shrink and material velocity increases, the limiting activity can turn out to be transaction processing. Increased demand, either from customers or through increased part commonality, can compound the problem.

As an example, a European consumer electronics company significantly cut the production time required to make a major high-volume component in response to increased demand. Product design changes and process capability improvements were both used to reduce setup and run times. Lot sizes were reduced, but lead times were not significantly reduced. The combination of smaller lot sizes and increasing volume simply meant that there were substantially more open orders on the floor being tracked by the MRP system, moving into and out of inventory, and being accounted for during the process. These "hidden factory" activities were limiting the improvements possible from the other activities.

When changes take place on the factory floor, PIM system changes may be a required response. These changes can come from internal actions, such as implementing a JIT program, or from external requirements that change the manufacturing task. In either case the need for a change in the production activity control system may be clear; the direction is most often from shop-order-based systems to kanban or other simple signals. A typical response is to backflush component usages at all levels triggered by receipt of completed items into finished-goods inventory.

FIGURE 13.13
Applicon's New Manufacturing Strategy

Market characteristics*	Manufacturing strategy	
	Manufacturing	
	Task*	Features
Customized products Wide product range Major design changes occurring monthly Quick response required to changes in product technology Need to reflect both price sensitivity and the price/performance ratio for a sophisticated customer base High product quality requirements Delivery responsiveness is critical	Low-cost manufacturing Short production lead times High product qualtiy Rapid engineering change capability	Straight-line flows of material Manufacturing cells dedicated to particular product families Short setup times Short manufacturing lead times (1 week) Short design change cycles Low work-in-process and finished-goods inventories Low flexibility to product family mix changes

*The market characteristics and manufacturing task are common to the old and new strategies.

Manufacturing strategy		
Production and inventory management		
Master production scheduling	*Detailed material planning*	*Shop-floor systems*
An assemble-to-order MPS is stated in top-level item terms and is coded by major model number.	MPS uses monthly time periods covering 5 future months to plan and order purchased materials, using family bills of material, MRP records, and bill of material explosion techniques.	Work orders are not scheduled for in-ternally manufac-tured items.
The company plans using forecast information in the MPS, but builds product only to customer orders using a final assembly schedule.	No stockrooms because material is located in the manufacturing cells.	Material is pulled through the production process using JIT methods. Delivery of 70 percent of supplier items directly onto the shop floor.
Customer order promising is a key activity. Available-to-promise records are used.	MPC system is run weekly, providing planning information to planners and buyers, and capacity planning information to plant work cells.	Customer orders, referred to as build cards, provide the basis for scheduling work cells and for pulling material through the plant.
Customer orders are used to convert the weekly production plan into specific daily requirements.	Only two inventory transactions are recorded—from suppliers into the stock bins, and out of stock bins as finished products are shipped from the plant.	

Physical Changes That Support Integration

One of the first requirements to support the JIT approaches in the factory is to reduce the inventory transaction volume. Cutting the number of times a lot has to be logged into and out of an inventory location not only reduces transactions, but also enables material to move to the next operation more quickly. This clearly helps increase the velocity and reduce lead times. Physically, this may mean making some changes in how lots get moved from department to department and how the need for the move gets signaled, but the major improvements are in making physical changes to the production process, such as the introduction of cellular manufacturing.

Cellular manufacturing supports integrating MRP and JIT approaches. The cell allows us to accomplish several routing steps as if they were a single step, and allows the shop floor to be scheduled at the level of part numbers instead of at the level of routing steps. More encompassing cellular manufacturing approaches permit the cell to be planned and controlled at the level of assemblies instead of at the part number level. One key objective is to reduce the need for inventory accounting and the other hidden factory transactions. Control of the cell is straightforward, and does not need the detailed tracking necessary when parts move all over the factory.

The choice of where to implement cellular manufacturing is important because we can create islands of velocity, like the islands of automation prevalent in the early installations of some computer-integrated manufacturing schemes. These islands might be quite successful on their own, but may not be well integrated into the system as a whole. Increasingly, we have found firms in this position needing to make more than cosmetic changes to their overall PIM systems.

Some Techniques for Integrating MRP and JIT

Whenever there is a combination of MRP and JIT in the shop, we need to move back and forth between the systems. A JIT cell in the middle of a process under MRP control must communicate with the MRP system. There must be a handoff from MRP to JIT at the start of the JIT process, and a transfer back to MRP at the end.

One way of supporting this need is to create special bills of material for activities under JIT control. Material requirements planning records can be used to plan raw material requirements, with movement through the factory done with JIT approaches (no shop orders or tracking). The special bill would ignore the creation of the detailed parts and assemblies performed under JIT scheduling, and the MRP system would pick up the completed part or assembly as a part number on the bill of materials at completion.

Strategy for Combining MRP and JIT

We are often asked if you need to go through the agony of implementing MRP if, thereafter, the goal is to dismantle parts of it to use JIT. A typical question is, "Why can't we just go to JIT in the first place?"

For a long time our response was that conceptually, JIT could be implemented in a company with no formal PIM system, but it was difficult. First, you need the discipline of a system in which execution according to a schedule was part of the basic factory culture. The usual problems of month-end surges in output, inadequate data integrity, pulling dollars instead of products, and panic conditions must be eliminated before you can implement a system with virtually no buffers. Even MRP has small buffering. JIT, by design, "exposes the rocks" as a basic philosophy. Without the underlying discipline, the steady-state condition would be rocks showing; the factory would be shut down much of the time until JIT discipline was achieved. Maintaining commitment to a JIT philosophy under these circumstances would be difficult.

Now, however, we believe that a more balanced view toward MRP/JIT integration is required. We need to realize that JIT encompasses much more than managing material flows. You can start to work on work simplification and cellular manufacturing approaches at a fairly early point, either concomitant with JIT implementation or not. The result can be progress toward manufacturing excellence on more than one front.

Similarly, improved quality is a fundamental underpinning to JIT. One does not need to wait to get started on the quality improvement process. As quality is improved, the "surprises" in PIM systems are reduced, and more simple systems suffice.

CONCLUDING PRINCIPLES

Throughout this chapter we have emphasized the need to design PIM systems to best support the competitive strategy of the company. It is critical that production and inventory management decisions be viewed in an integrative way so that planning efforts of all of the business functions can be linked effectively. Furthermore, the PIM system should be chosen in terms of business specifications, as opposed to technical specifications.

Two major integration issues in designing PIM systems have been addressed in this chapter: how to link the design of PIM systems to a firm's corporate strategy and the requirements of its market, and how to integrate MRP and JIT approaches in designing PIM systems. The following principles summarize the major points:

- Because investment in PIM systems is large and fixed over a long period of time, its design must support the firm's competitive strategy.
- A wide range of options are available in designing PIM systems, and the choices must be governed by the company's competitive needs.
- Business and technical specifications need to be considered in designing a PIM system.
- PIM system design should begin with an analysis of the market requirements to support the firm's competitive strategy.
- Understanding the manufacturing task is critical in developing the production process design, the PIM system design, and other elements of the manufacturing infrastructure.
- The manufacturing process's particular features need to be considered when choosing among the options in PIM system design.
- MRP and JIT approaches can be effectively integrated in designing PIM systems.
- Improved company performance can result from matching PIM system design to the firm's competitive strategy.

INTEGRATED RESOURCE LINKAGES

Throughout this book we have described the linkages that exist between elements of the production and inventory management system and other parts of the firm. We have looked at integration with other corporate functions, such as marketing and sales or accounting and finance. Consideration was given to the integration of engineering and data processing into the PIM system design and application activities. We made mention of integration across organizational boundaries as well. All of these are important to an effectively functioning PIM system and the achievement of company goals.

The overarching integration issue, however, is that of supporting company strategy. It is not only necessary to have the PIM system aligned to support company goals; the strategic plans of *all* functions must be coherent. The ultimate test of resource integration is the consistency of all activities in defining, supporting, and reaching company goals in the marketplace.

REFERENCES

Belt, B. "MRP and KANBAN—A Possible Synergy?" *Production and Inventory Management Journal* 28, no.1 (1987), pp. 71–80.

Berry, W. L., and T. J. Hill. "Linking Systems to Strategy."*International Journal of Operations and Production Management* 12, no. 10, 1992.

Dixon, J. R.; A. J. Nanni; and T. E. Vollmann. *The New Performance Challenge*. Homewood, Ill.: Richard D. Irwin, Inc., 1990.

Fakhoury, E. A. F., and T. E. Vollmann. "Applicon Case Study." Boston: Boston University, School of Management, 1987.

Goddard, W. E. *Just-in-Time*. Essex Junction, Vt.: Oliver Wight Ltd., 1986, chapters 7, 9, and 12.

Hall, Robert W. "Kawasaki, U.S.A., Transferring Japanese Productivity Methods to the U.S.A." Case Study 08002. Falls Church, Va.: American Production and Inventory Control Society, 1982.

Hill, T. J. *Manufacturing Strategy: Text and Cases*. Homewood, Ill.: Richard D. Irwin, 1989, chapters 2 and 3.

Karmarkar, U. S. "Getting Control of Just-in-Time." *Harvard Business Review*, September–October 1989.

Louis, R. S. "MRPIII: Material Acquisition System." *Production and Inventory Management*, July 1991, pp. 26–27.

Melnick, S. A., and P. L. Carter. "Moog Inc., Space Products Division," in *Shop Floor Control Principles, Practices, and Case Studies*. Falls Church, Va.: American Production and Inventory Control Society, 1987.

Rao, A. "A Survey of MRPII Software Suppliers' Trends in Support of JIT." *Production and Inventory Management Journal* 30, no. 3 (3rd Quarter 1989), pp. 14–17.

Wemmerlöv, U. "Production Planning and Control Procedures for Cellular Manufacturing Systems: Concepts and Practice," Falls Church, Va.: APICS, 1987.

INDEX

ABOUT APICS

APICS, the educational society for resource management, offers the resources professionals need to succeed in the manufacturing community. With more than 35 years of experience. 70,000 members, and 260 local chapters, APICS is recognized worldwide for setting the standards for professional education. The society offers a full range of courses, conferences, educational programs, certification processes, and materials developed under the direction of industry experts.

APICS offers everything members need to enhance their careers and increase their professional value. Benefits include the following:

- Two internationally recognized educational certification processes—Certified in Production and Inventory Management (CPIM) and Certified in Integrated Resource Management (CIRM), which provide immediate recognition in the field and enhance members' work-related knowledge and skills. The CPIM process focuses on depth of knowledge in the core areas of production and inventory management, and the CIRM process supplies a breadth of knowledge in 13 functional areas of the business enterprise.

- The APICS Educational Materials Catalog—a handy collection of courses, proceedings, reprints, training materials, videos, software, and books written by industry experts, many of which are available to members at substantial discounts.

- *APICS The Performance Advantage*—a monthly magazine that focuses on improving competitiveness, quality, and productivity.

- Specific Industry Groups (SIGs)—suborganizations that develop educational programs, offer accompanying materials, and provide valuable networking opportunities.

- A multitude of educational workshops, employment referral, insurance, a retirement plan, and more.

To join APICS, or for complete information on the many benefits and services of APICS membership, **call 1-800-444-2742** or **703-237-8344.** Use extension 297.

Other titles of interest to you from The Business One Irwin/APICS Library of Integrated Resource Management . . .

PURCHASING
Continued Improvement through Integration
Joseph R. Carter

A complete, integrative resource for purchasing goods and services in the United States and abroad! As free trading zones open up around the world, the possibilities for sourcing nationally and internationally expand with them. This guide will help you enrich the buyer-supplier relationship that can lead to higher-quality products from suppliers and more lucrative contracts from buyers. (200 pages)
ISBN: 1-55623-535-6

EFFECTIVE PRODUCT DESIGN AND DEVELOPMENT
How to Cut Lead Time and Increase Customer Satisfaction
Stephen R. Rosenthal

Effective Product Design and Development will help you steer clear of long development delays by pointing out ways to detect design flaws early and by showing how to empower the entire work team to recognize time-absorbing mistakes. You will discover how to shorten the cycle of new product design and development and turn time into a strategic competitive advantage. (341 pages)
ISBN: 1-55623-603-4

INTEGRATED PROCESS DESIGN AND DEVELOPMENT
Dan L. Shunk

Shunk's book is a no-nonsense, reader-friendly guide that not only defines the information requirements for integrated process design but also outlines the procedures you must take to achieve it. You will discover ways your company can benefit from new and future technological trends, value-adding through design, value-added tracking, and more. (260 pages)
ISBN: 1-55623-556-9

FIELD SERVICE MANAGEMENT
An Integrated Approach to Increasing Customer Satisfaction
Arthur V. Hill

How do companies like 3M and Whirlpool consistently rate highly with customers in areas of field service repair? Hill, an established researcher and consultant in service operations management, examines their tactics and offers practical strategies to manage field service for high-quality results. (270 pages)
ISBN: 1-55623-547-X

INTEGRATED DISTRIBUTION MANAGEMENT
Competing on Customer Service, Time, and Cost
Christopher Gopal and Harold Cypress

Manufacturing professionals who strive to maximize the efficiency of their companies' distribution systems will instantly recognize the wealth of knowledge this guide provides. Gopal and Cypress direct you toward satisfying internal and external customer expectations and reveal strategies for improving efficiency and service using the powerful Integrating Link. (270 pages)
ISBN: 1-55623-578-X

Available in bookstores and libraries everywhere.